Ze'ev Maghen

After Hardship Cometh Ease

W
DE
G

Studien zur Geschichte und Kultur des islamischen Orients

Beihefte zur Zeitschrift „Der Islam"

Herausgegeben von

Lawrence I. Conrad

Neue Folge

Band 17

Walter de Gruyter · Berlin · New York

Ze'ev Maghen

After Hardship Cometh Ease

The Jews as Backdrop for Muslim Moderation

Walter de Gruyter · Berlin · New York

♾ Printed on acid-free paper which falls within the guidelines of the ANSI
to ensure permanence and durability.

ISBN-13: 978-3-11-018454-9
ISBN-10: 3-11-018454-0
ISSN 1862-1295

Bibliographic information published by Die Deutsche Bibliothek

Die Deutsche Bibliothek lists this publication in the Deutsche Nationalbibliografie; detailed bibliographic data is available in the Internet at <http://dnb.ddb.de>.

Printed in Germany
Cover design: Christopher Schneider, Berlin

For Yael and Yoav
May they have it easy

Table of Contents

Introduction

The texts and genres of Islam's sacred canon – especially Qur'ān, *tafsīr* (scriptural commentary), *ḥadīth* (prophetic tradition), *sharḥ* (*ḥadīth* commentary), *sīra* (prophetic biography), *maghāzī* (chronicles of military campaigns), *ṭabaqāt al-ṣaḥāba* (biographies of Companions), *ta'rīkh* (historiography) and *milal wa-niḥal* (heresiography) – evince an intense fascination with matters Jewish. Modern scholarship has, in turn, displayed considerable interest in this fascination, elucidating many of the themes that have percolated from the Judaic into the Islamic tradition (or, as current academic fashion would have it, that are *held in common* by the two traditions). Even before Abraham Geiger's pathbreaking *Was hat Mohammed aus dem Judenthume aufgenommen?* (1833),[1] students of Islam had noticed and expounded upon the numerous elements in Muḥammad's message both avowedly and unavowedly derived from Jewish sources (a full century earlier, George

1 Originally penned in Latin by the twenty-two year-old Geiger in response to an essay contest posted by his teacher Wilhelm Freytag, and soon after rendered into German by the author himself (who then moved on to other fields of inquiry), this eloquent and stimulating work – researched without the benefit of some ninety percent of the Muslim primary sources which later became available to scholars – has never been surpassed (though some of its inevitable shortcomings have been exposed). It was translated into English by F. M. Young in 1896 and is now available, with a prolegomenon by Moshe Pearlman, under the title *Judaism and Islam* (New York: Ktav Publishing House, 1970). On Geiger's contribution to the field see Jacob Lassner, "Abraham Geiger: A Nineteenth Century Jewish Reformer on the Origins of Islam" in Martin Kramer (ed.), *The Jewish Discovery of Islam: Studies in Honor of Bernard Lewis* (Tel-Aviv: Tel-Aviv University, 1999); and Reuven Firestone, "The Qur'ān and the Bible: Some Modern Studies of Their Relationship" in John Reeves, *Bible and Qur'ān* (Atlanta: Society of Biblical Literature, 2003). For his considerable influence on the doyen of Western Islamic studies, Ignaz Goldziher, see Lawrence Conrad, "The Pilgrim from Pest: Goldziher's Study Tour to the Near East (1873–1874)," in Ian Richard Netton (ed.), *Golden Roads: Migration, Pilgrimage and Travel in Mediaeval and Modern Islam* (Richmond, Surrey, 1993); and idem., "The Dervish's Disciple: On the Personality and Intellectual Milieu of the Young Ignaz Goldziher," *Journal of the Royal Asiatic Society*, 2 (1990).

Sale had offered a goodly number of perspicacious comments on this subject in the "Preliminary Discourse" to his translation of the Qur'ān, as well as throughout the notes to the translation itself). By the early years of the twentieth century some of the most prominent names in Western Islamic studies – Weil, Dozy, Hirschfeld, Wensinck, Wellhausen, Friedlander, Margoliouth, Goldziher – had rendered significant contributions to this discussion, and in ensuing decades Horovitz, Hirschberg, Le Strange, Torrey, Snouck Hurgronje, Vajda, Goitein, Watt, Abbott, Jeffery, Bousquet and Speyer deepened our understanding of the Judaic—Islamic relationship. Spearheading such research in the third and fourth academic generations have been scholars such as Kister, Rosenthal, Stillman, Katsch, Wansbrough, Cook, Crone, Lewis, Hawting, Lazarus-Yafeh, Brinner, Pearlman, Lecker, Newby, Adang, Nettler, Cohen, Firestone, Wheeler, Tottoli, Lassner, Wasserstrom, Bouman, Ben-Shammai, Rubin, Libson and others. Despite all this effort, however, much work remains to be done. The primary sources are brimming with relevant material as yet unexplored or unexploited by scholars, and certain sub-fields have received almost no attention. One of these last forms the subject of the present study: early Muslim conceptions of Jewish law and practice.

The treatments of the authors enumerated above may be divided into three main categories: (1) historical, dealing with the political, social and economic interaction between communities of Muslims and communities of Jews from seventh-century Arabia onward; (2) literary-cultural-theological-hagiological, concerning the stories, structures, paradigms and ideas shared in varying degrees by the two religious traditions; and (3) legal-ritual, examining the prescriptions, proscriptions, rites, customs and jurisprudence of Judaism in terms of their relationship to the early and evolving religio-legal system of Islam. This last category is the most underrepresented. The preponderence of research devoted to the intertexture of Judaism and Islam has focused on lore (*haggada*) not law (*halakha*). While a number of prominent orientalists, including Goldziher, Vajda, Schacht, Wansbrough, Cook, Crone and Burton, have pointed to the existence of analogous features in the methodology and content of the Jewish and Islamic behavioral codes, only a relatively small group – Wensinck, Kister, Goitein, Graf, Wegner, Hawting, Sohn, Astren, Lazarus-Yafeh, Libson and Crone herself – have actually attempted the comparison of particular provisions or principles in the two religious systems, or examined possible routes of transmission. Among these, Kister and Goitein alone have devoted a modicum of serious attention to Islamic *perceptions* of *halakha* and its specific ordinances, and their prolusory contributions have since been augmented by Adang (*Muslim Writers on Judaism and the Hebrew Bible,* 1996) and most recently by Wheeler ("Israel and the Torah of Muḥammad," 2003). This question is not central to the work of any of these scholars, however, and none has pursued it comprehensively.[2]

Like the legendary or "mythomorphic" material emerging out of the Rabbinic and entering into the Islamic milieu, Judaic legal norms and communal customs also impacted on their Muslim counterparts in a variety of ways: directly and indirectly, overtly and covertly, consciously and unconsciously, positively and antithetically. One method of learning about the interaction between the two faith communities, and specifically about the effect of Jewish praxis on Islamic observance as well as the outlook of early Muslim authorities on Torah (and Talmudic) law, is by comparing and contrasting similar precepts in *halakha* and *sharīʿa*. But such parallels are often elusive and deceptive, nor is it a simple matter to decide what specific conclusions should be drawn – in cases where genuine correspondence *can be* satisfactorily established – from evidence of adjustments made by the *sharīʿa* to this or that *halakhic* provision.

Fortunately, Muslim texts offer us a less tenuous and more straightforward method of discovering how Islamic tradition viewed Jewish law, and how it employed this view in order to assist in (or at least explain *post facto*) the construction of Islam's own legal system. Hundreds of direct statements and detailed discussions regarding what the Jews had been commanded (or *claimed* they had been commanded) combine in early Muslim sources to provide the nascent Arabian creed with the optimal religious anti-ideal, a negative launch-pad whence to embark upon the creation of the ultimate spiritual—practical corrective to humanity's errors and excesses. Curiosity about *halakha,* and inquiry into its ordinances and algorithms, thus played a major role in the formation and evolution (as well as elucidation and justification) of *sharīʿa,* and early Muslim authorities cited in *tafsīr* and other genres often demonstrate a level of familiarity with Jewish law that does not stop short of sophisticated rehearsals of complex Talmudic *sugyot.* (Even if this represents, ultimately, information provided by converts,

2 For a selective list of scholarly works bearing on the Jewish-Muslim and Judaic-Islamic relationship, see the bibliography.

it still says a great deal about the extent of Muslim interest in Judaism, as well as about the intellectual caliber of those converts themselves: the stories punctuating Ibn Isḥāq's *Sīra* about "learned rabbis" going over to Islam – even if they ultimately reflect more of an Iraqi than an Arabian reality – cannot have been far from the truth!).[3]

Side-by-side with such impressive accuracy regarding Jewish law, however, we also find a great deal of fantasy. At the same time that Islam was portrayed in Muslim classical literature as coalescing (at least partially) in antithetical response to Judaism, Judaism was retroactively re-created by those same texts in Islam's mirror image, to become the "anti-religion" *par excellence*. The exaggerated and even imaginary *halakha* that often resulted functioned as an epitome of the aberrance that had crept into the cultures and dispensations preceding God's revelations to Muḥammad. Although Muslim sources dwell upon numerous aspects of the process of spiritual decline that plagued the pre-Islamic period, none receives more coverage – with the possible exception of mankind's recurrent lapses into polytheism – than the deterioration of the pristine, easygoing relationship between God and His creatures (sometimes characterized in the sources by the term *fiṭra*) into a series of abstruse and arduous legal systems. The paramount example of such an oppressive code is that of the Jews, the more so as Allāh is often shown punishing the Israelite community for adopting unnatural rites and restrictions (as well as for a host of other transgressions) by heaping upon them *more* unnatural rites and restrictions. The net result of this combination of self-oppression and divine augmentation is Judaism: the most difficult religion on earth.

This book investigates the way in which the Muslim juristic tendency of extenuation (*rukhṣa*) enlisted the Muslim legal instrument of abrogation (*naskh*) to mediate the relationship between the idealized Torah of the Banū Isrā'īl/Yahūd and the nascent community and code of Islam. Drawing primarily on the influential Qur'ān commentaries of Abū Ja'far Muḥammad b. Jarīr al-Ṭabarī (d. 923 CE) and Abū 'Abd Allāh Muḥammad b. Aḥmad al-Anṣārī al-Qurṭubī (d. 1272 CE),[4] it be-

3 See Alfred Guillaume, *The Life of Muhammad: A Translation of Ibn Isḥaq's "Sirat Rasul Allah"* (Oxford: Oxford University Press, 1955), 240ff. One could also, of course, construe such phenomena as supporting the Cook—Crone *Hagarism* thesis according to which (to put it simplistically) early Islam *was* Judaism. This theory and its many detractors are, however, beyond the scope of the present study.

4 The choice of al-Ṭabarī needs no justification: he was and remains the univer-

gins by discussing the pattern of increasing leniency already discernable in the embryonic stages of Islamic *fiqh* (jurisprudential) development. The study then posits parallels to this "domestic" Muslim phenomenon on the "international" plane of human religious history, as this last is depicted by the same scriptural exegetes: here, too, things get progressively easier. Because Islam's emblematic counterweight in this regard is Judaism, the better part of this work analyzes Muslim conceptions of the provenance, evolution and specific statutes of *halakha*. Here, more than in any other area, Islam describes its mission – and even, to a certain extent, defines its identity – in lively response to Biblical and Rabbinic tradition.

---

sally acknowledged master of Qur'ān interpretation whose encyclopedic commentary (*Jāmi' al-Bayān 'an Ta'wīl Āy al-Qur'ān*) incorporated, summarized, organized and built upon the lion's share of important exegetical work carried out until his day. Jane Dammen McAuliffe calls al-Ṭabarī "the undisputed foundation upon which the edifice of classical *tafsīr* was erected," and quotes John Burton's description of his *Jāmi' al-Bayān* as having "abruptly scaled heights not previously glimpsed and never subsequently approached" (McAuliffe, "Christians in the Qur'ān and Tafsīr" in Jacques Waardenburg [ed.], *Muslim Perceptions of Other Religions* [Oxford: Oxford University Press, 1999], 107). The commentary of al-Qurṭubī (*Al-Jāmi' li-Aḥkām al-Qur'ān*) has also been held in particularly high regard throughout the Muslim world since the medieval period, and it has two additional advantages for the present research: (1) as its title implies, al-Qurṭubī's *Tafsīr* places a strong emphasis on the legal side of things, and (2) al-Qurṭubī is a reservoir of (mostly *ḥadīth*ic) material that managed to escape inclusion in the commentary of al-Ṭabarī (see *Encyclopedia of Islam*, second edition [henceforward *EI²*], *s. v.* "Ḳurṭubī" [R. Arnaldez]). These two *mufassirūn*, therefore, complement each other well and are excellent representatives of their genre. They reflect the "state of the field" up to their respective times and serve to define that field subsequently. (It is noteworthy, for instance, that the Islamist theoretician and creator of the conservative—revivalist *Ḥizb al-Taḥrīr*, Taqī al-Dīn al-Nabhānī [d. 1978], after enumerating various types and examples of what he sees as problematic *tafāsīr* – including, significantly for our purposes, those that "imbibe excessively from the *Isrā'īliyyāt* [Jewish lore]" – concludes his survey by singling out the commentaries of al-Ṭabarī and al-Qurṭubī [together with that of 'Abd Allāh b. Aḥmad al-Nasafī] as works that are innocent of such unorthodox biases or deviant inclinations, and that are "considered the founding texts of Qur'ān interpretation" [*tu'atabaru min ummuhāt kutub al-tafsīr*] whose authors were "the guides and masters" [*al-a'imma*] of the exegetical enterprise – Taqī al-Dīn al-Nabhānī, *al-Shakhṣiyya al-Islāmiyya* [Beirut: Dār al-Umma, 1994], vol. 1, pp. 297–8). Innumerable other classical Muslim sources of varying genres could be – and, in many instances throughout this study, have been – usefully consulted in connection with our subject, but limits must be set, and for the most part I have preferred to drop my line deep rather than cast my net wide.

The importance of studying the Islamic understanding and evaluation of the Pentateuchal and Talmudic legal systems should be self evident. Islam and Judaism are both systems that place an extremely heavy emphasis on law.[5] This means that the Muslim assessment of *halakha* is tantamount to the Muslim assessment of Judaism. It means, too, that the recorded Muslim reactions to *halakha* speak volumes about early Islamic *self*-perception. The investigation of classical Islamic statements and discussions regarding Jewish rules and regulations can also shed further light on the extent, context and quality of medieval Muslim—Jewish intellectual communication. Needless to say, all of this additionally harbours much significance for the Muslim world's present day attitudes to Jews and their religion.[6]

The best intentions do not always lead to the best results. A quest for thoroughness and a desire to share with the reader interesting material bearing directly and indirectly on the book's subject, have led to a situation in which many of the footnotes in this volume have burgeoned to the size of mini-excursuses. Those who take all or even most of these "detours" risk losing the thread of the argument in the main text. Readers are therefore urged to consult the notes only at convenient rest-stops – at the conclusion of discussions, or even of chapters – or whenever their curiosity gets the better of them.

I owe a debt of gratitude to my colleague and friend Professor David Powers of Cornell University, who read large parts of this manuscript and offered numerous suggestions that have improved it considerably. I am likewise beholden to Professor Etan Kohlberg of the Hebrew University, who braved much of what follows and whose vast erudition saved me from many an error. Profound thanks are due, as well, to Professor Dr. Lawrence Conrad, whose kindness, encouragement, pro-

5 Hava Lazarus-Yafeh calls Judaism and Islam "the only Halakhic religions in the world" (Lazarus-Yafeh, "Judaism and Islam," in *Some Religious Aspects of Islam* [Leiden: E.J. Brill, 1981], 85; see also idem., "The 'Ulamā of al-Azhar," in ibid., 93, where she describes Judaism as "the only other religion [besides Islam] in which religious law takes such a central place").

6 One hopes to be spared the knee-jerk accusations of "essentialism" that so often greet statements of this sort nowadays. Anyone even vaguely familiar with the workings of the Muslim world in our times – whatever his or her ideological or philosophical bent – will vouch without hesitation for how extensively (though not uniformly) that world's cultures, politics and general ethos are colored by their dynamic interaction with the classical heritage of Islam (see also, in this connection, Conclusion, n. 15).

found grasp of the field and vigilant attention to detail helped bring this book to completion. Dr. Sabine Vogt of De Gruyter has been the picture of patience and professionalism.

As for my wife – my life – Anita: there are no words. I can only refer her to the title of this volume, in the hope that it is true.

1. The Shadow of Turning

Revelation and Abrogation in Medieval Muslim Theology

"God is not a man to be capricious," Balaam chides Balak on the Plain of Moab, "or the son of a man, to tergiversate" (Numbers, 23:19). "The Eternal of Israel neither lies nor repents," Samuel scolds Saul some centuries later, "for He is not human that He should repent" (I Samuel, 15: 29). Such unambiguous pronouncements coexist uneasily in the Bible with the numerous instances in which the Deity does indeed appear to have reversed Himself: "The Lord *regretted* that He had made man upon the Earth, and His heart was saddened. He said: I will blot out from the earth the men whom I created" (Genesis, 6:6). After an emotional entreaty by Moses (we read on another occasion) "God *repented* of the evil that He had purposed to do unto His people" (Exodus, 32: 14). Jonah was sorely disappointed when the inhabitants of Nineveh turned from their wicked ways and the Almighty in consequence "*renounced* the punishment He had planned to bring upon them, and did not carry it out" (Jonah, 3: 10). Not twenty verses before Samuel admonished Saul that "[t]he Eternal of Israel neither lies nor repents (*lo yinaḥem*)," the Lord Himself had informed Samuel that "I repent (*niḥamti*) having made Saul king ..." (I Samuel, 15: 11). The discord between these opposing Biblical attitudes to the question of divine equivocality – a contradiction about contradiction – supplied grist for the mill of many a medieval Jewish commentator, most of whom (especially those under the spell of Platonic—Aristotelian theories of divine immutability) argued that the Supreme Being's *volte face* are an illusion.[1]

1 See, e.g., the commentary of RaDaQ (R. David Qimḥi, d. circa 1235 CE) to Genesis 6: 6: "Regarding the fact that it says 'And He repented,' [it must be realized that] the Torah spoke in language understandable to human beings, for in truth 'He is not a man that He should repent,' for there is with Him, may He be Praised and Exalted, no change of will" (*ma she'amar vayinaḥem, dibrah*

Not so in the case of Islamic tradition. Here the idea of God changing His mind – or, at least, regularly overturning His decrees – is widely established and deeply entrenched; indeed, it is perceived to be an indispensable catalyst in the formation of the last and best religion. This fundamental tenet derives, *inter alia,* from the problem posed by the considerable quantity of apparently conflicting statements found in Muslim sacred writ. Such ostensible inconstancy is tackled by the classical commentaries in two primary ways.

The first of these, known as *jamʿ* or synthesis, is in fact specifically designed to circumvent the notion of intra-scriptural contradiction. In his discussion of Q. 4: 82 – "Will they not ponder the Qur'ān? Had it been from other than Allāh, they would have discovered in it much incongruity" – the foremost exegete of the ʿAbbāsid period and perennial touchstone of *tafsīr*, Abū Jaʿfar Muḥammad b. Jarīr al-Ṭabarī (d. 923 CE), buttresses his own gloss with a statement of ʿAbd al-Raḥmān b. Zayd b. Aslam: "It is incumbent upon the believer to say: 'All of [the Qur'ān] is from God.' He must believe in the ambiguous passages, and not set some against others (*yu'minu bi'l-mutashābih wa-lā yaḍribu baʿḍan bi-baʿḍin*) ... and he must know that God the Exalted did not say a thing and then confute it (*lam yaqul qawlan wa-yanquḍuhu*)."[2] From what was originally an affirmation – meditating upon the miraculous uniformity of the Qur'ān will oblige one to believe – al-Ṭabarī (backed by Ibn Zayd) has turned this verse into an exhortation: one is

---

Torah kilshon b'nei adam, ki ʿal derekh ha'emet lo adam [hu] lehinaḥem, ki ayn bo shinui ḥefetz yitbarakh veyitʿaleh). See also R. Abraham b. Ezra (d. 1164 CE), RaSHI (R. Shlomo Yitzḥaqi, d. 1105 CE) and RaMBaN (R. Moshe b. Naḥman or Naḥmanides, d. 1270 CE) to the same verse (and RaDaQ to I Samuel 15: 29, as well as RaSHBaM [R. Samuel b. Meir, d. circa 1174] to Numbers 23: 19). Cf., however, Ḥizquni (R. Ḥizqiya b. Manoaḥ, d. 13th century CE) to Genesis 6: 6, who does seem to admit the possibility of divine rethinking, and also Deuteronomy Rabbah, 2: 8, where Moses – seeking to convince his Maker to rescind the divine decree barring him from entering the Promised Land – accuses God of going back on His word, but only when it is convenient for Him: "When You so desired, did You not violate Your oath? Did you not swear that You would eradicate Your children after they worshipped the calf, and then reverse Yourself? (*kshe-bikashta lo ḥilalta hashvuʿa? Lo nishbaʿta she'ata mekhaleh et banekha baʿegel veḥazarta bakh?*)." See, in addition, Genesis Rabbah, 13: 9, where God is said to have "changed His mind" (*veḥazar bo haQadosh Barukh Hu*) regarding the arrangement of certain ecological matters.

2 Muḥammad b. Jarīr al-Ṭabarī, *Jāmiʿ al-Bayān ʿan Ta'wīl Āy al-Qur'ān* (Beirut: Dār al-Fikr, 1995 – henceforward: "Ṭabarī"), 5: 246.

obliged to believe in the miraculous uniformity of the Qur'ān. This mandatory conviction both motivated and was buttressed by *jam'*, the effort to reconcile scriptural passages that do not tally with one another *prima facie*.

But al-Ṭabarī's interpretation of Q. 4: 82 was by no means intended to undermine the premise of divinely ordained modification. While the great commentator rejected the possibility that God should be caught in a *factual* contradiction – the omniscient Creator who taught men by the pen would never be guilty of error or deliberate deception, and therefore no mutually exclusive descriptions of reality can possibly coexist in the Qur'ān – at the same time there was no doubt in al-Ṭabarī's mind that the Deity certainly could, and regularly did, make adjustments in matters of *guidance* for humankind, promulgating particular laws at a certain time and then canceling them in favor of new laws at a later stage. This claim represents the second method of confronting internal inconsistency in the Qur'ān, the well-known principle of *naskh* or abrogation: "Such of Our revelations as We abrogate or cause to be forgotten, We bring in their place better or similar ones. Do you not know that Allāh is capable of all things?" (Q. 2: 106).[3]

3 The reputed centrality of *naskh* – also known as *al-nāsikh wa'l-mansūkh* – to the growth of Islam in its formative period has spawned a great many books by Muslim scholars, the earliest of which is Abū 'Ubayd b. Qāsim al-Sallām (d. 838 CE), *Kitāb al-Nāsikh wa'l-Mansūkh,* ed. John Burton (Cambridge: The Trustees of the E. J.W. Gibb Memorial Foundation, 1987). Burton has also penned the preeminent study on the subject: *The Sources of Islamic Law: Islamic Theories of Abrogation* (Edinburgh: Edinburgh University Press, 1990). This work must be read in tandem with the same author's *The Collection of the Qur'ān* (Cambridge: Cambridge University Press, 1977) – as well as his "The Exegesis of Q. 2: 106 and the Islamic Theories of *Naskh,*" *BSOAS* 48/3 (1985) – in order to understand Burton's ideas about *naskh* (for which see the appendix). In the introduction to *Sources* Burton avers that "Western scholars have hitherto shown an incomprehensible indifference to the Muslim discussions on abrogation" (p. ix). Nevertheless, see also K. I. Semaan, "Al-Nāsikh wa'l-Mansūkh: Abrogation and its Application in Islam," *Islamic Quarterly* 6 (1961); Ahmad Hasan "The Theory of Naskh," *Islamic Studies* 14 (1965); John Wansbrough, *Quranic Studies: Sources and Methods of Scriptural Interpretation* (Oxford: Oxford University Press, 1977); Andrew Rippin, "Al-Zuhrī, *Naskh al-Qur'ān* and the Problem of Early *Tafsīr* Texts," in *BSOAS* 47 (1984); David Powers, "The Exegetical Genre of Nāsikh al-Qur'ān wa-Mansūkhuhu" in Andrew Rippin (ed.), *Approaches to the History of the Interpretation of the Qur'ān* (Oxford: Clarendon Press, 1988); and Christopher Melchert, "Qur'ānic Abrogation across the Ninth Century: Shāfi'ī, Abū 'Ubayd, Muḥāsibī and Ibn Qutaybah" in Bernard G. Weiss (ed.), *Studies in Islamic Legal*

The distinction between God's strict immovability in matters of fact and His willingness to adapt in matters of legislation is made explicit at the outset of al-Ṭabarī's discussion of the latter verse:

Theory (Leiden: E.J. Brill, 2002). The issue of *naskh* in Qur'ānic exegesis and Islamic jurisprudence is vast and complicated, and the following précis is only useful if accompanied by the awareness that each statement in it is subject to debate and each category to further breakdown.

Qur'ān can be abrogated by Qur'ān, but also *ḥadīth* by *ḥadīth* ("*kāna rasūl Allāhi yansakhu ḥadīthuhu ba'ḍuhu ba'ḍan kamā yansakhu al-Qur'ānu ba'ḍuhu ba'ḍan*" – Abū 'Abd Allāh Muḥammad b. Aḥmad al-Anṣārī al-Qurṭubī, *Al-Jāmi' li-Aḥkām al-Qur'ān* [Cairo: Al-Maktaba al-Tawfiqiya, n.d. – henceforward: "Qurṭubī"], 5: 178; "'Urwa alleged that his father told him that the Prophet would regulate some matter, then, after some time, replace his first ruling with a second regulation – just as the Qur'ān did" [Burton, *Collection*, 60]). Additionally, *ḥadīth* can be abrogated by Qur'ān (as some claim was the case with the change of *qibla*, because while the original direction of prayer is not mentioned in scripture – and thus must have been derived from Prophetic *sunna* – the later reorientation is [Q. 2: 142 – see, however, Burton, *Sources*, 179–83. Several commentators maintain that this verse alludes to the even earlier *qibla*-switch from the Ka'ba to Jerusalem, an alteration which some consider to have taken place *after* the *hijra*!]). According to most authorities, Qur'ān can even be abrogated by *ḥadīth* (as when the punishment for adultery expressly stipulated in the Qur'ān – one hundred stripes [Q. 24: 2] or indefinite confinement to the home [Q. 4: 15] – was replaced by stoning [see Muslim, *Kitāb al-Ḥudūd*, 29: 1692–1695; Melchert, "Qur'ānic Abrogation," 85–7; and Burton, *Sources*, 144–58 (many believed, however, that a verse enjoining the stoning of adulterers – and supplanting the verses prescribing flogging or sequestration – had originally formed part of the Qur'ān, and that while its text had subsequently been abrogated, the norm it introduced still held). Burton seems to feel that this final form of *naskh* – the abrogation of scripture by tradition – was the most significant and widespread of all (*Sources*, 4–5 and *passim*; idem., *Collection*, chapters 2–3)]). Al-Shāfi'ī vehemently denied these last two possibilities, asserting (though perhaps disingenuously) that each sacred genre could only be modified by its own kind (Muḥammad b. Idrīs al-Shāfi'ī, *al-Risāla* [Beirut: Dār al-Kutub al-'Ilmiyya, n.d.], 106ff; his school disagreed with him [Christopher Melchert, "The Meaning of *Qāla al-Shāfi'ī* in Ninth Century Sources," *Occasional Papers of the School of 'Abbasid Studies at Cambridge*, 135 (2004), 289; Burton, "The Exegesis of Q. 2: 106," 467]; and see, for yet another nuance, the Prophet's declaration that "my word does not cancel out God's Word, but God's Word cancels out my word" (*kalāmī lā yansakhu kalām Allāhi, wa-kalām Allāhi yansakhu kalāmī* – Mawlāna Faḍl al-Karīm's modern arrangement of Walī al-Dīn Tibrīzī's *Mishkāt al-Maṣābīḥ* [Lahore, Mālik Sirāj al-Dīn, n.d. – itself a later medieval revision of Abū Muḥammad al-Ḥusayn b. Mas'ūd al-Baghawī's (d. 1122) *Maṣābīḥ al-Sunna*, 1: 121]. This work will henceforward be referred to as "Baghawī").

One may also distinguish between at least three different types of intra-Qur'ānic abrogation: (1) *naskh al-ḥukm wa'l-tilāwa*, in which both the letter

> This refers to God's transformation of the lawful into the prohibited and the prohibited into the lawful, of the permitted into the forbidden and the forbidden into the permitted (*wa-dhālika an yuḥawwila al-ḥalāl ḥarāman wa'l-ḥarām ḥalālan wa'l-mubāḥ maḥẓūran wa'l-maḥẓūr mubāḥan*). This transformation occurs, however, only in the context of prescription and proscription, restraint and release, interdiction and authorization. But as for informative statements, there is in this area neither abrogating nor abrogated (*fa-ammā al-akhbār fa-lā yakūnu fīhā nāsikh wa-lā mansūkh*).[4]

God never corrects Himself regarding the "is," but He constantly updates Himself regarding the "ought." Truth is essential; law is existential.[5]

(i.e. text) and spirit (i.e. force) of a law are removed (the passage thus obliterated remaining only in the recollection of certain Companions); (2) *naskh al-tilāwa dūna al-ḥukm,* in which the text is removed but the regulation remains (as with the supposed "stoning verse" aforementioned); (3) *naskh al-ḥukm dūna al-tilāwa,* in which the regulation is abrogated but the text remains. In what follows, we will be primarily concerned with this latter type, which al-Ḥāzimī called "the 'classic' mode of abrogation": the suppression of one scriptural provision by another scriptural provision (or by a prophetic exemplum) without the excision of the first from the Qur'ānic text (see Burton, *Sources,* chapter 5, and idem., *Collection,* chapter 3). Most of the examples we will adduce of this phenomenon are not mentioned by Burton (or in the list of al-Suyūṭī, cited in *Sources,* 184–5). Burton's own take on the verse to which the present note is appended requires a different translation than the one that we – together with almost all renderings of the Qur'ān into English – have offered. For a critique of his outlook on *naskh,* see the appendix.

4 Ṭabarī, 1:665. Some early exegetes do not seem to have made this distinction, finding contradiction – and applying *naskh* – in cases of exposition no less than in cases of exhortation (see Burton, *Sources,* 2–3).

5 The notion that "law is existential" must itself be qualified. See the exchange between the Mu'tazilite Ibrāhīm al-Naẓẓām and the the Jew Yassā b. Ṣāliḥ excerpted in John Wansbrough, *The Sectarian Milieu* (Oxford: Oxford University Press, 1978), 110–12, where in order to defend *naskh*, the Muslim sets up a dichotomy between non-contingent values (*lā li-'illa*) – such as charity, honesty, justice or faith – which are good in themselves (*li-a'yānihā*), and norms contingent upon divine commandment (*li-'illat al-'amr bihā*) – like prayer and fasting – which are good because God declared them to be so (at the time). These latter, which together constitute the revealed law, can be abrogated, asserts al-Naẓẓām, whereas the former, which are tantamount to natural law, cannot. This smacks somewhat of the distinction made in medieval Judaic hermeneutics between *mishpaṭim* or *mitzvot bayn adam le-ḥavero* (rational precepts that man would have enacted without divine inspiration and which govern the dynamics of human interaction: the prohibition against murder, the requirement of probity in business, etc.), and *ḥukim* or *mitzvot bayn adam la-maqom* (non-rational precepts that could only have come about through heavenly intervention and which govern the human relationship with God: in a

Even before the intervention of Hellenistic rationalism with its static vision of the Godhead as *Intellectus Intelligens Intellectum* (Thought Thinking Itself), the idea of such a "progressive" Deity, moving and changing with the times, was not palatable to everyone. "And when we exchange one revelation for another – and Allāh knows best what He reveals – they say [to you, O Muḥammad]: 'Lo! Thou art but a forger.' But most of them understand not" (Q. 16: 102).[6] The renowned thirteenth century traditionist and commentator, Abū 'Abd Allāh Muḥammad b. Aḥmad al-Anṣārī al-Qurṭubī (d. 1272 CE), describes the circumstances in which this verse, as well as the previously cited Q. 2: 106, were revealed:

> The Jews resented the Muslims' realignment [of the *qibla* or prayer direction from Jerusalem] to the Ka'ba (after the Battle of Badr in 624 CE), and they sought to discredit Islam in this regard, saying: "See how Muḥammad commands his followers to do something, and then afterwards forbids them to do that thing. This Qur'ān is nothing but his own invention, and that is why parts of it contradict other parts (*wa-li-hādhā yunāqiḍu ba'ḍuhu ba'ḍan*)." In response to this, Allāh revealed the verses: "When we exchange one revelation for another ..." and "Such of Our revelations as We abrogate ..."[7]

---

word, ritual), although in Judaism, of course, neither type can be abrogated (nor are all *mitzvot bayn adam la-maqom* considered *ḥuqim*). It has in fact been speculated that this Jewish breakdown was influenced by Mu'tazilism – see Goldziher's introduction to *Das Buch vom Wesen der Seele* (Berlin, 1907), 21–24. The similar Islamic bifurcation between *mu'āmalāt* and *'ibādāt* (or *ḥuqūq al-nās* and *ḥuqūq Allāh*, the latter sometimes styled *ta'abbud*, a logically inexplicable manner of worship) is also comparable to al-Naẓẓām's classification, but the comparison breaks down when we remember that many of the *mu'āmalāt* were abrogated as well.

6 For the role of this and other key verses in the construction of, and polemics surrounding, *naskh* theory, see Burton, *Sources*, esp. chapter 6, and idem., *Collection, passim.*

7 Qurṭubī, 2: 55. This explanation is found in al-Qurṭubī's discussion of Q. 2: 106. In his gloss to Q. 16: 102, however, he – like many other *mufassirūn* – identifies Muḥammad's challengers as Meccan polytheists (*kuffār Quraysh*; some even connect Q. 16: 102 to the incident of the Satanic Verses). The "*qiblatayn*" passage itself (Q. 2: 142–5) focuses on the fire drawn by Muḥammad as a result of this about-face: "The foolish among the people will say, 'What has turned them from the *qibla* which they formerly observed?' Say: 'Unto Allāh belong the East and the West. He guides those He will to a straight path'... And We appointed the *qibla* that you formerly observed only that We might distinguish him who truly follows the Messenger from him who turns on his heels. In truth, it was a hard test, save for those whom Allāh guided ... And now verily We shall make you turn toward a *qibla* which is dear to you. So turn your face

For the Jews as depicted by al-Qurṭubī and al-Ṭabarī, not only was the appearance of divine self-contradiction appalling, but the very idea of the Deity communicating His message piecemeal over time was absurd. "We have revealed the Qur'ān to you in stages," Allāh affirms (Q. 76: 23),[8] but "those who disbelieve say: Why is the Qur'ān not re-

---

toward the inviolable place of worship (*al-masjid al-ḥarām*) ... Lo! Those who have received the Scripture before you know that this is the truth from their Lord. And Allāh is not unaware of what they do. Even if you brought unto those who have received the Scripture all kinds of portents, they would not follow your *qibla*, nor can you be a follower of their *qibla* ..." (see also Ibn Isḥāq—Guillaume, 258–9, and Qurṭubī, 2: 131 ff). Jewish authors, including R. Sa'adya Gaon, Ibn Kammūna, the Karaite al-Qirqisānī and others, did in fact attack the Islamic notion of *naskh* (see Camilla Adang, *Muslim Writers on Judaism and the Hebrew Bible* [Leiden: E. J. Brill, 1996], 198–210 and *passim*; Moshe Perlmann (ed.), *Ibn Kammūna: Tanqīḥ al-Abḥāth li'l-Milal al-Thalāth* [Berkeley: University of California Press, 1967]; Wansbrough, *Sectarian Milieu,* 112–14; Hava Lazarus-Yafeh, *Intertwined Worlds* [Princeton: Princeton University Press, 1992], esp. 149). What may well be genuine reflections of such Jewish criticism in Islamic *naskh* literature credit its purveyors with elaborate philosophical arguments (see the examples adduced by Muṣṭafā Zayd, *Al-Naskh fī'l-Qur'ān al-Karīm* [Beirut: Dār al-Fikr al-'Arabī, n.d.], 81–2). For the issue of *qibla* change and its role in *naskh* debates, see Burton, *Sources,* 174–183 and Melchert, "Qur'ānic Abrogation," 84; for the same question as it impacted on the nature of early Muslim—Jewish relations, see Uri Rubin, "Kivvun ha-Tefilla be-Islam: le-Toldotav shel Ma'avak bayn Pulḥani," *Historiya* 6 (5460). While the Jews are portrayed as denying *naskh,* the Shi'ites are often accused of going to the opposite extreme in positing that God abrogates and replaces ("erases and rewrites") scriptural injunctions through sheer caprice (see, e.g., Muḥammad al-'Atā'iqī, *al-Nāsikh wa'l-Mansūkh* [Cairo: Maktabat Wahba, 2000], 9–12).

8 Cp. Q. 25: 32: "*wa-ratalnāhu tartīlan.*" Although the "*nazzalnā 'alayka al-Qur'āna tanzīlan*" of Q. 76: 23 might be interpreted otherwise, Ibn 'Abbās, for one, explains this verse to mean: "He revealed the Qur'ān discontinuously, verse after verse; it did not come down in one bunch" (*anzala al-Qur'āna mutafarriqan, āya ba'da āya, wa-lam yanzil jumla wāḥida* – Qurṭubī, 19: 112). Al-Ṭabarī quotes Ibn 'Abbās elsewhere to the opposite effect, however, unless the following should be read as a more detailed formulation (or apologetic rewrite) of the above statement: "God sent down the Qur'ān in one bunch on the Night of Destiny from the upper heaven to the lower heaven [the sky of our world], and it lingered at the level of the stars, and God dispensed it to His Messenger one passage after another ..." (*anzala al-Qur'āna jumlatan wāḥidatan fī laylat al-qadr min al-samā' al-'ulyā ilā'l-samā' al-dunyā fa-kāna bi-mawqi' al-nujūm, fa-kāna Allāhu yunziluhu 'alā rasūlihi ba'ḍuhu fī ithra ba'ḍin ...* – Ṭabarī, 30: 328). If this latter description is merely an elaborate version of the preceding one – and if it should not be viewed as deliberate "spin" – then Ibn 'Abbās does *not* believe in divine mind changing. If it is *antithetical* to the

vealed to him all at once?" (Q. 25: 32). Elaborates al-Qurṭubī: "When the Jews saw how the Qur'ān came down bit by bit, they asked: 'Why did God not vouchsafe it to [Muḥammad] in one fell swoop (*jumla wāḥida*), as He did the Torah to Moses, the Evangel to Jesus and the Psalms to David?"[9] Still worse in Jewish eyes, Allāh appeared to be as much a *reactive* as an initiative-taking Divinity, "sometimes revealing a single verse, sometimes two or more, in order to answer [the believers or others]: when they would inquire about something, God would send down verses in response (*idhā sa'alū 'an shay'in anzalahu Allāhu jawāban lahum*)."[10] Indeed, if we are to believe Muḥammad's earliest surviving biography, the Jews themselves were responsible for the lion's share of the instigative questions that provoked the divine revelations eventually integrated into Muslim scripture:

> It was the Jewish rabbis who used to annoy the Apostle with questions and introduce confusion, so as to confound the truth with falsity. The Qur'ān used to come down in reference to these questions of theirs, though some of the questions about what was allowed and forbidden came from the Muslims themselves.[11]

---

former statement, then we are back to our polemic (for which see below, notes 25 and 27; chap. 3, n. 8; chap. 7, notes 47 and 51).

9 Qurṭubī, 13: 25. Similarly, Ibn Isḥāq portrays the Jews as dissatisfied by what they saw as the disorder in the revelations received by Muḥammad (*lā narāhu muttasiqan kamā tattasiq al-Tawrāt* – Wansbrough, *Sectarian Milieu*, 21). See also Ibn Isḥāq—Guillaume, 269, where the Jews ask, "Is it true, Muḥammad, that what you have brought is the truth from God? For our part, we cannot see that it is arranged as the Torah is." On modes of revelation of the Qur'ān, see Wansbrough, *Quranic Studies*, esp. 30 ff. Not only the structure, but also the style of Muslim scripture evoked Jewish jeering: "*ḍaḥikat al-Yahūd wa-qālū: mā yashbahu hādhā kalām Allāh!*" – Qurṭubī, 1: 239.

10 Ṭabarī, 19: 15. As we shall see, al-Qurṭubī is more gingerly in his description of this archetypal *istiftā'-fatwā* process. That the forging of the Islamic religion was a process – at least from the vantage point of the believers – is suggested, *inter alia*, by the wording of what is considered by Muslim tradition to be the final revelation, vouchsafed unto Muḥammad eighty-two days before his death: "Today I have completed (*akmaltu*) your religion for you and finished (*atmamtu*) dispensing My favor upon you ..." (Q. 5: 3).

11 Ibn Isḥāq—Guillaume, 239. The original reads: "*kānat aḥbār Yahūd humu lladhīna yas'alūna rasūl Allāhi, ṣallā Allāhu 'alayhi wa-sallam, wa-yata'annatūnahu wa-ya'tūnahu bi'l-labs li-yalbisū'l-ḥaqqa bi'l-bāṭili* (see Q. 2: 42) *fa-kāna al-Qur'ānu yanzilu fīhim fīmā yas'alūna 'anhu illā qalīlan min al-masā'il fī'l-ḥalāl wa'l-ḥarām kāna al-Muslimūna yas'alūna 'anhā*" (Abū Muḥammad 'Abd al-Mālik b. Hishām al-Ma'āfirī, *Al-Sīra al-Nabawiyya* [Cairo: Maktabat al-Kulliyāt al-Azhariyya, n.d.], 2: 115). The qualification at the end – "though

It was such unwelcome (though ultimately fruitful) pestering that earned the Jews the pithy sobriquet, *aṣḥāb al-mas'ala* – "the people who ask questions."[12] Regardless, however, of which party can take credit for

some few of the questions ... came from the Muslims themselves" – implies that the Jews posed the majority of queries that led to the reactive revelations that currently comprise the better part of the Qur'ān. Interesting in this vein is the resemblance between the Israelites' persistent questioning of Moses concerning the sacrificial heifer (Q. 2: 67–71 – see below, chapter 7) and 'Umar b. al-Khaṭṭāb's repeated requests for further divine elucidation of the policy on wine (Qurṭubī, 5: 174). The two interrogations employ suggestively similar terminology (*ud'u lanā Rabbaka yubayyin lanā mā hiya ... Allāhumma bayyin lanā fī'l-khamri bayānan shāfiyan*); both involve exactly three demands for increasing clarification of a heavenly prescription (or *takhṣīṣ*, as certain exegetes would call it), after which the inquirers are avowedly satisfied (*qālū: al'āna ji'ta bi'l-ḥaqqi fa-dhabaḥūhā ... qāla 'Umar: intahaynā*); and both are the proximate cause of celestial communications eventually included in the *muṣḥaf* or Qur'ānic codex. Like the Jews – although to a far lesser extent – 'Umar is what we might call a *muhbiṭ al-waḥy*, an "instigator of divine revelation" (see below, chap. 2, n. 33 and chap. 7, notes 51 and 55).

12 Ibn Isḥāq—Guillaume, 240; Ibn Hishām, 2: 117 (this essential characteristic of the Jews in early Islamic literature is taken up at length below, in chapter 7). David Powers reminds me that in Sūrat al-Kahf, Moses himself is portrayed as singularly incapable of *not* asking questions (of "one of our servants whom We had granted mercy and knowledge," generally construed as Khiḍr [Q. 18: 66–82], in a story that itself has Jewish parallels. On Moses and Khiḍr see Gordon Newby, *The Making of the Last Prophet: A Reconstruction of the Earliest Biography of Muhammad* [Columbia: University of South Carolina Press, 1989], 182 ff; Bernhard Heller, "Chadhir und der Prophet Elijahu als wundertätige Baumeister," *Monatsschrift für Geschichte und Wissenschaft des Judentums* 81 [1937]; Mark Lidzbarski, "Wer ist Chadhir?" *Zeitschrift für Assyriologie* 8 [1893]; Karl Vollers, "Chidher," *Archiv für Religionwissenschaft* 12 [1909]; Jacob Lassner, *Demonizing the Queen of Sheba: Boundaries of Gender and Culture in Postbiblical Judaism and Medieval Islam* (Chicago: Cicago University Press, 1993), 243, n. 75; Brannon Wheeler, "Moses or Alexander: Early Islamic Exegesis of Qur'ān 18: 60–65," *Journal of Near Eastern Studies* 57 no. 3 [1998], and now the same author's *Moses in the Quran and Islamic Exegesis* [London: RoutledgeCurzon, 2002], chapter one). As they did in the New Testament and Christian tradition, the Jews of Qur'ān and *ḥadīth* play the role of irritating gadfly, relentlessly bombarding Muḥammad with picayune questions designed to trip him up (one Jew even challenged the descriptions of culinary paradisiacal recompense found in Q. 55 and 56 by raising the objection that "so much eating and drinking must necessarily require proper evacuations, an act unworthy of the holiness of heaven." Muḥammad responded that in the World to Come all human waste-products will exit the body as perspiration, "a sweat as odoriferous as musk" – (George Sale, *The Koran* [London: Frederick Warne & Co., n.d.], *Preliminary Discourse*, 77). For

eliciting the greatest number of heavenly *fatāwā* (responsa), it is al-Qurṭubī's justification of this "continuous revelation" in the face of reputed Jewish criticism that is of interest to us. That justification includes, albeit, the claim that Muḥammad, unlike the previous *rusul* or recipients of scriptures, was illiterate (*ummī*), and could therefore absorb the Creator's message only in small, periodic doses; but the commentator's premier rejoinder to this challenge is that only if revelation is a prolonged process can there be sufficient room for *nāsikh* and *mansūkh.*[13]

Al-Qurṭubī waxes fervid about the significance of the institution of abrogation for Islamic law and life:

> Knowledge of this discipline is imperative, and its utility enormous. No religious scholar may dispense with it, and only ignorant persons and fools contest it. An abundance of regulations arise from it, and without it one cannot distinguish the permitted from the forbidden.[14]

---

a selective list of scholarly works illuminating aspects of the Jewish-Muslim and Judaic-Islamic relationship, see the bibliography of the present work.

13 Qurṭubī, 13:25.

14 Qurṭubī, 2:55. The "ignorant persons and fools," we find out further along in al-Qurṭubī's discussion, are "certain latter-day groups affiliated with Islam that deny the legitimacy [of *naskh*], and they are refuted by the consensus of the earlier generations of scholars regarding its occurrence and significance in the framework of the law (*ankarat ṭawā'if min al-muntamīn li'l-Islām al-muta'akhkhirīn jawāzahu wa-hum maḥjūjūn bi-ijmā' al-salaf al-sābiq 'alā wuqū'ihi fī'l-sharī'a* – Ibid., 2:56). Muslim opponents of *naskh* are still encountered in modern times, from Sir Sayyid Aḥmad Khan and Muḥammad 'Abduh onward. See, as one instance among many, Maulana Muhammad Ali, *The Holy Qur'ān: Arabic Text, English Translation and Commentary* (Lahore: Ahmadiyyah Anjuman Isha'at Islam, 1995 [first published 1917]), *passim,* in which the well known Aḥmadī translator-commentator engages in a veritable crusade against the concept of abrogation. The earliest opponent of *naskh* was evidently the famed Qur'ān reader (*sayyid al-qurrā'*) and secretary to the Prophet, Ubayy b. Ka'b, of whom 'Umar b. al-Khaṭṭāb reputedly said: "We abandon some of the statements of Ubayy, because he is unwilling to abandon any of the statements of Allāh" (Bukhārī, 6:60 [8]; cf. Burton, *Collection,* 165 and 179–80).

One is tempted to speculate on the possible connection between criticism by the *aṣḥāb al-ḥadīth* (conservative, precedent-touting "traditionalists") of the fickleness of the *aṣḥāb al-ra'y* (early purveyors of an independent rationalist methodology in jurisprudence) and the historical development of the opposition to *naskh.* The Khurāsānī *muḥaddith* Abū Ḥamza al-Sukkarī told of having asked Abū Ḥanīfa, the pivotal figure of early *ra'y,* a series of legal questions. "I went away for some twenty years, then returned to him, and lo, he had gone back on those questions! [In the meantime] I had given [his original answers] to people as juridical opinions (*aftaytu bihā al-nās*), and I informed Abū Ḥanīfa

He relates an anecdote in which 'Alī b. Abī Ṭālib entered the mosque to find an unfamiliar man haranguing the crowd (*rajul yudhakkiru wa-yukhawwifu al-nās*). Angered, the Commander of the Faithful sent to the preacher: "Do you know *nāsikh* from *mansūkh*?" The man admitted that he did not. "Then," said 'Alī, "you have ruined yourself and others" (*halakta wa-ahlakta*).[15] Al-Qurṭubī's enthusiasm for *naskh* – a term he defines as "the annulment and elimination of a thing and the substitution of another thing for it, as when the sun replaces (*nasakhat*) the shade or old age replaces youth" – leads him to take up the aforementioned gauntlet purportedly thrown down by the Jews, and offer a more elaborate refutation of their critique than the terse dismissal of Q. 16: 102 ("But most of them understand not"):

> Certain parties among the Jews rejected the validity [of *naskh*], but they are refuted by what is found in their own scriptures. For it is there asserted that God the Exalted declared to Noah upon his egress from the ark: "Behold, I have made all beasts food for you and for your descendents (*innī qad ja'altu*

---

of this. He said, 'We see one view (*narā al-ra'y*) one day, then the next day we see another view and take the first one back." Similarly, the qāḍī Ḥafṣ b. Ghiyāth reported seeing Abū Ḥanīfa "state ten positions, then go back on all of them." (Christopher Melchert, *The Formation of the Sunni Schools of Law, 9th–10th Centuries CE* [Leiden: E.J. Brill, 1997], 11–12). 'Abd Allāh b. Dāwūd al-Khuraybī justified this tendency of Abū Ḥanīfa, saying that it "indicates the breadth of his learning: if his learning had been narrow, his answer would have been one; however, his affair was broad, so he would treat it however he liked." (ibid., 52). The resolute search for stability on the part of the *aṣḥāb al-ḥadīth* may have led some of them to recoil from descriptions of Allāh that made Him sound as wishy-washy as Abū Ḥanīfa. In the event, however, the majority of traditionalists seem to have been strong supporters of *naskh*, and the resistance to (what I would claim was) the pristine Islamic notion of an open-minded, swayable Deity seems to have emerged primarily within the *opposing* camp: among the circles of the *mutakallimūn/mu'tazilūn* who were associated with the *aṣḥāb al-ra'y* (see below, note 27, and the appendix).

15 Qurṭubī, 2:55. For other recensions of this report, involving various protagonists in place of 'Alī, see Burton, *Sources*, 22–3. "*Halakta wa-ahlakta*" is reminiscent of the *khoṭe u makhṭi et ha-rabim* (the one who sins and causes others to sin) of Jewish tradition, as well as of the *yuḍallūn wa-yaḍullūn* of the *ḥadīth*. The version of this anecdote in Abū Bakr Muḥammad b. 'Abd Allāh al-Ma'āfirī b. al-'Arabī, *Al-Nāsikh wa'l-Mansūkh fī'l-Qur'ān al-Karīm* (Cairo: Maktabat al-Thaqāfa al-Dīniyya, n.d.), 1: 14, lays even more stress on the hellfire and brimstone character of the unidentified man's preaching and thus on the lenient orientation of 'Alī's response.

16 Genesis, 9: 3–4: "Every creature that lives shall be yours to eat; as with the green grasses, I give you all these. You must not, however, eat flesh with its life-blood in it." Al-Qurṭubī's rendering is quite close to the Hebrew original.

kulla dābbatin ma'kal laka wa-li-dhurriyyatika), and I have given you free rein [to consume] these just as [you have heretofore eaten] herbage – with the exception of blood, which you shall not eat."[16] Then, subsequently, God forbade Moses and the Children of Israel a great many animals. [It is also alleged in the Torah] that Adam used to affiance brothers to their sisters, and afterwards [the same sacred document states that] God prohibited this to Moses and others.[17] [The Pentateuch additionally avers] that God commanded Abraham, the Friend of God, to sacrifice his son, and then afterwards He said to him: Do not sacrifice him;[18] and that Moses ordered the Children of Israel to kill those among them who had worshipped the calf, and then ordered them to withhold their swords from the same;[19] and that

17 Rabbinic tradition (not the Pentateuch itself) indeed posits that humankind is descended from the union of siblings, i.e. Adam's children (see Soṭa 10a; Sanhedrin 57a–58b; Genesis Rabbah 18:3 and 20:5). The prohibitions against such incest are found in the eighteenth chapter of Leviticus. For the stories of Cain, Abel and their sisters in Islamic historiography, see Newby, *Last Prophet,* 38–41 and 71, and Brannon Wheeler, *Prophets in the Qur'ān: An Introduction to the Qur'ān and Muslim Exegesis* (London: Continuum, 2002), 36–42; also Adang, *Muslim Writers,* 121. The Midrash avers, moreover, that all of *Jacob's* sons were born together with a female twin to whom they were eventually married and with whom they cohabited in order to produce the ensuing generations of the Children of Israel (see RaSHI, drawing on Midrash Rabbah, to Genesis, 37:35: "And [Jacob's] sons *and daughters* rose up to comfort him ..." Rabbi Judah says: *aḥayot te'omot noldu 'im kol shevеṭ ve-shevеṭ u-nesa'um*).

18 Genesis, 22:1–19.

19 The Bible nowhere says this. Moses is shown giving the original order, but he neither countermands it nor limits it at any point. How did al-Qurṭubī arrive at his conclusion? Several possibilities suggest themselves. In the opening verses of Exodus, Chapter 32, we read that when Moses tarried on the mountain, "the people" demanded that Aaron fashion them a substitute deity; then "all the people" donated their jewelry for the same purpose; and finally "the people" offered sacrifices to, and otherwise adored, the calf that Aaron had made. Later on in the chapter, when Moses hurried down the mountain and caught his nation in the act of idolatry, he commanded the Levites who had rallied to him to "go back and forth from gate to gate throughout the camp, and slay brother, neighbor and kin." The text continues: "Some three thousand of the people fell that day" (32:27–8). Perhaps al-Qurṭubī was impressed by the discrepancy: far more than three thousand had worshipped the calf (the Israelites – "all the people" – numbered six hundred thousand men of army age alone [see Numbers, 1:46] and al-Qurṭubī knew this, as is evidenced elsewhere in his commentary: "*wa-hum sittu-mi'a alf min al-muqātila siwā al-shuyūkh wa'l-dhurriyya wa'l-nisā'* [Qurṭubī, 1:375]). God had purposed to eradicate them *all* in the wake of their mass betrayal (Exodus, 32:9–10), yet, in the end, only three thousand were killed. We should remember, also, the midrash cited above (note 1) in which Moses challenges God: "Did you not swear that You would eradicate your children after they worshipped the calf, and then reverse Yourself?" (Deut. Rabbah, 2:8). Al-Qurṭubī is focusing on what he claims to

Moses was not pledged to his prophetic office before receiving the call, but then became beholden to it afterward.[20]

---

be the Biblical version of these events, so as to turn the Jews' own weapon against themselves in the matter of *naskh*, but he may additionally have been influenced by the Qur'ānic summary of the incident: "... and when We appointed for Moses forty nights [on the mountain], and then you chose the calf when he had gone from you, and were wrongdoers. Then, even after that, We pardoned you in order that you might give thanks" (Q. 2: 51–2).
It is al-Qurṭubī's commentary to Q. 2: 54, however – in which Moses is depicted ordering the people to "kill themselves" in repentance for their idolatrous betrayal and God is depicted "turning to them in mercy" immediately afterward – which may provide a clue to what really happened here. In this gloss al-Qurṭubī adduces an opinion to the effect that all of those who had worshipped the calf were originally slated for slaughter, but that "when the number of slain reached 70,000, God forgave them" [Qurṭubī, 1: 385–6]). Now, the opening verses of *Ki Tisa,* the Pentateuchal "portion of the week" containing the story of the golden calf, read as follows: "The Lord spoke to Moses, saying: 'When you take a census of the Israelite people according to their count, each shall pay the Lord a ransom for himself upon being counted, so that no plague may come upon them as a result of being counted'" (Exodus, 30: 11). In II Samuel, an angry God "incites" David to take an additional census of his subjects, and the king commands Joab: "Go number Israel and Judah." After Joab reluctantly fulfills this mission, "the Lord sent a pestilence upon Israel from morning until the set time, and 70,000 of the people died from Dan to Be'er Sheva'. But when the angel extended his hand against Jerusalem to destroy it, the Lord renounced further punishment and said to the *angel* who was destroying the people, 'Enough! Stay your hand!'"(II Samuel, 24: 15–6; cf. Chron. 1 21: 1 where the "inciter" is Satan). Returning to the conclusion of the golden calf story in Exodus, we find that after the Levites had killed 3,000 of their Israelite brethren – and Moses had tried to extract a pardon for the remainder from his Lord – God enjoined: "'Go now, lead the people where I tell you. Behold, My *angel* shall go before you, and when I choose to make an accounting, then will I bring them to account for their sins.' Then the Lord sent a plague upon the people for what they did with the calf that Aaron made" (Exodus, 32: 34–5). Nothing is said regarding the results of this plague, nor are we told *when* the Lord sent it (did He delay it until David's time?). At any rate, the close relationship between the story in Exodus and the story in II Samuel (the latter almost definitely harks back to the former) was apparently not lost on certain of the authorities consulted by al-Qurṭubī, and he himself may have conflated the two narratives (characteristically, as we shall see) in order to arrive at his conception of the calf-worshippers' fate, and his conclusion that the slaughter had been aborted. 70,000 is a common number in Muslim—Jewish legend, see Newby, *Last Prophet,* 131, 141 and 187–8, and Qurṭubī, 19: 221.

20 Qurṭubī, 2: 56–7. My rendering of this last clause – "*wa-bi-anna nubuwwatahu ghayr muta'abbadu bihā qabla ba'thihi thumma tu'abbidu bihā ba'da dhālika*" – is a guess. For similar arguments employed by other exegetes and authors to combat the Jewish ridicule of *naskh,* see Adang, *Muslim Writers,* 79 and

The remainder of al-Qurṭubī's defense of *naskh* focuses on what he sees as the fine but essential distinction between the valid phenomenon of divine abrogation and the illegitimate notion of celestial vacillation. In the course of clarifying this issue, he employs phraseology that sounds almost as if it were lifted from the manifesto of a modern-day religious reformer:

> Nor is [the institution of *naskh*] tantamount to heavenly wavering (*al-badā'*).[21] Rather, it consists of the transfer of human beings from one rite to the next and from one regulation to the next according to what is in their best interests (*naql al-'ubbād min 'ibāda ilā 'ibāda wa-ḥukm ilā ḥukm li-ḍarbin min al-maṣlaḥa*), [in a process that] gives evidence of God's infinite wisdom and unmitigated sovereignty. And there is no disagreement among reasonable people that the legal systems of the prophets were designed in order to serve both the sacred and mundane interests of humanity (*sharā'i' al-anbiyā' quṣida bihā maṣāliḥ al-khalq al-dīniyya wa'l-dunyawiyya*). Now, this [transfer from dispensation to dispensation] would necessarily entail a change of mind, were [the one effecting the transfer] unaware of the ultimate outcome (*ma'āl*) of the process. However, in the case of one who *is* aware [of the ultimate outcome – i.e., God – it may be said that] His mes-

chapter six; Lazarus-Yafeh, 40–1; Moshe Pearlman, "Ha-Pulmus bayn ha-Islam la-Yahadut bi-Yemei ha-Baynayim," in Lazarus-Yafeh (ed.), *Sofrim Muslemim 'al Yehudim ve-Yahadut* (Jerusalem: Mercaz Zalman Shazar le-Toldot Yisrael, 1995), 137–8; and Brannon Wheeler, "Israel and the Torah of Muḥammad" in Reeves, *Bible and Qur'ān,* 81. It might be a fruitful avenue of investigation to compare the general notion of *naskh* with a Qur'ānic statement seen by many Muslim commentators as a reference to the Satanic Verses (which were themselves, in a sense, abrogated): "We have not sent before you [O Muḥammad] any Apostle or Prophet but when he longed, Satan cast suggestions [into his heart to satisfy] his longing. But God annuls (*fa-yansakhu Allāhu*) that which Satan suggests and then firmly establishes His revelations (*yuḥkimu Allāhu ayātihi*); and He makes that which Satan had suggested a trial (*fitna*) for those whose hearts are diseased and hardened" (Q. 22: 52; see also Q. 17: 73 and 16: 102; for the "official" Muslim outlook on the import of *n.s.kh.* in this verse see Burton, *Collection,* 62 and 235). "What kind of idea is He?" Salman Rushdie's "Mahound" wonders aloud about God. "What kind am I? An idea strong and immovable, or an idea that bends?" "Mahound" finally decides that he and his God are the former; Muslim tradition portrays both as in every way the latter (see below, chapter 2).

21 Lane defines *badā'* as "an opinion that occurs to one or arises in the mind, and particularly one that is different from a former opinion" (E.W. Lane, *An Arabic-English Lexicon* [London: Williams and Norgate, 1863], 1: 171, col. 1; see also I. Goldziher/A. S. Tritton, *s. v.* "Badā'" in *EI*²). For the issue of *badā'* in Muslim—Jewish polemic and Bible criticism see Adang, *Muslim Writers,* chapter six and *passim,* and Lazarus-Yafeh, *Intertwined Worlds,* 38, where other relevant secondary literature is also cited (n. 55).

> sages are modified in accordance with shifts in the requirements [of the people] (*tatabaddalu khiṭābātuhu bi-ḥasabi tabaddul al-maṣāliḥ*), in the same way that a physician observing the varying conditions of his patient [adjusts his treatment accordingly]. Thus did the Creator observe the varying conditions of His creatures [and alter the "prescription" to suit the situation] in accordance with His desire – there is no god but He! His message mutates, but His knowledge and will remain the same.[22]

How can God alter His decrees without changing His mind? Al-Qurṭubī's analogy to the doctor-patient relationship seems to indicate that his solution to this conundrum is as follows. An experienced physician has acquired a certain body of medical knowledge, which (more so in al-Qurṭubī's time than our own) remains essentially static. This knowledge is manipulated by a Boolean method of deduction: *if* the patient is suffering from streptococcus, *then* he should be put on antibiotics; *if* the strep-throat is aggravated and turns into the flu, *then* amantadine and three days rest must be prescribed instead. In such a scenario, the body of medicinal knowledge remains constant, while the patient's ailments and the physician's curative measures vary. Even though the doctor tailors the treatment he administers to fit the patient's fluctuating condition, it would be inaccurate to say that he changes his mind (which he would do only if he caught himself in an error).[23]

Similarly, God enjoins upon His believers those rules and rituals which are suitable to their situation at a given time. When circumstances change and different guidelines are required, He is ready and willing to issue a fresh injunction or impose a novel order. In His omniscience, the Deity (unlike the doctor) is, moreover, fully apprised from the outset of the various stages through which a given community will pass (including the final stage, *ma'āl*).[24] The problems that will

---

22 Qurṭubī, 2:57. Adang has noted this conclusion of al-Qurṭubī's (Adang, *Muslim Writers,* 209). See also Pearlman, "Pulmus," 130.

23 For another health-related analogy designed to explain and justify *naskh,* see Adang, *Muslim Writers,* 214. Many more similar arguments to this effect may be found in the theoretical literature, e.g., Abū Bakr Muḥammad b. Mūsā al-Ḥāzimī, *Al-I'tibār fī'l-Nāsikh wa'l-Mansūkh min al-Āthār* (n. p., n. d.), 6 ff; or 'Abd Allāh Shams al-Dīn al-Ḥanbalī, *Ṣafwat al-Rāsikh fī 'Ilm al-Mansukh wa'l-Nāsikh* (Beirut: Dār al-Fikr, n. d.), 2:35 ff and *passim.*

24 In a certain sense the doctor, too, can anticipate the requisite changes in treatment. That is, he knows (or ideally should know) what therapy will be needed for any given scenario – there being a finite set of possibilities – and in many cases may even be able to predict the progression of an illness. Still, this is a far cry from the Deity's level of knowledge, or from the Qurṭubīan conception of historical events "lingering in the womb of time, waiting to be delivered" (as

arise are all expected and the solutions to them prepared ahead of time. Long before the world came into being, the successive regimes that would govern humankind during different periods were already lined up and set to descend down to earth intermittently. Both *nāsikh* and *mansūkh,* both the original provisions and their eventual replacements, were inscribed on the Preserved Tablet and recorded from aforetime in the uncreated *Umm al-Kitāb* (Heavenly Codex), anticipating all the exigencies of the future.[25] To Allāh belongeth East and West, beginning

---

Shakespeare phrased it). The early victory of the outlook known as *qadar,* the divine predestination of all things, facilitated the defense of the Qur'ān as *ghayr makhlūq* (uncreated) despite its having been parceled out in response to circumstances, the argument being easily made that – as Sale formulates it – "all the accidents for the sake of which these occasional passages were revealed, were predetermined by God from all eternity" and thus the passages themselves could have existed from all eternity (Sale, "Preliminary Discourse," 50).

25 The first word of the first revelation vouchsafed unto the Prophet Muḥammad in 610 CE was: *iqra'!* – "Recite!" (or perhaps: "Read!"). Even according to the well known *ḥadīth*ic interpolation in which Muḥammad asks, "What shall I recite?" and the angel responds "Recite in the name of your Lord!", etc. (Ṭabarī, 30: 318; Qurṭubī, 20: 91; see Isaiah, 40: 6), we still aren't told *whence* the newly appointed Messenger should recite the material that would eventually be redacted into the Qur'ānic codex (some traditions do have Gabriel hold out a piece of silk covered with writing on that august occasion or show Muḥammad – then and once a year from that point on until "the final check" – the whole of scripture on scrolls wrapped in silk embroidered with precious stones [see the commentaries to Q. 97]). Perhaps a reference may be discerned in this to the idea, already adumbrated elsewhere in the Qur'ān, that every one of the revelations, including the abrogated and abrogating verses, was already present and accounted for (in the *Umm al-Kitāb* or on the *Lawḥ al-Maḥfūẓ*) ages before the Apostle's initial epiphany. The script had been composed long ago (or had existed eternally): Gabriel merely read his lines on cue (see again the commentaries to Q. 97).

Even al-Ṭabarī sometimes seems to support this notion: "The [entire] Qur'ān descended from the Preserved Tablet to the lowest heaven (*samā' al-dunya* – or, as some say, from the *zibr/zubr* [= the Writing] to the *bayt al-ma'mūr*) on the Night of Destiny in the month of Ramaḍān, and thence it was subsequently dispensed to Muḥammad whenever God willed" (Ṭabarī, 2: 196. Interestingly, many of al-Ṭabarī's proof-texts stipulate that this "pre-revelation" occurred *fī jumla wāḥida,* in one fell swoop. See also Ṭabarī, 30: 327–8, where the ready-made Revelation descended complete on *laylat al-qadr* and "hovered amongst the stars," whence it was parceled out over time to Muḥammad). The Mu'tazilites basically concurred with this outlook (see Majid Fakhry, *A History of Islamic Philosophy* [New York: Columbia University Press, 1970], 62), but they nevertheless utilized the phenomenon of abrogation to argue that the Qur'ān was not eternally pre-existent (see David Powers, *Studies in Qur'ān and Ḥa-*

and end: in His infinite wisdom and unlimited sovereignty He "effaces what He pleases and establishes what He pleases" (Q. 13:39), adapting and exchanging His ordinances as He sees fit – and as He had, indeed, planned to do from time immemorial – for the ultimate benefit of mankind. Thus, though His Knowledge, Will and even Word (all of which may be said, according to Ash'arite theology, to comprise integral parts of Himself)[26] are never modified in an absolute sense, His Message is nevertheless regularly "modernized" from the perspective of human beings, through the medium of a staggered release of already extant material. *Pace* Aristotle, then (and the Jews), "God is capable of all things" – including (transitive) change.[27]

---

dīth: The Formation of the Islamic Law of Inheritance [Berkeley: University of California Press, 1986], 143.

26 See Richard J. McCarthy, *The Theology of al-Ash'arī* (Beirut: Imprimerie Catholique, 1953), chapter 2.

27 By al-Qurṭubī's time (13th century CE), the infiltration of Greek philosophical rationalism into Islam, Christianity and Judaism had succeeded in demythologizing and dehumanizing the Deity even more than the Semitic monotheisms themselves had done, enforcing a perception of divine omniscience and immutability in the minds of many *mutakallimūn* that went so far as to preclude any genuine interaction between God and His creatures. Al-Qurṭubī was at least partially "infected": he maintained the *form* of the pristine Muslim conception of Allāh as regularly and truly responsive – a unique outlook, I would argue, in the history of religious thought – but his own thesis (which evolved out of those of certain of his predecessors) deracinated it. Al-Ṭabarī, on the other hand, writing around the turn of the tenth century CE (and seemingly as innocent of the post-Socratic perception of divine infallibility as he was of the later Islamic notion of the Prophet's *'iṣma*), still appears, for the most part, to be working with what I would argue was the earliest understanding of *naskh* (but cf. note 25, above, as well as Patricia Crone and Martin Hinds, who assume that al-Ṭabarī did support the doctrine of *iṣma* – see their *God's Caliph: Religious Authority in the First Centuries of Islam* [Cambridge: Cambridge University Press, 1986], p. 5. n. 5). That pristine conception of *naskh* is difficult for the modern religious mentality to retrieve after centuries of indoctrination by Aristotelian-based theology. It held, one imagines, a sentiment not too far removed from Emerson's famous assertion that "[a] foolish consistency is the hobgoblin of little minds ... With consistency a great soul has simply nothing to do ... Speak what you think today in hard words; and to-morrow, speak what tomorrow thinks in hard words again, though it contradict everything you said to-day" (Emerson, "Self Reliance"). The great soul of God interacts with the world and is genuinely affected and even edified by what it experiences there. Allāh, no less than the Biblical Deity (at least according to a plain reading of the Old Testament), is man enough to admit His mistakes. This, it seems to me, was the original, blissfully "unexamined" outlook eventually swept away by the Hellenistic logic-chopping of medieval scholasticism.

2. Clemency as Policy

Naskh, Rukhṣa and the Incubation of Islamic Law

Unlike the method of *jam'* or synthesis, *naskh* serves not so much to *defuse* the tension between apparently conflicting scriptural passages as to harness the energy produced by that tension in order to construct the traditional narrative of early Islamic legal development. A few examples of the application of this technique to verses perceived by many exegetes as irreconcilable will help clarify the matter. "O you, wrapped in your mantle!" we read at the outset of Sūrat al-Muzzammil, "Arise [to prayer], and continue [therein] all night, save a small part: a half thereof, or a little less, or a little more ..." (Q. 73: 1–3).[1] The concluding lines of the same chapter, however, read as follows:

> Your Lord knows that you sometimes keep vigil nearly two-thirds of the night, and sometimes half or one third of it, as do others among your followers. Now, God measures the night and day [with precision]. He knows that you [believers] cannot calculate [the length of your vigil accurately – *'alima an lan tuḥṣūhu*], and He turns to you in mercy: Recite [during the night], therefore, as much of the Qur'ān as is easy for you (*iqra'ū mā tayassara min al-Qur'ān*) ... (Q. 73: 20).

These two passages seem to evince divergent attitudes to *tahajjud*, "passing the night in prayer," a *hapax legomenon* in the Qur'ān appearing only in a third passage from Sūrat al-Isrā': "Pray also during the night [in addition to the quotidian *ṣalāt* sessions],[2] as a supererogation

---

1 It is, of course, *ḥadīth*, *fiqh*, and *asbāb al-nuzūl* that connect these verses to nocturnal prayer. A critical perspective, bypassing the guidance of tradition, may certainly propose alternate referents. Muir, for example, sees this passage as describing long nights spent by Muḥammad labouring over the composition of the Qur'ān itself (Sir William Muir, *The Life of Moḥammad* [revised edition by T. H. Weir; Edinburgh: John Grant, 1923], 102). This is evidently his way of portraying what tradition describes as the nights of Ramaḍān during which Gabriel taught Muḥammad the Qur'ān.

2 My parenthetical clarification is itself problematic: according to some opinions

for you (*wa-min al-layli fa-tahajjad bihi nāfilatan laka*), for the fulfillment of which your Lord may exalt you to a high station" (Q. 17: 79).

Although the issue of nocturnal devotions is highly complex and shot-through with exegetical and juristic disputes,[3] the following composite sketch may responsibly be offered. Based on the fact that Q. 73: 1 addresses "you, wrapped in your mantle" and appropriately employs the singular (*qum al-layl* ... *aw unquṣ* ... *aw zid* ... *wa-rattil* ...) – as does Q. 17: 79 (*tahajjad* ... *nāfilatan laka*) – al-Ṭabarī sides with those early experts among the *ṣaḥāba* (Companions), *tābiʿūn* (successors) and *tābiʿū al-tābiʿīn* (third generation Muslim authorities) who claim that the original injunction to pray at night was directed at the Prophet alone, and did not obligate the rest of the believers (*laka khāliṣatan dūna ummatika*); or, put differently, that this practice, while mandatory for Muḥammad, was only optional for his followers (*farīḍa ʿalayhi wa-li-ghayrihi taṭawwuʿ*).[4] This distinction did not last long, however,

---

it was *this* verse that ultimately abrogated the obligatory nature of night prayer originally established by Q. 73: 1–3, such that it represents the *end* of a process. Since Q. 17: 79 is directly preceded by, and connected to, one of the launch-verses for the establishment of *awqāt al-ṣalāt* (the times for the prescribed *day-time* prayers), we can therefore understand the determination of al-Māwardī (and many other jurists) that "the first [prayer service] imposed by God on his Prophet was the night vigil" (*awwal mā faraḍa Allāhu ʿalā nabiyihi qiyām al-layl* – Abū'l-Ḥasan ʿAlī b. Muḥammad b. Ḥabīb al-Māwardī, *Al-Ḥāwi al-Kabīr* [Beirut: Dār al-Fikr, 1994], 2: 4. Henceforward: Māwardī). If one follows the (more popular) opinion of Ibn ʿAbbās, however, that the beginning of *Sūrat al-Muzzammil* was abrogated by its ending, then the place and function of Q. 17: 79 is somewhat harder to locate, and the chronology of the establishment of the various components of prescribed prayer all the more bewildering. All told, some seven different verses are suggested by as many commentators and *fuqahā'* as occasioning the abrogation of Q. 73: 1–3.

3 For a thorough (but difficult) exposition of these, see Qurṭubī, 19: 25–30 and 40–45. The complexity of the divine process of prayer-law promulgation is reflected in the one-sentence summary offered by al-Shāfiʿī in the introduction to his discussion of the same: "I heard from one whose transmissions are trustworthy that God revealed an ordinance regarding prescribed prayer, then abrogated that ordinance in favor of another ordinance, then abrogated the second ordinance in favor of the obligation to perform the five daily prayers" (Muḥammad b. Idrīs al-Shāfiʿī, *Kitāb al-Umm* [Beirut: Dār al-Fikr, n.d], 1: 86).

4 Ṭabarī, 15: 176, 178. Cf. al-Qummī al-Naysābūrī's general rule – which he stipulates in connection with the *witr* prayer – that "if it was mandated for [the Prophet], then it was mandated for his community (*idhā wajaba ʿalayhi wajaba ʿalā ummatihi*), as it is written: 'Follow him!'" (Q. 6: 156 – in scriptural context this actually means "follow it," i.e. the Qur'ān). Niẓām al-Dīn Ḥasan b. Muḥammad al-Qummī al-Naysābūrī, *Tafsīr Gharā'ib al-Qur'ān* (Beirut: Dār

as we learn from the same commentator's gloss to the aforementioned verses of Sūrat al-Muzzammil, where varying versions of the following *ḥadīth* of 'Ā'isha are cited:

> I used to weave a mat for the Messenger of God upon which he would pray at night. Word got out about this and the people assembled [in, or just outside of, the Prophet's Mosque adjoining 'Ā'isha's quarters] during his prayer, and they began coughing and clearing their throats (*ja'alū yatanaḥnaḥūn wa-yatfulūn*).[5] [The Prophet thereupon] went out to them as one angered (*kharaja ka'l-mughḍab*) – in truth he did this out of compassion for them, fearing that nocturnal devotions would be prescribed for them also – and he said to them: "O people! Take upon yourselves only those acts of which you are capable (*iklafū min al-a'māl mā tuṭīqūn*), for God does not tire of dispensing rewards until such time as you yourselves tire of performing good deeds, and [thus] the best of actions are those in which you can persevere (*khayr al-a'māl mā dumtum 'alayhi*)." [Despite his best efforts, however, the Prophet's fears were in short order realized, for] the revelation then came down: "O you, wrapped in your mantle! Arise to prayer, and continue therein all night, save a small part: a half thereof, or a little less, or a little more..." (Q. 73: 1–3) – and [nocturnal devotions] were made incumbent upon them (*fa-kutibat 'alayhim*; in other versions: And God commanded His Prophet *and the believers* to rise for prayer at night...).[6]

---

al-Fikr, 1996), 4: 57. Another way to phrase this principle that underlies the institution of *sunna* is attributed to Ibn 'Abbās: *nabiyyakum mimman umira an yaqtadī bihi* (Qurṭubī, 15: 147). Al-Bayḍāwī restores the balance: *ḥukmuhu wa-ḥukm al-umma wāḥida illā mā khaṣṣahu al-dalīl* (Bayḍāwī, *Tafsīr,* 2: 247).

5 See Qurṭubī, 19: 29. Both of these are specifically acceptable methods of *isti'nās* (asking permission to enter or warning tenants of one's presence) required by Q. 24: 27–9 (see Ṭabarī, 9: 297–9). But because the crowd outside was clearly not requesting entrance into 'Ā'isha's tiny chamber (nor would they have ventured to interrupt their prophet's devotions); and as *isti'nās* is not required for entering a mosque (Qurṭubī, 15: 137); and, finally, since Muḥammad is said to have coughed/cleared his throat often during prayer (*kāna yatanaḥnaḥu fī ṣalātihi,* see, e.g., Ibn Ḥanbal, 10: 574); given all this, it is at least possible that the intent here is that the Muslims gathered outside had already begun "praying" in imitation of the sounds they heard emanating from their spiritual leader behind the door.

6 Ṭabarī, 29: 155–6. Although Q. 73: 1–3 is formulated in the singular, the *ḥadīth* perceives its addressees to be the Muslims at large. Alternate versions of this report are sometimes connected to the special nocturnal prayers of Ramaḍān (*tarāwīḥ*), and depict a gradual convergence of the believers on the Prophet's mosque over a three day period during that month, as word spread of their leader's exceptional practice. By the fourth night, the congregation of supererogatory supplicants had reached considerable dimensions, and on that occa-

What began as a personal precept intended for Muḥammad alone was thus expanded into a universal statute. (It is interesting that the Muslims' zeal to imitate their Prophet and enhance their service of God was the occasion for a divine fiat rendering that imitation and enhancement compulsory, a point to which we shall return later). This, however, was not Allāh's last word on the matter. Required to devote a considerable portion of their sleep-time to supplementary worship – worship that involved both numerous prostrations and prolonged standing[7] – the pious members of the community soon began to suffer from exhaustion and swollen feet, resorted to suspending themselves with ropes, and in general found this observance increasingly arduous.[8] The law remained in force for anywhere from eight months to ten years,[9] until

---

sion Muḥammad either refrained from performing nocturnal devotions, or did not show up at the mosque to do so publicly, or both. On the morrow, he explained to his perplexed followers that "the only thing that prevented me from coming out to you [last night] is that I feared that doing so might lead to [this precept] being declared obligatory for you" (*lam yamnaʿnī min al-khurūj ilaykum illā annī khashītu an tufraḍa ʿalaykum*) – either because the practice would thereby become a known *sunna* of the Prophet, or because Muḥammad's presence might lead to a situation in which the already mandatory nature of *his* night prayer would somehow "rub off" on the congregation as a whole (Ṣaḥīḥ Muslim, *Kitāb Ṣalāt al-Musāfirīn, Bāb Qiyām Ramaḍān – al-Tarāwīḥ*, 25: 177 [761]. All of this should probably be read with the development of the Jewish evening prayer [*maʿariv*] in mind, which began as an optional rite but became, as a result of increasingly regular performance, mandatory by late Talmudic times). See also Māwardī, 2: 4, where we read that after receiving (privately) the revelation at the outset of *al-Muzzammil* (Q. 73: 1–3), "*qāma rasūl Allāh naḥwan min qiyām shahr Ramaḍān ...*" If this means that the Prophet rose nights all year round the way he (or his community) *used to do* only during Ramaḍān, then it seems as if *qiyām al-layl* was an outgrowth of *tarāwīḥ*. If it means that he rose nights the way that we Muslims *now do* only during Ramaḍān, then *qiyām al-layl* appears to have chronological precedence, and the special nocturnal devotions of Ramaḍān are the vestige thereof. The entire issue is highly confused in the sources.

7 See Ṭabarī (19: 46) to Q. 25: 64: "[The servants of the Beneficent are they that] pass the night before their Lord prostrate and standing."

8 Ṭabarī, 29: 155–6: "*intafakhat sūquhum wa-warimat aqdāmuhum ... ḥattā kāna al-rajul yarbuṭ al-ḥabl wa-yataʿallaq ... fa-shaqqa dhālika ʿalā al-muʾminīn.*" Ibid., 16: 172: "Mujāhid said: 'This verse [i.e. Q. 20: 1] is similar to His injunction, "Recite [during the night] therefore, as much of the Qurʾān as is easy for you" (Q. 73: 20), for they used to suspend themselves by ropes tied around their chests [to keep them awake and erect] during [night] prayer'" (*kānū yuʿalliqūn al-ḥibāl fī ṣudūrihim fīʾl-ṣalāt*).

9 Ṭabarī, 29: 156–7, nos. 27260, 27264 and 27262. Those – like ʿAbd b. Ḥamīd and

such time as "God had mercy upon the believers" and "lightened their burden" and "revealed the amelioration at the end of the chapter" which "abrogated [the ordinance at] the beginning [of the chapter]" and "restored the prescribed prayer and abandoned the supererogatory supplication" ... "and the people rested."[10]

Ibn Abī Ḥātim – who proposed the ten year option must have envisioned the original imposition of *qiyām al-layl* as occurring earlier than indicated in the aforementioned hadīth of 'Ā'isha, who was married to the Prophet in 623 CE, and the remaining *aḥādīth* supplied by al-Ṭabarī to explain the onset of the night-prayer obligation indeed do not involve the Prophet's favorite wife. Another problem in this regard is that according to most accounts, *al-Muzzammil* is a Meccan *sūra* (some, however, except verse 20, as it discusses fighting in the way of Allāh), and certain opinions therefore place the entire process of the promulgation and cancellation of *qiyām al-layl* and its replacement by the five daily prayers *before* the *hijra* (e.g., Māwardī, 2: 5). This would leave 'Ā'isha out of the picture entirely. Still, upon arrival in Madīna after the *hijra,* the Prophet is reported to have urged the *anṣār* who swarmed to greet him to "show your joy by giving your neighbours the salutation of peace; send portions to the poor; bind close the ties of kinship; *and offer up your prayers while others sleep.* Thus shall you enter paradise in peace" (Muir, *Life of Mohammad,* 168. Emphasis added).

10 Ṭabarī, 29: 156–7, nos. 27260, 27261, 27264, 27263, 27260 and 27265 respectively. Another cycle of *ḥadīths* shows the Prophet himself "overdoing it" in the matter of *tahajjud* and being reproved for this by a divine revelation. Abū Ja'far (either Muḥammad al-Bāqir, the fifth Shī'ite Imām, or Muḥammad al-Taqī, the ninth Shī'ite Imām, probably the former) recounted: "The Messenger of God, may God's peace and blessings be upon him, was at 'Ā'isha's house on her night, and she said to him, 'O Messenger of God, why do you wear yourself out [standing in prayer until dawn]? After all, God has already forgiven you all of your past and present sins!' (*lima tut'ibu nafsaka wa-qad ghafara Allāhu laka mā taqaddama min dhanbika wa-mā ta'akhkhara* – see Q. 48: 2). He replied, 'O 'Ā'isha, shall I not be a thankful servant of God?'" [Abū Ja'far] said: "The Messenger of God used to stand up [praying all night] on the tips of his toes (*kāna yaqūmu 'alā aṭrāf aṣābi' rijlayhi*) until God the Exalted sent down: 'Ṭā Hā – We have not revealed the Qur'ān to you so that you should be distressed!'" (*mā anzalnā 'alayka al-Qur'ān li-tashqā* – Q. 20: 1. Muḥammad Bāqir al-Majlisī, *Biḥār al-Anwār* [Beirut: Mu'assasat al-Wafā', 1983], 68: 24. 'Ā'isha's query is also placed in the mouth of 'Umar, and elicits the self-same response from the Prophet, at Muḥammad's death-bed, when the latter continues reciting lengthy Qur'ānic passages despite his final agony – a suggestive conjunction of hypnos and thanatos [Muir, *Life of Mohammad,* 488]). Qatāda said: "[Muḥammad] would supplicate the whole night through and suspend himself by tying a rope around his chest so that sleep would not overcome him (*kāna yuṣallī al-layl kullahu wa-yu'alliqu ṣadrahu bi-ḥabl ḥattā lā yaghlibahu al-nawm*). And God, may He be Praised, commanded him to take it easy on himself (*amara an yukhaffifa 'an nafsihi*), and it is said that no revelations came

So al-Ṭabarī. The version of these events preferred by al-Qurṭubī omits the initial stage in which *qiyām al-layl* was converted from an individual to a collective precept, asserting that *tahajjud* was immediately made obligatory for Muḥammad and the entire congregation with the descent of the first verses of Sūrat al-Muzzammil (Q. 73: 1–3). In the wake of this revelation, "the Prophet and his Companions stood up (or woke up – *fa-qāmū*)[11] during the night for an entire year ... as they had been wont to do previously only during the month of Ramaḍān."[12] Moreover, unlike God who "measures the night and day [with

---

to him [during the period when he would pray all night] as a result of his abject exhaustion ... The Prophet was tired out from long night vigils in which he remained standing on his feet (*kathrat al-tahajjud wa-qiyām 'alā sāq*) ... and when the unbelievers saw the extent of his worship, they said: 'You have made your life hard through world-renunciation (*tark al-dunya*), and this Qur'ān was revealed to you only in order to make you miserable'" (Majlisī, 68: 27). Al-Ṭabarī to Q. 20: 1: "The interpretation of these words is ... 'We did not reveal it (*viz.*, the Qur'ān) to you in order to charge you with tasks of which you are not capable' (*fa-nukallifuka mā lā ṭāqa laka bihi min al-'amal*). It is said that this was communicated to him (*viz.*, Muḥammad) because of his fatiguing exertions and insomnia in the context of nocturnal devotions" (Ṭabarī, 16: 172). Al-Qurṭubī comments on the same verse: "The Messenger of God, may God's peace and blessings be upon him, remained praying at night until his legs became lean and emaciated (? *ismakhaddat qadamāhu*), and Gabriel said to him: 'Spare yourself [this undue effort], for your soul has a claim on you,' meaning, 'We did not reveal the Qur'ān to you so that you should tire yourself out in worship and expose your soul to oppressive burdens (*li-tanhaka nafsaka fī'l-'ibāda wa-tudhīqahā al-mashaqqa al-fādiḥa*), but rather [you were sent] in the spirit of the true, liberal Creed'" (*al-ḥanīfiyya al-samḥa* – Qurṭubī, 11: 143).

11 The Prophet is sometimes depicted as waking up for a session of *tahajjud*, then returning to bed, then rising for a second round, followed by more sleep, and so on (of King David, Ibn 'Abbās says that he would "sleep half the night, rise for a third, then sleep again for a sixth," see Geiger, *Judaism and Islam*, 146; Qurṭubī, 15: 150; and Psalms, 119: 62). The term "*qiyām*" in this context may indicate (1) rising from sleep, (2) preparing for prayer and/or (3) remaining in a standing position (just as the opening clause of Q. 4: 43 and Q. 5: 6 – *idhā qumtum ilā al-ṣalāt* – may harbor either or both of the first two meanings, for which *ikhtilāf* see Marion Holmes Katz, *Body of Text* [Albany: State University of New York Press, 2002], 60–75).

12 Cf., however, al-Ya'qūbī's statement that nightly prayer rituals in Ramaḍān were instituted by 'Umar b. al-Khaṭṭāb. When challenged that "neither the Messenger of God nor Abū Bakr ever practiced this," 'Umar reputedly replied: "If this is a *bid'a*, it is an excellent one!" (G. H. A. Juynboll, *Studies on the Origins and Uses of Islamic Ḥadīth* [Aldershot: Variorum, 1996], 3: 309). The apparent contradiction might be removed by positing that the special *tahajjud* or night prayers of Ramaḍān – known as *tarāwīḥ* – were originally an optional, in-

precision]," the believers "could not calculate [the length of their vigil accurately]" (Q. 73: 20), and they therefore ended up worshipping even longer than the maximum time required in their anxiety to avoid transgression.[13] Al-Qurṭubī's formulation of Allāh's eventual abrogation of this difficult rite is consistent with his general theory of *naskh*, which envisions innovations, reversals and surprises here on earth, but not in the mind of the Creator or on the pages of the celestial Qur'ānic "Urtext." He quotes 'Ā'isha as explaining to Sa'd b. Hishām that "God imposed the performance of the night-prayer at the beginning of this chapter (i.e. *al-Muzzammil*), and He withheld its concluding verses in the heavens for a period of twelve months (*amsaka khātimatahā ithnay 'ashara shahran fī'l-samā'*), until He sent down the alleviation found at the end of this chapter, at which time nocturnal devotions became voluntary after having been mandatory (*fa-ṣāra qiyām al-layl taṭawwu'an ba'da farīḍatin*)."[14]

---

dividual observance adopted by the exceptionally pious, but were turned into a collective duty by the second righteous caliph. The story of the extension of the *farīḍa* of *qiyām al-layl* from the Prophet to the believers could well be a telescoping of this legal-historical development.

13 Qurṭubī, 19: 41. The fear of not praying long enough because of imprecise time-keeping was compounded by the confusing formulation found in Q. 73: 1–3: "Arise to prayer, and continue therein all night, save a small part: a half thereof, or a little less, or a little more ..." Even if understood in terms of the corresponding reference in 73: 20 – "two thirds of the night, or half of it, or one third" – how is a praying Muslim supposed to accurately gauge such periods? More importantly, which was best? Should the believer stay up a third, or a half, or two thirds of the night? Unclear on this, many of the pious remained awake even beyond the two thirds maximum, just to be sure. For further elaboration of certain issues surrounding *qiyām al-layl*, see Burton, *Sources*, 186–8.

14 Qurṭubī, 19: 27. See also Ṣaḥīḥ Muslim, *Kitāb Ṣalāt al-Musāfirīn wa-Qaṣruhā, Bāb Ṣalāt al-Layl wa'l-Witr*, 17: 139 (746). Sums up al-Shāfi'ī: *nasakha [Allāhu] qiyām al-layl... bimā tayassara* – "[God] cancelled the duty to rise at night... in favor of something easier" (*Umm*, 1: 86). Al-Asqalānī, basing himself on the future tense usage of Q. 73: 20: *lan tuḥṣūhu* ("you *will* not be able to calculate it/manage it"), even has Allāh abrogate the night prayer already in Mecca, in anticipation of the difficulties He knows it will eventually occasion in Madīna (where believers are going to be occupied in *jihād* and will need to be fresh for battle in the morning – see Aḥmad b. Nūr al-Dīn 'Alī b. Ḥajar al-'Asqalānī, *Fatḥ al-Bārī bi-Sharḥ Saḥīḥ al-Bukhārī* [Beirut: Dār al-Fikr, 1970], 1: 460). Another source goes further still by suggesting that God sought to *prevent* the imposition of the requirement of *qiyām al-layl* ahead of time: "It is possible that Allāh revealed unto [Muḥammad]: 'If you persevere in such [supererogatory nocturnal] prayer together with them (*viz.*, the believers), I will [be forced to] obligate them in it, whereas I prefer to allay [rather than compound] their

Many similar instances of later divine decrees overturning earlier ones may be found throughout the sources, almost invariably connected to perceived contradictions in scripture. "O you who believe," we read in Sūrat al-Tawba, "what aileth you when it is said to you: 'Go forth (*infirū*) in the way of Allāh'?" (that is, participate in wars of *jihād*)... If you do not go forth, He will afflict you with a painful chastisement and will choose instead of you a folk other than you ..." (Q. 9: 38–9). Later on in the same chapter, however, a somewhat different note is struck: "The believers should not all go forth (*yanfirū*) to fight; of every group of them, a party only should go forth, so that [those remaining] may obtain understanding in religion (*yatafaqqahū fī al-dīn*) ..." (Q. 9: 122). The former passage is said to have descended in order to reprove those who did not flock to the Prophet's standard on the eve of the Battle of Tabūk (630 CE), pleading the impending harvest and late summer heat ("The fire of hell is hotter!" Allāh's Messenger was instructed to retort [Q. 9: 81]; the expedition, which set out nonetheless, was dubbed *ghazwat al-'usra*, "the raid of hardship"). The remorseful Muslims from that time forward marched out on every campaign one and all without exception, in obedience to God's chastening command. This, however, led to other troubles, including the widespread neglect of religious studies in favor of service at the front. To rectify this problem, Allāh sent down the latter verse, which freed up a portion of the populace to engage in the sacred sciences. Thus, "*jihād* was, at the inception of Islam, an individual duty (*farḍ 'ayn*), incumbent upon each and every Muslim, no-one being permitted to stay behind (*lā yasa'u aḥadan al-takhalluf 'anhu*) ... then, afterwards, this regulation was relaxed (*rukhkhiṣa*) for those who were excused [on just grounds from enlisting], and became a *farḍ kifāya* (a collective duty to which not everyone need attend)."[15] Draft exemptions had been issued on a wide scale.

---

burden'" (*in wāẓibta 'alā hādhihi al-ṣalāt ma'ahum aftariḍuhā 'alayhim fa-uḥibbu al-takhfīf 'anhum* – I have unfortunately mislaid this reference). The triumph of the less over the more arduous practice manifest in the supercession of Q. 73: 1–3 by the later directive to "[r]ecite, therefore, as much of the Qur'ān as is easy for you" (*mā tayassara min al-Qur'ān* [Q. 73: 20]) influenced more than just nocturnal devotions. To this day, when a *mujawwid* or Qur'ān reciter is introduced on Arabic radio the formula most often employed is: "And now, so-and-so will chant for us *mimma yatayassaru min sūrat fuṣṣilat*..."

15 Zayn al-Dīn Abū'l-Faraj b. Rajab al-Ḥanbalī, *Fatḥ al-Bārī: Sharḥ Ṣaḥīḥ al-Bukhārī* (Madīna: Maktabat Taḥqīq Dār al-Ḥaramayn, 1996), 4: 527. See also

Verse 221 of the Qur'ān's second chapter admonishes the faithful: "Marry not idolatresses (*mushrikāt*) until they believe ..." Since the People of the Book are subsumed under the rubric of idolatry for a wide variety of purposes (among other reasons because: "The Jews say 'Ezra is the son of God,' and the Christians say 'the Messiah is the son of God'"),[16] it is considered problematic that – side-by-side with the above excerpt – the fifth verse of the Qur'ān's fifth chapter announces: "[Lawful unto you in marriage] are the virtuous women from among the believers and the virtuous women from among those who have received the scriptures before you ..." In this latter passage the women of the *ahl al-kitāb* are directly contrasted with "believers," yet both types are permitted in marriage, whereas in the former passage the Muslims are specifically warned not to wed women "until they believe." Some *fuqahā'* (jurists) and *mufassirūn* (commentators) proposed a "synthetic" resolution (*jam'*) to this conflict, claiming that Q. 2: 221 – the "general" verse (*'āmm*) – already harbored within it the exception of *kitābiyyāt* made manifest in Q. 5: 5 – the "particular" verse (*khāṣṣ*) – and thus there was no contradiction between them. Others, reversing the widely accepted chronology according to which the contents of Sūrat al-Baqara were revealed earlier than those of Sūrat al-Mā'ida,

---

Ibn Isḥāq—Guillaume, 602–5, and the commentaries to Q. 9: 117–8. As the Prophet died less than two years after the excursion to Tabūk, the original promulgation and subsequent abrogation must have taken place within a short time (despite the usage "at the inception of Islam ... then afterward ..."). For a related "reduction" arising out of Q. 8: 65–6, according to which (in al-Shāfi'ī's words) "God made it clear in His book that He had relieved the Muslims of the obligation to fight the unbelievers in the ratio of one against ten, and had imposed upon them [instead] the obligation to fight only in a ratio of one against two," see Burton, *Sources,* 27, and Christopher Melchert, "The Ḥanbalī law of Ĝihād," *The Maghreb Review* 29 (2004), 26–7. When Q. 4: 95 – "Not equal are those who stay at home and those who strive in God's cause ..." – was revealed, Muḥammad called for his secretary Zayd b. Thābit and began dictating it to him. Just then the blind man 'Abd Allāh (or 'Amr) b. Umm Maktūm (for frowning at whom the Prophet was famously chastised, Q. 80: 1–11) approached and protested: "O Messenger of God! Had I the power I would certainly participate in *jihād*!" Immediately Allāh sent down: "... except for those who are disabled" (i.e. the continuation of the verse – Bukhārī, 4: 52 [85]).

16 Q. 9: 30. See Yohanan Friedmann, "Classification of Unbelievers in Sunnī Muslim Law and Tradition," *Jerusalem Studies in Arabic and Islam,* 22 (1998); and Lazarus-Yafeh, *Intertwined Worlds,* chapter three. Ibn 'Abbās averred regarding Q. 2: 221: "This verse constitutes a general statement encompassing female idol-worshippers (*wathaniyyāt*), female Zoroastrians (*majūsiyyāt*) and female scriptuaries (*kitābiyyāt*)" – Qurṭubī, 3: 59.

asserted that Q. 2: 221 had abolished Q. 5: 5 and that Muslim men from that time forward must cease marrying Jewish and Christian women. But the majority held the opposite view: that the blanket prohibition in Q. 2: 221 was *mansūkh,* abrogated – or, rather, mitigated – by the concession granted in Q. 5: 5.[17]

Allāh sent down verses to protect the weakest element of society: "Approach not the property of the orphan save with the proper motivation (*illā bi'llatī hiya aḥsanu* – Q. 6: 153)"; and "Lo! Those who devour the wealth of orphans wrongfully, they do but swallow fire into their bellies, and they will burn in blazing flame" (Q. 4: 10).[18] When apprised of these divine admonitions, those Muslims who had orphans in their care began to separate their own fare from that of their wards, lest they inadvertantly encroach upon the portion of a parentless child and incur eternal damnation. Guardians ceased supping with their dependents, and in some cases even stayed shy of their own homes during meal time. Moreover, if the food and drink earmarked for the orphan exceeded what he could consume at a single sitting, they would store away the remainder until he became hungry again, or, alternately, until it rotted (*idhā faḍula min ṭa'ām al-yatīm wa-sharābihi shay'un ḥabasa lahu ḥattā ya'kulahu aw yafsuda*). This practice was found to be extremely wasteful and arduous (*fa-ishtadda dhālika 'alayhim*) and the believers came complaining to Muḥammad. God thereupon revealed: "They question you concerning orphans. Say: To improve their lot is best. And if you mingle your affairs with theirs (*fa-in tukhāliṭūhum*), then they are your brethren" (Q. 2: 220). The dire warnings having lapsed into obsolescence, all food was henceforward taken in common.[19]

---

17 Qurṭubī, 3: 58. Etan Kohlberg informs me that Q. 60: 10 is also said to have abrogated Q. 5: 5. On the ensuing jurisprudence surrounding interfaith marriages, see Yohanan Friedmann, *Tolerance and Coercion in Islam* (Cambridge: Cambridge University Press, 2003), chapter 5; and Suzan A. Spectorsky, "Women of the People of the Book: Intermarriage in Early *Fiqh* Texts" in Benjamin H. Hary *et al* (eds.), *Judaism and Islam: Boundaries, Communication and Interaction – Essays in Honor of William M. Brinner* (Leiden: E. J. Brill, 2000), 269–78.

18 Visiting the second "heaven" during his celebrated *mi'rāj* (ascension), Muḥammad indeed witnessed "men with lips like camels, with pieces of fire like stones in their hands. They thrust them into their mouths and they come out their posteriors. Gabriel said: these are those who devoured the property of orphans" (Ibn Isḥāq — Guillaume, 185).

19 Baghawī, 3: 4.

The "incident of the necklace" in about 5 AH was the occasion for yet another divine modification. Until that time, the only substance with which Muslims could purify themselves in preparation for prayer was water: "O ye, who believe, when you prepare for the *ṣalāt*, wash your faces and your hands up to the elbows and wipe (i.e., moisten) your head and your feet up to the ankles ..." (Q. 5: 6). But these parameters were destined to be widened, as 'Ā'isha recounts:

> I accompanied the Messenger of God on a military excursion. [On our way back to Madīna] my necklace (which Muḥammad had given her from the booty, or, according to other versions, which she had borrowed from her elder sister Asmā') went missing. I informed the Messenger of God of this, and he commanded [those present, or the entire division] to search for it, and they did so but it was not found. So the Prophet and the people set up camp for the night (the search had taken so long that the sun was already setting). The people said: 'Ā'isha has encumbered the Messenger of God! (*ḥabasat 'Ā'isha al-nabī*). Abū Bakr ('Ā'isha's father) came [to our tent], and the head of the Prophet was in my lap and he was sleeping, and he (Abū Bakr) began to poke me and pinch me, exclaiming: On account of a necklace you prevent the progress of the Prophet!? (In another version: You have brought hardship upon the people!). I ('Ā'isha) did my best not to move, for fear that the Prophet's sleep would be disturbed, and then [Abū Bakr] really caused me pain and I didn't know what to do (*qad awja'anī fa-lā adrī kayfa aṣna'*). When [Abū Bakr] saw that I did not react or answer him, he turned and left. Then the Prophet woke up, and he wanted to pray, but there was no water available (what supplies were left were no doubt reserved for drinking, but milk was the staple beverage anyway). At which point ('Ā'isha concludes) Allāh sent down the verse about *tayammum* (rubbing with sand in place of washing with water – "... if you find not water, then go to clean, high ground and rub your faces and your hands with some of it ..." [Q. 5: 6]).[20]

Ultimately, the necklace was found – under 'Ā'isha's own camel – when the camp pulled up stakes the following morning.[21] 'Ā'isha was lauded for bringing fortune upon the Muslims, in the form of the ameliorative provision (*rukhṣa, 'udhr*) of *tayammum*, as a result of what she had

20 Ṭabarī, 5: 149 (no. 7617); Muslim, *Kitāb al-Ḥayḍ, Bāb al-Tayammum*, 28: 108 (367). Other versions of this *ḥadīth* – such as that retold by Ibn Isḥāq/Ibn Hishām in the *Sīra* (Guillaume 493 ff) – have it segue into the story of 'Ā'isha's unintentional abandonment in the desert, her rescue by Ṣafwān b. al-Mu'aṭṭal al-Sulamī, and the well-known subsequent crisis. There are alternate suggestions for the circumstances of this revelation, see Ṭabarī, 5: 146 ff.

21 Ṭabarī, 5: 150 (no. 7619).

thought was her own misfortune.[22] The second half of Q. 5: 6 had abrogated (in this case by augmenting) the first half.

Scores of additional examples could be adduced, among them the famous "reduction" from fifty daily prayer sessions to five, granted Muḥammad in the course of his Night Journey and Ascent to the seventh heaven,[23] as well as the revocation of the requirement to perform ritual ablutions before each and every one of those sessions.[24] It will have been noticed by now that all of the cases discussed so far involve extenuation. This is in line with what Islamic tradition proudly puts forth as one of its central tenets and defining characteristics: *rukhṣa*, the inclination toward leniency.[25] "Allāh would not place a

22 Māwardī, 1: 283. See also Ṭabarī, 5: 150 (no. 7621), and Shams al-Dīn al-Sarakhsī, *Al-Mabsūṭ* (Beirut: Dār al-Fikr, 1989), 1: 106: "*Yā 'Ā'isha,*" exclaimed Usayd b. Ḥuḍayr, "*mā nazala biki amrun takrahīnahu illā ja'ala Allāhu li'l-Muslimīn fīhi farajan.*" In other versions it is Abū Bakr himself who, having vented his fury on his daughter only moments earlier, was the first to congratulate her for this achievement (Ṭabarī, 5: 158, no. 7648: "*innaki la-mubāraka nazala fīki rukhṣa!*").

23 For the question whether an edict rescinded even before it was carried out may be said to have been "abrogated," see the discussion in Ibn Ḥajar, *Fatḥ al-Bārī*, 1: 463–4, which revolves around the specific case of the *takhfīf* bestowed by Allāh during the *mi'rāj*. See also below, p. 141.

24 For the cancellation of the obligation to perform *wuḍū' li-kulli ṣalāt* – a revision involving either the abrogation of Qur'ān by *sunna* or of *sunna* by *sunna* – see Katz, *Body*, 66 ff.

25 Despite the seminal and central role played by *rukhṣa* in the formation of Islamic religion, the subject has been virtually ignored by Western scholarship. The sole exception is M. J. Kister, "On 'concessions' and conduct: A study in early *ḥadīth*," originally published in *Studies on the First Century of Islamic Society*, ed. G. H. A. Juynboll (Carbondale: South Illinois University Press, 1982), and reprinted in M. J. Kister, *Society and Religion from Jāhiliyya to Islam* (Aldershot: Variorum, 1990). Kister, spartan as ever, manages to compress into this short study a large amount of material from a wide variety of sources, thus providing a sizeable reservoir to scholars who would fill in this lacuna. One who has begun to do so is David Powers: for *rukhṣa* (or at least *'udhr*) in action – as it was applied in genuine judicial cases – see chapters 2 and 5 of his *Law, Society and Culture in the Maghrib, 1300–1500* (Cambridge: Cambridge University Press, 2002). See also Satoe Horii, "Reconsideration of Legal Devices (*Ḥiyal*) in Islamic Jurisprudence: The Ḥanafīs and their 'Exits' (*Makhārij*)," *Islamic Law and Society* 9: 3 (2002). *Ḥiyal* aren't really *rukhaṣ*, but they do share a common impetus, and the terminology of *makhraj*/*makhārij* is often found in connection with the alleviative enterprise as well. Even more recently, Michael Cook's *Forbidding Wrong in Islam* (Cambridge: Cambridge University Press, 2003) is a good place to look for examples of "easygoing" re-

burden upon you," the Qur'ān regularly reassures the believers (Q. 5:6). "Allāh desires ease for you; He does not desire hardship for you" (Q. 2:185).[26] "God the Exalted did not send me to sow difficulties or cause vexation," testified the Prophet. "Rather, He sent me to instruct and to facilitate."[27] Because, in the final analysis, "Allāh imposes

---

ligious and political authorities who resist the enforcement of the strict letter of the law on many occasions.

26 The former declaration is appended to the permission afforded those sick or traveling to perform ablutions with sand when water is unavailable; the latter statement follows the clause allowing those sick or traveling to make up missed Ramaḍān fast days on an equivalent number of alternate days (a substitution somewhat reminiscent of the right, granted by the Pentateuch to those "defiled by a corpse or on a long journey," to observe a "second Passover" [Numbers, 9:6–8]). It was later debated just how sick one had to be in order to break the Ramaḍān fast, but the preponderance of jurists insisted that even minor indispositions were sufficient to activate this exemption. Ṭarīf b. Tamām al-'Uṭāridī went to visit Muḥammad b. Sīrīn in the daytime during the holy month, and found him eating. "This finger hurts," explained Ibn Sīrīn (*waja'at iṣba'ī hādhihi* – Ṭabarī, 2:204).

The *dīn al-yusr* refrain pervades the primary literature: "'Urwa al-Faqīmī said: We were once waiting for the Prophet, may God's peace and blessings be upon him, and he emerged [into the mosque from one of his wives' rooms] with his head dripping either from *wuḍū'* or from *ghusl,* and then he prayed, and when he had finished praying, the people asked him: "Shall we strain/constrain ourselves in such matters?" (*a-'alaynā min ḥarajin fī kadhā?*). And he – may God's peace and blessings be upon him – responded: "No, O people! For the religion of Allāh is one of ease, the religion of Allāh is one of ease, the religion of Allāh is one of ease!" (*inna dīn Allāhi fī'l-yusr* – Ibn Ḥanbal, 5:68). "God the Exalted desires ease for this community," echoed the Prophet on another occasion, "and He dislikes hardship for it" (*inna Allāhu ta'āla raḍiya li-hādhihi'l-umma al-yusr wa-kariha lahā al-'usr* – Aḥmad b. 'Alī b. Ḥajar al-'Asqalānī, *Al-Iṣāba fī Tamyīz al-Ṣaḥāba* [Cairo: Maṭba'a al-Sa'āda, 1328], 3:366).

27 Abū Zakariyā' Yaḥyā Muḥyī al-Dīn al-Nawawī, *Sharḥ Saḥīḥ Muslim* (Cairo: Maṭba'at al-Ḥalabī, 1349 AH), 10:81: "*inna Allāha ta'āla lam yab'athnī mu'annitan wa-lā muta'annitan, wa-lākin ba'athanī mu'alliman muyassiran.*" The need to instruct and facilitate underlay, among other concessions, the right to maintain multiple Qur'ān readings, granted by God in response to Muḥammad's plea that he had been sent to a nation of illiterates (Burton, *Collection,* 152). The Prophet certainly engaged in *imitatio Dei* in the matter of *rukhṣa,* ever striving to "be merciful as He is merciful" (to borrow a Rabbinic phrase). Muḥammad's inclination toward leniency, willingness to accommodate, readiness to retract and indomitable soft-spot form a central motif in Muslim classical literature, whether of the legal or legendary variety. He shortened congregational services for the sake of a mother with a difficult child (and cancelled them altogether when it was too hot, too cold or too rainy), instructed a young man who found it hard to rise early to "pray whenever you get up," turned a

not on any soul that which is beyond its scope" (Q. 2:286),[28] He there-

---

blind eye to a warrior who wolfed down some common booty, and threatened to thrash a maid-servant who returned late from an errand... with a tooth-pick. He regularly sought to avoid inflicting prescribed penalties on transgressors by having them acquitted on "technicalities" (*idra'ū al-ḥudūd 'an al-Muslimīn mā istaṭa'tum, fa-in kāna lahu makhraj fa-khallū sabīlahu*). He forgave the high treason of one of his followers – and the longstanding opposition of his fiercest enemy – on the eve of the invasion of Mecca (his treatment of which city he compared to Joseph absolving his brethren: "*al-yawm aqūlu lakum mā qāla akhī Yūsuf min qablu: lā tathrību 'alaykum al-yawm...*"). He granted amnesty to Waḥshī, the slave contracted by Abū Sufyān's wife Hind to assassinate his uncle Ḥamza (even though he cried the bitterest tears of his life over the latter) and eventually excused his erstwhile amanuensis, 'Abd Allāh b. Abi Sarḥ, who had defected from Islam and called him an imposter. He even pardoned the Qurashite who had attacked his daughter and caused her to miscarry.
Muḥammad was a man of much laughter, throwing his head back in hilarity until one could see his molars, but also a man of tears, shed in compassion. Once, he and his Companions stopped at a Bedouin camp, and the Prophet began to preach about the various types of hellfire awaiting sinners: *nār, laẓā, saqar, ḥuṭama,* etc. Meanwhile, a bedouin woman with a baby tied to her hip crouched down nearby and baked bread for the visitors over a flame. At one point some grease fell into the fire and it surged. The woman leapt back to protect her infant, and then turned on Muḥammad: "Are you the one they call the Messenger of God?" she demanded. "I am," he replied. "And you claim that He is 'the Merciful, the Benificent'?" she pressed on. "He is," confirmed the Prophet. "If so," continued the woman, "then you are a liar. A loving parent would never throw His children into the fire!" So saying, she stormed off – and Muḥammad wept. On a different occasion, passing by a group of bereaved women after Badr, Allāh's Apostle declared: "Any mother who has lost three sons in battle, will go straight to the Garden of Eden!" One woman turned to him with tears in her eyes and queried, "O Messenger of God! – and if she lost only two?" Muhammad immediately melted: "Yes, of course: two as well, two as well..." (He made a similar adjustment, in response to a similar query, to the number of daughters or sisters one should sustain in order to gain entrance to Paradise). Elaborating on the many activities forbidden in Mecca's Sacred Precinct, Muḥammad reached the subject of flora: "... neither shall there be any gathering of shrubs or grasses there, for such was forbidden by God himself on the day He created heaven and earth, and it will *remain* thus forbidden *forever*, from now until Resurrection Day!" Interrupted Ibn 'Abbās: "O Messenger of God – except for the Idhkhir bush, yes? For it is used by the people to ornament their persons and their houses?" "Except for the Idhkhir bush" retreated Muḥammad, without losing a beat. Examples of the Prophet's clemency, forbearance and pliability abound in the literature.
Instances of the opposite tendency, however, are also not lacking. Muḥammad turned a deaf ear to the desperate appeals of the women of al-Ṭā'if to spare their idol of al-Lāt if only for a few months (he had not forgotten his treatment at the hands of the city's Thaqīfite natives a decade earlier) and sent al-Mughīra to de-

fore closely monitors the fate of His own newly promulgated legislation. If the community shows itself equal to the task of fulfilling a given commandment, well and good; if not, the load must be lightened.[29] "It is by God's mercy that you dealt with [the believers] gently,"

---

stroy it forthwith. Nor did he agree to relieve them, even in part, of the obligation to pray five times daily. Ignoring the impassioned beseechments of al-Ḥārith b. Suwayd, a Muslim who had killed his own father's murderer, the Prophet issued orders for his beheading. To the Badr prisoner 'Uqba b. Abī Mu'ayṭ's heart-rending plea, "And my little girl? *Who will take care of her?*" Muḥammad answered, "Hell fire!" and had him immediately executed (his orphaned daughter, Umm Kulthum, eventually made her way to Madīna as a Muslim, and in a painfully ironic twist, offered herself to her father's killer in marriage. The Prophet, however, added insult to injury by rejecting her proposal and affiancing her instead to his freed slave Zayd). When a believer reported stabbing his pregnant slave girl in her belly for slandering God's Apostle, the latter declared coldly that "no recompense was payable for her blood." The Prophet's hearty ratification of Sa'd b. Mu'ādh's verdict condemning eight (or seven, or six, or nine) hundred men of the Jewish tribe of Banū Qurayẓa to death and their women and children to be sold on the open slave market – a decree that turned the *maydān* of Madīna into a Babi Yar-like charnel house for an entire day and evening as the Jews were paraded out in groups of six and beheaded over mass graves – should also not be forgotten.

28 See also Q. 2: 233: "... No soul shall be burdened beyond its capacity ..." Echoes Jār Allāh Maḥmūd b. 'Umar al-Zamakhsharī in his *Al-Kashshāf 'an Ḥaqā'iq Ghawāmiḍ al-Tanzīl* (Cairo: Al-Maktaba al-Tijāriya al-Kubrā, 1934), 1: 408: "*Allāh lā yukallif al-nafs illā mā yattasi'u fīhi ṭawquhā wa-yatayassaru 'alayhā.*"

29 Our language here is somewhat misleading, of course, from the perspective represented by al-Qurṭubī, at least if he is to be kept to consistency. According to his outlook, after all, no divine monitoring is necessary, as all failures of the community to cope with one or another regulation are anticipated ahead of time. What often appears, on the other hand, to be al-Ṭabarī's conception (or that of most of the authorities he cites) of bona fide divine experimentation is closer to our intent here, and to what Burton had in mind when he described "the construction of the ideal human society between AD 613–32" as having taken place "under God's personal day-to-day supervision" (Burton, *Sources*, 9). On the following page Burton speaks of problems that arose among the ranks of the believers being "resolved by the *ad hoc* revelation of a divine ruling on the matter." An apt illustration of this latter phenomenon, which does not constitute abrogation *per se* but is akin to it, may be had from the traditional contextualization of Q. 4: 11, which lays down certain particulars of inheritance law. The commentators tie this verse to the demise of Sa'd b. Rabī', who was martyred at Uḥud and whose brother – as was the custom before Islam when a man had no sons – took possession of all of his property. Sa'd's penniless widow and daughters made a moving appeal to Muḥammad, who replied that God would in due course decide regarding their financial fate, as "no command has yet been revealed to me in this matter." Soon afterward the

Allāh informs His Apostle at one point, "for had you been stern and fierce with them, they would surely have deserted you" (Q. 3: 158). "Religion is ease," seconds Muḥammad himself, "and anyone who makes religion rigorous will in the end be overcome by it."[30] Leniency, we note, is both principle and strategy.

"Allāh desires to decrease your difficulties, for man was created weak" (Q. 4: 28). "Allāh has lightened your burden, since He knows there is feebleness in you" (Q. 8: 66). Confronted with manifestations of human frailty, the God of Islamic tradition almost invariably "goes soft." On one of the nights of Ramaḍān, ʿUmar b. al-Khaṭṭāb returned home after conversing into the small hours with the Prophet. His wife was already fast asleep, but he wanted her (*arādahā*) and proceeded to wake her up. "But I have slept!," she protested (*innī qad nimtu* – by which she meant that cohabitation was permitted during the holy month only from sunset to slumber, which was the divinely ordained norm at the time. Once one dozed off after dark, all of the prohibitions of Ramaḍān – against eating, drinking and sexual relations – were reactivated until the following evening).[31] "No, you have *not* slept!," ʿUmar insisted – and he took her (*fa-qāla: mā nimti! thumma waqaʿa bihā*).[32] After sho-

---

Prophet received the revelation contained in Q. 4: 11, as a result of which he directed that two thirds of Saʿd's property be conferred upon his female heirs. The divine decision in regard to this *specific* case henceforth became enshrined as a *general* law, valid for all time. Compare Numbers, 27: 1–10: "The daughters of Tzelophehad ... came forward. They stood before Moses ... and said: 'Our father died in the wilderness ... Let not our father's name be lost to his clan just because he had no son! Give us a holding among our father's kinsmen.' Moses brought their case before the Lord, and the Lord said: 'The plea of Tzelophehad's daughters is just. You should give them a hereditary holding among their father's kinsmen; transfer their father's share to them. Further, speak to the Children of Israel, saying: If a man dies without leaving a son, you shall transfer the property to his daughter. If he has no daughter, you shall assign his property to his brothers. If he has no brothers ...'" Here, too, a particular verdict set a permanent precedent. Such a reactive ruling on the Deity's part is the exception in the Bible, the rule in the Qur'ān. In Jewish tradition the initiative is God's; in Islam it is man's.

30 Baghawī, 4: 144: "*inna al-dīna yusrun wa-lan yushādda al-dīna aḥadun illā ghalabahu.*"

31 "*Kāna aṣḥāb Muḥammad idhā kāna al-rajul ṣā'iman fa-ḥaḍara al-ifṭār fa-nāma qabla an yuftira lam ya'kul laylatahu wa-lā yawmahu ḥattā yumsiya ...*" (Abū Zakariyā' Yaḥyā Muḥyī al-Dīn al-Nawawī, *Al-Majmūʿ Sharḥ al-Muhadhdhab* [Beirut: Dār al-Kutub al-ʿIlmiyya, 2002], 7: 412).

32 Since the text is not vocalized, ʿUmar's retort to his wife's claim that she had slept might alternately be rendered: *mā nimtu* – "Well *I* haven't slept!"

wering ritually in the wake of intercourse, ʿUmar, wracked with guilt over his violation, burst into tears (*fa-lammā ightasala akhadha yabkī wa-yalūmu nafsahu ka-ashaddi mā ra'ayta min al-malāma*). He wept his way over to the Prophet's house, where he confessed his misdeed: "My wife appeared beautiful to me and I lay with her!" He begged forgiveness and, according to one version of this report, even went so far as to plead: "Might you find me some sort of indulgence, O Messenger of God?" (*hal tajidu lī min rukhṣa yā rasūl Allāh?*). A new revelation, abolishing the onerous restriction, descended shortly thereafter:

> It is made lawful for you to go in unto your wives on the night of the fast (*uḥilla lakum laylata al-ṣiyāmi al-rafathu ilā nisā'ikum*). They are a raiment for you and you are a raiment for them. God is aware that you have been undermining yourselves (i.e. that due to your inability to abstain from sexual relations after sleep you have been accumulating violations of the law as it currently stands), and He has turned in mercy toward you and pardoned you (*tāba ʿalaykum wa-ʿafā ʿankum*). So from now on have intercourse with them (*fa'l'āna bāshirūhunna*) and seek that which God has ordained for you, and eat and drink until the white thread becomes distinct from the black thread at dawn.[33]

33 Q. 2: 187. Various versions of this anecdote appear in Ṭabarī, 2: 225 ff (a similar story is told with the same protagonists concerning kissing during a fast [Mawardī, 3: 295]). What Western polemicists have often mocked as Muḥammad's "convenient revelations" – the type of timely divine dispensations concerning which ʿĀ'isha herself (referring to the Zaynab affair) once quipped sardonically at her husband, "Verily, your Lord hastens to do your pleasure!" (Ibn Ḥanbal, 6: 158) – may be viewed from a different angle as the divine *fatāwā* of a uniquely responsive religion. ʿUmar b. al-Khaṭṭāb appears to have played a central role in eliciting such responsa. He once "boasted innocently of having three times given advice which turned out miraculously to correspond with the dictates of heaven" (Maxime Rodinson, *Mohammed* [New York: Penguin Books, 1971], 219). On another occasion the rumour spread among the believers that "ʿUmar had had an idea and the Qur'ān came down accordingly" (Hava Lazarus-Yafeh, "ʿUmar b. al-Khaṭṭāb – Paul of Islam?" in *Some Religious Aspects*, 6). These are the *muwāfaqāt ʿUmar*, the concurrences of ʿUmar's will or perception with certain divine revelations – see Avraham Hakim, "Conflicting Images of Lawgivers: *Sunnat ʿUmar* and *Sunnat Muḥammad*" in Herbert Berg (ed.), *Method and Theory in the Study of Islamic Origins* (Leiden: E.J. Brill, 2003): 159–177, esp. 160. We have already seen how ʿUmar demanded and received increasingly clearer revelations concerning wine (above, chap. 1, n. 11). Although this last ultimately led to a stricter policy (as was the case, according to most sources, in the matter of *mutʿa*, which ʿUmar outlawed as caliph; of *ḥijāb*, the imposition of which he requested directly from On High; and of stoning adulterers, which he "would have written into the text of the Qur'ān" were it not for fear of scandal); and although ʿUmar has a widespread

Divine legislation regarding the proper disposal of booty is similarly linked to – or, at least, provides the occasion for a widely circulated story concerning – the accomodation of the wishes of a prominent

---

reputation in the literature as stern and puritanical (*rajul jalīd,* they called him [a strict man], as well as *dhū al-dirra,* they called him, "he with the whip." [A. J. Wensinck, "Muḥammad und die Propheten," *Acta Orientalia* 2 (1924), esp. 195–8, and Lazarus-Yafeh, "'Umar b. al-Khaṭṭāb," *passim*]); nevertheless Islam's strongman seems to have been at least as responsible for eliciting *rukhaṣ* as he was for tightening up religion (Abū Bakr Muḥammad b. 'Abd Allāh al-Ma'āfirī b. al-'Arabī [d. 1148], *Aḥkām al-Qur'ān* [Cairo: 'Īsā al-Bābī al-ḥalabī, 1967], 2: 348: "*wa-kāna 'Umaru yaṭlubu min al-nabī, ṣalla Allāhu 'alayhi wa-sallam, al-naṣṣ al-qāṭi' li'l-'udhr...*"). When the verse against the hoarding of gold and silver was revealed (Q. 9: 34), "it proved too difficult for the Muslims (*kabura dhālika 'alā al-Muslimīn*). So 'Umar said, 'I will bring you relief' (*anā ufarriju 'ankum*)." He went and described the people's predicament to the Prophet, who reconstrued the verse and explained that hoarding must in fact be legitimate, else whence would come the surplus of possessions taxed in *zakāt*? (Baghawī, 2: 38). 'Umar it was who, though in general insisting on the punctilious performance of ritual, validated *al-masḥ 'alā'l-khuffayn,* wiping over one's shoes to avoid the inconvenience of removing them during ablutions (in response to a query put by his son, who opposed this practice – see Joseph Schacht, *The Origins of Muhammadan Jurisprudence* [Oxford: Clarendon Press, third edition, 1967], 263). As we shall see below, the divine carte blanche to have vaginal intercourse in an endless variety of positions was also credited by many to 'Umar's powerful libido, no less than the concession to which the present note is appended. Even with regard to the stoning of adulterers – the bit of severity for which 'Umar later became so well known – we read that he once shoved Ubayy in the chest with the words, "Are you asking [the Prophet] to permit the recitation of the stoning verse when the people are as randy as donkeys?" (Burton, *Collection of the Qur'ān,* 81). Revealingly in regard to 'Umar's predilection for moderation, when Ḥafṣa, 'Umar's daughter and Muḥammad's wife, broke her fast early one Ramaḍān afternoon and inveigled 'Ā'isha into doing the same, the latter's subsequent comment was: "She was indeed the daughter of her father!" (Nabia Abbott, *Aishah: The Beloved of Mohammad* [Chicago: University of Chicago Press, 1942], 11). 'Umar's son also broke fasts early (see Abū Ḥāmid Muḥammad al-Ghazālī, *Iḥyā 'Ulūm al-Dīn* [Cairo: Mu'assasat al-Ḥalabī li'l-Nashr wa'l-Tawzī', 1967], 1: 184). So, for that matter, did the Prophet (Bukhārī, *Kitāb al-Ṣawm, passim*). The relaxed spirit of *rukhṣa* pervades all of these anecdotes. Even Lazarus-Yafeh admits (via a citation from al-Tirmidhī) that "whenever a problem arose, the people would say: Oh that the revelation may come down according to what 'Umar said!" (Lazarus-Yafeh, "'Umar b. al-Khaṭṭāb," 6–7). Since "the people" – as opposed to occasional pious individuals – are almost always presented as seeking the *extenuation* of religious law (see, e.g., below p. 47), their desire as reflected in this statement that God "follow the advice" of 'Umar certainly seems to indicate – contrary to popular belief over ensuing centuries and down to the present day – that even 'Umar b. al-Khaṭṭāb leaned toward leniency.

Companion. The brother of Sa'd b. Abī Waqqāṣ, 'Umayr, had been slain at Badr, and Sa'd had avenged his death on the same battlefield by killing Sa'īd b. al-'Āṣ.[34] Having despoiled the dead man of his celebrated sword (known as "That of the Broad Iron Blade"),[35] Sa'd afterwards encountered the Prophet and exclaimed: "O Messenger of God! With this sword God has quenched [my thirst for vengeance against] the polytheists!" (*hādhā al-sayf qad shafā Allāhu bihi min al-mushrikīn*). Muḥammad, however, chided him: "That sword is neither mine nor thine – go and throw it in with the common booty! (*idhhab fa'ṭraḥahu fī'l-qabḍ*). "So I went there and threw it in," recounts Sa'd, "and then I turned to go, my heart heavy with that which only God knows because of the murder of my brother and the confiscation of my plunder. I had not gone more than a few steps [away from the Prophet, however,] when the Chapter of Spoils was revealed unto him, [and he called out to me] and said: "Go and take your sword!" (*fa-mā jāwaztu illā qarīban ḥattā nazalat 'alayhi Sūrat al-Anfāl, fa-qāla: idhhab fa-khudhu sayfaka*).[36] The pain of a pious Muslim was the trigger for a major legislative overhaul.

Not even scriptural passages the specific purpose of which was to exhort to diligence could escape the tranquilizing sting of abrogation-based alleviation. "Strive for Allāh with the striving that is His due," enjoins Q. 22: 78, which is bolstered by Q. 3: 102: "O you who believe!

---

34 Father of the famous 'Amrū. Another of Sa'īd's sons, an infant at the time of his father's death, was also named Sa'īd (and like his father – and brother – is referred to in the sources as "Ibn al-'Āṣ"), and grew up to become an important Muslim figure, sitting together with Zayd b. Thābit on the committee to oversee the transcription of the Qur'ān under 'Uthmān, supervising the Meccan market with 'Umar b. al-Khaṭṭāb, governing the city of Kūfa, etc.

35 If we read "*dha al-katīfa*," but al-Ṭabarī's modern editor has placed a ḍamma over the kāf, so perhaps we should render the sword's name *dha al-kutayfa*, "Possessor of the Little Shoulder."

36 Ṭabarī, 9: 230–31. For the context of this anecdote see 'Alī b. Burhān al-Dīn al-Ḥalabī, *Insān al-'Uyūn fī Sīrat al-Ma'mūn* (Beirut: Dār Iḥyā' al-Turāb, n.d. – also known as "*al-Sīra al-Ḥalabiya*"), 2: 186. Details are not given, but since the verse being glossed (Q. 8: 1) reads in part: "They ask you about the spoils. Say: The spoils belong to God and His Apostle...", the implied justification for the Prophet's reversal seems to be that since the new rules granted ownership of war booty to Muḥammad, he was now free to dispose of what had become his personal property as he saw fit. Alternately, since some consider even Q. 8: 1 to have been superseded by Q. 8: 42, which specified that a fifth of the booty should go to the Prophet, it may have been the revelation of this latter verse that facilitated the return of Sa'd's sword.

Observe your duty to Allāh with right observance." But God soon found both of these formulations overly demanding, and repealed them in favor of Q. 64: 16: "Keep your duty to Allāh *as best you can* ..."[37] Indeed, the confluence of *naskh* and *rukhṣa* in the texts often leads to a portrayal of the Deity as a veritable "pushover." When al-Ḥārith b. Suwayd al-Anṣārī recidivated (*kafara baʿd īmānihi* – according to other versions the apostate was "a man from the clan of ʿAmrū b. ʿAwf," who "went to Byzantine territory and converted to Christianity"), Allāh waxed wroth and, as it were, hurled down the following verses:

> How shall God guide those who lapse into unbelief after embracing the Faith, and after acknowledging the Apostle and receiving veritable truths? God does not guide the evil-doers! Their reward shall be the curse of God, of the angels and of all men; under it they will abide forever. Their punishment shall not be lightened, neither shall they be granted a reprieve ... (Q. 3: 86–8).

All possibility of pardon having been expressly denied, one would have expected this prototypical *murtadd* to remain in *Rūm*. Instead, al-Ḥārith soon thereafter wrote to his folk, requesting them: "Send to the Messenger of God and ask: Is there any repentance for me? (*hal lī tawba?*)." Immediately, "Allāh abrogated those verses, and revealed [their counteractive conclusion]: '... except for those who repent and mend their ways, for God is forgiving and merciful'" (Q. 3: 89).[38]

---

37 "*Fa'ttaqū Allāha mā istaṭaʿtum ...*" Qurṭubī, 12: 83. Even the second clause of 22: 78, which is *rukhṣa* oriented ("... He has chosen you and has not laid any hardship upon you in religion ..."), could not save the first clause from abrogation.

38 Ṭabarī, 3: 460–62. The following verse, Q. 3: 90, reads like an amended version of what came just before it: "Those who disbelieve after their profession of belief, *and afterward grow violent in their disbelief,* their repentance will not be accepted ..." For another recension of this anecdote, in which the Khazrajite al-Ḥārith treacherously murders one (or two) of his Awsite comrades-in-arms at the Battle of Uḥud (in retaliation for the earlier murder of his own father at the Battle of Buʿāth, 615 CE), then defects to Quraysh and later begs forgiveness through his believing brother Julās, see Ibn Isḥāq/Guillaume, 242–3. Interestingly, in this version al-Ḥārith is not explicitly said to have been redeemed (and may, indeed, have been executed – see above, end of note 27). Julās, sometimes styled a "hypocrite" (*munāfiq*) like his sibling, was himself accused at one point of backsliding after conversion to the faith, and of gross perjury besides. While on a trip with his step-son Muṣʿab b. ʿUmayr (Muḥammad's chosen emissary to the earliest converts of Madīna) he had exclaimed: "If what Muḥammad preaches is true, then we are worse than these asses upon which we ride!" (*in kāna mā jā'a bihi Muḥammadun ḥaqqan, la-naḥnu asharr min ḥamīrinā*

From the very beginning, then, Islam has seen itself as *dīn al-yusr*: not just the religion of ease, but the religion of easing, of an evolution-

---

hādhihi allatī naḥnu ʿalayhā! – Ṭabarī, 10: 236; Ibn Isḥāq—Guillaume, 242). Muṣʿab later informed the Prophet of this, the latter confronted Julās, and Julās swore a solemn oath that he had never uttered such words. The revelation promptly came down: "They swear by Allāh that they said nothing. And certainly they did speak the word of disbelief, and disbelieved after their adoption of Islam ... but if they repent, it will be good for them ..." (Q. 9: 74). Julās did indeed repent, and, as usual, all was forgiven.

See also the commentaries to Q. 39: 54 – "O My servants who have transgressed against your own souls, despair not of the mercy of God; for God forgiveth sins wholly" – where the story is recounted of ʿAyāsh b. Abī Rabīʿa who was kidnapped by his family just before the *hijra* and relapsed into idolatry, only returning to the faith and to the bosom of the *umma* after the revelation of the verse in question many years later, which his old friend ʿUmar copied out and sent to him forthwith (a similar story is told of Hishām b. al-ʿĀṣ, brother of the famous ʿAmr). Q. 16: 106 – "He who denies God after having believed, *except him who is forcibly compelled thereto though his heart remains steadfast in the faith,* on such rests the wrath of God and a terrible chastisement" – is a *rukhṣa,* as it were, for those who temporarily recant under duress (such as ʿAmmār, son of Yāsir and Sumayya, whose parents were horribly murdered in front of his eyes for their faith and who himself broke down under torture and acknowledged the Meccan idols – Ṭabarī, 14: 237; Qurṭubī, 10: 148).

All of this leniency coexists with the fact that apostasy particularly infuriated both Muḥammad and his Maker (a Jew who had become a Muslim and then returned to Judaism was put to death, Bukhārī, 9: 84 [60]). On apostasy, its punishments and the possibility of repentance in the further *fiqh*, see Friedmann, *Tolerance,* p. 5, note 16, and especially chapter 4.

A great many Qur'ānic verses follow this pattern, in which harsh admonitions of interminable agony are immediately softened by qualifications and reservations, whether the mitigating factor involves human repentance, divine compassion, or both (see, e.g., Q. 11: 106–7: "[The sinners] shall be in the Fire; for them shall be a sighing and groaning in it, and they shall abide therein as long as the heavens and earth shall endure – except as thy Lord please [*mā dāmat al-samawāt wa'l-arḍ – illā mā shā'a rabbuka*]"; Q. 4: 145–6: "The hypocrites are surely in the lowest depths of the Fire, and you will find no helper for them – save for those that repent and amend and hold fast to Allāh ..."). Q. 25: 69–70 contains yet another instance of what initially sounds like the ruling out of any possible clemency followed by an immediate retreat and relaxation, in this case in connection with the three most serious felonies of all (in Islam as in Judaism): "The chastisement [of him who commits the sins of idolatry, murder or fornication] will be doubled on the Day of Resurrection, and he shall abide therein forever in abasement – except him who repents and believes and does good deeds; for the sake of such, Allāh changes their evil deeds to good ones." The principle embodied in this latter passage is illustrated, *inter alia,* by the inquiry of one Abū Ṭawīl: "O Messenger of God! What would you say about a

ary progression toward palliation.[39] Long before the *fuqahā'* standardized and applied the notions of *'udhr* (exemption), *takhfīf* (reduction), *istiḥsān* (discretion, equity), *istiṣlāḥ* (considerations of public weal), *'umūm al-balwa* (ubiquity of hardship or hardship due to ubiquity) and many other related concepts,[40] Allāh Himself had already set the

---

man who has committed every sin in the book, omitting no transgression, large or small – is there any repentance for him?" (*a-ra'ayta rajulan 'amila al-dhunūb kullahā wa-lam yatruk minhā shay'an, wa-huwa fī dhālika lam yatruk ḥājatan wa-lā dājatan illā iqtaṭa'ahā – fa-hal lahu min tawba?*). "Have you become a believer?" asked Muḥammad (*hal aslamta?*). Abū Ṭawīl recited the *shahāda* in answer, and the Prophet enjoined him to act uprightly from that point on, and assured him that all of his sins were not only forgiven, but turned into good deeds. Abū Ṭawīl was incredulous: "Even all my perfidiousness and profligacy?!" (*ghadrātī wa-fajrātī*). Upon receiving an affirmative reply, he exclaimed, "God is great!" and went on repeating the *takbīr* until Muḥammad had disappeared from view (Qurṭubī, 13: 67). See also the commentaries to Q. 9: 117–18, where God's willingness to turn in mercy and pardon even the most serious offenses is repeatedly emphasized. The *ḥadīth* literature is full of statements and anecdotes describing not only Allāh's inclination to forgive, but the profound pleasure He receives, as it were, from doing so. One tradition even goes as far as to quote the Prophet thus: "If you [Muslims] were not to commit sins, God would have wiped you out of existence and replaced you by another people who *do* commit sins, and then ask for pardon" (Muslim, *Kitāb al-Tawba*, 37: 6621).

39 Since, however, as we shall see, Islam claims not only to have relaxed its own provisions over time but also to constitute itself a relaxation of the demands imposed by earlier religious dispensations, we should certainly not go as far as Goitein in declaring that "the policy of world renunciation and adventist asceticism (*hinazrut min ha-'olam ve-sagfanut adventistit*) that characterized the earliest stage of Islam was soon distorted by a brazen opportunism and pragmatism already evident in Mecca" (S. D. Goitein, "Ha-dat ha-zo'efet: qavim lidmut ha-yahadut ba-sifrut ha-muslemit ha-qduma" in *Sefer Dinaburg* [Jerusalem: Qiryat Sefer, 1950], 2). The former half of this statement greatly exaggerates the extent of rigor and abstinence informing Islam at its inception; the latter half is a curious value judgement, especially coming from a man who was himself far from a stickler in matters of religious observance (and see Abraham Udovitch's reflections – in the forward to the fifth, posthumously published volume of Goitein's monumental *A Mediterranean Society*, p. xv – on Goitein's aspirations for religious reform. What is *rukhṣa-naskh* if not religious reform?).

40 What Abraham Udovitch asserts regarding Ḥanafī jurists is largely true of the *fuqahā'* of other schools as well: "While the passage from Sarakhsī quoted above is an unusually candid statement of the concessions which Ḥanafī law was prepared or forced to make to popular business usages, it is by no means unique. Throughout their discussion of partnership (and also of other commercial contracts and practices), Ḥanafī writers, from Shaybānī on, frequently invoke customary practice or the needs of merchants as a justification for their

tone in His capacity as archetypal and eminently malleable Muftī On

---

exercise of juristic preference in the face of the occasionally confining effects of systematic legal reasoning. The total effect of this greater leniency was to enlarge the area of legitimacy for transactions and contracts, thereby giving merchants and others a much freer hand in the conduct of their affairs." Abraham L. Udovitch, *Partnership and Profit in Medieval Islam* (Princeton: Princeton University Press, 1970), 73. Elsewhere in the same work Udovitch writes simply that "the requirements of the law yielded in the face of the people's need" (ibid., 251). It should, however, be remembered that there may be a difference between *rukhṣa* – which often involves a permanent alteration of the law and appears, with several exceptions, to be the sole prerogative of Allāh, His Apostle and a few other important *ṣaḥāba* and *tābiʿūn* – and the tendency of the later *fuqahā'* and *quḍāh* to temporarily suspend, mitigate or reinterpret certain regulations due to changed or extenuating circumstances. That having been said, it is the jurists who debate and decide the question when a particular "relaxation" may be legitimately applied (*yatarakhkhaṣu / lā yatarakhkhaṣu* – see, e.g., Abū Zakariyā' Yaḥyā Muḥyī al-Dīn al-Nawawī, *Rawḍat al-Ṭālibīn* [Beirut: Dār al-Kutub al-ʿIlmiya], 1:483–4), and moreover the term *rukhṣa* is in fact used freely in describing *fiqh* activity (see, e.g., Kister, "Concessions," 11, where Sulaymān b. Ṭarkhān is quoted to the effect that "anyone who would adopt every *rukhṣa of the fuqahā* would turn out a libertine"). For issues of judicial discretion, see also Wael Hallaq, *A History of Islamic Legal Theories* (Cambridge: Cambridge University Press, 1997), 107ff; and Gideon Libson, *Jewish and Islamic Law: A Comparative Study of Custom during the Geonic Period* (Cambridge: Harvard University Press, 2003), chapter 3.

The Prophet himself could come back from the grave to reinforce even the most minor *rukhaṣ*. For instance, the law had originally stipulated that all instances of reverse peristalsis – the return of food from stomach to mouth – violated a believer's ritual fitness (*naqaḍa al-wuḍū'*). However, the devout Muslim performs at least seventeen *rakaʿāt* spread across five prayer services from dawn to dusk, and will therefore probably have eaten not long before genuflecting. Since such a combination of pre-digestion and forehead-to-floor prostration often leads to egestion (food coming up into the throat), the *fuqahā'* (or their predecessors) for the most part decided to differentiate between *qay'*, vomit that bursts the bounds of the mouth and is declared polluting, and *qils*, eructation that only partially fills the oral cavity and then recedes, and which does not require the renewal of ablutions (*fa-inna man yamla'u min al-ṭaʿām idhā rakaʿa fī'l-ṣalāt yaʿlu shay'un ilā ḥalqihi fa-li'l-balwā jaʿalnā al-qalīl ʿafwan* – here is a jurists' *rukhṣa*). In this connection, al-Sarakhsī records the following incident: "ʿĀbid bi-Balkh alias ʿAlī b. Yūnus recounted: My daughter asked me, 'What should I do if something comes up out of my throat [into my mouth – *in kharaja min ḥalqī shay'un*]?' I answered her, 'If you taste its flavor in your throat, then repeat your ablution.' ʿĀbid continued: '[That night] the Prophet came to me in a dream (*ra'aytu al-nabī fī'l-manām*) and said, "No, ʿAlī! Only if it fills up the mouth!"' (*lā, yā ʿAli, ḥattā yamla'u al-fam!*). From that moment, I took it upon myself never to deliver another legal opinion" (Sarakhsī, *Mabsūṭ*, 1:75).

High, handing down indulgences in response to, and in compassion for, the endemic weaknesses of human flesh. "God's mercy was made manifest," writes al-Ṭabarī, "in that He charged [the Muslims] with obligations, and then relieved them of the same, not burdening them with more than they could handle."[41] The preeminent methodology employed in the bestowal of these divine dispensations was *naskh.* With its help, countless prohibitions were punctured by loopholes, rigid restrictions were bent and strenuous observances tempered or eliminated. So frequent, in fact, were such celestial reprieves that the Muslims began to take them for granted. When the Prophet, on the strength of the recently revealed Q. 4: 43 ("... Draw not near unto [the place of] prayer ... when you are sexually impure ..."),[42] instructed his flock to reposition their domiciles so that their doors faced away from the mosque, lest that edifice become a thoroughfare, "the people did nothing, expecting the alleviation that would be revealed."[43] Experience had taught them that it was only a matter of time until Allāh's characteristic benevolence won out. Although there were exceptions to this unidirectional tendency – the Qur'ānic attitude to wine became more, not less, prohibitive over time[44] and the penalty for imbibing this beverage was doubled;[45] the punishment for adultery was eventually stiffened;[46] inheritance law turned increasingly restrictive;[47] donkey-flesh

41 Ṭabarī, 4: 428: "... *'raḥīman' bihim fī-mā kallafahum min al-farā'iḍi wa-khaffafa 'anhum fa-lam yuḥammilhum fawqa ṭāqatihim.*"

42 For the legal debates revolving around the different possible translations of various parts of this verse, see the present writer's "Strangers and Brothers: The Ritual Status of Unbelievers in Early Islamic Jurisprudence," forthcoming in *Medieval Encounters,* summer 2006.

43 Qurṭubī, 5: 180: "*wa-lam yaṣna' al-qawm shay'an rajā'an an tanzila lahum rukhṣa.*" On this occasion, for a change, it did not arrive.

44 Qurṭubī, 5: 173.

45 M. M. Bravmann, *The Spiritual Background of Early Islam* (Leiden: E. J. Brill, 1972), 131.

46 According to most opinions – see Qurṭubī, 3: 72. For the whole story, see Burton, *Sources,* chapter 7, which is introduced by the author with the following declaration: "Of all the disputed questions in the *Fiḳh,* and especially in the *uṣūl,* none is richer in variety of treatment, or fuller in its appeal to Ḳur'ān and *Sunna* sources, or more acute in tension as to the relative weight that the *fuḳahā'* were alleged to have accorded to each of the sources, than that of the penalties for fornication and adultery." See also Burton, *Collection,* chapter 4, and Melchert, "Qur'ānic Abrogation," 84–9.

47 David Powers, *Studies in Qur'an and Ḥadīth: The Formation of the Islamic Law of Inheritance* (Berkeley: University of Caifornia Press, 1986), 145–158.

was forbidden after having been permitted[48] and wild beasts and birds of prey were added to the list of prohibited foodstuffs;[49] coition without seminal emission was declared ritually defiling, then this provision was revoked, and finally it was reinstated[50] – nevertheless, the overall

Still, important aspects of inheritance law were specifically subjected to alleviation through abrogation (see, e.g., the commentaries to Q. 8: 74–5).

48 Nasā'ī, *Ṭahāra,* 54; Bukhārī, *Jihād,* 48:130: "... from Anas, may God be pleased with him: that someone came to the Messenger of God at [the siege of] Khaybar, and said: I have eaten of donkey meat – and the Prophet was silent. A second man came, and said: I have eaten of donkey meat – and the Prophet was silent. Then a third man came, and said: [Many] donkeys have been gobbled up! (*ufniyat ḥumuran*). [This was evidently too much for the Prophet, and] he commanded a crier to announce among the people: Lo, God and his Messenger forbid to you the meat of the domestic donkey! And they overturned their cooking pots, which had been simmering with [donkey] flesh (*fa-ukfi'at al-qudūr wa-innahā li-tafūr bi'l-laḥm*)." Still, even in the midst of increasing stringency, *rukhṣa* will out: in other versions of this story the Prophet commands that the meat-stew be thrown out *and* the pots smashed. The people appeal to him, and ask whether it is not sufficient to *wash* the pots. He responds – in typical "softy" style – "Very well, that will do." Muslim, *al-Jihād wa'l-Siyar,* 43:1802.

49 Burton, *Collection,* 55.

50 For the vacillation on *inivit sed non emisit*, see Qurṭubī, 5:178–9; Manṣūr b. Yunus al-Buhūtī, *Kashshāf al-Qinā' 'an Matn al-Iqnā'* (Riyāḍ: Maktabat al-Naṣr al-Ḥadītha, n.d.), 1:142; Sarakhsī, *Mabsūṭ,* 1:68–9; Nawawī, *Sharḥ,* 2:30; Abū Muḥammad 'Abd Allāh b. Aḥmad b. Muḥammad ("Muwaffaq al-Dīn") b. Qudāma al-Maqdisī, *Kitāb al-Mughnī* (Beirut: 'Ālam al-Kutub, n.d.), 1:204 ff; and 'Alī al-Qārī al-Harawī, *Fatḥ Bāb al-'Ināya* (Aleppo: Maktab al-Maṭbū'āt al-Islāmiya, 1967), 1:94–6. Regarding the right to engage in *mut'a* ("temporary marriage" for purposes of sexual release), the title of the third chapter in Muslim's *Kitāb al-Nikāḥ* describes an even greater shilly-shallying: "*Bāb Nikāḥ al-Mut'a wa-Bayān annahu Ubīḥa, thumma Nusikha, thumma Ubīḥa, thumma Nusikha, thumma Istaqarra Taḥrīmuhu ilā Yawm al-Qiyāma.*" One of the reports recorded in this chapter includes the statement that "[*mut'a*] was a concession granted during the early days of Islam for the sake of those who were in dire need [of sexual satisfaction], just as [one may, in situations of severe necessity, eat] carrion, blood and swine-flesh; then God fortified (i.e. toughened) religion and forbade it" (*thumma aḥkama Allāhu al-dīn wa-nahā 'anhā* – Muslim, *Nikāḥ,* 3:27 [1406]). On *mut'a* in this connection, see also Hakim, "Conflicting Images," 171–3 and 176–7. Ibn Ḥazm's discussion of *mulāmasa* – the act of "touching another" by which ritual impurity is incurred according to Q. 4:43 and Q. 5:6 – includes the claim that this clause abrogated a previous dispensation in which such contact caused no ceremonial impairment (Abū Muḥammad 'Alī b. Aḥmad b. Ḥazm, *Al-Muḥallā* [Beirut: Manshūrāt al-Maktab al-Tijārī li'l-Ṭibā'a wa'l-Nashr wa'l-Tawzī', n.d.], 1:246). Another precept that was made more difficult, according to some authorities, was the fast, which at

trend in abrogation was decidedly toward abatement. "After hardship, Allāh bringeth ease" (Q. 65: 7).[51]

---

first was vaguely limited to "a certain number of days" (Q. 2: 183) but then was extended to the entire month of Ramaḍān (Q. 2: 184).

It should be noted that the classification of a particular instance of abrogation as either relaxing or restrictive is often a matter of perspective. "Many of the People of the Book long to make you disbelievers after your belief..." explains Q. 2: 109, "... but forgive them and be indulgent toward them *until Allāh commands.*" Some time after this passage was revealed, Allāh did indeed command: "Kill the *mushrikūn* (here construed as including scriptuaries) wherever you find them" (Q. 9: 5), putting an end to the previously ordained patient approach (see Qurṭubī, 6: 104). The replacement of the forebearance-oriented injunction with this comparatively merciless "sword verse" may not look like *rukhṣa* to the modern ecumenical eye – and it certainly didn't make the lives of Islam's enemies any easier – but it may well have come as a considerable relief to the ideologically zealous and honor-driven Arab-Muslims of the time, eager to fight for their faith and frustrated by the ignominy of longstanding restraint. The same may be said of the increasingly aggressive interpretations of the precept of *jihād* described, e.g., in Qurṭubī, 2: 312 ff and 8: 37–8 (for which development see also Uri Rubin, "Bara'a: A Study of Some Quranic Passages," *Jerusalem Studies in Arabic and Islam,* 5 [1984], 18–20); as well as of the revelation permitting warfare in the Sacred Months found in Q. 2: 214 (which some writers consider to have itself been cancelled, or at least qualified, later on). In another example of such relativity, most authorities hold that the requirement to maintain a widow for the period of a year from the proceeds of her deceased husband's estate (Q. 2: 240) was abrogated by the commandment to herit her one fourth of his property if he dies without offspring and one eighth if he has children (Q. 4: 12 – see, e.g., Muqātil b. Sulaymān, *Kitāb Tafsīr al-Khams Mi'at Āya min al-Qur'ān al-Karīm* [ed. Isaiah Goldfeld. Shfar'am: Al-Mashriq Press, 1980], 192). Depending on the dead spouse's worth – and depending upon our point of view (that of the widow versus that of the children or the executors) – this modification may be seen as ameliorating or not. In many cases, in other words, *rukhṣa* is in the eye of the beholder (but see next note).

51 The versatile and prolific ninth century CE theologian and *adīb,* Abū Muḥammad 'Abd Allah b. Muslim b. Qutayba, advanced a helpful criterion for determining the abrogating from the abrogated precept: "The ruling which is easier to perform is usually the one abrogating an earlier, more exacting one" (Adang, *Muslim Writers,* 197; and see, on Ibn Qutayba's general theory of abrogation, Melchert, "Qurānic Abrogation," 80–1). Qatāda explained that Q. 2: 106 – "... We bring [in place of verses We abrogate] better or similar ones..." – means "[We bring] a verse containing a reduction, containing mercy, containing a 'Thou shalt' or a 'Thou shalt not'" (*yaqūlu: āya fīhā takhfīf, fīhā raḥma, fīhā amr, fīhā nahy* – Ṭabarī, 1: 671). "By [al-Shāfi'ī's] day," writes Burton, "[the word 'alleviation'] had already become a quasi-technical term denoting *naskh,* or rather, the rationalization of *naskh.* He himself uses it on occasion as a synonym for *naskh*" (Burton, *Sources,* 29). "For Shāfi'ī," he adds further along, "*naskh* is an integral aspect of the divine revelatory activity, motivated by a di-

vine desire to alleviate the burdens He had placed upon men" (ibid., 32). Even more simply: "The definition of *naskh* is: God abandoned an obligation He had earlier imposed" (Burton, quoting al-Shāfiʿī, ibid., 34). See also al-Shāfiʿī's representative enumeration of Qur'ānic clauses beginning with the phrase "it is no sin for you..." (*laysa ʿalaykum junāḥun / lā junāḥun ʿalaykum*), all of which he appears to consider *rukhaṣ* (*takhfīfun min Allāhi... rukhṣatun min Allāhi... – Umm,* 1:206–7). Al-Ghazālī, elucidating the implications of Q. 2:106, maintained that "God did not mean to say that He proposed to bring a *verse* superior to the first, for no part of the Qur'ān is superior to another. He meant to state that he would bring a *ruling* superior to the first, in the sense of *its being easier to perform,* or richer in terms of reward" (cited in Burton, *Collection,* 57). The dominant trend in *naskh*, then, is clearly the entropic one of *al-faraj baʿda al-shidda* (relief after exertion).

It may be significant for this, that a not uncommon method of dealing with contradictory *aḥādīth* involves presuming alleviation through abrogation even when the same is not directly mentioned. For example, Ibn ʿAbbās affirmed that "the Prophet drank milk, then called for some water and gargled, saying, 'It contains fat' (*inna lahu dasaman*)." Anas b. Mālik, on the other hand, remembers that "the Messenger of God drank milk and neither gargled nor performed ablutions afterward, and then he prayed." In Shams al-Ḥaqq al-ʿAẓīm Ābādī's *ʿAwn al-Maʿbūd: Sharḥ Sunan Abī Dā'ūd* (Beirut: Dār al-Fikr, 1979), 1:331, the first of these reports is entitled: "*Bāb al-Wuḍū' min al-Laban*" and the second: "*Bāb al-Rukhṣa min Dhālika.*" This classification involves a double assumption: (1) that both reports are *ṣaḥīḥ* and therefore must be reconciled (either through *jamʿ* or through *naskh,* the method of *tarjīḥ* being inapplicable in such a case – see Muḥammad b. Rushd, *Bidāyat al-Mujtahid wa-Nihāyat al-Muqtaṣid* [Fez: al-Maṭbaʿa al-Mawlawiya, 1909], 1:31), and (2) that the report harboring the more lenient implications describes the Prophet's later practice, and consequently abrogates the report containing the relative stringency. There seems to be some basis for the former assumption, but not for the latter (see, e.g., *Mughnī,* 1:191, where Ibn Qudāma confirms the soundness of both the conflicting traditions relevant to the question whether milk is a *nāqiḍ al-wuḍū'*, but concludes that the issue itself is unclear). Thus, we appear to have here, in the caption chosen by ʿAẓīm Ābādī, what amounts to a "presumption of *rukhṣa.*" A similar attitude may be manifest in Abū Dā'ūd's chapter heading concerning ablutions after eating cooked food: "*Bāb fī Tark al-Wuḍū' mimma Massat al-Nār*" (Abū Dā'ūd Sulaymān b. al-Ashʿath b. Isḥāq al-Azdī al-Sijistānī, *Sunan Abū Dā'ūd* [Cairo: Muṣṭafā al-Bābī al-Ḥalabī wa-Awlāduhu, n.d.], 1:43. For methods of *ḥadīth* harmonization in general see now Eerik Dickinson, *The Development of Early Sunnite* Ḥadīth *Criticism: The* Taqdima *of Ibn Abī Ḥātim al-Rāzi (240/854–327/938)* (Leiden: E. J. Brill, 2001), especially chapter one.

3. New Things under the Sun

Community, Humanity and Teleology

In the ninety-fourth chapter of the Qur'ān, Allāh addresses His Apostle:

> Have We not expanded your breast, and removed from you your burden (*waḍa'na 'anka wizraka*) which weighed down your back, and have We not exalted your fame? Verily, in the wake of hardship cometh ease; in the wake of hardship cometh ease (*inna ma' al-'usri yusran* – Q. 94: 1–6).

On the immediate level, these lines are taken by the classical commentators to refer to developments in Muḥammad's personal life: either his metamorphosis from a state of ignorance and sin in the *jāhiliyya* (pre-Islamic period) to a state of gnosis and righteousness in the prophetic period; or his meteoric rise from wretched and persecuted outcast in Mecca to triumphant and prosperous leader in Madīna; or both.[1] It is

1 See Nāsir al-Dīn Abū Sa'īd 'Abd Allāh b. 'Umar al-Shīrāzī al-Bayḍāwī, *Tafsīr al-Bayḍāwī* (Beirut: Dār al-Kutub al-'Ilmiya, 1988), 2: 605; Ṭabarī, 30: 295; Qurṭubī, 20: 80; and elsewhere. "Expansion of the breast" (*sharḥ al-ṣadr*) is sometimes used as a metaphor for Islam in general, and because the root *sh.r.ḥ.* also denotes slicing, this phrase later gave rise to the celebrated story of the extraction from his chest and lavation by angels of the child (or man) Muḥammad's heart. For the extension of this "prosperity after adversity" theme to the lives of other major prophets, see the commentaries to Q. 33: 38, where we read that "it has ever been the custom of Allāh to remove straitness from the lives of His messengers by permitting them things [denied to others]" (*nafiy al-ḥaraj 'anhum fīmā abāḥa lahum*). This includes the right to marry without furnishing a dowry (*tazwīj al-anbiyā' bi-ghayr ṣidāq* – Qurṭubī, 15: 142). See also, in this connection, Abū 'Alī al-Muḥassin b. 'Alī al-Tanūkhī, *Al-Faraj ba'da al-Shidda* (Beirut: Dar Ṣādir, n. d.), where a lengthy analysis of the grammer of Q. 94: 5–6 is also offered (pp. 59–64. I thank Camilla Adang for bringing this work to my attention). Making Muḥammad's own life easier is itself a persistent preoccupation of Revelation, the most famous (because most controversial) examples of which being God's release of the Prophet from his vow, uttered in haste to placate his enraged wife Ḥafṣa, never again to sleep with Mary the Copt (see the commentaries to the opening verses of Q. 66), and the divine censure of Muḥammad for denying himself Zaynab bint Jaḥsh (see the commen-

interesting, however, that at least one account of the Prophet's remarks upon receiving this divine communication has him go out to the people and proclaim: "Rejoice at the glad tidings! Ease has come to you: one 'hardship' will never vanquish two 'ease's" (*ibshirū, atākum al-yusr, lan yaghliba 'usr yusrayn*).[2] This statement probably means that the Qur'ān's twofold reiteration of the supersession of hardship by ease locks Muslim history onto a liberalizing course that brooks no future reversals.[3] It *definitely* means that with respect to the principle of *rukhṣa,* the line dividing the general from the particular is not very clear. The Islamic orientation and progression toward leniency is perceived to exist concurrently on a number of levels, including (1) Muḥammad's individual career and (2) the career of the *umma*. Just as the Messenger of God, in his own life, moved inexorably from a stage of difficulty to a stage of facility, so, too, did the Community of God. But the analogy must be expanded further still: the third level on which *rukhṣa* and *naskh* are portrayed as cooperating to fuel the forward march of history is that of humanity as a whole.

The process of divine revelation followed by divine revision that honed and perfected the legal system in the Islamic microcosm is paralleled by the phenomenon of successive creeds – as it were, mega-revelations – amending and supplanting their predecessors in the universal macrocosm.[4] This grand-scale procession, too, is characterized by extenuation. "The hardships and strict applications of the law were the lot of the faith communities that preceded us," explains the less well known of the two Ibn al-'Arabīs, "whereas God has bestowed upon this community a degree of liberalism and flexibility not afforded to any community before it, as a sign of His mercy and favor."[5] Com-

taries to Q. 33: 37), the latter leading to an "expanding" (*tawsa'a*) of the law for the benefit of all Muslims.

2 Ibn Ḥajar, *Iṣāba,* 8: 711.

3 A tendency we tried to illustrate in the previous chapter.

4 Fascinating in this regard is Q. 5: 19: "O People of the Book! Our Messenger has come to you to make things plain after an interval devoid of prophets (*qad jā'akum rasūlunā yubayyin lakum 'alā* fatratin *min al-rusuli*)..." The maddening interval between Muḥammad's first and second revelations is also famous as the *fatra,* a prolonged period of time between divine communications. The parallelism is inescapable: ontogenesis recapitulates philogenesis.

5 [Abū Bakr Muḥammad b. 'Abd Allāh al-Ma'āfirī] b. al-'Arabī, *Aḥkām al-Qur'ān,* 2: 76: "*Inna al-shadā'id wa'l-'azā'im kānat fī'l-umam qablanā, fa-a'ṭā Allāhu hādhihi'l-ummata min al-musāmaḥa wa'l-līn mā lam yu'ṭi ummatan qablahā raḥmatan minhu wa-faḍlan.*"

menting on Q. 22:78 – "God has chosen you [Muslims] and has not laid upon you any constriction in your faith" – al-Qurṭubī asserts that the institution of *rukhṣa* serves to distinguish Islam from all other dispensations: "This verse is integral to a great many regulations, and it is among those hallmarks by which God has singled out this nation."[6] "Our Lord!," prayed the believers, "Do not lay upon us a burden, as You did upon those who came before us!" (*la taḥmilu ʿalaynā iṣran kamā ḥamaltahu ʿalā alladhīna min qablinā* – Q. 2:286). Their prayers were answered: God made Islam the easiest religion.[7]

Al-Qurṭubī's aforementioned doctor—patient analogy might therefore be improved upon. The venerated exegete was at pains, it will be recalled, to reconcile God's impeccable stability of mind with the evident vicissitudes in His lawgiving. He argued that these two phenomena could coexist because God's all-encompassing foreknowledge allowed Him to anticipate (if He did not actually predestine) the various stages of communal or overall human development that would punctuate the march of history, and to prearrange the periodic deployment of regulations or systems appropriate to each stage. In a certain sense, this is indeed what doctors do. Medical science endeavors to foresee all of the maladies that might conceivably threaten an individual's well-being, and prepares treatments for each. These treatments are held in abeyance until such time as they are needed, at which point they are administered. But a doctor cannot predict the order of the disorders he will be called upon to treat, nor can he forecast with certainty the trajectory of a patient's disease. He knows neither the *ma'āl* (final outcome) nor the road leading up to it. Consequently, it is impossible to sketch the progress of his prescriptions before the fact, even in the broadest of outlines, for they will perforce describe an erratic and sometimes even circuitous line.

Though one hesitates to second-guess a thirteenth-century *mufassir*, a better analogy might have been the parent—child or teacher—pupil

6 Qurṭubī, 12: 84: "*hādhihi'l-āya tadkhul fī kathīr min al-aḥkām wa-hiya mimmā khaṣṣa Allāhu bihā hādhihi'l-umma.*" See also Ṭabarī, 17:270: "God made Islam capacious, He did not make it narrow" (*ja'ala al-dīn wāsiʿan wa-lam yajʿalhu ḍayyiqan*).

7 "Rukhaṣ represent, in the opinion of Muslim scholars, the characteristic way of Islam as opposed to Judaism and Christianity" (Kister, "Concessions," 91). The Prophet said: "The best part of your religion [Islam] is the easiest part" (*khayru dīnikum aysaruhu* – Qurṭubī, 12: 84). The principle is naturally extended: the best of mankind's religions is the easiest one.

relationship. Here, in normal cases, a roughly linear chart may be plotted beginning at birth or matriculation: the child will grow physically and intellectually in a more-or-less predictable fashion, and home and school curricula may be planned in accordance from the outset. More importantly, this simile sits better with the trend of *rukhṣa* through *naskh* that al-Qurṭubī sought to portray, especially as it pertains to the macrocosmic plane. Parents naturally surround a juvenile with a dense network of rules and a full program of activities. As the child grows and approaches adulthood, both of these categories are significantly scaled down: less supervision is required and more independence is granted. When humanity was young it needed a plethora of regulations to keep it in line and an abundance of rituals to keep it busy. When mankind matured, much of this could be dispensed with.[8]

What are the stages of this Islamic brand of dialectical materialism? Statements like those of Ibn al-ʿArabī (above) that "the hardships and strict applications of the law were the lot of the faith communities that preceded us" give the impression of either (1) a parade of confessional denominations leading up to Islam, each stepping into the shoes, and mitigating the harshness, of the system that preceded it,[9] or – and the wording seems to support this interpretation slightly better – (2) Islam

8 This construction does not, however, completely eliminate the problems with al-Qurṭubī's outlook. Many provisions were abrogated, as we have seen, because they were considered too onerous, and the abrogation usually took place quite soon after the promulgation (sometimes on the same night). Neither the parent-child analogy nor the physician-patient analogy really works with this process. Most of al-Ṭabarī's informants, who are still able to accept what amounts to a divine methodology of trial and error, can dispense with such acrobatics.

9 Muslim tradition generally conceives of a chronological series of divinely ordained religio-legal systems prior to the advent of Islam that includes those vouchsafed unto Adam, Noah, Abraham, Moses and Jesus (and perhaps also Ṣāliḥ, Hūd, Shuʿayb and several other *rusul* or *ulū al-ʿazm*), each dispensation abrogating the previous one. But since very little is said regarding the nature of the confessions introduced through Adam, Noah, the Arab apostles and even Abraham, nor do we have much information about the manner in which those systems were ostensibly subverted (thus making new heavenly messages necessary), it is difficult to know whether the historical process of abrogation is perceived as proceeding in the direction of *rukhṣa* from the very beginning, or only from the onset of Judaism. One gets the sense that, if anything, a bell-curve is (vaguely) envisioned, with Adam's simple monotheism at one end, the Torah's incomparably complex and demanding religion in the middle, and Islam's return to easy, pristine *fiṭra* at the other end.

as a direct and synchronic reaction to the excesses marring *all* of the religio-cultural administrations it encountered in the first decades of its existence, especially Judaism, Christianity, Zoroastrianism and Arab paganism. Although there are some traces in the literature of the former, multi-stage conception, these are primarily concerned with progress (or, at least, repeated rectification) on the theological plane. The references in such passages to incremental improvement in the *legal* sphere are, for the most part, general and superficial.[10] The latter image, in

10 See Lazarus-Yafeh, *Intertwined Worlds,* 37, and especially 109, n. 110, where she mentions Ibn Taymiyya's comparison of the Torah to the break of dawn, the Gospel to the rising sun, and the Qur'ān to its midday brilliance (this simile may itself derive indirectly from a famous eschatological midrash: "Rabbi Ḥiyya, Rava and Rabbi Samuel b. Ḥananya were walking in the valley of Arbel at dawn [*be-qritzta*] when they espied the day's first rays. Rabbi Ḥiyya said to Rabbi Samuel, "So indeed shall be the redemption of Israel: at first it will glow faintly, then gradually increase in incandescence, and finally it will show forth in all its splendor" [*metzaftzefet ba-teḥila kim'a kim'a, kol ma she-hi menatznetzet hi raba ve-holekhet* – Yerushalmi Berakhot, 1:1]). See also Ṭabarī, 1:461: "The [genuine] faith of the Jews prescribed cleaving to the Torah and to the *sunna* of Moses until such time as Jesus would come. Once Jesus came, whoever continued to cleave to the Torah and hold fast to the *sunna* of Moses, and did not reject these and follow Jesus, was lost (*kāna hālikan*). The [genuine] faith of the Christians consisted of cleaving to the Evangel and to the laws of Jesus (*sharā'i' 'Īsā*) until such time as Muḥammad would come. Once Muḥammad came, whoever among them did not follow Muḥammad and reject his earlier allegiance to the *sunna* of Jesus and the Evangel, was lost." (Islam itself will never be superceded: it is the *sharī'a nāsikha ghayr mansūkha,* "the abrogating but never to be abrogated Law"). See also, in this connection, Ṭabarī, 3:383.

It is true that the passage of al-Ṭabarī just quoted alludes to a process of legal as well as theological evolution, and indeed, the Qur'ān itself implies that *legal* systems may vary, but *theology* is stable and universal: "For each nation We have ordained a rite (*mansik*) of their own, that they may pronounce the name of God over the cattle which He has given them for food – but your [*viz.,* all human beings'] God is the same God" (Q. 22:35). Sale explains, regarding the procession of monotheistic faiths, that in the eyes of Islam "there never was nor ever can be more than one orthodox religion. For though the particular laws or ceremonies are only temporary, and subject to alteration according to the divine direction, yet the substance of it being eternal truth, is not liable to change, but continues immutably the same" (Sale, "Preliminary Discourse," 49). Further on Sale elaborates: "As to the matter of practice, [orthodox Muslim belief consists in] the observance of the immutable and eternal laws of right and wrong, together with such other precepts and ceremonies as God should think fit to order for the time being, according to the different dispensations in different ages of the world: for these last, [the Muslim] allowed, were things indif-

which the religion revealed through Muḥammad challenges the normative severity of an array of doctrines all at once, appears to be more common in the sources. It also tallies better with the nature of the *naskh-rukhṣa* process on the microcosmic, intra-Islamic plane, where – save for several important exceptions[11] – only two steps were involved: the issuance by God of (what turned out to be) an overtaxing injunction, and the imminent substitution of a more feasible law.[12] Unlike

---

ferent in their own nature, and became obligatory by God's positive precept only; and were therefore temporary, and subject to alteration according to His will and pleasure" (ibid., 55 – see above, chap. 1, n. 5). Similarly, Friedmann writes: "Though [Allāh's] message was identical in its essentials because all prophets preached absolute monotheism, it varied in particulars and the detailed laws imposed on the various communities were not identical ... It goes without saying that the abrogation of the former laws does not apply to the basic principles of religion, such as the belief in one God, which are common to all prophets" (*Tolerance,* 14, 23). This is what Jacques Waardenburg calls "the one primordial, eternal religion which perpetuates itself through multiple histories" (Waardenburg, "Muslim Studies of Other Religions" in Geert Jan van Gelder and Ed de Moor [eds.], *Orientations: The Middle East and Europe, Encounters and Exchanges* [Amsterdam: Rodopi, 1992], 15). It also tallies with al-Ṭabarī's bifurcation, that we noted in chap. 1, between the absolute immutability of divine *information* and the contingent nature of divine *legislation.* Nevertheless, from another angle it is specifically theology that evolves; or, at least, we may say that there are occasional depictions of multi-stage theological development (or regression) *in the minds of men,* such as the desultory advance toward an ever purer monotheism (regularly held up, or diverted, by covenant neglect); instances of resurgent polytheism (including trinitarianism); and crimes of text distortion. In contrast to this, I have yet to come across an instance in which a law or ritual is shown to be gradually ameliorated *by God* as it filters through *more than two* religious systems (see, however, Friedmann, *Tolerance,* 21–2, where notions of the *divergence* between specific laws spread across the three Semitic monotheisms are presented). Furthermore, on the following page [23] Friedmann points out that "[t]here is some difference of opinion whether it was Islam that abrogated both Judaism and Christianity, or first Christianity abrogated Judaism and then Islam abrogated Christianity"). Texts like Q. 5:48 – "... for every one of you We appointed a law and a way ..." – can indeed be construed, as Friedmann states, to support the view "according to which each prophet abrogates the laws of his predecessor," (*Tolerance,* 22). Still, this idea ever remains general and vague. See below, n. 47.

11 E. g., the multi-stage process characterizing (a) the development of prayer rites, (b) the law regarding intoxicating beverages, and (c) the regulations concerning coitus interruptus, all mentioned above in chapter 2.

12 On the other hand, it must be admitted that such substitutions took place over and over again in connection with diverse precepts throughout Muḥammad's

Marx, then, Islamic tradition on the whole envisions what amounts to only two *über*-phases in the forward march of humankind: (1) the world under the spiritual sovereignty of a wide range of sinfully innovative and harmfully excessive doctrines; (2) the world under the spiritual sovereignty of the restorative and moderating doctrine of Islam.[13]

Which were those harmfully excessive doctrines in line for replacement? A widespread theme in the literature represents some of the existing ideologies as too hot, some as too cold, and Islam as just right. "O People of the Book," Allāh admonishes, "do not be extreme in your religion! (*lā taghlū fī dīnikum*)" (Q. 4: 171). "Those who went before you," preached the Prophet to his followers, "came to ruin because of extremism in their religion (*halaka man qablakum bi'l-ghuluwwi fī'l-dīn*)."[14] The extremism of the Christians was their apotheosis of Jesus[15] coupled with the "monkery which they invented for themselves, and which We did not prescribe for them" (Q. 57: 27). The extremism of the Jews was their defamation of Jesus[16] on top of their inordinate passion which induced them to sanction marriage to half-sisters.[17] "The true religion of God," on the other hand, "is midway be-

---

prophetic career, and the path toward the perfection of the Islamic religion may therefore be seen as involving many stages.

13 To the extent that the pristine, *fiṭra*-based faith of Adam – and its later reincarnation, the *millat Ibrāhīm* – are included in this legendary historical process, we might better speak of a bell-curve in three stages: (1) the reign of right religion, (2) doctrinal deviation/innovation across the board, and (3) return to Truth with Islam. This study is, however, primarily concerned with the relationship between the latter two phases.

14 Jaṣṣāṣ, *Aḥkām*, 2: 367. According to al-Jaṣṣāṣ, the Prophet made this statement to Ibn 'Abbās after the latter supplied him with some pebbles with which to pelt the pillars during (what was probably) the farewell pilgrimage. Muḥammad approved of the size of the stones, saying, "Just like these, just like these [and no bigger]: beware of exaggeration in religion ..." (*bi-mithlihinna, bi-mithlihinna, iyyākum wa'l-ghuluww fī'l-dīn ...*).

15 Ibid., 2: 366: "*jāwazū bihi manzilat al-anbiyā ḥattā ittakhadhūhu ilāhan.*" See also Q. 4: 171.

16 Ibid.: "*ja'alūhu li-ghayr rishdatin*" (they called him illegitimate).

17 Ṭabarī, 5: 41 (no. 7254). See the various commentaries and midrashim surrounding Abraham's justification to Avimelekh for having claimed that his wife Sarah was his sister: "... and besides, she is in truth my sister, my father's daughter though not my mother's; and she became my wife" (Genesis, 20: 12). In his *Tārīkh*, al-Ṭabarī justifies Abraham's statement by saying that "all believers are brothers and sisters" (*Annales*, 1: 189). In the passage to which this note is appended, the division of labor is different than that generally encountered. Here the Christians are portrayed as overly restrictive, the Jews as

tween the slack and the fanatic."[18] Scripture, albeit, urges: "Forbid not the good things which God has made lawful for you ..."; but in the same breath admonishes: "... and exceed not the limits" (Q. 5: 87). "We have appointed you a middle nation," Allāh advised the Muslims (Q. 2: 143); and, as His Apostle regularly affirmed (echoing Aristotle), "the best of things is their middle."[19]

Here, too, the relationship of the *ummī* Prophet to his *umma* in the microcosm corresponds to the relationship between the believers and the rest of humanity in the macrocosm, for the latter verse (Q. 2: 143) continues: "... so that you may bear witness against the peoples, and the Messenger may bear witness against you."[20] Just as Muḥammad regularly chided his followers for heaping stringencies upon themselves, and urged them to seek the path of least resistance ("Watch and learn, take it easy and do not burden yourselves!" [*ta'allam wa-yassirū wa-lā tu'assirū*]),[21] those same followers were charged with flaunting the advantages of *rukhṣa*-based religion for the benefit of the members of the remaining Semitic faiths:

> ... from 'Ā'isha, that the Abyssinian believers used to play games with their spears on the holiday (some recensions add: in the mosque) in the presence of the Prophet, may God's peace and blessings be upon him, and he called

---

overly permissive. Usually, either both religions are described as excessively difficult (compared to Islam), or else Judaism is made out to be too demanding and Christianity not demanding enough (see below, chap. 5, notes 22 and 33 [clause 7]; and above, end of n. 10).

18 Jaṣṣāṣ, *Aḥkām*, 2: 367: "*dīn Allāhi bayna al-muqaṣṣir wa'l-ghāly.*"

19 Baghawī, 4: 142: "*khayr al-umūr awṣatuhā,*" and see Q. 25: 67.

20 This parallelism is almost explicit in Qurṭubī, 12: 84, and is evocative of God's designation of Israel as "a kingdom of priests and a holy nation" (*mamlekhet kohanim ve-goy kadosh* – Exodus, 19: 6): the Israelites are to be to the world community as Aaron's family is to them.

21 Nasā'ī, *Ṭahāra*, 1: 47–8; Bukhārī, *Bāb Ṣabb al-Mā' 'alā'l-Bawl fī'l-Masjid*, 1: 323; and elsewhere (see the list provided by al-Māwardī's modern editor, Māwardī, 1: 367). The Prophet's remonstrations in this regard are sufficiently ubiquitous to form a genre of their own. This particular exhortation forms the conclusion of a famous *rukhṣa*-oriented anecdote in which a bedouin enters the Prophet's mosque, makes a beeline for the corner and proceeds to urinate. The Companions rush at him, but Muḥammad commands: "Leave him alone until he is finished!" (*da'ūhu ḥattā idhā faragha*). The Prophet then instructs them to bring a bucket of water, wash the affected area and forget the whole matter. (This is one of many exempla regularly adduced by latter-day Muslim preachers to prove Muḥammad's prophethood, since modern medicine has determined that interrupting urination is harmful to one's health!).

> me over and put me on his shoulders and I watched them play (in other versions: and 'Umar arrived and pelted them with stones, but the Messenger of God said: Leave them be!). And Muḥammad said to the Abyssinians: Play on, O sons of Arfida! So that the Jews and Christians may know that ours is a religion of liberality, and that I have been sent with the True Creed of Tolerance (*li-ya'lamu al-Yahūd wa'l-Naṣāra anna fī dīninā fusḥa, innī bu'ithtu bi'l-ḥanīfiyya al-samḥā'*).[22]

Muslim mildness is not merely a protest against the exaggerated practices of the surrounding nations; it is often presented as the mirror image of those practices. Once, when the Prophet was ill, he led the prayers in a seated position. When he turned around and saw the congregation standing, he motioned for them to sit. Afterwards he explained that "Persians and Byzantines stand in the presence of their sitting kings. You must not do so." This was, of course, *mukhālafa* – acting in conscious contrast to the usage of neighboring societies – but it was also a statement of liberalism.[23] The same combination of anti-as-

22 Ibn Ḥajar, *Iṣāba,* 2: 44, and see Hava Lazarus-Yafeh, "Muslim Festivals" in *Some Religious Aspects,* 43, and now M. J. Kister, "Exert Yourselves, O Banu Arfida! Some Notes on Entertainment in the Islamic Tradition," *Jerusalem Studies in Arabic and Islam* 23 (1999). Arfida is a nickname for Abyssinians. On Abyssinians in the ḥijāz see the literature cited in F. E. Peters, *Muhammad and the Origins of Islam* (Albany: State University of New York Press, 1994), 296, n. 8. A similarly kerygmatic indulgence is described in an anecdote recorded by al-Qurṭubī: "Tambourines are permitted. Al-Qushayrī said: [The women] played them in front of the Prophet on the day he entered Madīna, and Abū Bakr was on the point of scolding them, but the Messenger of God said: Let them be, Abū Bakr, so that the Jews may know that ours is a broadminded religion! (*al-duff mubāḥ, qāla al-Qushayrī: ḍuriba bayna yaday al-nabiyy yawm dakhala al-Madīna, fa-hamma Abū Bakr bi'l-zajr, fa-qāla rasūl Allāh: da'hunna yā Abā Bakr, ḥattā ta'lam al-Yahūd anna dīnanā fasīḥ*). And [the women] would beat [the tambourines] and sing: We are the daughters of Najjār, what a wonderful neighbor is Muḥammad!" (*naḥnū banāt al-Najjār, ḥabbadhā Muḥammad min jār!* – Qurṭūbī, 14: 46–7). The figures of Abū Bakr and 'Umar are often interchanged and even seemingly conflated in early Muslim literature.

23 Taqī al-Dīn Aḥmad b. Taymiyya, *Iqtiḍā' al-Ṣirāṭ al-Mustaqīm: Mukhālafat Aṣḥāb al-Jaḥīm* (Cairo: Dār al-Ḥadīth, n.d. – henceforth: "Ibn Taymiyya"), 65–6. It was also an exhortation to egalitarianism: "Human beings are equal," the Prophet famously said, "like the teeth of a comb" (*al-nās sawāsī ka-asnān al-mushṭ*). On *mukhālafa* see M. J. Kister, "Do not Assimilate Yourselves," in *Jerusalem Studies in Arabic and Islam,* 12 (1989) (it should be noted that *mukhālafa* was far from being a consistent policy; indeed, Muḥammad often leaned toward *following* the People of the Book in matters concerning which he had no express command). Some claimed that the precept of sitting with a sitting imām – instituted on this occasion – was ultimately abrogated (see Burton,

similatory policy with the inclination toward *rukhṣa* may be detected in Muḥammad's affirmation that "Religion will remain victorious as long as the people hasten the breaking of the fast (at sunset during Ramaḍān); for the Jews and Christians push it off until late."[24]

Islam is also said to have moderated many of the excesses adopted by Muḥammad's own people, the Arabs. The Prophet's prohibition against the inordinate mourning (*niyāḥa*) of the *jāhiliyya* is well known,[25] as is his relaxation of many of the rigors connected with pre-

---

Sources, 28; also Christopher Melchert, "The Etiquette of Learning in the Early Islamic Study Circle," in Joseph E. Lowry *et al* [eds.], *Law and Education in Medieval Islam: Studies in Memory of George Makdisi* [Warminster: E. J.W. Gibb Memorial Trust, 2004], 37. In the same essay [p. 39] Melchert cites from Ibn Abī Shayba another instance of *mukhālafa* in the matter of sitting: "[The Jews] said that God created the heavens and earth in six days, then settled on the Sabbath and sat in that posture (i.e. cross-legged)." The Jews therefore "used to dislike [sitting thus], so the Muslims contradicted them [and do sit thus]"). On another occasion the Prophet was less latitudinarian: many of the *muhājirūn* were stricken with fever after their exposure to the comparatively humid climate of Madīna, and at one point Muḥammad found himself almost the only person in the mosque able to stand up; he nevertheless admonished: "The prayer of one who sits is worth only half the prayer of one who stands," so they all made efforts to stand up (Muir, *Life of Mohammad,* 174).

24 Ibn Taymiyya, 60: "*Lā yazālu al-dīn ẓāhiran mā 'ajjala al-nās al-fiṭr li-anna al-Yahūd wa'l-Naṣārā yu'akhkhirūn.*" The referent is obviously the Jews' and Christians' own break-fasts, which they postpone far into the evening. As we saw above (chap. 2, n. 33) the Prophet and his Companions were famous for ending the Ramaḍān fast often even *before* its official conclusion at sunset (this despite the great importance Muḥammad assigned to this particular *rukn*, calling it, among other things, "the gate of religion"). See also Māwardī, 3: 301, who cites a widely circulated variant of the report to which this note is appended according to which Muḥammad promised perennial success to those who hasten the end of the fast "and do not delay it as do the people of the East" (*ahl al-mashriq*).

25 See, e.g., Abū Zakariyā' Yaḥyā Muḥyī al-Dīn al-Nawawī, *Al-Minhāj: Sharḥ Ṣaḥīḥ Muslim b. al-Ḥajjāj* (Damascus: Dār al-Khayr, 1994), 2: 522 ff (*Kitāb al-Janā'iz*, 11: 10 [922 ff]); Goldziher, *Muslim Studies* (trans. C. R. Barber and S. M. Stern. London: Allen & Unwin, 1971), vol. 1, 217 ff; and G. H. A. Juynboll, *Muslim Tradition: Studies in Chronology, Provenance and Authorship of Early Ḥadīth* (Cambridge: Cambridge University Press, 1983), 96 and the literature cited there; see now also Fred Astren, "Depaganizing Death: Aspects of Mourning in Rabbinic Judaism and Early Islam" in Reeves, *Bible and Qur'ān*. "The Messenger of God cursed, among the [mourning] women, the howler (*sāliqa*), the shaver (*ḥāliqa*), the ripper (*ḥāriqa*) and the scratcher" (*mumtahisha* – Māwardī, 3: 236). Al-Shāfi'ī specifically designates this new policy of milder mourning rites a *rukhṣa* (ibid., 3: 235).

Islamic *ḥajj* rituals[26] and his abolition of the stringencies adopted by the *ḥums* association.[27] In al-Qurṭubī's commentary to Q. 7:31 – "Who has forbidden you to wear the decent clothes and eat the good things which God has provided for his servants?" – he explains that this rhetorical query refers to "the slit-eared camel-calves, free-roaming she-camels, barren camel mares and old camel stallions the meat of which the people of the Time of Ignorance used to forbid themselves" and which Islam subsequently permitted.[28]

Such instances, taken together, depict Islam as having loosened the fetters fastened upon human societies by a *wide variety* of surrounding religio-cultural systems. But this is misleading. Neither Ḥijāzī poly-

26 Qurṭubī, 12:85. See also Abū 'Umar Yūsuf b. 'Abd al-Barr, *Al-Tamhīd li-mā fī'l-Muwaṭṭa' min al-Ma'ānī wa'l-Asānīd* (Fez: Tab' Wizārat al-Awqāf, n.d.), 7:264; and Kister, "Concessions," 103.

27 The Prophet's declaration to one of the *anṣār* during the year of Ḥudaybiya that he, too, was an *aḥmasī*, was accompanied by a demonstrative act geared toward relieving that same *anṣārī* of one of the *ḥums* restrictions he still followed (*scil.*, entering a house from behind through a hole in the ground when ritually impure – see Peters, *Muhammad*, 97 – or when in the *iḥrām* state [see the commentaries to Q. 2:189]). The *ḥums*, who are vaguely reminiscent of the Tannaitic *ḥaverim*, had introduced in the pre-Islamic period "innovations for which they had no warrant. They thought it wrong that they should eat cheese made of sour milk or clarify butter while they were in a state of taboo. They would not enter tents of camel hair or seek shelter from the sun except in leather tents when they were in this state. They went further and refused to allow those outside the *ḥarām* to bring food in with them when they came to the great or little pilgrimage. Nor could they circumambulate the House except in the garments of the Ḥums. If they had no such garments they had to go round naked. If any man or woman felt scruples when they had no *ḥums* garments, then they could go around in their ordinary clothes; but they had to throw them away afterwards so that neither they nor anyone else could make use of them ... They imposed all these restrictions on the Arabs, who accepted them" (Ibn Isḥāq-Guillume, 87–8). Islam did away with every one of these rules. On the *ḥums* see R. Simon, "Ḥums et Īlāf ou Commerce sans Guerre," *Acta Orientalia* 18 (1970) and M. J. Kister, "Mecca and Tamīm," *JESHO* 8 (1965).

28 Abū 'Abd Allāh Muḥammad b. Aḥmad al-Anṣārī al-Qurṭubī, *Jāmi' al-Aḥkām al-Fiqhiyya* (Beirut: Dār al-Kutub al-'Ilmiyya, 1994), 3:238. See Q. 5:103 and Q. 6:139–40. For various definitions of *baḥā'ir, sawā'ib, waṣā'il* and *ḥawāmī*, see the relevant entries in Lane, as well as Sale, "Preliminary Discourse," 100–101). Reputedly connected to such dietary prohibitions, which some of the pre-Islamic Arabs had imposed upon themselves (*ḥarramūhu 'alā anfusihim*), is Q. 2:168: "O people! Eat the lawful and good things from what is in the earth, and follow not in the footsteps of Satan." Unnecessary restriction is of the devil.

theism nor Iranian Zoroastrianism, nor yet even Byzantine or other forms of Christianity were the true targets of the Muslim moderation campaign, or formed the background against which that campaign proceeded. For one thing, Islam appears to have forbidden as many practices permitted by the *ahl al- jāhiliyya* as it permitted practices forbidden by them,[29] and much the same may be said regarding the *majūs* (Magians).[30] Indeed, most such Islamic "counter-legislation" cannot be – and, in fact, is not – defined as more lenient or less lenient than the purported norms it came to replace. Thus, the Qur'ānic ban on the pre-Islamic practice (reputedly common in some Arabian tribes) of burying female infants alive (*wa'd*), while unquestionably constituting a significant moral reform, represented neither *rukhṣa* nor its opposite.[31] The same may be said of not shaving the nape of the neck as the Zoroastrians were wont to do,[32] not offering devotions with the dawn's first rays as the sun-worshippers did,[33] not greeting one another according to the custom of the bedouin,[34] not praying[35] for rain in the manner of

29 See Ṭabarī, 8: 92–4. Moreover, a large number of precepts were simply transferred over intact from the pre-Islamic period, the most famous being hand-amputation (Q. 5: 33 and 5: 38). Patricia Crone calls "Arab law, and above all the customary law of the Ḥijāz ... the single most important source of the substantive law of the Sharī'a" (Crone, "Jāhilī and Jewish Law: The *Qasāma*," *Jerusalem Studies in Arabic and Islam* 4 [1984], 153).

30 See the examples in Ibn Taymiyya, *Iqtiḍā'*, 56–64 and *passim*, and in Qurṭubī, *al-Jāmi' li-Aḥkām al-Qur'ān*, 7: 124–5 and 3: 309–10.

31 See, e.g., Q. 6: 138 and 6: 141. Even from the perspective of the newborn girl (if one can speak of such a perspective) the right to life is not exactly a "relaxation," while for her father – especially if we accept the economic explanations commonly offered for the practice of *wa'd* – rearing her instead of killing her was actually a hardship (the Prophet had to assure his followers that "whoever has a female child and does not bury her alive ... will be sent by God to the Garden of Eden" [Baghawī, 2: 24]). The custom among certain Arab tribes, according to many sources, had been to dig a pit whither the woman in labor was brought and delivered. If the child was a daughter, they threw her into the pit and covered it up with earth; if a son, they saved him alive. It is interesting that this is the mirror image of what Pharaoh did to the Children of Israel (Q. 2: 49).

32 Ibn Taymiyya, *Iqtiḍā'*, 59.

33 Muslim, 6 (*Kitāb Ṣalāt al-Musāfirīn*): 51 (*Bāb al-Awqāt allatī Nuhiya 'an al-Ṣalāt fīhā*) [828 (290)]), vol. 2, p. 432. See also the commentaries to Q. 20: 130 and Q. 50: 39–40, and Sale on the Sabeans, "Preliminary Discourse," 11 ff. This was the rite of the Queen of Sheba and her people according to Muslim tradition (Lassner, *Queen of Sheba*, 52).

34 Kister, "Do not Assimilate," 323.

the Arabs,[35] and a host of other deliberately antithetical enactments. Such new norms were different, not necessarily easier or harder.[36]

There is, of course, a far simpler and more fundamental reason why Arab paganism and Persian Mazdaism could not partake of the macrocosmic *naskh-rukhṣa* process: their deities were not Allāh.[37] Of the Zoroastrians it could not be said – as it was of the Jews – that "God, praise Him, prohibited to them (a list of acts and things) ... then God abrogated all of that in favor of the law of Muḥammad (*thumma nasakha Allāhu dhālika kullahu bi-sharīʿati Muḥammadin*), permitting them that which had been forbidden to them and removing the straitness (*ḥaraj*) through Muḥammad."[38] The historical trend of alleviation-through-abrogation entailed the periodic emanation from the *same* Deity of successive spiritual messages, by means of each of which He

35 Suliman Bashear, *Arabs and Others in Early Islam* (Princeton: The Darwin Press, 1997), 13.

36 It is perhaps equally important to remember that "many negatives associated with pagans originated in a polemical environment as anti-Jewish but were later retrojected to Arabian pagans" (Firestone summarizing Wansbrough, "Qur'ān and Bible," p. 20, n. 59). This point was made earlier by Vajda: "Ce ne serait pas le seul exemple de la transposition dans le paganisme d'une coutume dont les Musulmans ne tenaient pas a reconnaître la provenance juive" (G. J. Vajda, "Juifs et Musulmans selon le Hadit" in *Journal Asiatique*, 179 [Jan.-Mar., 1937], 75). In other words, some of the stringencies attributed to the pre-Islamic Arabs and abolished by Islam may not have been Arabian at all. One of the many possible instances of this phenomenon is *nasā'/nasī'*, the supposed *jāhilī* practice of calendrical intercalation or commutation abolished by Q. 9: 36–7. While the Arab philologists have found a local derivation for this in the root *n.s.'.*, meaning to postpone (and even quote Arabian tribesmen beseeching their chiefs: *ansi'nā shahran*, "postpone us a month!") – or alternately connect it to the *aw nunsihā* of our very own Q. 2: 106 – still, it is quite possible that the term comes from the Hebrew title of the officer in charge of the analogous Jewish institution (*nasi ha-sanhedrin*). Thus, the Qur'ānic ban on this practice may have been a hardening *vis à vis* the *jāhiliyya*, or, alternately, a cancellation of a Jewish custom considered odious in the eyes of Allāh.

37 *Jāhilī* Arabs were purportedly aware of an overarching, transcendental god named Allāh, but had on the whole a vague and distant relationship with Him, being more directly involved with the comparatively immanent deities of the Ḥijāzī pantheon. At any rate, even if the one and only true God is conceived as having communicated with certain Arabian peoples prior to the advent of Islam – through the likes of Hūd, Ṣāliḥ, Shuʿayb, etc. – the religio-legal systems revealed through those communications are nowhere (to my knowledge) fleshed out in the literature, and thus no comparison for the sake of demonstrating Islam's relative leniency was possible.

38 Qurṭubī, 7: 103.

would revise His *own* previously promulgated statutes. Arabian idolatry and Iranian dualism obviously had no share in this. Their religious systems could never be the objects of *naskh,* because *naskh* is the substitution of what God considers suitable in the present for what God considered suitable in the past. At no point did God consider heathenism suitable.

Despite initial appearances, Christianity, as well, had virtually no role to play in the historical saga of evolving ease. True, the Deity who sent down the original, undistorted *Injīl* (Evangel) was none other than Allāh Himself:

> Allāh, there is no God but He, the Eternal, the Everlasting. He revealed to you the Book with truth, a confirmation of that which was sent down previously; and He revealed the Torah *and the Gospel* aforetime, a guidance for the people, and He sent down the Discrimination (i.e., the Qur'ān) (Q. 3: 3).

Thus, unlike Zoroastrianism and Jāhilism, Christianity – as one of God's acknowledged temporary prescriptions or interim regimes – qualified in principle for the position of stepping-stone toward Muslim mildness, and thus could conceivably serve as the focus of much *rukhṣa*-through-*naskh* activity. And indeed, Q. 7: 157 speaks of

> those who follow the illiterate Messenger-Prophet whom they find mentioned in the Torah *and the Gospel* – he enjoins the good and forbids the evil, and makes lawful to them the good things and prohibits to them the foul things, and removes from them their heavy load [or: their covenant[39] – *yaḍa'u 'anhum iṣrahum*] and the shackles that were upon them (*wa'l-aghlāl allatī kānat 'alayhim*)...

In his gloss to this verse, al-Ṭabarī describes God and His Messenger as having "unburdened [those who chose Islam] of the compacts and covenants to which they were bound by the Torah *and the Evangel.*"[40] Elsewhere the same exegete speaks of the "laws of Jesus" (*sharā'i' 'Īsā*), of which the Christians have been relieved since the advent of Muḥammad,[41] and in still another context avers that "whoso followed Muḥammad and his religion from among *the People of the Book* were freed from the difficult requirements of their erstwhile faith (*wuḍi'a 'anhum mā*

39 Al-Ṭabarī prefers this understanding of *iṣr* (Ṭabarī, 9: 115).

40 Ṭabarī, 9: 114. Compare the formulation here – "*'uhūdahum wa-mawāthīqahum allatī ukhidhat 'alayhim*" – with Q. 2: 63 and 2: 83: "And when We made a covenant with you (*wa-idh akhadhnā mīthāqakum*)..."

41 Ṭabarī, 1: 461.

kāna ʿalayhim min al-tashdīd fī dīnihim)."[42] While the term *ahl al-kitāb* often refers to Jews alone, it can certainly indicate Christians as well, and the latter are also included on many occasions in the designation Banū Isrāʾīl.[43] Such is the case, for instance, when the *ḥadīth* speaks of "a people from among the Children of Israel who placed hardships upon themselves, and Allāh consequently placed hardships upon them; and this refers to their observances/seclusions in their convents and cells (*baqāyāhum fīʾl-ṣawāmiʿ waʾl-diyār*)."[44] In lines he composed that have

42 Ṭabarī, 9:115.

43 E.g., Q. 43:59, 61:14, 27:76, and the *ḥadīth* of Abū Dharr: "The Children of Israel's first prophet was Moses and their last was Jesus" (Qurṭubī, 4:84). See Daniel Madigan, *The Qur'ān's Self-Image: Writing and Authority in Islam's Scripture* (Princeton: Princeton University Press, 2001), esp. the appendix: "The people of the *kitāb*"; also McAuliffe, "Christians," in Waardenburg (ed.), *Muslim Perceptions*, 116; and Waardenburg's introductory essay to the same volume: "The Early Period: 610–650," 6–7. See in addition Friedmann, *Tolerance*, 58–69, and Newby, *Last Prophet*, 210–11 and *passim*. Despite such widespread "lumping together" many verses lay down a clear dichotomy between Jews and Christians on a number of levels (e.g., Q. 2:113, Q. 5:82). From a certain perspective, of course, the Banū Isrāʾīl are *Muslims*, and are often styled thus in early Islamic texts, especially when they (or at least certain righteous individuals among them) behave as proper monotheists (see, e.g., al-Rāzī to Q. 38:24, where the commentator notes that David stands accused of "conspiracy to murder a Muslim man" [*al-saʿy fī qatl rajul Muslim*], i.e., Uriah); or the statement that "Aaron remained steadfast [and did not worship the calf] along with *those of the Muslims* who were not seduced" [Newby, *Last Prophet*, 133]; or al-Thaʿlabī's description of two of the four parts into which David would divide his week as *yawman li-qaḍāʾ ḥawāʾij al-Muslimīn wa-yawman li-Banī Isrāʾīl yudhākiruhum*... [Abū Isḥāq Aḥmad b. Muḥammad al-Thaʿlabī, *Kitāb Qiṣaṣ al-Anbiyā* (Cairo: Al-Maṭbaʿa al-Bahiyya al-Miṣriyya, 1951), 231]; or al-Ṭabarī's history and commentary, in both of which Abraham is depicted as justifying his problematic claim that his wife is his sister by telling her: "You are, after all, my sister in faith, for there is *no Muslim* in this land save us" [cited in Moshe Tzuker, "Ha-efshar sheh Navi Yekheṭa? ʿAl Baʿayat "Iṣmat al-Nabī" ba-Islam uva-Yahadut," *Tarbitz* 35 (5726), p. 152]). Muslims, for their part, occasionally refer to themselves as "the Children of Israel" (see EI^2, *s. v.* "Banū Isrāʾīl" [Goitein]).

44 Baghawī, 4:137. See also the Israelite in his hermitage described in Bukhārī, *Kitāb al-Anbiyāʾ*, 4:55 (645). Another reason why Christianity is not a suitable target for abrogation is because Muslim tradition is ambivalent about asceticism, the quality with which Christianity is most frequently identified in that tradition. Thus, despite statements like the one to which this note is appended – and despite scriptural condemnation, as we saw, of the "monkery which [the Christians] invented for themselves and which We did not prescribe for them" (Q. 57:27) – the Qur'ān nevertheless evinces appreciation for the qualities of people who appear to be Christian monks (*qissīsīn*, Q. 5:82; see also Q. 22:40,

relevance to *rukhṣa,* the pious *ḥanīf*-turned-Muslim Abū Qays b. Abū Anas also put Christians and Jews on a par:

Praise God at every dawn
When His sun rises and at the new moon...
His are the birds which fly to and fro and shelter
In nests in their mountain retreats.
His are the wild creatures of the desert
Which you see on the dunes and in the shade of sandhills.
Him the Jews worship and follow
Every dreary custom you can think of (*kullu dīni idhā dhakarta ʿuḍāl*).
Him the Christians adore and keep
Every feast and festival to their Lord.
His is the self-denying monk you see
A prisoner of misery though once right happy (*rahnu bi'si wa-kāna nāʿim bāl*).[45]

All of these juxtapositions notwithstanding, Christianity was never a genuine candidate for alleviation through abrogation. Statements such as al-Ṭabarī's about the superseded "compacts of the Evangel" or "laws of Jesus" are rarely fleshed out in the literature, and the perception of Christianity as a purveyor of oppressive institutions that were

---

where cloisters are mentioned positively), and there are many instances in *ḥadīth* and *tafsīr* in which Christianity is specifically *commended* for numbering among its adherents "a people diligent in worship, living monastically in cells and hermitages" (*tarahhub fī diyārāt wa'l-ṣawāmiʿ* – al-Ṭabarī, cited in Mcauliffe, "Christians," 114), who "renounce temporal satisfactions" (*mu'riḍūn ʿan al-dunya* – al-Rāzī, cited in ibid.) and who practice various forms of *zuhd* (ibid., 115). Mary herself was "made a hermit in the church" by her mother "so that she would make no use of the matters of this world." She met Joseph there (Newby, *Last Prophet*, 207). This positive outlook on Christian monasticism is perhaps most pronounced in the cycle of narratives that grew up around the mysterious "people of the trench" (*aṣḥāb al-ukhdūd*) mentioned in Q. 85:4, in almost all versions of which the spiritual influence of a monk (*rāhib*) is responsible for setting off a chain of events that lead to the conversion to monotheism (or to Islam: "*islām*") of entire populations, who are then thrown into flaming trenches for their faith (according to most versions, by the Jewish tyrant Dhū Nuwās) – see Qurṭubī, 19:216–221. For a five line history of Christian monasticism, and the circumstances which transformed it from a praiseworthy tendency into an excessively self-abnegating ideology, see Qurṭubī, 17:199.

45 Ibn Isḥāq—Guillaume, 237; Ibn Hishām, 2: 114. See also the poem of Abū Qays b. al-Aslat, which includes the lines: "Were it not for our Lord we should be Jews / And the religion of Jews is not convenient / Were it not for our Lord we should be Christians / Along with the monks on Mount Jalīl" (Ibn Isḥāq-Guillaume, 201; Ibn Hishām, 2: 60).

ultimately abrogated remains on the level of generality.[46] There is good

46 Save for the institution of monasticism itself, which is regularly and roundly criticized (but see above, n. 44). Wansbrough states correctly that in the *Sīra*, the context of Muslim polemic against other faiths is "emphatically Jewish: allusions to Christianity and to Christian opposition are inconsistent and confused and, save for the Christological dispute with the delegation from Najrān, appear only in the framework of Jewish polemic" (Wansbrough, *Sectarian Milieu*, 40). A survey of the classical Islamic attitude to Christianity that never wanders far from the Qur'ānic text may be had from Richard Bell, *The Origin of Islam in its Christian Environment* (London: Frank Cass, 1968), chapter 5. The arguments of Bell, Ahrens, Andrae, Rudolph, Sweetman, Trimingham and others to the effect that Christianity was more influential than Judaism in molding the Prophet's persona and shaping classical Islamic doctrine and practice are, to this writer's mind, ill-founded. Though it is true that the early Muslims were sitting in a sea of Christianity – churches, populations, hierarchies, theologies, polemics, etc. – while Jews were nowhere as prominent (except in Madīna, if we accept the traditional accounts, a fact that is highly significant), nevertheless the comparatively rare Jew and his religious tradition made a significantly stronger impression on Islam than the ubiquitous Christian and the institutions of his faith. Much speculation could be devoted to answering the question why this happened, but that such was the case is hard to deny after perusing the Muslim sources. Well over a century ago, the extremely thorough (and devoutly Christian) Muir could state that Muḥammad "never showed the same interest in the Christian as in the Jewish faith, nor indeed had he the same means of learning its history and doctrines" (Muir, *Life of Mohammad*, 123, and see 148–50 where he speaks of Muslim tradition's "few passing observations regarding our faith" as opposed to its "familiar knowledge of Jewish Scripture and tradition" and asserts that "[w]e do not find a single ceremony or doctrine of Islam in any way moulded, or even tinged, by the particular tenents of Christianity; while, on the contrary, Judaism has given its colour to the whole system, and lent to it the shape and type, if not the actual substance, of many ordinances"). While the claim of Muir's contemporary, T. P. Hughes, that "[t]he teachings of Jesus form no part of [Islam's] religious system" which is "nothing more nor less than Judaism plus the Apostleship of Muḥammad" is obviously exaggerated and probably agenda-driven, one understands how someone could get this idea (*A Dictionary of Islam* [originally published in 1886, reprinted by KAZI publications, 1994], *s. v.* "Jews"). Kister points out more soberly that "[t]he influence of Christianity on the ḥadīth is not as apparent" as that of Judaism (*Encyclopedia Judaica*, s. v. "Ḥadīth"). Hodgson did not hesitate to declare that "much of the spirit that formed Muslim expectations of what a religion should be was inspired by Jewish example" (Marshall Hodgson, *The Venture of Islam* [Chicago: University of Chicago Press, 1974], vol. 1, p. 317. Most recently, Donner notes regarding al-Ṭabarī's *Tārīkh* that its author "gives lengthy discussions of the history of the Old Testament prophets and the Children of Israel, but passes quickly over Jesus and tales about the Christian community" (Fred M. Donner, *Narratives of Islamic Origins: The Beginnings of Islamic Historical*

reason for this, of course. Christianity had centuries earlier applied its own equivalent of the *naskh-rukhṣa* treatment to what it saw – in terms often strikingly similar to those later employed by Islam – as the cumbersome stringencies and boggling intricacies of Jewish law, trimming down the corpus of *halakha* considerably and placing much of what remained justiciable into the hands of Caesar. The Qur'ān acknowledges this: "I (Jesus) am a verifier of what came before me in the Torah, and *I allow you part of what was forbidden to you* (in that document – *wa-li-uḥilla lakum ba'ḍa alladhī ḥurrima 'alaykum*, Q. 3:49). In the area of civil and criminal law (*mu'āmalāt*), no less than in the realm of ritual (*'ibādāt*), very little survived in terms of a Christian legal system to function as a backboard or "control" to offset Muslim mitigation. Indeed, anything more than a superficial confrontation with Christianity on this score might have detracted from the uniqueness of Islam's achievement in the sphere of extenuation: it had all been done before.[47]

Writing [Princeton: The Darwin Press, 1998], 128). For a helpful overview of the shifting scholarly positions on this question, see Moshe Pearlman's Prolegomenon to Geiger's *Judaism and Islam*, pp. xx–xxiv. For a rather unconvincing argument that Muḥammad's message was for the most part original and owed little to either Judaism or Christianity, see Johann Fück, "The Originality of the Arabian Prophet" in Merlin L. Schwartz (ed. and trans.), *Studies on Islam* (Oxford: Oxford University Press, 1981). It might be argued, I suppose, that Islam was influenced by Christianity specifically in its desire to shed Jewish restrictions (see next note).

47 It is interesting in this connection that Ibn Ḥazm, in explaining why Muslims may eat (what is defined and disallowed by Jews as) *terefa* meat, argues that "Jewish laws with regard to the consumption of meat, along with all other Jewish laws, were abrogated first by Jesus and finally by Muḥammad" (Adang, *Muslim Writers*, 221 – see ibid., p. 195 for a similar statement by Ibn Rabban). Credit is occasionally given to Christianity for initiating the process of macrocosmic *rukhṣa*. Commenting on Q. 57:27: "... and we instilled compassion and mercy into the hearts of those who followed [Jesus] ...," al-Qurṭubī writes: "This refers to the fact that they commanded peace in the Evangel and an end to the oppression of the people, and God had softened their hearts for that purpose (*amarū fī'l-Injīl bi'l-ṣulḥ wa-tark īdhā' al-nās wa-alāna Allāhu qulūbahum li-dhālika*). This is in contradistinction to the Jews whose hearts became hardened [*qasat qulūbuhum* – see Q. 2:74 and esp. Q. 5:13] and who corrupted their scriptures [in the direction of severity and/or denial of Muḥammad]" (Qurṭubī, 17:199 and 6:104). "Jesus, may God's prayers be upon him, was a believer in the Torah who held steadfastly to it ... and never violated any of its laws, save for those of them that God mitigated for the benefit of the people of the Torah in the Evangel (*'Īsā ṣalawāt Allāhu 'alayhi kāna mu'minan bi'l-Tawrāt muqarran bihā ... lam yukhālif shay'an min aḥkāmihi*

This left the Jews. They were the only community encountered by Islam possessing *both* of the cardinal qualifications for the job of "strait" man in the ongoing comi-drama of progressive palliation: (1) Allāh had spoken to them, and (2) He had spoken to them as Law-Giver, not Law-Remover. Thus, what we boiled down (above) to the two-stage *naskh-rukhṣa* process in history may also be said to involve only two real players: Judaism and Islam. Even if, from a certain angle, Judaism may be conceived as an aberrational interregnum of exaggerated austerity between the previous reign of *fiṭra*-based *millat Ibrāhīm* (the "religion of Abraham") and the later onset of restorative and relax-

---

illā mā khaffafa Allāhu 'an ahlihā fī'l-Injīl) ... Jesus was an adherant of the Law of Moses, he would keep the Sabbath and face Jerusalem in prayer (*wa-kāna yasbutu wa-yastaqbilu bayt al-maqdis*), and he said to the Children of Israel: 'Verily I do not call you to the abandonment of even a single letter of the Torah; I come only to permit you some of those things which you are forbidden, and to remove burdens from you'" (Ṭabarī, 3:383. The patent contradiction here – a cogent reflection of the same unresolved paradox manifest in the New Testament [see Matt. 5:18 and Luke 16:17] – is nowhere addressed). "That which Jesus brought was milder (*alyan*) than that which Moses brought ... The Jews were forbidden by the Torah to eat camel flesh, suet, certain types of fish and birds that do not have spurs (*mimmā lā ṣīṣīya lahu*), and their lives were made difficult by the prohibition of other things as well, and Jesus came with relief from all this in the Evangel" (Ṭabarī, 3:384. According to al-Qurṭubī's informants, Jesus was sent to lift prohibitions that were not inscribed in the Torah but were only rabbinical decrees [*aḥalla lahum ashyā' ḥarramathā 'alayhim al-aḥbār wa-lam takun fī'l-Tawrāt*] – Qurṭubī, 4:86. Birds without spurs [*etzba' yetera*] are indeed an example of this category, see Mishna Ḥulin, 3:6. This would perhaps solve the paradox noted immediately above. On the same page al-Qurṭubī even quotes Ibrāhīm al-Nakha'ī as making what sounds like the claim that *wine* was eventually placed by the rabbis on the prohibited list, and that this period of "Prohibition" was ended by the advent of Jesus). This Christian characteristic of comparative mildness – *līn* – is part of the reason why "[Muḥammad] used [the Jews], for the latter part of his life, much worse than he did the Christians, and frequently exclaims against them in his Koran; his followers to this day observe the same difference between them and the Christians, treating the former as the most abject and contemptible people on earth" (Sale, "Preliminary Discourse," 27. It is interesting, however, that Muslim sources almost invariably locate Christians in a hotter hell than Jews – ibid. 72). See also Jane Dammen McAuliffe, "The Abrogation of Judaism and Christianity in Islam: A Christian Perspective," *Concilium* (1994). On Jesus in Muslim sources see now T. Khalidi, *The Muslim Jesus: Sayings and Stories in Islamic Literature* (Cambridge: Harvard University Press, 2001). It should be noted that, historically speaking, Christianity disposed of a greater number of "burdensome" Jewish precepts overall than did Islam.

ing Islam, nevertheless: since that same *millat Ibrāhīm* is, for all intents and purposes, itself nothing other than Islam from the perspective of Muslim classical sources, this still leaves only two primary participants.[48] The remainder of this study will examine aspects of how Muslim sources cast the Banū Isrā'īl and Yahūd in the role of backdrop for, and negative image of, Muslim moderation.[49]

48 On *millat Ibrāhīm* see Arthur Jeffery, *The Qur'ān as Scripture* (New York: Books for Libraries, 1980), 76ff; and Roberro Tottoli, *Biblical Prophets in the Qur'ān and Muslim Literature* (Richmond: Curzon Press, 2002), 10–11, and especially the literature cited there in n. 18. Muslim tradition is neither clear nor unanimous on the idea that Islam was both first and last. See, e.g., Bukhārī, *Kitāb Ṣalāt al-Jum'a,* 2: 13 [1]: "We Muslims are the last to come, but will be the first on the Day of Resurrection."

49 An instructive analysis of the overall attitudes of six of her nine exegetes to the issue of the abrogation of Mosaic law (with the added bonus of reactions thereto on the part of R. Sa'adya Gaon) is provided by Adang, *Muslim Writers,* chapter six. I cannot agree, however, with Professor Adang's assessment – which leads her to exclude al-Ṭabarī from her survey – that "al-Ṭabarī goes into the internal Islamic abrogation, but not into that of the earlier scriptures by the Qur'ān" (p. 194), or that (as she asserts earlier) "one does not gain the impression that al-Ṭabarī was much interested in the beliefs and practices of the Israelites and the Jews. This is not really surprising, since providing information on different cultures and religions was not on al-Ṭabarī's agenda, and in his *Tafsīr,* of course, even less so than in the *Annales*" (p. 76). In what follows, we shall witness al-Ṭabarī – in his *Tafsīr* – displaying extensive interest in both of these related topics. Similarly, I must take exception to Fred Astren's generalization that "[t]he increasingly powerful 'ulamā', whose socio-legal views were typified by Sharī'a and Qur'ān commentary, preferred an agglutinative and segmentary world-view that was typical of their literature and that excluded narrative genres such as the *Isrā'īliyyāt.* Al-Tha'labī himself is a perplexing figure, since in addition to compiling tales of the prophets, he was a traditional Qur'ān commentator ..." (Astren, "A Tribute to Professor William M. Brinner" in Benjamin Hary *et al* [eds.], *Judaism and Islam: Boundaries, Communication and Interaction* [Leiden: E. J. Brill, 2000], xxiv). Classical *Tafsīr,* even those versions of it produced in later periods and utilized by the *fuqahā',* is often saturated with *Isrā'īliyāt* and *qiṣaṣ al-anbiyā',* the material adduced in the present essay representing only the tip of the iceberg (see below, chap. 4, n. 8). Moshe Pearlman, who concedes that "even some early post-Quranic Muslim exegesis on occasion reflects such [Judaic] sources of inspiration," still heavily understates the case (Pearlman, Prolegomenon to Geiger, *Judaism and Islam,* xix).

4. The "Strait" Man

Judaism as anti-Ideal in Islamic Classical Discourse

Muḥammad was both thesis and antithesis. The many juristic disputes that punctuated early *fiqh,* coupled with the gradual recognition of the Prophet's status as Excellent Exemplar (*uswa ḥasana*), saw to it that the image of the Messenger of God became heavily polarized. He performed ablutions after eating cooked food; he did not perform ablutions after eating cooked food.[1] He took a ritual bath in between sexual encounters; he did not take a ritual bath in between sexual encounters.[2] He said: "The fast of the Day of 'Arafāt absolves [the sins of] this year and the next"; he did not fast on the Day of 'Arafāt.[3] He drank from a silver vessel;[4] he threatened that "anyone who drinks from a silver vessel, the fire of hell will rumble in his belly."[5] He was wont to lie in the mosque with legs crossed; he prohibited the crossing of legs.[6] He dyed his hair jet-black; he warned that "those who dye their hair black shall never smell the fragrance of paradise."[7] The perennial dialectic powering Islamic legal evolution meant that Allāh's Apostle was regularly enlisted to prove a thing and its opposite.

---

1 Abū Bakr 'Abd Allāh b. Muḥammad b. Abī Shayba al-Kūfī, *Al-Kitāb al-Muṣannaf fi'l-Aḥādīth wa'l-Āthār* (Beirut: Dār al-Fikr, 1989), 1:68 and 65.

2 Bukhārī, *Ghusl,* 13: 268; Muslim, 3: 28 (309); Abū Dā'ūd, 85: 215 (*Bāb fi'l-Junub Ya'ūdu*); Bukhārī, *Ghusl,* 24: 284.

3 Kister, "Concessions," 104.

4 Muḥammad b. 'Alī al-Shawkānī, *Nayl al-Awṭār: Sharḥ Muntaqā al-Akhbār min Aḥādīth Sayyid al-Akhyār* (Cairo: Mujtama' Majlis Dā'irat al-Ma'ārif, 1953), 1:85.

5 Aḥmad b. Muḥammad b. Faraḥ al-Lakhmī al-Ishbīlī, *Mukhtaṣar Khilāfiyāt al-Bayhaqī* (Riyāḍ: Maktabat al-Rushd, 1997), 1:164: "*yujarjiru fī baṭnihi nār al-jahannam.*" Some of these contradictory reports about Muḥammad's practices were themselves reconciled by resorting to *naskh.*

6 Melchert, "Etiquette," 39.

7 Muir, *Life of Mohammad,* lxvii, n. 1.

The Banū Isrā'īl performed a similar function. They, too, were an exemplar – though not an excellent one. Despite growing disapproval on the part of Muslim purists, the genre known as *Isrā'īliyyāt* or *qiṣaṣ al-anbiyā'* (stories of the prophets) not only continued to entertain and edify the Muslim masses for centuries after Muḥammad's death,[8] but

8 See S. D. Goitein, "Isrā'īliyyāt," *Tarbitz*, 6 (1934–5); T. Nagel, *Die Qiṣaṣ al-Anbiyā': Ein Beitrag zur Arabischen Literaturgeschichte* (Bonn: Selbstverlag des orientalischen Seminars der Universitat Bonn, 1967); M. J. Kister, "Ḥaddithū 'an banī isrā'īla wa-lā ḥaraja," in *Israel Oriental Studies*, 2 (1972); R. G. Khoury, *Les Légendes Prophétiques dans l'Islam depuis le Ier jusqu'au IIIe Siecle de l'Hégire* (Wiesbaden: O. Harassowitz, 1978); W. M. Thackston, Jr. (trans), *The Tales of the Prophets of al-Kisa'i* (Boston, 1978); G. D. Newby, "Tafsir Isra'iliyyat," *Journal of the American Academy of Religion*, 47 (1979); W. M. Brinner, "Prophets and Prophecy in the Islamic and Jewish Traditions," in Brinner and Ricks, *Studies*; Adang, *Muslim Writers*, 8–14 and *passim*; Tottoli, *Biblical Prophets*, Part II, and idem, "The Origin and Use of the Term Isrā'īliyyāt in Muslim Literature," *Arabica* 46 (1999); Norman Calder, "*Tafsīr* from Ṭabarī to Ibn Kathīr," in G. R. Hawting and Abdul-Kader A. Shareef (eds.), *Approaches to the Qur'ān* (London: Routledge, 1993); and Jane Dammen McAuliffe, "Assessing the Isrā'īliyyāt: An Exegetical Conundrum" in S. Leder (ed.), *Story-Telling in the Framework of Non-Fictinal Arabic Literature* (Wiesbaden: Harrassowitz, 1988). For a selective list of primary sources comprising this genre, see Brian M. Hauglid, "On the Early Life of Abraham: Biblical and Qur'ānic Intertextuality and the Anticipation of Muḥammad" in Reeves, *Bible and Qur'ān*, 91, n. 11.

Brannon Wheeler has done the scholarly community a significant service in arranging and translating passages from many seminal *tafāsīr* connected to the Biblical prophets (Wheeler, *Prophets*). Equally important is Gordon Newby's masterful reconstruction of the *Kitāb al-Mubtada'*, the missing first section of Ibn Isḥāq's *Sīra* (Newby, *Last Prophet*), which was itself eliminated by Ibn Hishām as a result of the anti-*Isrā'īliyyāt* climate that prevailed in his day. Interestingly, according to at least one authority permission to narrate stories about the Banū Isrā'īl was granted – after having earlier been denied – as a result of *naskh* based on changed circumstances (after the Islamic religion consolidated itself, the danger to its separate identity posed by Jewish notions and narratives was no longer serious. See Kister, "Ḥaddithū," 220–1. This is, intriguingly enough, post-Prophetic *naskh*). We might posit Ibn Isḥāq (d. circa 767 CE) as a rough *terminus ad quem* for the free and open imbibing from Jewish (and Christian) sources, followed by a period of comparative insularity which for some circles lasted until the present day (and was intensified by the likes of Ibn Ḥazm and Ibn Taymiyya), but for others wound down once Islamic identity and ideology and Muslim institutions and laws crystallized around the ninth and tenth centuries CE. Thus Newby can reconstruct the *Kitāb al-Mubtada'*, which relies so heavily on Jewish tradition, almost entirely from the history and commentary of al-Ṭabarī (d. 923 CE), and we can also read so much about the Islamic view of Judaism and the semi-legendary history of

also found its way into the legal literature. An example is the following *ḥadīth*:

> ... from Abu Hurayra, from the Prophet, who said: The Children of Israel used to bathe naked in full view of one another, whereas Moses would bathe alone. They (*viz.*, the Children of Israel) said: By God! The only thing preventing Moses from bathing with us is that he's got a scrotal hernia (*mā yamnaʿ Mūsā an yaghtasila maʿanā illā annahu ādar*). And [Moses] went out once to bathe, and lay his garment on a rock – and the rock ran away with his garment (*farra al-ḥajaru bi-thawbihi*). Moses started after it, shouting: My clothes, O rock, My clothes, O rock! The Children of Israel looked at him [running naked through the camp] and said: By God, there is not a blemish on Moses! (*mā bi-Mūsā min ba'si*). And Moses took his garment back, and began to beat the rock. Abu Hurayra said: By God, there are [to this day] six or seven scars on that rock from that beating.[9]

This anecdote was harnessed by the *muḥaddithūn*, *shurrāḥ* and *fuqahā'* to hammer home the importance of modesty in general, and especially during ritual immersion. It is catalogued in al-Bukhārī's *Book of Major*

---

the Israelites in al-Qurṭubī (d. 1272 CE). This "reinstatement," however, was accompanied to some degree by an Islamization of the material, a process reflected, *inter alia*, by the increasing replacement of the term *Isrā'īliyyāt* with the term *qiṣaṣ al-anbiyā'*.

Many modern Muslim thinkers have tried (again) to devalue the Isrā'īliyyātic elements – the *abāṭil al-Yahūd* or "Jewish fairy-tales" – that pervade early Islamic literature, and not just as a result of the Arab-Israeli conflict. Muḥammad ʿAbduh, for one, was already engaged in such a "purification" process before the turn of the twentieth century (as his Qur'ān commentary bears eminent witness), largely as a result of his rationalist and reformist tendencies (see an excellent example of ʿAbduh's method in this regard in Lazarus-Yafeh, "Modern Attitudes to the ḥadjdj," *Some Religious Aspects*, 115–116). There is a considerable literature on the *quṣṣāṣ* in general, beginning with Goldziher, *Muslim Studies*, vol. 2, 149–59 and ending (to date) with Jonathan Berkey, *Popular Preaching and Religious Authority in the Medieval Islamic Near East* (Seattle: University of Washington Press, 2001). These storytellers at certain times acquired larger followings and had greater authority among the rank and file than the *ʿulamā'*, just as the purveyors of *haggada* often attracted more impressive crowds than the teachers of *halakha* in the rabbinic milieu. Finally, it should be noted that there is a sense in which the genre of *Isrā'īliyyāt* is conceived by Muslim tradition as a collection of vestigial excerpts from the long-lost, uncorrupted Torah, before this divine document was revised by the Jews/Ezra/Solomon's demons/ *kahana* in order to serve their own deplorable ends (see below, n. 28).

9 Bukhari, *Ghusl*, 21:277. See Kister, "Concessions," 3, where "[t]he Prophet is said to have denied the believers permission to enter baths, but later granted them a *rukhṣa* to enter them, provided they wear loincloths, *ma'āzir.*"

Purification under the heading: "Chapter on Concealing Oneself from People while Bathing" (*Bāb al-Tasattur fī'l-Ghusl 'inda al-Nās*). Here the Banū Isrā'īl set the standard for how *not* to act, while Moses is made the model of correct behavior. The latter half of this story may derive from a conflation of the famous Biblical/Qur'ānic incident in which Moses smote the rock to obtain water[10] and the Rabbinic legend of Miriam's mobile well (in the form of a rolling boulder) that accompanied the Israelites whithersoever they roamed.[11] The former half, however – about the collective nude bathing – is a purely Muslim invention. Another such imaginary depiction of Jewish practice may be found in a report that owes its preservation to an early Islamic (and pre-Islamic) debate concerning the appropriate posture to assume during urination:

> From 'Abd al-Raḥmān b. Ḥasana, who related: The Messenger of God came out to us, and he was holding a leather shield (*daraqa*) in his hand. He placed it on the ground and proceeded to squat down and urinate into it. One of those present said: Look at him, he urinates like a woman! (*unẓurū ilayhi, yabūlu kamā tabūlu al-mar'a*). When the Prophet heard this, he said: Woe unto you! Do you not know what overtook the *ṣāḥib* of the Children of Israel? If they bespattered themselves with urine, they would excise [the bespattered portion of their flesh] with cutters (*qaraḍahā bi'l-maqārīḍ*) – and he (the *ṣāḥib*) forbade them to do that, and he was [consequently] punished in his grave (*fa-nahāhum 'an dhālika fa-'udhdhiba fī qabrihi*).[12]

The roles have been reversed here. Unlike the shameless Israelites bathing publicly in the buff, the Banū Isrā'īl of this report would appear to have treaded the proper, pious path, at least at first; and unlike the modest Moses of the previously cited tradition, the anonymous spiritual—temporal leader of this *ḥadīth* (for thus we must call such a *ṣāḥib amrin wa-nahyin* – one who possesses the authority to command and forbid) is accused of *derailing* his flock from the straight and narrow in

10 Numbers 20:7–11 and Exodus 17:1–7; Q. 2:60.

11 Louis Ginzberg, *Legends of the Jews* (Philadelphia: Jewish Publication Society, 1968), 3:50–3. See also al-Ṭabarī's commentary to Q. 2:60 in which he adduces a number of versions of the anecdote about the rock that the Banū Isrā'īl used to carry with them as a water source throughout their wanderings in the wilderness (*ja'ala bayna ẓahrānayhim ḥajar murabba'/ṭūrī* – Ṭabarī, 1:438).

12 Ibn Mājah, *Kitāb al-Ṭahāra,* 26:286. That at least some Arab men urinated in a squatting position is evidenced in Wāqidī, 2: 533, where a member of the posse chasing 'Abd Allāh b. Unays turns into the cave where the latter is hiding and (Saul-like) *jalasa yabūlu 'alā bāb al-ghār.*

the matter of micturition.[13] Up to that time, they had meticulously avoided *najāsat al-bawl,* surgically removing any spot splashed by urine (Muḥammad himself preferred an ounce of prevention to a pound of flesh: he urinated in a seated position to reduce the chance of "ricochet"). The *ṣāḥib* put an end to this severe practice, and is criticized for this. The unfortunate fate of those led astray by his new policy may well be alluded to in the following narration of Ibn 'Abbās:

> The Prophet once passed by two graves and said: "These two are undergoing torture, and they are not being tortured for a major sin (*kabīra*). Rather, one of them did not shield himself (*lam yastatir*) from urine, and the other went around spreading calumnies." Then the Prophet took a green palm leaf, broke it in twain and planted one piece on each grave. They said: "O Apostle of God! Why have you done this?" He replied: "Perhaps [their suffering] will be eased as long as these remain fresh."[14]

It is important to note that in both the above cases – that concerning the right environment for *ghusl* and that regarding the correct position for passing water – the upshot of the anecdotes is the Banū Isrā'īl as anti-ideal. Whether in spite of their leader or because of him, the Biblical Jews end up acting improperly and furnishing a negative example. This is no less true for the counter-*ḥadīth* put about by those who advocated moderation in matters of *najāsat al-bawl,* and who accordingly supported urination in a standing position (even though the chances of "back-spray" were greater):[15]

> ... from Yaḥyā b. Yaḥyā, who said: Abū Mūsā [al-Ash'arī] used to behave stringently in the matter of urination, and would urinate into a bottle, and say: "If the skin of one of the Banū Isrā'īl was bespattered with urine, he would excise [the affected portion] with a cutter." Ḥudhayfa said: Would that your companion (Abū Mūsā) did not act so severely (*la-wadidtu anna ṣāḥibakum lā yushaddid hādhā al-tashdīd*), for you know that I and the Messenger of God once walked together until we came to a place where sweepings and filth are thrown (*subāṭatun*)[16] behind a wall, and [the Prophet] stood just as one of you stands and he urinated (*fa-qāma kamā*

13 From a similar usage in a different anecdote cited by Newby, *Last Prophet,* 118, it would appear that the "*ṣāḥib*" here is Moses (despite the problem that might be posed by the image of an Apostle of God being punished in the afterlife), thus heightening the thesis-antithesis aspect of these two traditions.

14 Bukhārī, *Wuḍū',* 59:217; Muslim, *Ṭahāra,* 34:292.

15 It is difficult to know whether the original impetus for this debate was a gender issue or a purity issue.

16 So according to Lane, 1295, col. 3.

> *yaqūmu aḥadukum fa-bāla*). And I hastened to withdraw from him, but he beckoned to me, so I came to him and stood at his back until he had finished.[17]

This report is *rukhṣa* oriented (the final sentence reflects a lenient line as well), and again enlists a badly behaving (because overly strict) Banū Isrā'īl as a foil for proper Muslim conduct. Thus, like Muḥammad, imagined Israel was regularly called upon by antagonistic parties to support a thing and its opposite. The difference is, that while the Prophet's *sunna* was probed in search of effective examples of the right thing to do, the Children of Israel's *sunna* was dredged for vivid illustrations of the wrong thing to do.

The particular type of wrong thing to do at which the Biblical/Rabbinic Jews excelled was overzealousness and hyper-piety. Although we have so far seen two instances in this section of the opposite tendency – the uninhibited balneation and the lapsed fastidiousness in urination – and although the Jews are occasionally taken to task for laxity and the exploitation of loopholes (one source even accuses Israelite "court-jurists" of granting Henry VIII-style *rukhaṣ* to dissolute Hebrew monarchs),[18] still: such references are relatively rare. In the majority of cases, the Banū Isrā'īl and their religion are presented in early Islamic literature as the unsurpassed embodiment of excessive rigidity and punctiliousness. Even in the case of the polemic over the acceptable manner of relieving oneself which produced the two contradictory *aḥādīth* adduced above, the report showing the Israelites as too easygoing (after the intervention of the *ṣāḥib*) was largely ignored by commentators and jurists. Only the report displaying their fanaticism was sustained, and employed in warnings against untoward anxiety (and undue rigor) in matters of *najāsat al-bawl.* Commenting on Q. 7: 157 – "Those who follow the Messenger ... [God] will make lawful for them all good things" – al-Ṭabarī explains that these words refer to "the unlettered prophet" (i.e. Muḥammad) who will "put away

17 Muslim, *Ṭahāra, Bāb al-Masḥ 'alā'l-Khuffayn*, 22: 273. Abū Mūsā was a Companion of the Prophet from Yemen, governor of Baṣra under 'Umar and 'Uthmān, and lukewarm representative of 'Alī at the famous arbitration of Adhruḥ.

18 'Abū al-Faḍl 'Abd al-Raḥmān b. Abī Bakr Jalāl al-Dīn al-Suyūṭī, *Al-Durr al-Manthūr fī'l-Tafsīr bi'l-Ma'thūr* (Cairo: Dār Iḥyā' al-Kutub al-'Arabiyya, 1314), 2: 109; partially cited in Kister, "Concessions ...," 10–11. There are several other instances where Jews and Israelites are described as having tampered with religious law specifically with a view toward making their lives *easier*: see below, chapter 5, n. 11 and p. 154–6.

the covenant which God had made with the Children of Israel concerning the obligation to fulfill the laws of the Torah, especially the stringencies found therein such as the cutting of the skin because of [its having been bespattered by] urine (*al-'amal bimā fīhā min al-a'māl al-shadīda ka-qaṭ' al-jild min al-bawl*) ... and all like manner of difficult acts that were imposed upon them [by the Torah], and he (*viz.*, Muḥammad) will replace them with the [more lenient] law of the Qur'ān (*nasakhahā ḥukm al-Qur'ān*).[19] Echoes al-Qurṭubī:

> The Children of Israel were obligated by a covenant to carry out burdensome acts (*kāna ukhidha 'alayhim 'ahd an yaqūmū bi-a'māl thiqāl*), but they were relieved of that covenant by [the advent of] Muḥammad, and those difficult acts [were replaced, *inter alia,* by the permission] to merely *wash* off urine (*ghasl al-bawl*); by the legalization of booty (*taḥlīl al-ghanā'im*); and by [leave to] sit, eat and sleep with a menstruant. For if the clothing of one of [the Children of Israel] was spattered by urine, he would cut off [the affected piece of his garment] – and it is also narrated: if the *skin* of one of them [was spattered by urine, he would excise the affected portion of it]; and when they would gather booty together, fire would descend from the sky and consume it (*nazalat nār min al-samā' wa-akalathā*); and when a women menstruated, they would not approach her; and there are many other examples [of such oppressive burdens that had been imposed upon the Banū Isrā'īl] in the sound *ḥadīth* and elsewhere.[20]

Israel's lot was an unenviable one: like a first-born child, they were subjected to the maximum in discipline and limitation. The Muslims – like a second or third child – were given much greater leeway. This, of course, is not to imply that Islam was lacking in strictures and prescriptions. In his impassioned speech before the Negus of Ethiopia during what is known as the first *hijra* (615 CE), 'Alī's brother Ja'far al-Ṭayyār related how the Prophet whom God had sent amongst them had

> commanded us to speak the truth, to be faithful in our engagements and mindful of the ties of kinship and of kindly hospitality, and to refrain from crimes and from blood; and he forbade us to commit abominations and to speak lies, and to devour the property of orphans, and to vilify chaste women; and he commanded us to worship God alone, and not to associate anything else with Him, and he gave us orders about prayer, and almsgiving, and fasting.[21]

19 Ṭabarī, 9:115.
20 Qurṭubī, 7:241–2.
21 Ibn Isḥāq—Guillaume, 151–2.

Islam is without doubt a religion of law. But compared to the extremely complicated and overly demanding norms of Judaism (as perceived by Muslim sources), the precepts of Islam are simple, sensible and practicable. "Is there no 'difficulty' involved in our religion's proscription of fornication and theft?" Abū Hurayra once inquired of Ibn 'Abbās, wondering aloud how the divine imposition of even such reasonable strictures jibed with God's repeated renunciation of the ways of *ḥaraj*. "There is indeed," responded Ibn 'Abbās, "but the burden that weighed upon the Children of Israel has been lifted from our shoulders."[22]

The Jews toiled more and earned less; the Muslims toiled less and earned more: "There was amongst the Israelites," explains Mujāhid, in one of the many contextualizations of Q. 97: 3, "a man who would stand up in prayer all night until morning, and then do battle with the enemy all day until evening, and he continued in this manner for a thousand months. So Allāh revealed: 'The Night of Destiny is *better* than a thousand months!' – that is, wakefulness on that single night is greater than all the works of that man."[23]

> Allah's Apostle said: [The comparison between] you [Muslims] and the People of the Book who came before you is like a man who hired a labourer who worked from morning until noon (*min al-ghadā ilā al-ẓuhr*), and was paid one qīrāṭ – this was the case with the Jews. The man then hired another labourer who worked from noon until mid-afternoon (*min al-ẓuhr ilā al-'aṣr*) and was also paid one qīrāṭ – this was the case with the Christians. Finally he hired a labourer who worked from mid-afternoon until evening (*min al-'aṣr ilā al-maghrib*) and was paid two qīrāṭs – this is the case with you [Muslims]. The Jews and Christians became angry, saying: "How is it

22 Ṭabarī, 9: 115. A minority opinion attributed to al-Ḥasan al-Baṣrī states that even one of Islam's most fundamental precepts – "commanding the right and forbidding the wrong" (*al-amr bi'l-ma'rūf wa'l-nahy 'an al-munkar*) – had been obligatory (*farīḍa*) for Israelites, but was now only supererogatory (*nāfila*) for Muslims (Cook, *Forbidding Wrong*, 84).

23 Ṭabarī, 30: 329. The actions of this Hebrew warrior-worshipper (probably David – see Qurṭubī, 15: 150) are described in terminology that rings positively in Muslim ears – *yaqūmu al-layl … yujāhidu al-'adū* – but he appears to have overdone it (compare Q. 73: 20, where God relieves the Muslims of the previous obligation to rise in prayer for much of the night, *inter alia* because "some among you … will be fighting in God's cause"; and see also above, chap. 2, n. 14). The Muslim rite of *tarāwīḥ*, the nocturnal vigil kept during the month of Ramaḍān, is Islam's practical alternative to such Israelite excess, garnering even more merit with a fraction of the effort.

> that we worked more and received less wages?" (*mā bālunā naḥnu aktharu ʿamalan wa-aqallu ajran*). [The employer responded]: "Was your own salary in any way diminished?" So it is with the favour of God: He grants it to whom He wishes.[24]

Islam's very identity is often tied to this offsetting of its own easy ways from the hardship characterizing the previous dispensations, especially Judaism. Aḥmad b. Muḥammad al-Qasṭallānī (d. 1517 CE) defined *al-ḥanīfiyya al-samḥa* (i.e. Islam) as "the *ḥanīfiyya* which is opposed to the religion of the Children of Israel and the arduous duties (*shadāʾid*) imposed upon them."[25] "What wonderful brothers are the Banū Isrāʾīl to you," exclaimed Ḥudhayfa b. al-Yamān to his fellow Muslims. "They endured the bitter, whereas you enjoy the sweet."[26]

Our description of Islam's perception of the norms of Judaism as "overly demanding" raises at least one important question: if it was none other than God Himself who revealed the ordinances and injunctions found in the Torah, then how could these same be excessive or in any other way imperfect? Perhaps the intent of the Muslim texts is that the Pentateuchal regulations, while perfectly appropriate for the Banū Isrāʾīl in their own times and circumstances, have since been superseded (al-Qurṭubī would add: according to plan), and must now be abandoned in favor of the more advanced system of Islam.[27] Alternately, the idea

---

24 Different versions of this *ḥadīth* appear in various contexts in the collections of al-Bukhārī and al-Tirmidhī in one of which the Jews quit in the midst of the work and are replaced by the Christians. When these, too, abandon the task without completing it, the Muslims take over and finish the job. The recension to which this note is appended is from Māwardī, 2:20, where the analogy is literalized and employed by opposing sides in a debate over the exact definition of prayer times. The period from dawn to noon is the greatest interval represented here: the Jews worked longest and hardest.

25 Aḥmad b. Muḥammad b. Ḥusayn al-Qasṭallānī, *Irshād al-Sārī Sharḥ Ṣaḥīḥ al-Bukhārī* (Cairo: Al-Maṭbaʿa al-Kubrā al-Amīriya, 1304 AH), 1:123.

26 Abū Nuʿaym Aḥmad b. ʿAbd Allah al-Iṣbahānī, *Ḥilyat al-Awliyāʾ wa-Ṭabaqāt al-Aṣfiyāʾ* (Beirut: Dār al-Kitāb al-ʿArabiyya, 1967), 3:50: "*Niʿma al-ikhwa lakum Banū Isrāʾīl, kānat fīhim al-mirra wa-fīkum al-ḥilwa.*" Cf., however, the "*sunna* statements" of ʿAbd Allāh b. ʿAmr b. al-ʿĀṣ and others to the effect that "You [Muslims] will surely follow the *sunna* of those before you – the sweet as well as the bitter" (cited in Rubin, *Between Bible and Qurʾān*, 172). Ḥudhayfa was married to a Jewess (Friedmann, *Tolerance*, 181).

27 "O People of the Book! Now has our Messenger come to you, expounding much of that which you concealed in your scriptures [see next note], but also alleviating much (*wa-yaʿfū ʿan kathīrin*). Indeed, there has come to you from Allāh a light and a clear Book" (Q. 5:15). This option may challenge the widely

may be that Allāh never did, in fact, issue any of those impossible commands, and that the written records of such divine enactments in the Torah are merely another instance of the Jews' well-known corruption of, or dissimulation about, their scriptures.[28] Finally, since one cannot argue that the Deity erred, could it be that He *deliberately* embittered

accepted claim that "[t]heoretically, at least, there can be no discrepancy in the content of [the successive divine revelations to humanity] because they all proceed from the same source" (Jane Dammen McAuliffe, "The Prediction and Prefiguration of Muḥammad" in Reeves, *Bible and Qur'ān,* 108). The radical understanding of macrocosmic *naskh* certainly seems to posit such a discrepancy, in content as well as in form.

28 For the longstanding accusations of *taḥrīf* (corruption, distortion) and *tabdīl* (alteration, substitution) see Adang, *Muslim Writers,* chapter 7; N. Roth, "Forgery and Abrogation of the Torah" in *Proceedings of the American Academy of Jewish Research,* 54 (1987); David Powers, "Reading/Misreading One Another's Scriptures: Ibn Ḥazm's Refutation of Ibn Nagrella al-Yahūdī" in Brinner and Ricks, *Studies*; Lazarus-Yafeh, *Intertwined Worlds,* 19–35; Jean-Marie Gaudeul and Robert Caspar, "Textes de la Tradition Musulmane concernant le *Taḥrīf* (falsification) des Ecritures," *Islamo-Christiana* 6 (1980); Ignazio de Matteo, "Tahrif or the Alteration of the Bible according to the Muslims," *Muslim World* 14 (1924); and Maimonides' well known "Epistle to Yemen." See also the commentaries to Q. 4:48. Al-Suddī asserts that "the Tawrāt and the Qur'ān were [originally] in agreement, but the Jews cast off the Tawrāt and adopted the book of Āṣaf" (also spelled Āṣāf, son of Barakhyā, supposed *wazīr* of Solomon – Qurṭubī, 2:37). In the Bible Asaph is a Levite appointed by King David to oversee the liturgical music in the Temple, see 1 Chronicles 15:17, Nehemia 12:46, and the "Asaphic" psalms (50 and 73–83). On Āṣaf in Muslim literature see Jacob Lassner, "The 'One who had Knowledge of the Book' and the 'Mightiest Name' of God: Qur'ānic Exegesis and Jewish Cultural Artifacts" in Ronald L. Netter (ed.), *Studies in Muslim-Jewish Relations: Vol. 1* (Camberwell: Harwood Academic Publishers, 1993), 63–65; idem., *Queen of Sheba,* 106 ff; and Newby, *Last Prophet,* 166–70. For what appears to be a fuller version of the development described by al-Suddī – in which Āṣaf (who was, according to most Muslim accounts, a pious figure) is replaced with Solomon's demons – see Ṭabarī, 1:623 ff. There we read that those demons eavesdrop on angels (see the commentaries to Q. 67:5, 37:7 and 72:8, and compare tractate Ḥagigah, 16a, where demons are said to "listen behind the curtain" [*shom'in me'aḥoray ha-pargod*]). They then whisper a combination of true and false prophesies to the *kahana* (priests/soothsayers), who in turn write them down on scrolls and thereby fashion a false Torah. The most significant point of consensus between the original Tawrāt and the Qur'ān according to these reports (and scores of others) was their common affirmation of the apostleship of Muḥammad (see, e.g., Ṭabarī, 4:268 ff and the other commentaries to Q. 3:187; also Uri Rubin, *The Eye of the Beholder: The Life of Muḥammad as viewed by the Early Muslims* [Princeton: Darwin Press, 1995], chap. 1; and McAuliffe, "Prediction," as well as below, chap. 5, n. 15, and chap. 8, n. 35).

the lives of the Israelites with stressful and superfluous regulations? In what follows we will detect elements of all three of these solutions, separately and in conjunction, in the discussions of al-Ṭabarī and al-Qurṭubī.

The widespread claim that the Jews (and specifically Ezra, or the *shayāṭīn* and *kahana* of Solomon's time) rewrote their scriptures to suit their needs and erase the explicit support for Islam originally found therein (*taḥrīf* – see Q. 2:75; Ibn Isḥāq—Guillaume, 241), has a problematic but tenacious relationship with the equally pervasive assertion that the Jews concealed inconvenient, but still extant, sections of their sacred literature (*kitmān* – see Q. 6:92; Ibn Isḥāq—Guillaume, 259). This latter outlook is manifest in the notion that the Jewish conspiracy of silence about the contents of the Pentateuch can be exposed by demanding that they "bring forth the Torah and read it to us, if you are truthful!" (Q. 3:93), or by lifting a rabbi's hand that had been hiding a Biblical clause commanding the stoning of adulterers, as Muḥammad famously did (Ṭabarī, 6:340; Ibn Isḥāq—Guillaume, 266–7; Burton, *Sources*, 129–134). The reconciliation of these seemingly contradictory positions may not be essential, but could perhaps be achieved by averring that the Jews changed some parts of their *Kitāb* while keeping quiet about others. On the other hand, al-Māwardī (for instance) envisions a less reconcilable relationship between these two conceptions when he cites the opinion that a temporarily impure individual (*muḥdith*) may not carry a Torah scroll "because it is the writing of God the Exalted no less than the Qur'ān" (*li-annahā katb Allāh ta'āla manzila ka'l-Qur'ān*), and then contraposes this opinion to a ruling that such ritually polluted persons may indeed carry a Torah scroll "because it is altered (*mubdila*)... and an altered scripture has no sanctity" (*lā ḥurma lahu* – Māwardī, 1:176). See also, on the question of *taḥrīf* versus *kitmān*, McAuliffe, "Prediction," 120–23, and Lassner, *Queen of Sheba*, 121.

5. The Bread of Adversity

The Jews Refuse the *Dīn al-Yusr*

On the eve of the Theophany at Sinai – so a well-known midrash relates – God traveled to all the nations of the world, offering each of them the Torah. The people of Edom demurred when informed that the divine law book contained the commandment "Thou shalt not murder." "Master of the Universe!," they exclaimed in dismay. "The promise of greatness bestowed upon our father (Esau) by his father (Isaac) was rooted in murder (Genesis 27:40: 'By your sword you shall live ...'). We cannot, in consequence, accept the Torah." Moab declined when apprized of the clause prohibiting incest: "We are nothing," they admitted, "if not products of incest" (Genesis 19:36: "And the two daughters of Lot were impregnated by their father ..." – *Mo-av* sounds like Heb. *meh-av*, "from father"). The Ishmaelites rejected God's gift when they discovered that it included the injunction "Thou shalt not steal." "But our livelihood is based on theft and plunder!" they protested (Genesis 16:12, describing Ishmael: "His hand against everyman, and everyman's hand against him ...").[1] Thus matters continued, failure after failure, until God finally approached the Israelites, who accepted His overture without hesitation, vowing: "We will do and we will hearken" (Exodus, 24:7).[2]

---

1 George Sale, writing in 1734: "As the Arabs have their excellencies, so have they, like other nations, their defects and vices ... The frequent robberies committed by these people on merchants and travellers have rendered the name Arab almost infamous in Europe; this they are sensible of, and endeavor to excuse themselves by alleging the hard usage of their father Ismael ..." (Sale, "Preliminary Discourse," 24).

2 Sifri VeZot HaBrakha, no. 343. This story arises out of the commentary on Deut. 33:2: "The Lord came from Sinai, He shone upon them from Se'ir, He appeared from Mount Paran, and approached from Rivevot Kodesh." It is certainly significant that this is the Pentateuchal passage most often cited by Muslim authors in order to anchor in the Bible the Islamic conception of humanity's religious history, according to which Judaism (Sinai) and Christianity

To listen to al-Ṭabarī and al-Qurṭubī, the Qur'ān – or something very much like it – was also offered to at least one other candidate before being bestowed by God upon the Muslims. In this case, however, the community first in line to receive (what would instead become the last installment of) the *Kalām Allāh* rejected the religio-legal system originally held out to it not because its precepts were too hard, but because they were too easy:

> Yaḥyā b. Abī Kathīr narrated from Nawf al-Bikālī the Ḥimyarite: When Moses chose seventy men of his people for the appointed rendezvous with his Lord,[3] God the Exalted said to him: "O Moses! I hereby grant you (i.e. the Israelites) the ground as a place of prostration and as a medium of purification (*innī aj'alu lakum al-arḍa masjidan wa-ṭahūran*), that you may pray wherever the onset of the prayer-time catches you – save in the lavatory, bath or at a gravesite; and I shall infuse the Divine Presence into your bosoms (*aj'alu al-sakīna fī qulūbikum*);[4] and I shall make it so that you recite the Torah from your innermost hearts (or: from the tablets of your hearts, or: by heart – *'an ẓahri qulūbikum*), and it shall be recited by the women among you as well as the men, by free folk and slaves, by young

(Se'ir – because Se'ir = Edom = Rome) are superseded by Islam, which was revealed to the sons of Ishmael who dwelt in Paran (Lazarus-Yafeh, *Intertwined Worlds*, 109; Adang, Appendix Two. The opening verses of Q. 95 – "By the fig and the olive and by Mount Sinai, and by this city made secure…" – are often seen as a Qur'ānic parallel to this Pentateuchal passage). The Qur'ān famously depicts the Children of Israel as responding to God's offer by declaring: "We hear and we *disobey*" (*sami'nā wa-'aṣaynā* – Q. 2: 93 and elsewhere, probably a play on the Hebrew *shama'nu ve-'asinu* of Deut. 5: 24 rather than the *na'ase ve-nishma'* of Exodus 24: 7. See Brannon Wheeler's summary of the debate on this subject [Wheeler, *Moses,* 1–3]. Some reports attribute this rebellious response to the Christians as well.)

3 This is a paraphrase of Q. 7: 155. Cp. Exodus, 24: 1–2, 9–11: "The Lord said to Moses: Come up to God, with Aaron, Nadav and Avihu, and seventy elders of Israel, and bow low from afar. But only Moses shall come near the Lord. The others shall not come near; and the people shall not come up with him at all… Then Moses and Aaron, Nadav and Avihu, and seventy elders of Israel ascended. And they saw the God of Israel: under His feet there was the likeness of a pavement of sapphire like the very sky for purity. Yet He did not raise His hand against the leaders of the Israelites; they beheld God, and they ate and drank." See C. Sirat, "Un midras juif en habit musulman: la vision de Moïse sur le mont Sinai," *Revue de l'histoire des religions* 168 (1965).

4 Q. 48: 4: "He it is who sent down tranquility into the hearts of the believers, that they might add faith unto their faith (*huwa alladhī anzala al-sakīna fī qulūb al-mu'minīn li-yazdādū īmānan ma' īmānihim*)…" See the similar formulation in Q. 48: 18, which is connected to the Ḥudaybiya pledge. On the term *sakīna,* see Geiger, 39–41.

> and old." Moses conveyed God's words to his people, and they replied: "We do not want to be able to pray anywhere except in the synagogues; and we are not capable of carrying the divine presence in our hearts – we would rather it remained as it had been, in the ark (*nurīdu an takūna kamā kānat fī'l-tābūt*);[5] and we cannot recite the Torah by heart: we wish to recite it only from the text (*lā nurīdu an naqra'ahā illā naẓaran*)." [Upon hearing this response,] God the Exalted declared: "I shall therefore ordain it for those who ward off evil [and pay the poor due, and those who believe in Our revelations, and follow the Messenger-Prophet who can neither read nor write... he will make lawful for them all good things and prohibit only the foul, and he will relieve them of their burden and the shackles that were upon them]," up to His words: "... [such as these shall be] the successful" (Q. 7: 156–7) – and God made it over to this community (*fa-ja'alahā li-hādhihi'l-umma*).[6]

There are many more influences on, and allusions in, this pregnant passage than we have space to expand upon here: the dwelling of the Divine Presence in the midst the Israelites (Exodus, 25: 8 and 29: 25), its subsequent departure therefrom (Deut., 31: 17) and eventual return thereto (Ezekiel, 43: 9; Zechariah, 8: 3); the "new covenant" heralded by Jeremiah and its "circumcision of the heart" so beloved of Christian doctrine (Jeremiah, 31: 31–4);[7] Solomon's exhortation to his son to

5 Q. 2: 248: "And their prophet said to [the Banū Isrā'īl]: Lo! The token of [Saul's] kingdom is that there shall come unto you the ark wherein is tranquility from your Lord (*ya'tīkum al-tābūt fīhi sakīnatun min Rabbikum*)..." Interestingly, the word *tābūt* – apparently connected to the Hebrew *tayva* (ark) – can also mean "innards" and thus "heart" in Arabic (and see Geiger, 31, on this term).

6 Qurṭubī, 7: 239. Compare McAuliffe's translation of al-Ṭabarī's nearly identical version of this report (McAuliffe, "Prediction," 117).

7 Compare Q. 2: 88: "And they [*viz.*, the Jews] say: 'Our hearts are uncircumcised!'..." (*wa-qālū qulūbunā ghulfu* ...); Leviticus, 26: 41: "When I [the Lord]... have removed them into the land of their enemies, then at last shall their uncircumcised heart humble itself"; and Deut., 10: 16: "Circumcise, therefore, the foreskin of your heart, and be no more stiffnecked..." See also Asher Z. Lopatin, "The Uncircumcised Jewish Heart" in Nettler, *Studies*, 75–84, also Brannon Wheeler, "The 'New Torah': Some Early Islamic Views of the Quran and Other Revealed Books," *Graeco-Arabica* 7–8 (1999–2000). Interestingly for our purposes in this study, Kathryn Kueny points out that the absence of any mention of circumcision in the Qur'ān and the relative de-corporealization of this institution in Islamic law and lore may partake of the process, initiated by Paul, of diminishing the importance of the physical aspect of this rite: "This route toward a reinterpretation of circumcision would certainly coincide with several qur'ānic injunctions that lift many of the rules and restrictions imposed upon the Jews by the Torah, a rhetorical move that parallels

"bind [my commandments] on your fingers, and write them on the tablets of your heart" (Proverbs, 7:2–3); Moses' petition, "Would that all the Lord's people were prophets, that the Lord put His spirit upon them!" (Numbers, 11:29) coupled with Joel's effusion, "I (God) will pour out My spirit on all flesh; your sons and daughters shall prophesy; your old men shall dream dreams and your young men shall see visions. I will even pour out My spirit upon male and female slaves in those days" (Joel 3:1–2); the recoiling of the Hebrews at Sinai from their direct encounter with the divine, and their entreaty of Moses to mediate between themselves and God (Exodus, 20:15–18);[8] the Rabbinic ruling that "things which are written down must not be recited from memory" (*dvarim shebikhtav iy ata rashai le'omram 'al peh* – Gittin 60b); and much else besides. Here we need comment only on that which bears directly on our subject. The main points of Nawf al-Bikālī's disquisition are (1) that the representatives of the Children of Israel were granted first refusal of the *dīn al-yusr* (the religion of ease); (2) that they did indeed refuse it; and (3) that God, in view of such ungratefulness, announced forthwith that He would instead "ordain it for those who ward off evil ... and follow the Messenger-Prophet who can neither read nor write" – in other words, He would give it to the Muslims.[9]

What specific aspects of the "religion of ease" repelled the Israelites? *Tayammum,* for one. God proposed to "grant them the ground ... as a medium of purification" – that is, allow them to substitute sand ablutions if water was unavailable[10] – but (as al-Qurṭubī informs us in his

---

the same efforts in the Christian tradition" (Kueny, "Abraham's Test: Islamic Male Circumcision as Anti/Ante-Covenantal Practice" in Reeves, *Bible and Qur'ān,* 167).

8 Contrast Q.2:55: "And when you [Israelites] said, 'O Moses! We will not believe in you until we see God manifestly ..." (although many commentaries see this as referring to the same incident alluded to in Q.7:155 – see Katsh, *HaYahadut Ba-Islam,* 53). See also Ibn Isḥāq—Guillaume, 251.

9 "In the widely current tradition about the supplications of Moses," writes Kister, "he implored the Lord to grant his people, the Children of Israel, the excellent qualities and merits which were enumerated in the Torah; God preferred, however, to choose the Muslim community and grant them these qualities and merits." Kister, "Ḥaddithū," 222. Nawf al-Bikālī is said to be the son of the wife of Ka'b al-Aḥbār, the famous Yemenite-Jewish convert to Islam (although Fakhr al-Dīn al-Rāzī may have another Ka'b in mind – see Wheeler, *Prophets,* 226; also Newby, *Last Prophet,* 118).

10 Q.4:43 and Q.5:6: "And if ye be ill, or on a journey, or one of you comes from the privy, or you have touched women, and you find not water, then go to

elaboration) the Jews would have none of this: "No, only with water!" (*lā, illā bi'l-mā'*). God would also make the whole world their hall of worship, but they preferred confinement: "No, only in the synagogues!" (*lā, illā fī'l-kanā'is*). He additionally offered to "accept the prayer of lone individuals, wherever they might be found," but they insisted on collective devotions: "No, only in a quorum!" (*lā, illā bi'l-jamā'a*).[11] The Banū Isrā'īl were gluttons for punishment.

The Jews were saddled with additional encumbrances as a result of having turned their backs on what was, essentially, the *millat Ibrāhīm*. "Among the burdens [that Israel had to bear] was refraining from productive activity on the Sabbath (*tark al-ishtighāl yawm al-sabt*) – and it is told that Moses, upon him be peace, saw a man carrying reeds on the Sabbath and executed him."[12] Noteworthy here is the foregrounding of

---

clean, high soil and rub your faces and your hands therewith ..." "Dust," declared the Prophet, "is the ceremonial detergent of the Muslim, even for ten years running, in a case where he (lit. 'you') cannot find water," for "the earth has been made a mosque for my sake, and a ritual cleanser, so that wherever the time for prescribed prayer catches up with me, I will daub my face and limbs with dust and pray" (*al-turāb ṭahūr al-Muslim wa-law ilā 'ashara ḥijaj ma lam tajid al-mā'... ju'ilat lī al-arḍ masjidan wa-ṭahūran aynamā adrakatnī al-ṣalāt tayammamtu wa-ṣalaytu*) – Sarakhsī, *Mabsūṭ*, 1:106.

11 Qurṭubī, 7:239. There is, however, a different echo of this encounter in the tradition according to which at least some Israelites misrepresented the divine communication vouchsafed unto them specifically with a view toward *loosening* the yoke of heaven. Glossing Q.2:75 – "Did you hope that they would believe in you, when *a party from among them* used to hear the word of Allāh and then *knowingly alter it* after having understood it?" – al-Wāḥidī adduces the opinion of Muqātil and Ibn 'Abbās to the effect that "[t]his verse was revealed in connection with the seventy men Moses chose to accompany him to his Lord. Upon arrival they perceived the word of God, commanding and forbidding. Then they returned to their people, and while the truthful among them accurately conveyed what they had heard, a certain faction said: 'We heard from God's own mouth the words: "If you are capable of doing these things, then do them; but if you prefer, you may leave off doing them – no harm done!" (*in istaṭa'tum an taf'alū hādhihi al-ashyā' faf'alū wa-in shi'tum fa-lā taf'alū wa-lā ba's*. Wāḥidī, *Asbāb al-Nuzūl* to Q.2:75).

12 Qurṭubī, 7:242: "*yurwā anna Mūsā, 'alayhi al-salām, ra'a yawm al-sabt rajulan yaḥmilu qaṣaban fa-ḍaraba 'unuqahu.*" See Numbers, 15:32. The tension between the negative attitude to the rigorous provisions of the Jewish religion and the simultaneous recognition that they emanate from God and are therefore deserving of fulfillment is well illustrated by the contrast between a statement like the one to which this note is appended and the message of Q.2:65: "You know what happened to those [of the Children of Israel] who broke the Sabbath, how We said unto them: Be ye apes, despised and hated!" Combining this verse with

nabī Mūsā, who plays a presiding role in the Israelite *dīn al-ʿusr* (re-

---

Q. 7: 163–166 – "And ask them about the town by the sea, when they violated the Sabbath: when their fish came to them on the surface on their Sabbath day, and when it was not the Sabbath they came not to them ... And when they revoltingly persisted in that which they had been forbidden, We said to them: 'Be ye apes, despised and hated!'" – al-Ṭabarī and al-Qurṭubī tell slightly different versions of the following story. God commanded the Israelites through Moses to observe Friday as their special day, but they refused and demanded Saturday (*yawm al-sabt,* the Sabbath. Q. 50: 37 – "We created the heavens and the earth and what is between them in six days, and *no weariness affected us* [*wa-mā massanā min lughūb*]" – is construed by the commentaries as a rejection of the Jewish claim that God rested on the seventh day [see Lazarus-Yafeh, "Muslim Festivals," p. 41, and n. 8 where she reminds us that the Midrash itself had already asked: "Is God liable to weariness?" (Mekhilta Exodus, 20: 11)]). "In chastisement for their stubbornness in insisting on the Sabbath (as opposed to Friday), God afflicted the Jews on that day, and forbade them what was permitted to them on other days" (note the use of prohibitions as a punishment). One of the acts forbidden to them on that day was fishing.

The narrative now shifts to a town called "Madyan" on an unidentified coast where many Jews lived (for speculation in the *tafsīr* regarding the location of this town, see Wheeler, *Prophets,* 218–20, and Qurṭubī, 7: 202. Al-Ṭabarī locates it "between Ayla [Elat/ʿAqaba] and al-Ṭūr [on the South-Western coast of the Sinai peninsula]," and many medieval geographers place a town by that name just north of Tabūk near the present day Jordanian-Saudi border. The sea in question would therefore be the Red Sea, although the Dead Sea – in which no fish can live – is a more interesting possibility, as we shall now see). To exacerbate the misery of the Jewish denizens of Madyan, Allāh saw to it that fish were scarcely found in the sea during the week, when they could legally be caught, whereas on the Sabbath thousands of them floated languidly on the surface directly off-shore, taunting the hungry inhabitants (compare the midrash about the River Sambatyon – literally, the Sabbath river – which ceases to flow on the Sabbath, and the fish of which lounge on its banks during the Day of Rest). One fellow could stand this torture no longer. He crept down to the sea on a Sabbath and caught one of the numerous fish. He then pierced it with a hook at the end of a string, threw it thus transfixed back into the water, tied the other end to a tent peg in the sand, and headed home leaving the whole contraption in place. Returning the following morning, he reeled in his catch and enjoyed a delicious breakfast ("as if to say" injects Ibn ʿAbbās, al-Ṭabarī's source for this tale, "'I didn't catch it on the Sabbath!'" [*ay innī lam aʾkhudhhu fī yawm al-sabt*]. In other versions this fed-up fisherman baits his hook and casts his line out on a *Friday,* leaving it anchored to the tent-peg over the Sabbath. The following day he comes back and feasts on the fish that had been caught on the Sabbath – not by him, but by the device. This is closer to the type of "*ḥiyal*" or circumventions generally considered legitimate by the *halakha,* such as modern day Sabbath timers and the like). Other Jews began to follow their co-religionist's example, employing a variety of ruses of this sort, and soon the markets were filled with fish.

ligion of hardship) despite having applied (according to an earlier aside of al-Qurṭubī's) for what can only be described as a "transfer." Upon hearing of God's decision to withdraw His offer of easy religion and resubmit it to "those who ward off evil" – i.e. to the future Muslims – Moses pleaded: "O Lord: make me *their* Prophet!" (*ij'alnī nabiyya-*

At this point al-Qurṭubī picks up the story and relates that the more pious elements of the town were incensed by this surreptitious infraction of Sabbath law. They came out openly in opposition to such activity, and broke away from that segment of the populace that sanctioned it or participated in it (*qāmat firqa fa-nahat wa-jāharat bi'l-nahy wa-'tazalat*; and see also Qurṭubī, 7: 316, where they are said to have actually departed [like good Muslims]: "*hajarū al-'āṣīn wa-qālū lā nusākinukum*"). In order to prevent all intercourse with such sinners, these more meticulous members of the community erected a wall that divided the town in half. Peering over that same wall soon afterward, they discovered that the "Sabbath-fishers" on the other side had all been turned into apes. Upon subsequently entering the "ghetto" they had created, the strict Sabbath observers were accosted by their metamorphosed countrymen, each of which ran up to his relatives – whom he recognized, though they did not recognize him – and took to sniffing their garments and weeping. "Did we not warn you?" the humans scolded. The sorrowful simians nodded their assent (Ṭabarī, 1: 470; Qurṭubī, 1: 418; see also, for another reference to the ape and swine metamorphosis, Wheeler, *Prophets,* 218–220, and Q. 5: 60, and see William Brinner, "The Image of the Jew as *Other* in Medieval Arabic Texts" in Ilai Alon *et al* [eds.], *Israel Oriental Studies XIV: Concepts of the Other in Near Eastern Religions,* 227–40. The Prophet reputedly refrained from eating the large lizard, fearing that this was another species into which "a party of the Children of Israel" had been changed (Muir, *Life of Mohammad,* 527). Still other sources speak of the Ten Lost Tribes having been turned into rodents, noting that these last "do not drink camel's milk when it is placed before them, but do drink goat's milk" (kosher-keeping rats! – Bukhārī, 4: 524)]).

It is significant that in the Madyan story not the sticklers, but rather those who transgressed the law were *mamsūkhīn* (transformed): God's regulations, difficult as they may be (and even when they are enacted as punishments), must be obeyed ("Hold fast to [the commandments] We have given you!" Allāh adjures the Israelites [Q. 2: 63]). Another animal comparison makes this point: "The likeness of those who were charged with the Torah but observe it not, is as the likeness of an ass carrying books" (*mathalu'llladhīna ḥummilū al-Tawrāta thumma lam yaḥmilūhā ka-mathali'l-ḥimāri yaḥmilu asfāran* – Q. 62: 5. See also Qurṭubī, 6: 208: "*wabbakha [Allāhu] 'ulamā'ahum* [the jurists/spiritual leaders of the Jews and Christians, or just of the Jews] *fī tark nahyihim,*" and ibid., 10: 177: "*al-murād bi'l-fasād mukhālafat aḥkām al-Tawrāt.*" Similarly, one of the main categories of iniquity for which "Bukhtnaṣr" [Nebukhadnezzar] was sent to destroy the first Jewish commonwealth was that its leaders "*istaḥallū al-maḥārim,*" rendered the forbidden permissible [ibid., 10: 179], an accusation that repeats itself often [see, e.g., Newby, *Last Prophet,* 179 and 183, as well as 192, where observance even of the post-Ezra Torah is approved of and

hum). God denied his request: "Their Prophet will be from among them" (*nabiyyuhum minhum*). "Then at least make me *one* of them!," begged Moses.[13] "No – you will not reach them," regrets the Lord (that is, you will die long before they arrive on the stage of history). Moses had to be satisfied with his less than perfect lot as leader of what was, essentially, a warm-up act.[14]

---

lauded). Cf., however, the story of the "learned rabbi" Mukhayriq who reminded his fellow Jews of their contractual obligation to assist Muḥammad on the day of the battle of Uḥud. "But it is the Sabbath!" the Jews objected. "May you *have* no Sabbath!" Mukhayriq answered, and went off immediately to fight, and die, for the Prophet (Ibn Isḥāq — Guillaume, 241 [the battle of Uḥud took place on the second Sabbath of Shawwāl – ibid., 389]). See also the consultation reputedly held among the Banū Qurayẓa, in the course of which the suggestion made by one of them that they attack Muḥammad on the Sabbath when he would least expect it is rejected by the assembly (ibid., 462); here it is hard to tell whether the text intends to praise or demean the Jews for this decision. In Q. 4:47 Allāh threatens the People of the Book that if they do not "believe in what We have revealed" then "We will curse [you] as We cursed the Sabbath breakers."

13 Admittedly, another way to render "*ij'alnī minhum*" here would be: "[Since their Prophet can only be from among them, then] make me one of them [so that I can be their Prophet]." See, however, a related tale recorded by Ibn Qayyim al-Jawziyya in which Moses is agog at all the good that God will someday bestow upon the Muslims and asks to be made one of Muḥammad's Companions (cited in Lazarus-Yafeh, *Intertwined Worlds*, 25). This would militate for the first interpretation, as would the Prophet's well-known statement that "if Moses were alive today, he would follow me" (e.g., Abū Bakr Muḥammad b. Aḥmad al-Sarakhsī, *Uṣūl* [Beirut: Dār al-Ma'rifa li'l-Ṭibā'a wa'l-Nashr, 1973], 2: 102. In other traditions, however, Muḥammad asserts Moses' superiority over himself, butressing this claim, *inter alia*, with the assertion that the Biblical prophet will rise from the eschatological state of unconsciousness before he [Muḥammad himself] does).

14 Qurṭubī, 7: 239. Another way to translate "*lan tudrikahum*" might be "you will not comprehend them" or "you will not reach their level." The remainder of the dialogue in al-Qurṭubī has Moses complain before God that "Here I have come to You with a delegation of the Children of Israel, and you have bestowed the hospitality due us upon others! (*ataytuka bi-wafd Banī Isrā'īl fa-ja'alta wifādatanā li-ghayrinā*), at which point Allāh revealed: "And of Moses' folk there is a community who guide with truth and establish justice therewith" (Q. 7: 159) – and Moses was satisfied (*fa-raḍiya Mūsā*). When combined with the rendering "you will not comprehend them" for *lan tudrikahum*, this portion of al-Qurṭubī's discourse is evocative of the rhythm of yet another famous Midrash: "When Moses ascended to heaven, he found God occupied ornamenting the letters in which the Torah was written with little crown-like decorations ... and he inquired as to their significance. 'Hereafter there shall live a man called 'Aqiva son of Joseph,' God explained, 'who will erect gigantic

Here, too, there is a plethora of cross-cultural influences at work, upon only one of which we can remark. In Q. 2: 129, Ibrāhīm and Ismāʿīl pray regarding their distant descendants: "O Lord, raise up in their midst a Messenger from among them (*rasūlan minhum*), who shall recite to them Your revelations and instruct them in the Scripture and in wisdom ..." This verse is an acknowledged and deliberate echo of Deuteronomy, 18: 18, in which God informs Moses that "I will raise up for them a Prophet from among their own people (*navi aqim lahem mi-qerev aḥayhem*), like yourself, and I will put my words in His mouth and he will speak to them all that I command him." Islamic tradition sees the Biblical statement, no less than the Qur'ānic one, as a reference to Muḥammad,[15] but more important for our purposes is the fact that God's promise of this up-and-coming, messianic seer-leader refers – in its context in Deuteronomy – to the period after "you have entered the land that the Lord your God is giving you" (Deut., 18: 9). This being the case, attention should be paid to the following midrash.

When God informed Moses that his death was imminent, and that he would not be privileged to enter the Land, the great guide of the desert turned to his Creator and attempted to plea-bargain: "Master of the Universe! Your judgment against me reads that I may not enter the Land *as a king*; for to Aaron and me You did say: 'Ye shall not *bring* this

---

mountains of *halakhot* on every jot and tittle of these letters.' Moses said to God, 'Show me this man.' God said, 'Turn thee round.' Moses did, and found himself sitting in the eighteenth row of the study hall of Rabbi Akiba, who was discussing the law with his students. Moses was unable to follow these discussions (*veh-lo haya yodeʿa ma hem omrim*), and this grieved him deeply. Just then, however, he heard one of the disciples question his master in regard to a certain subject: 'Whence do you know this?' 'This is a statute given to Moses at Sinai,' Akiba replied – and Moses was content (*nityashva daʿato* – Menaḥot 29b)."

15 Together with Deut., 33:2, this is the verse most commonly invoked by Muslim authors seeking proof of Muḥammad's prophethood in the Bible (see Adang, *Muslim Writers*, 264 [Appendix Two]). Upon his conversion to Islam, the Madīnan ʿAbd Allāh b. Salām – the Jews' "chief, son of our chief; our rabbi and our learned man" – accused his former co-religionists of hiding the fact that Muḥammad "is described in your Torah and even named" (Ibn Isḥāq—Guillaume, 241; and see Lazarus-Yafeh, *Intertwined Worlds*, chapter 4; also chap. 4, n. 28 and chap. 8, n. 35 of the present study). "A copt, reading his uncle's Bible, was struck by finding two leaves closely glued together. On opening them, he discovered copious details regarding Moḥammad, as a prophet about to appear. His uncle was displeased at his curiosity and beat him, saying that the Prophet had not yet arisen" (Muir, *Life of Mohammad*, lxiii, n. 2).

people into the land which I have given them.' Permit me then, at least, to enter it as a common person (*hedyoṭ*)."[16] The Lord turned down His servant's request, but the resemblance to al-Qurṭubī's story is intriguing. Moses in the midrash yearns to cross a *spatial* boundary – the distance between his present location and the Gilgal region on the opposite side of the Jordan – in order to enter into "the rest and inheritance" (*ha-menuḥah ve-ha-naḥalah*, Deut. 12: 9) of which he has so long dreamed. Al-Qurṭubī's Moses yearns to cross a *temporal* divide – the centuries that stretch between his own time and the inception of Islam – in order to enter into the "religion of relaxation" (*dīn al-rukhṣa*), the advent of which also represents a chiliasm of sorts. In both cases, when he is denied access in his capacity as leader, Moses declares his willingness to be demoted from his high station and join the rank and file ("then at least make me *one* of them!"), preferring, as it were, to be a tail among lions than a head among foxes.[17] If such a connection can plausibly be made between the two narratives, then a significant parallel is being drawn between moderation in the law and eschatological repose. *Rukhṣa* is the high road to the Promised Land.[18]

---

16 Ginzberg, *Legends*, 3:421.

17 Avot, 4:20.

18 Characterizations of *al-arḍ al-muqaddasa* in Muslim classical literature are often reminiscent of paradise, as in the case of the milk and honey motif (see, e.g., Muslim, 30:5702). Before leaving the subject of Moses ascending to receive the Torah, it should be noted that Q. 7: 154 relates that "when Moses' anger calmed down [after the calf incident] he took up the tablets [again? See Exodus 32:19 and 34:1 ff]; and in the writing thereof was guidance, and mercy for those who fear their Lord." The Arabic word rendered here by "the writing thereof" is *nuskhatihā.* Although *nuskha* certainly means "transcription, copy" (like the Hebrew *nuskha,* formulation), still, there is perhaps an evocation here of *naskh,* and therefore, perhaps, even an allegorical hint to Islam's supersession of Judaism: the new law replacing the old as the second set of tablets replaced the first. Interestingly in this connection, Lazarus-Yafeh notes that Samau'al al-Maghribī – the ex-Jewish author of *Ifḥām al-Yahūd* (Silencing the Jews) – referred to the scribe who had rewritten Jewish scripture ('Uzayr, but not Ezra, in his dissenting opinion) as a *nāsikh.* Lazarus-Yafeh comments: "[This is] a word that the Islamic reader could not fail to associate with the theory of abrogation" (Lazarus-Yafeh, *Intertwined Worlds,* 69). Also, the optional rendering of the root *n.s.kh.* as "to transfer" (whence is derived the sense of "to transcribe" and therefore "to write") gives us the common description of the Qur'ān in the sources as *mansūkh*: here meaning not "abrogated," of course, but "transferred" from the upper to a lower heaven or "transmitted" from the *lawḥ al-maḥfūẓ* (the Preserved Tablet) to the Prophet, and thence to the codex itself.

There were additional "discounts" ostensibly forfeited by the Jews as a result of having rejected God's generous offer: the wergild, for instance. "They did not possess the precept of blood money (*diya*) but only the *lex talionis* (*qiṣāṣ*)," asserts al-Qurṭubī.[19] Indeed, the Pentateuch not only admonishes that "[y]ou shall not accept a ransom for the life of a murderer who is guilty of a capital crime; he must be put to death" (Numbers, 35:31), but also famously demands "an eye for an eye, a tooth for a tooth, a hand for a hand, a foot for a foot" (Exodus, 21:24; Leviticus, 24:20).[20] The Qur'ān confirms this: "Lo! We revealed

19 Qurṭubī, 7:242.

20 The Rabbis interpreted "an eye for an eye" as "the *worth* of an eye for an eye," thereby certainly supporting the equivalent of *diya* (see Baba Qama 83b–84a). Rabbinic modifications of Biblical law – real and imagined – are often the butt of criticism in Muslim commentaries (see, e.g., Lazarus-Yafeh, *Intertwined Worlds*, 138 and especially 41, where the rabbis of the Talmud are accused by Samau'al al-Maghribī – the Jewish apostate author of *Ifḥām al-Yahūd* [Silencing the Jews] – of "increasing the burden" of law upon the Jewish people, and thereby ignoring Deut. 13:7 in which all augmentation of Biblical regulations is forbidden). This phenomenon has encouraged certain scholars to see Karaite, Samaritan and/or Christian influence at work (see Adang, *Muslim Writers*, 80–83 and *passim*; Lazarus-Yafeh, *Intertwined Worlds*, throughout chapters 1–3, where the relevant articles and monographs are given in the notes; and Goitein, "Ha-dat ha-zo'efet," 6). In the case of the *lex talionis*, in which the Talmudic take on the matter would have spoiled the favorable contrast to Judaism, it has apparently been ignored by al-Qurṭubī. Al-Ṭabarī, on the other hand, attacks the Jews of Muḥammad's time for overdoing it in the opposite direction: he portrays them as flouting Torah law and accepting the wergild even for murder (Ṭabarī, 6:342).

The need to portray the Jewish religion as harsh and thereby throw into relief the lenient ways of Islam may also have influenced the exegesis of what is probably a Qur'ānic reference to the Pentateuchal penalty for stealing. We read in Q. 12:75 that when Joseph's emissaries catch up with his brothers, into the bag of one of which (Benjamin, according to the Bible) the king's drinking cup had been planted, they accuse them of theft. When the brothers deny such a possibility, the emissaries ask: "What is the penalty for this (i.e. for stealing), if you are liars?" The brothers – the Children of Israel – respond: "The penalty for this is that the person in whose bag it is found shall himself be the penalty for it. Thus do we punish the wrongdoers." Al-Ṭabarī explains that Joseph's siblings meant that "he in whose possession the stolen object is discovered is himself the recompense, that is, he in whose saddlebags it is found is delivered up to him from whom he stole it and is enslaved by him" (*yuslamu bi-sirqatihi ilā man saraqa minhu ḥattā yastariqqahu*). Mu'ammar is cited by al-Ṭabarī to the same effect, with an interesting addition: "The brothers informed [the messengers of] Joseph of *the law of their land* (*bimā yuḥkamu fī bilādihim*), which was that he who steals is consigned to servitude" (*ukhidha 'abdan* – Ṭabarī,

the Torah, wherein is guidance and light ... and We prescribed therein the life for the life, the eye for the eye, the nose for the nose, the ear for the ear and the tooth for the tooth ..." (Q. 5: 44–5). Islam harbours a different, more *rukhṣa*-driven outlook on this issue:

> O you who believe! Retaliation is prescribed for you in the matter of the murdered: the freeman for the freeman, the slave for the slave, and the female for the female. But for him who is forgiven somewhat by his brother, payment of the blood-wit is prescribed with handsome compensation. This is an alleviation and a mercy from your Lord (*dhālika takhfīf min Rabbikum wa-raḥmatun* – Q. 2: 178).[21]

Here, too, Islam is described as occupying a happy medium between the Jewish extreme – in which the only option is executing the murderer – and the Christian extreme – in which the only option is forgiving the murderer, neither executing him *nor* demanding the wergild (*wa-ḥakama 'alā ahl al-injīl al-'afw wa-lā yuqtalu bi'l-qiṣāṣ wa-lā yu'khadhu al-diya*). In contrast to these two constricting norms, the *sharī'a* leaves all doors open: "God, the Mighty and Majestic, granted a 'reduction' to the nation of Muḥammad: if he wishes, the relative of

13: 29). The Biblical punishment for theft is outlined in Exodus, 22: 1–3: "If a man steals an ox or a sheep, and slaughters it or sells it, he shall pay five oxen for the ox and four sheep for the sheep ... If he lacks the means [to pay this fine] he shall be sold [into slavery] for his theft ... but if what he stole – whether ox or ass or sheep – is found alive in his possession, he shall pay double." Indenture is thus a last recourse (and, as refined by the Talmud, applies only in the case of failure to pay the *principle* of – not the "interest" on – the theft). However, given that servitude might well be considered harsher than hand amputation, while paying double or even quintuple restitution certainly seems less severe than the loss of a limb, it is possible that Muslim sources chose to highlight the "understudy," i.e. bondage, thereby adding one more component to the favorable contrast between the *dīn al-'usr* and the *dīn al-yusr.* It is true that in the Biblical text the brothers swear that "whichever of [us the goblet] is found with shall die, and the rest of us shall become slaves to my lord," and Joseph's steward responds, "Although what you propose is right, only the one with whom it is found shall be my slave, and the rest of you shall go free" (Gen. 44: 9–10), and therefore the Qur'ānic version may represent little more than a (relatively) faithful reproduction of the Biblical narrative. But it is significant that in the *tafsīr* Mu'ammar, as we saw, turns the conclusion of this exchange between the brothers and the emissaries into "*the law of their land* which was that *he who steals is consigned to servitude.*"

21 For *qiṣāṣ* and *diya,* especially as applied by Muslim law to *dhimmīs*, see Friedmann, *Tolerance,* 39–53. There is much controversy over the proper parsing and interpretation of this verse.

the murdered man may kill the murderer; if he wishes, he may forgive the murderer altogether; and if he wishes, he may accept the blood price."[22]

Even the method of atonement prescribed for the Jews was exceedingly harsh, for "they were commanded to kill themselves as a sign of their repentance."[23] Here al-Qurṭubī clearly refers to Q. 2: 54: "And when Moses said unto his people: O my people! You have wronged yourselves by choosing the calf, so turn in penitence to your Creator/Acquitter, and kill yourselves (*tūbū ilā bāri'ikum fa'qtulū anfusakum*).[24] That will be best for you in the sight of your Creator/Acquitter; and He will relent toward you. Lo! He is the relenting, the Merciful." Seeing that the Israelites were unwilling to slay themselves – or, alternately, that they remained obstinate and unbelieving despite such auto-slaughter – God took matters into His own hands:

> And remember when you [Israelites] said: "O Moses! We shall never believe in you until we behold Allāh manifestly"; and even while you gazed the lightning struck you. Then We revived you after your death, that perchance you might be grateful (Q. 2: 55).[25]

---

22 Muqātil b. Sulaymān, *Tafsīr al-Khams Mi'at Āya* [ed. Goldfeld], 118, n. 345. This may refer, however, to one who kills without intent. Muslim sources are generally under the impression, or make the claim, that Torah law prescribed execution even in cases of accidental killing. Once again it is hard to define the purported Christian position: is it too lax, in that it lets all murderers live, or too demanding, because it restricts one's choices? See above, chap. 3, n. 10, and below, n. 33, clause 7.

23 Qurṭubī, 7: 242.

24 Many – especially moderns but also a handful of medieval commentators – have attempted to reread this phrase, suggesting alternatives such as "kill [the guilty] yourselves" (a rendering which would require the vocalization *anfus*u*kum* as opposed to *anfusakum*, and would still then be forced) or "kill your souls" (in repentance). Al-Qurṭubī's employment of this verse shows that he understands Moses' command literally to mean "kill one another" or "kill your own people." It will be recalled that al-Qurṭubī used this same scene as a refutation of the Jewish arguments against *naskh*: "Moses ordered the Children of Israel to kill those among them who had worshipped the calf, and then he ordered them to withhold their swords from these." In the context of what he calls the fatalistic "*sunna* statement" – the eschatological notion that the Muslims are doomed to imitate the experience of the Banū Isrā'īl willy-nilly – Uri Rubin shows Ibn Mas'ūd predicting that the Muslims themselves will worship the calf in the future (Rubin, *Between Bible and Qur'ān*, 174). See also, in this connection, Kister, "ḥaddithū," 232.

25 Compare Q. 7: 155 (the first line of which was already cited above by al-Qur-

Death by their own hands and/or death by the hand of heaven: even when followed by an immediate resurrection, this is a stiff price to pay for a return to God's graces. Adam's atonement had been a much milder affair: "Adam received words [of revelation] from his Lord (immediately after the Fall), and He relented toward him. Lo! God is the relenting, the merciful" (Q. 2: 37). That of the later Muslims was also comparatively painless: "Those who, when they do an evil thing or wrong themselves, remember Allāh and implore forgiveness for their sins (who forgives sins save Allāh?) and will not knowingly repeat the wrong they did – the reward of such will be forgiveness (*maghfira*) from their Lord, and Gardens underneath which rivers flow, wherein they will abide forever" (Q. 3: 135–6).[26] Indeed, upon revival (after the aforementioned extinction by lightning), the Banū Isrā'īl were themselves given first rights to what would ultimately become the more facile, Islamic route to repentance: "And when We said: Enter this township and eat freely of that which is therein, and enter the gate prostrate, and say: *ḥiṭṭa* – We will then forgive you your sins and increase the reward for those who do right" (Q. 2: 58).[27] But the Jews – "those

ṭubī): "And Moses chose of his people seventy men for Our appointed meeting. And when the trembling came upon them, he said: My Lord! Had You so willed, You would have destroyed them before, and me with them. Will You destroy us for that which the foolish among us have done? It is but Your trial of us. You send whom You will astray and guide whom You will. You are our Protecting Friend. Therefore forgive us and have mercy upon us, You, the best of all who show forgiveness." See Exodus, 19: 16ff. It is interesting to note, in connection with the death and revival of the Banū Isrā'īl in Q. 2: 55, that the Talmud and Midrash embellish the fear expressed by the Israelites at the foot of mount Sinai: "You [Moses] speak to us, and we will obey; but let not God speak to us, lest we die" (Exodus, 20: 16 – this is the diametric antithesis of their demand, according to the Qur'ān [2: 55], to "see God manifestly"). The rabbis claim that "when they came to Sinai and God appeared before them, *their souls departed at His speech* ... the Torah, however, interceded for them, saying, 'The whole world rejoices [at my appearance], and shall the Children of Israel die?' At once their souls were restored to them ..."

26 Commenting on Q. 22: 78, al-Ṭabarī reminds his readership that "God did not leave you without a 'safety valve' (*makhraj*) in your religion: He set up repentance (*tawba*) as one way out, and *kaffāra* as another ..." (Ṭabarī, 17: 268). *Kaffāra* involves the manumission of a slave in expiation for a misdeed. If this is not practical, one may fast instead (*man 'adima al-raqaba fī'l-kaffāra yantaqilu ilā ṣawm* – Abū Zakariyā' Yaḥyā Muhyī al-Dīn al-Nawawī, *Kitāb al-Majmū' (Sharḥ al-Muhadhdhab)* [Cairo: Al-Azhar, n.d.], 2: 249). Here is a leniency within a leniency.

27 On this verse and the meaning and provenance of the term *ḥiṭṭa*, see the intri-

who did wrong" – played their habitual word games[28] and "exchanged the utterance that had been spoken to them (*viz. ḥiṭṭa*) for a different expression ..." (Q. 2: 59) – one of rebellion or mockery.[29]

Once again, the Israelites had bitten the divine hand extended to them in mercy and had masochistically disdained the less painful method of making amends in favor of excruciating chastisement. And chastisement they duly received (as the second half of the same verse indicates), and they received it in punishment, one would have to say (given the above), for the specific crime of *demanding to be punished*: "... and we sent down upon the evildoers *rijz* from the heavens because of their depravity" (Q. 2: 59). *Rijz* is here interpreted by al-Ṭabarī and others to mean a plague (*ṭāʿūn*), which either "killed off the older generation [of Hebrews] leaving only the children"[30] or eradicated the people altogether (*lam yubqi minhum aḥadan*).[31]

---

guing suggestions of Uri Rubin, *Between Bible and Qur'an*, 83–99. The "township" is variously interpreted, some commentators speculating that it refers to the entire territory of the Holy Land (an area the location and extent of which is also a matter of dispute), others that it indicates specific cities such as Jerusalem or Jericho.

28 See, e.g., Q. 2: 75, 2: 93, 2: 104, 4: 46 and Geiger, 12–13. Instead of "*al-salāmu ʿalaykum*" the Jews would swallow the "lām" and greet their Muslim neighbors with "*al-sāmu ʿalaykum*," that is, "mischief be upon you" (Bukhārī, 9: 84 [60]; the Muslims in such a case are instructed by Muḥammad to shoot back with: "*wa-ʿalaykum!*"). Arabic *samm* is poison and *sāmm* is poisonous, perhaps connected, speculates Geiger, to Hebrew *sam ha-mavet*, "the drug of death." The Jews would also sneeze deliberately in the Prophet's presence in the hopes that he would respond instinctively: "God have mercy upon you! (*yarḥamuk Allāh*)," but Muḥammad didn't fall for this ruse (Abū Dāwūd, *Kitāb al-Adab*, 41: 5020).

29 Ṭabarī, 1: 433–5. *Ḥiṭṭa* may have been changed by the Banū Isrāʾīl into *khaṭīʾa*, Arabic (and, with slight alteration, Hebrew) for sin, or into Arabic *ḥinta* (Hebrew *khiṭa*) meaning wheat (the forbidden fruit of Eden according to one opinion in the Midrash – Bereishit Rabbah, 15: 7 – and a symbol of the sedentary life stubbornly demanded by the Israelites and decried by Moses in Q. 2: 61). See Bukhārī, 6: 60 (6) and Ṭabarī, 1: 463, where instead of entering prostrate, as commanded, the Israelites dragged themselves on their buttocks and uttered the word "grain" (*ḥabbatun* – i.e. *khiṭa*, wheat?) in place of "*ḥiṭṭatun*," and see Newby, *Last Prophet*, 33–4.

30 See Numbers, 14: 32. The punishment of wandering in the desert until the older generation died off was a direct result, according to the Biblical narrative, of the people's lack of faith upon hearing the discouraging report of the men sent to spy out the land in preparation for the Israelite invasion (Numbers chap. 13–14). It is thus interesting that al-Ṭabarī connects it specifically to this Qur'ānic verse, in which the Israelites are encouraged to "enter this township

Suicide, genocide, and resurrection followed by a second liquidation – such were the trials and tribulations of the Israelites in connection with repentance, another example, according to al-Qurṭubī, of "the chains that bound them." They had brought all of this misery upon themselves by scorning the Lord's largess, and would, in fact, continue to do so even after Islam arrived on the scene: "The Jews were envious of Muḥammad because of what God in His mercy had bestowed upon his followers – for Muḥammad had come with the 'removal of burdens and fetters from them' – and this envy instigated the Jews to deny Muḥammad's prophethood and reject the [world-view and code of] 'reduction' (*tark qabūl al-takhfīf*)."[32]

It remains to point out, before proceeding, that of the various "encumbrances" attributed by al-Qurṭubī to Judaism thus far – (1) the excision of flesh bespattered by urine, (2) the regular denial of booty after battle, (3) the exclusive use of water in ablutions, (4) the restriction of prayer to the synagogues, (5) the right to worship only in a group, (6) the literal understanding of the law of retribution, (7) the thoroughgoing avoidance of women during their periods, (8) the requirement to read the Torah from the text and (9) the strict observance of the Sab-

---

and eat freely of that which is therein ..." (Q. 2:58). The "township" in question is alternately identified as Jericho, Jerusalem, Syria (*shām*) or – according to al-Ḍaḥḥāk – "Ramla, Jordan, Palestine and Tadmor" (Qurṭubī, 1:392).

31 Ṭabarī, 1:436 (see also Qurṭubī, 4:119: "*qāla al-Kalbī: wa-kānat Banū Isrā'īl idhā aṣābū dhanban 'aẓīman ... ṣabba 'Allāhu 'alayhim rijzan, wa-huwa al-mawt*"). After this they were, perhaps, revived yet again. See Newby, *Last Prophet*, 134, where those eradicated and then revivified were only Moses' entourage of seventy, and ibid., 190–1 and 204, where the Children of Israel are annihilated and then resurrected in Babylon.

32 Ṭabarī, 9:116. This, however, did not prevent the Jews from seeking to take advantage of Muḥammad's new lenient direction when it was convenient for them. When a certain Jew and Jewess committed adultery – in the well known story already noted (chap. 4, end of n. 28) – and the Jewish community wished to avoid carrying out the stoning penalty prescribed in such cases by the Torah, "they consulted amongst themselves and said: 'Let us go to this Prophet, for he is a prophet who has been sent in a spirit of indulgence (*fa-innahu nabiyy bu'itha bi-takhfīf*), and if he issues an opinion prescribing a punishment lighter than lapidation, we will accept it (*fa-in aftānā bi-futyā dūna al-rajm qabilnā-hā*) and we will use it to defend our position before God, saying: Behold! The responsum of one of Your own prophets!'" (Ṭabarī, 6:338. See also Q. 5:43 and the commentaries to 2:75. The rabbi's hiding of the Biblical stoning verse with his hand in the continuation of the story unquestionably bears some interesting relationship to the controversial "suppression" of the Qur'ānic stoning verse [see above, chap. 1, toward the end of n. 3]).

bath – less than half correspond to the actual *halakhic* position.[33] Judaism is hard; Islam's Judaism is harder.

---

33 (1) Vajda mistakenly saw Muslim's *ḥadīth* about the Banū Isrā'īl cutting out urine-spattered flesh as an instance of Jewish → Muslim antithetical influence (i.e. *mukhālafa* – Vajda, "Juifs et Musulmans ...," 75). In fact, there exists no such precept in Jewish law and no Jew on record ever did this. Urine is not a ritually defiling substance in the *halakha* (see Makhshirin 6:7; Yerushalmi Pesakhim 35b, and Tevul Yom 2:1, where the point is made that the urine of all but the most severely impure persons is not the least bit contaminating [i.e. cannot even *transmit* the defilement of the impure individual to other things/people: "*ush'ar kol haṭeme'in, bayn kalin bayn ḥamurin, hamashkin hayotz'in mehen kamashkin shehu noge'a bahen: elu ve-elu aynan meṭam'in.*"]. See also M.Y. and Menaḥem Kister, "'Al Yehudei 'Arav – He'arot," *Tarbitz*, 49 [5739 (1980)], 239, n. 38). Even were Jews inordinately wary about contact with urine, cutting oneself is expressly prohibited in Jewish law (see especially the commentary of RaShbA to Baba Qama 91b. He concludes that this is true even if inflicting a wound were to give someone pleasure. Circumcision is an obvious exception to this rule, though significantly, a circumcision performed in other than the prescribed manner or circumstances – e.g., earlier than the eighth day of life – is considered nothing less than an assault on the child [RaSHI to Shabbat 137a, beginning with the words *ve-shakhaḥ va-mal*]. Certain authorities dispute the absolute prohibition of inflicting pain or a wound upon oneself, permitting it, for instance, in cases of fulfilling vows of penitence and the like).

(2) Al-Qurṭubī's ideas about the Israelite experience with, and divine policy regarding, booty – "when they would gather booty together, fire would descend from the sky and consume it" – can be traced as far back as Muqātil (Muqātil b. Sulaymān, *Tafsīr* [Cairo: Al-Hay'a al-Miṣriyya al-'Āmma li'l-Kitāb, 1978], 2:125–6). This notion may derive from a conflation of the passage concerning the "subverted city" (*'ir nidaḥat* – Deut., 13:13–19) and the events at Jericho (Joshua, 6) and Ai (Joshua, 7). Regarding the "subverted city" – one in which the Israelite inhabitants have gone over *en masse* to other gods – the Pentateuch instructs: "Put the inhabitants of that town to the sword and put its cattle to the sword. Doom it and all that is in it to destruction. Gather all its spoil into the open square, and burn the town and all its spoil as a holocaust to the Lord your God ..." Issuing orders just before the tumbling of Jericho's walls, Joshua warned that "the city and everything in it are to be proscribed for the Lord ... if you take anything from that which is proscribed (*ḥerem*), you will cause the camp of Israel to be proscribed; you will bring calamity upon it. All the silver and gold and objects of copper and iron are consecrated to the Lord; they must go into the treasury of the Lord." God informed Joshua that the initial debacle at Ai, the next town, was due to the presence among the Israelites of one who had taken from that which was proscribed at Jericho. This traitor must be found and "he and all that is his shall be put to the fire because he broke the covenant of the Lord and committed an outrage in Israel ... Then Joshua, and all Israel with him, took Achan son of Zerah – and the silver, the mantle and the wedge of gold [the booty he had illicitly taken] – and his sons and daughters, his ox, his ass, his flock, his tent and all his belongings,

---

and ... they put them to the fire and stoned them." The "fire from the Lord" that "descended and consumed the burnt offering, the wood, stones and earth, and licked the water that was in the trench" at the climax of Elijah's duel with the priests of Ba'al (I Kings, 18:38) may also have found its way into al-Qurṭubī's blend (this was, in fact, God's habitual manner of consuming sacrifices – see Leviticus, 9:24, and note Genesis Rabbah, 22:5, where fire descends fom heaven to devour Abel's offering), and even the mass donation of jewelery to Aaron which he melted down with fire to form the golden calf may have contributed here (Exodus, 32:1–4; see also Goitein, "Ha-dat ha-zo'efet," 8, n. 6, and Ibn Isḥāq—Guillaume, 326, where Muḥammad declares that "booty was made lawful to me as to no prophet before me"). Be that as it may, the regulations concerning the booty of the subverted city, Jericho and Ai are all situation-specific in the Biblical (and *halakhic*) view. As far as the norm went, the Israelites were in no way deprived of the spoils of their conquests: "The Lord said to Moses: 'You and Eleazar the Priest and the family heads of the community take an inventory of the booty that was captured [in the raid on Midyan], man and beast. And divide the booty equally between the combatants who engaged in the campaign and the rest of the community ...'" (Numbers, 31:25–7). See also 1 Samuel, 30:21–25, where the dispute over the spoils between those who had remained behind to guard the camp and those who had marched forward to fight is remarkably similar to that alluded to in the third and eighth chapters of the Qur'ān in connection with the Battle of Badr. The solution – a precedent-setting equal division of the booty between the two parties – is also the same in both cases. Note that in at least one other context – that of the question of the provenance of Solomon's magnificent horses (Q. 38:31) – many Muslim exegetes assume that Israelites took booty (Lassner, *Queen of Sheba*, 100 and n. 49).

(3) Earth, pebbles and chips (*'afar, tzror, qismit*) are expressly permitted as substitutes for water in "ablutions" (that is, for the purpose of obtaining *yadayim nekiyot*, "clean hands"). See Berakhot 15a.

(4, 5) Jews may pray anywhere ("Every place where I cause My name to be mentioned I will come to you and bless you," Exodus, 20:21) and alone (although collective worship – *tefilla be-tzibur* – is preferable, and there are elements of the service – *kol davar she-bi-kedusha* – which are omitted when a quorum of ten is lacking. A Jew must literally "walk a mile for a *minyan*"). It should be noted that Islamic law sees collective prayer as similarly preferable ("*qāla rasūl Allāh: ṣalāt al-jamā'a tafḍulu 'alā ṣalāt al-qadh bi-sab'in wa-'ashrīna daraja*") and al-Shāfi'ī, for one, considers it mandatory ("*lā urakhkhiṣu liman qadara 'alā ṣalāt al-jamā'a fī tark ityānihā illā min 'udhr*" – Māwardī, 2:378 ff). "He who hears the call to prayer and does not come [to the mosque]," warned the Prophet, "prays an invalid prayer (*lā ṣalāt lahu*), unless he has an acceptable excuse" (Dāraquṭnī, 1:460; Bayhaqī, 3:57).

(6) We saw above that the *lex talionis* was applied only to murder – as in the *sharī'a* – at least according to Talmudic law (Baba Qama 83b–84a).

(7) The Muslim conception that "among the Jews, when a woman began to menstruate, they would send her out of the house, and they would not eat with her, and would not drink with her, and would not remain with her in their houses" (*lā yu'ākilūhā wa-lā yushāribūhā wa-lā yujāmi'ūhā* [here denoting "be with" and not "have sex with"] *fī'l-buyūt* – Suyūṭī, 1: 258), is somewhat exaggerated, but correct in broad outline (the same may be said of the Islamic idea of the Christian attitude to the same issue, to wit, that they permit full sexual relations even in the very midst of menstruation). While mainstream Jews have never put their wives out of the house during menses, the *halakha* does prohibit eating from the same vessel as a menstruant (as a *siyag* or "fence" against being drawn into more intimate activity), and since "eat with" in the pre-modern Middle East usually meant sitting around a common bowl and taking victuals out of it all together, one could say that Jewish law forbids a man to eat with his wife during her period. Rabbinic sources frown on other types of interaction between a man and his menstruating spouse, including "idle chatter" (Avot de-Rabbi Natan 8 ff). See the comments of the Kisters, "'Al Yehudei 'Arav," 240–2. Muslim men are allowed not only to eat and fraternize with their menstruating wives, but even to engage in every intimacy with them save full-blown sexual intercourse.

(8) The Torah is indeed to be chanted in the synagogue from the text, even if one has memorized it. The rabbis conduct a lengthy discussion about whether one may cite Pentateuchal and other Biblical passages from memory (in many circumstances they ruled that one could – Gittin 60a). In a largely oral culture where Biblical scrolls and codices were hard to come by, the requirement to read from the text could certainly be considered an inconvenience.

(9) The description of Jewish Sabbath observance is on the mark.

6. Tendon of Contention

Jacob's Sciatica and Israel's Masochism[1]

Jurists and traditionists spent long hours and spilled much ink debating the question whether touching one's penis (*mass al-dhakar*) should be included among the "defiling events" (*aḥdāth*) that render a Muslim unfit for prayer until he performs ablutions (*wuḍū'*). Most of the evidence mustered by both sides in this polemic consisted of *aḥādīth al-qawl* (reports of statements) to the effect that contact with one's member did, or did not, violate ritual fitness, interspersed with occasional *aḥādīth al-fi'l* (anecdotal reports) showing important personages acting in accordance with this or that opinion.[2] To my knowledge, only one attempt was made to peg the purported *ḥadath* of *mass al-dhakar* onto a scriptural source, and it was a bold attempt.

Q. 4:43 and 5:6 both contain what is known in the *ṭahāra* code as the *mulāmasa* clause, declaring a devotee to be in need of minor purification if he has "touched women" (*lāmastum al-nisā'*).[3] Ibn Abī Shay-

---

1 Since writing this chapter I have come upon Brannon Wheeler's "Israel and the Torah of Muḥammad" in Reeves, *Bible and Qur'ān* (2003). In that essay, Wheeler investigates aspects of Jacob's sciatica and the foods he did or did not prohibit himself in its wake, albeit from somewhat different angles of approach than we have taken here. The following may thus be seen as a supplement to his discussion.

2 See, e.g., Abū Bakr Muḥammad b. Ibrāhīm b. al-Mundhir al-Naysābūrī, *Al-Awsaṭ fi'l-Sunan wa'l-Ijmā' wa'l-Ikhtilāf* (Riyāḍ: Dār al-Ṭayba, 1993), 1:193 ff; and 'Abd al-Razzāq al-Ṣan'ānī, *Muṣannaf* (Beirut: Al-Majlis al-'Ilmī, 1970), 1:87.

3 Q. 5:6 reads in full: "O ye, who believe, when you prepare for the *ṣalāt*, wash your faces and your hands up to the elbows and wipe your head and your feet up to the ankles. And if you are sexually defiled (*junuban*), purify yourselves. And if you are sick, or on a journey, or one of you cometh from the privy, or you have touched women (*aw lāmastum al-nisā'*), and you find not water, then go to clean, high ground and rub your faces and your hands with some of it. Allāh would not place a burden upon you, but He would purify you and perfect His grace upon you, that you may give thanks." On *mulāmasa* see Katz, *Body*, 87–96 and 149–155, and Maghen, *Virtues of the Flesh: Passion and Purity*

ba's *Muṣannaf* records the following tradition under the heading "Those who Opined that Feeling the Phallus Requires *Wuḍū'*":

> ... Ibn Sīrīn said: I asked 'Abīda [al-Salmānī] about God the Exalted's words: *aw lāmastum al-nisā'*. He answered by motioning with his hand, and I guessed his meaning and didn't ask him about it (*fa-qāla bi-yadihi fa-ẓanantu mā 'anā fa-lam as'alhu*). I knew that Ibn 'Umar would, if he touched his genitals, perform ablutions, and – continued Muḥammad [b. Sīrīn] – I surmised that the position of Ibn 'Umar and the position of 'Abīda were identical (*shay'un wāḥidun*).[4]

Given the context in which this *ḥadīth* is adduced; the link established by Ibn Sīrīn between what he witnessed and the practice of Ibn 'Umar; and the atmosphere of euphemism and indirect speech ("I guessed his meaning and didn't ask him about it"), we can safely assume that 'Abīda had pointed to his groin. But what has this to do with the scriptural phrase he was asked about?

To answer this question, we proceed to al-Ṭabarī's commentary on Q. 3: 93. The verse itself reads, in part: "All food was lawful to the Children of Israel, save that which Israel forbade himself (*illā mā ḥarrama Isrā'īlu 'alā nafsihi*)." What did Israel forbid himself? Al-Ṭabarī explains with the help of al-Ḍaḥḥāk [b. Muzāḥim], who said:

> Israel – that is, Jacob[5] – was seized by a pain in his sciatic tendon (*akhadhahu 'irq al-nasā*),[6] and it kept him awake at night but did not disturb him during the day (*fa-kāna lā yathbutu al-layl min al-waja' wa-kāna lā*

---

in Early Islamic Jurisprudence (Leiden: E. J. Brill, 2004). The Ḥanafiyya reject the notion that mere bodily contact between the sexes induces ritual preclusion.

4 Ibn Abī Shayba, 1: 189 (196, no. 4). It is remotely possible that *fa-qāla bi-yadihi* should be translated "and he said: 'with his hand,'" meaning that 'Abīda upheld the minority juristic position that only touching a woman with one's hand (*al-lams bi'l-yad*) – or, according to others, with any limb involved in *wuḍū'* – constitutes a prayer-precluding *ḥadath*. Were this the intent a different intepretation of the *ḥadīth* than the one we will advance would be necessary.

5 In the two places in the Qur'ān in which the name "Isrā'īl" appears alone, without the preceding "Banū" – Q. 3: 93 and Q. 19: 58 – it is considered by exegetical tradition (with good reason, given the context) to refer to Jacob.

6 Arabic *'irq* means a blood-vessel (like the Hebrew *'oreq*, artery), but can also denote a stem, a root, a sinew or a duct – including (and this is important for what follows) the spermatic duct. See Lane, 2019, col. 2. The sciatic tendon or nerve is "either of a pair of nerves, the largest in the body, that originate in the sacral plexus of the lower back and extend down the buttocks to the back of the knees ... the sciatic nerve and its branches innervate large areas of the pelvis, leg and foot" (Webster).

> *yu'dhīhi bi'l-nahār*).[7] He swore that if God cured him he would never again eat the [sciatic] tendon [in animals].[8]

Al-Qurṭubī tells a fuller story, relying on ('Abd Allāh) b. 'Abbās, Mujāhid (b. Jabr al-Makkī), Qatāda (b. Di'āma al-Sadūsī) and (Ismā'īl b. 'Abd al-Raḥmān) al-Suddī:[9]

> When Jacob – upon whom be peace – was coming back from Ḥarrān on his way to Jerusalem (*bayt al-maqdis*), fleeing from his brother Esau, who was a strong bully of a man, an angel accosted him. Jacob mistook the angel for a highwayman and strove with him to fell him (*ẓanna Ya'qūb annahu liṣṣ fa-'ālajahu an yaṣra'ahu*).[10] But the angel touched Jacob's thigh (*ghamaza*

7 Al-Ṭabarī's modern editor suggests the emendation *yabītu* for *yathbutu*, but since the Arabic root *th-b-t* is intimately related to the Hebrew *sh.b.t.*, meaning to rest or remain in one place, it is quite possible that *yathbutu* is the right reading. Other recensions of this report indeed have: "*fa-kāna yabītu wa-lahu zuqā*," (the latter word is said by Sufyān al-Thawrī to mean screaming [*ṣiyāḥ*] and is probably related to the Hebrew *z'aqa/tza'qa*). The idea that Jacob's sciatica acted up during the night and calmed down during the day is almost certainly rooted in a cycle of midrashim connected to Genesis, 32:32 ("The sun rose upon him as he passed Penuel, limping on his hip"), wherein it is claimed that "God brought the dawn two hours early that morning" (Genesis Rabbah, 68:10), and also – since the Hebrew original literally means "the sun rose *for* him" (*va-yizraḥ* lo *ha-shamesh*) – that "the sun rose *for his sake*, that is, in order to heal him (*lirfu'ato*)" (ibid., 78:5). "Behold," prophesies Malachi, "a day cometh, blazing like a furnace, and all the arrogant and all the doers of evil shall be straw, and the day that cometh shall burn them to ashes ... but unto you that fear My name, a sun of righteousness shall rise, with healing in its wings" (Malachi, 3:19–20). R. Huna said: "The sun cured Jacob, but seared Esau and his champions" (see RaDaQ to Genesis, 32:32). Another distant, antithetical contributor to these *aḥādīth* might be the quaint notion reflected in the commentary of al-Suddī, who avers that Jacob was renamed Israel at this crucial juncture because he had left Be'er Sheba' "traveling by night (*isrā' bi'l-layl* = 'Isra-el') and hiding by day" (see Wheeler, *Prophets*, 113; the seventeenth chapter of the Qur'ān is named both "Isrā'" and "Banū Isrā'īl").

8 Ṭabarī, 4:4. Other versions add: "*min al-dawābb.*" The link in the transmission chain just above al-Ḍaḥḥāk is 'Ābīd b. Sulaymān, and al-Ṭabarī's direct informant is al-Ḥusayn b. Faraj.

9 These early exegetes and traditionists died in c. 687 CE, c. 720 CE, c. 734 CE and 745 CE, respectively. I have consulted Brannon Wheeler's translation of this passage (Wheeler, *Prophets*, 115).

10 Greek-Aramaic *lisṭa*, robber, bandit. The Talmud has the angel Michael beseech Jacob, "Let me go for the day breaks." Jacob responds, "Are you a thief (*ganav*) or a gambler with dice (*kubiyostos* – Rashi: a kidnapper) that you fear the daylight?" (Ḥullin 91b). Rabbi Samuel b. Naḥmani avers that the angel appeared to Jacob disguised "as a heathen" (*'oved kokhavim*). The Biblical text does not specifically mention Jacob's attempt to "fell" the angel, relating only that they "struggled" (which, however, might be the meaning of Arabic *yaṣra'*

al-malak fakhdh Ya'qūb) and then ascended to the heavens with Jacob looking on. Jacob's sciatic tendon (*'irq al-nasā*) thereafter began to burn,[11] and he suffered intensely. He could not sleep because of the pain and he spent the night screaming (*yabītu wa-lahu zuqā' ay ṣiyāḥ*). Jacob took an oath that if God, the Mighty and Majestic, would restore him to health, he would avoid eating [that] tendon itself, and he would never again eat food containing it.[12] [After recovering] he indeed forbade it to himself, and his children after him observed [this rule regarding sciatic] tendons, removing them from their meat. And the reason why the angel touched Jacob [on that spot] was because Jacob had vowed that if God bestowed upon him twelve sons – and if he reached Jerusalem in safety – he would sacrifice the twelfth son.[13] And this [gesture of the angel] absolved him of his vow; so says Ḍaḥḥāk (*fa-kāna dhālika li'l-makhraji min nadhrihi 'an al-Ḍaḥḥāk*).[14]

---

here also), but the Midrash mentions it: "Jacob sought to overcome the angel and threw him to the ground (*hipilo*). What did the angel do? He grabbed the sciatic tendon that is in the hollow of the thigh, and Jacob's sciatic tendon was dislocated (*nashah gid ha-nasheh shelo* – Pirkei de-Rabbi Eliezer, 37 [a source post-dating the Islamic advent]).

11 At least one other commentator, when telling this story, calls the affected tissue not *'irq* but *ḥirq al-nasā* (Ibn Abī Ḥātim al-Rāzī, cited in Uri Rubin, *s. v.* "Israel," in Jane Dammen McAuliffe [ed.], *Encyclopedia of the Qur'ān* [Leiden: Brill, 2001], 2:571). The letters ḥā/he and 'ayn/'ayin are often interchangeable in Semitic languages (note, e.g., *ḥūg-'ūg* or *ḥanaq-'anaq* in Hebrew and even the *ḥilm-'ilm* association in Arabic) and Lane defines *ḥāriqa* as "the sinew that connects the thigh and the hip … it is said that when the *ḥāriqa* is displaced, a man becomes lame." The Arabic root *ḥ-r-q* means "to burn" (probably related to Hebrew *ḥ-r-kh*, "to scorch"), and this may have something to do with why Jacob's sciatic tendon became inflamed (although the verb employed by al-Qurṭubī is "*hajja*").

12 Compare Ḥizkuni to Genesis, 32:33: "It is like a person who is ailed by his head or one of his limbs, who takes upon himself never again to eat that limb [in animals], so that [this oath] will bring him a cure" (*mashal le-adam she-ḥash be-rosho o be-eḥad me-evarav, she-meqabel alav she-lo le'ekhol me-oto evar me-olam, kedei she-yehe lo ha-davar li'rfua*).

13 In Genesis 28:20–22, Jacob, having wakened from his celebrated ladder dream at Bethel, does indeed make a vow: "If God remains with me, if He protects me on this journey that I am making and gives me bread to eat and clothing to wear, and if I return safely to my father's house – the Lord shall be my God. And this stone, which I have set up as a pillar, shall be God's abode; and of all that You give me, I will set aside a tithe for you." The place where Jacob slept that night is, according to most Rabbinic opinions, the future site of the Temple Mount in Jerusalem (Genesis Rabbah, 68:9: "*va-yifga' ba-maqom – tzali be-Bayt ha-Mikdash*") – and thus al-Qurṭubī has him make his vow conditional upon returning thither – as well as the past site of Abraham's binding of Isaac (Ḥullin 91b) – and thus, perhaps, the added element of an oath to sacrifice the youngest child. This last may also have drawn upon a midrash citing the angel

Why would the angel choose specifically to touch Jacob's thigh and af-

---

Michael's reminder to Jacob at the end of their struggle that "'you promised to give a tithe of your possessions to God.' At once Jacob separated out five-hundred fifty cattle from his herds, which consisted of 5, 500 head. 'But you have sons,' continued the angel, 'and you have yet to tithe *them*.'" Jacob thereupon handed over his son Levi to the angel, who took him up to heaven, where he received the tidings that his descendants would be dedicated to the Temple (Pirkei de-Rabbi Eliezer, 27, which is, however, a very late Midrashic source. See Wheeler, "Israel and the Torah," 68–70 for Jacob's vow in general and an interesting elaboration of the tithe motif in particular). Jephtaḥ may have found his way into al-Qurṭubī's mix, as well. This mighty man of valor pledged that "whatever comes out of the door of my house to meet me *on my safe return* from [the battle against] the Ammonites shall be the Lord's, and shall be offered by me as a burnt offering" (Judges, 11:31). What came out of his door was his daughter.

Perhaps even more important than the above sources in terms of its potential *direct* influence on al-Qurṭubī's narrative is the story of ʿAbd al-Muṭṭalib – Muḥammad's grandfather – and the (re-) digging of the well of Zamzam. Encountering much opposition during this operation from the remainder of Quraysh, and having only one son at the time to support him against them, ʿAbd al-Muṭṭalib vowed that "if he should have ten sons to grow up and protect him, he would sacrifice one of them to God at the Kaʿba" (see Q. 6:138). He was indeed blessed thereafter with ten sons, and when the last of these was born, he assembled his progeny in front of the god Hubal to see which of them was to be offered up. The arrows were cast and the lot fell on ʿAbd Allāh, the youngest and his father's favorite. ʿAbd al-Muṭṭalib led ʿAbd Allāh to the feet of Isāf and Nā'ila [two idols at which the Quraysh would offer their animal oblations] and took a large knife with which to sacrifice his son. At the last moment his hand was stayed by his fellow Qurashites, who warned ʿAbd al-Muṭṭalib against such a drastic deed and the terrible, decimating precedent it would set, and offered to redeem his son "though his ransom be all our property." After consulting, at their urging, a certain Khaybarian sorceress (whose heritage no doubt afforded her a suggestion for how to end the story happily), ʿAbd al-Muṭṭalib returned to the *ḥarām* and proposed ten camels to Hubal against the life of ʿAbd Allāh. The arrows indicating that the idol still preferred the boy's blood, ʿAbd al-Muṭṭalib added ten more camels to the pot for a total of twenty, and so on until Hubal was finally satisfied with the offer of one hundred camels. These were slaughtered instead of ʿAbd Allāh, Muḥammad's father, whom ʿAbd al-Muṭṭalib had sought to sacrifice, just as a ram was slaughtered instead of Isaac, Jacob's father, whom Abraham had sought to sacrifice (Ibn Isḥāq — Guillaume, 66–8; Ibn Hishām, 1:140–3; Genesis, 22; see G. R. Hawting, "The Disappearance and Rediscovery of Zamzam and the 'Well of the Kaʿba'," *BSOAS* 43 [1980]). For such "mythomorphism" in general see Newby, *Last Prophet*, introduction, esp. 21–3. Sale points out that ʿAbd Allāh was not the youngest son, since Hamza and al-ʿĀbbās were younger (Sale, "Preliminary Discourse," 29, n. 2), but they may have been born after these events.

14 Qurṭubī, 4:118.

flict his sciatic tendon in order to signify that the eponymous begetter of the twelve tribes was released from the vow to sacrifice his last-born son? Let us glance quickly at the Biblical version of the story. On the eve of his much feared reunion with his brother, Jacob sent his wives, children and possessions across the ford of Jabbok, after which

> Jacob remained alone. And a man wrestled with him until the break of day. When [the man] saw that he could not prevail against [Jacob], he touched the hollow of his thigh (*va-yiga' be-khaf yerekho*), and the hollow of Jacob's thigh was strained as he wrestled with him. Then [the man] said, "Let me go, for the dawn is breaking." Jacob answered, "I will not let you go unless you bless me." "What is your name?" asked the other. "Jacob," he replied. "Your name shall no longer be Jacob, but Israel (*yisra El*), for you have striven with God and with men, and have prevailed"... And the sun rose upon [Jacob-Israel] as he passed over Peniel, limping on his thigh. Therefore the Children of Israel do not eat the sciatic sinew which is upon the hollow of the thigh (*gid ha-nasheh asher 'al kaf ha-yarekh*), because [the "man"] had touched the hollow of Jacob's thigh at the place of the sciatic sinew (Genesis, 32:25–33).

One widely circulated midrash interprets the words "he touched the hollow of his thigh," to mean "he touched the righteous men and women, prophets and prophetesses who would descend from him (*naga' ba-tzadikim u-va-tzadikot, ba-nevi'im u-va-nevi'ot she-hen 'atidin lavo mimenu*)."[15] Just as in the conclusion of al-Qurṭubī's description of the same events, so in this midrash: contact with the sciatic tendon (*gid ha-nasheh*) on the inside of the thigh (*kaf ha-yarekh*) is taken to imply a statement about progeny. It should by now be clear, then, that this body part can be employed as a euphemism for the male genitalia (the "touching" – i.e., striking or grabbing – of which is a classic resort of those losing a fight). Support for this hypothesis may be found in other contexts, such as the inventory taken in Genesis 46:26 of "all the people who came down to Egypt with Jacob, his own offspring (*yotz'ei yerekho*, lit. 'those who issued from his thigh,'), aside from his daughters-in-law ..."[16]; or Abraham's request of his servant in Gen-

---

15 Genesis Rabbah, 77:3. Nachmanides, who adopts the tradition that the "man" grappling with Jacob was "Esau's angel," explains his touching of the sciatic tendon as a foreshadowing of the horrors that Rome (Esau) would inflict on Israel's *descendents* (see his commentary to Genesis 32:33).

16 The Talmudic statement that "the foetus is [like] the thigh of its mother" (*'ubar yarekh imo*), though intended to express the notion that an unborn child is not an independent entity, may also harbor relevance for this metaphoric thigh-

esis 24: 2: "Place, I pray thee, thy hand underneath my thigh (*taḥat yerekhi*), and swear to me ..." (whence "*testi*-mony"). The Hebrew *gid* (sinew, tendon, vein) is itself regularly employed by the Talmud as a metonym for the penis.[17]

The *gid ha-nasheh* is, of course, the *ʿirq al-nasā*, and we are now in a better position to venture a guess about ʿAbīda al-Salmānī's employment of the Qur'ānic clause "*aw lāmastum al-nisā'*" (in the *ḥadīth* of Ibn Sīrīn with which we launched this discussion) to support the pollutive potency of *mass al-dhakar.* ʿAbīda, it seems, either made a play on words or followed a different "reading" of this scriptural phrase: not "[you must perform ablutions if] you touched *women* (*lāmastum al-*

---

genitalia connection. See also Megilla, 13a: "*ayn ha-isha mitqan'a ela be-yarekh ḥavertah,*" where the thigh clearly represents the uterus, and Ḥizquni to the priest's adjuration of the "wayward woman" (*isha soṭa*) in Numbers 5: 22 (*scil.*, "May the Lord make you a curse and an imprecation among your people, as He causes your thigh to sag and your belly to distend"): "*yerekhekh – hi bayt ha-rekhem.*"

17 E.g., Qiddushin 25a ("*sirus de-gid*"); Rashi to Deut., 23: 2 ("*u-khrut shofkha – she-nikhrat ha-gid ve-shuv aino yore kiluaḥ zera*ʿ"). The Biblical exegete Moses b. Ezra specifically mentions the theory that *gid ha-nasheh* refers to the male member, although he appears to disapprove of it (see his commentary to Genesis, 32: 33, where the text may be deficient: "There is no doubt that [the term *gid ha-nasheh* is derived from *nasha,* 'was dislocated'], except among fools and children [?] who interpret it to mean the member [*ha-evar*]"). Note, also, RaDaQ to Genesis, 32: 26: "'And he touched the hollow of his thigh,' – [by this act the angel] hinted to Jacob that he would be pained by [the fate of] one of those who issued from his thigh (*ramaz lo be-ze she-yikh'av me-eḥad me-yotz'ei yerekho*), and this refers to his daughter [Dina] who was raped by a Canaanite [Sheḥem son of Ḥamor]." It should be remembered, however, as a counter to all this theorizing, that in the end (as the Bible itself tells us) the Jews refrained from eating not testicles, but the sciatic nerve.

We might, it is true, suggest an alternative understanding of al-Qurṭubī's statement that "Jacob had vowed that if God bestowed upon him twelve sons, *and if he reached Jerusalem in safety,* he would sacrifice the twelfth son. And this [gesture of the angel] absolved him of his vow." The Arabic for "reaching Jerusalem in safety" is *atā bayt al-maqdis* saḥīḥan, which might be better translated "[if he] reached Jerusalem *in good health.*" If this is the correct rendering, then we need not posit that the angel touched Jacob's *genitals*, thereby indicating that he should refrain from sacrificing his progeny. Rather, we can stay with the literal text and accept that the angel injured Jacob's sciatic nerve, thus causing him to be in a state of *ill health* and thereby releasing him from his vow. Nevertheless, the parallel in the Hebrew original is *ve-shavti be-shalom,* which is probably closer to "and I return safely." *W'Allāhu aʿlam.*

nisā')," but "[you must perform ablutions if] you touched *the sciatic tendon*, i.e., *the penis* (*lāmastum al-nasā*)."[18]

The prohibition against consuming the *'irq al-nasā* is, of course, merely another link in the heavy chain that once bound the Banū Isrā'īl and still binds the Yahūd.[19] The Muslims were assured by Q. 6: 146 that this

18 Both Katz (*Body*, 129) and Wheeler ("Israel and the Torah," 62–9) have remarked instructively on aspects of the *nisā-nasā* relationship, the latter even adducing evidence that suggests a connection between Jacob's injury and circumcision. The transposition or word play may even go in the opposite direction, i.e. from "sciatic tendon/phallus" to "women." Ibn Ezra mentions the claim (though he dismisses it) that *nasheh* is from *nashim*, women. RaDaQ on Genesis, 32: 26 notes that "the word 'hollow' [in 'hollow of the thigh'] connotes the feminine" (*'kaf' lashon nekeva* – perhaps because it evokes concavity; and we just saw the RaDaQ, in the previous note, associate it with Dina); the Talmud explains the etymology of *nasheh* thus: "It [*viz.*, Jacob's tendon] slipped away [*nasha*] from its place and rose up, as it is written, "Their strength has slipped away, they are become as women" (*nashta gevuratam hayu le-nashim* – Jeremiah, 51: 30). Al-Ṭabarī adduces a report about a bedouin (that is, a bumpkin) who approached Ibn 'Abbās and informed him that he had forbidden his wife to himself (*innahu ja'ala imra'tahu 'alayhi ḥarāman*). Ibn 'Abbās rejected his interlocutor's right to declare such a ban: "She is *not* prohibited to you," he scolded (cp. Q. 2: 226: "Those who swear that they will not have intercourse with their wives should wait no more than four months ..." This was evidently a common *jāhilī* oath, regarding which Ibn 'Abbās held a lone dissenting opinion [see Qurṭubī, 3: 93; cp. Ketubot 70a and Nedarim 15b]). The Bedouin protested: "But does not God – by God! – state clearly in His Book that 'All food was lawful to the Children of Israel, save that which Israel forbade himself?'" Ibn 'Abbās laughed heartily: "Don't you know what it was that Israel [i.e. Jacob] forbade to himself?!" Then he went out to speak to the people, explaining: "Jacob was afflicted by his sciatic tendon (*'irq al-nasā*), and he swore that if God cured him of this that he would never again eat this tendon. [Turning to the bedouin, he concluded:] So your wife is not prohibited to you!" (Ṭabarī, 4: 5–6). It is probable that all the bedouin meant by his citation of scripture was that if Jacob could forbid himself things that were not originally forbidden by God, then he, the bedouin, could do the same. But there is a slight possibility that Ibn 'Abbās was so entertained because the bedouin had heard the story of Jacob prohibiting to himself the *nasā* and (especially given his probable ignorance of such technical – and probably calqued – anatomical terms) mistakenly concluded that Jacob had sworn off of his *nisā'*, his wives – bringing us full circle to 'Abīda and Q. 4: 43/5: 6.

19 In general – and there are many exceptions to this – one may say that the "Banū Isrā'īl" lived in ancient days, whereas the "Yahūd" are their descendents of either Muḥammad's time (or thereabouts), or the time at which a given medieval writer is writing (see Goitein's excellent review of this issue in *EI*², *s. v.* "Banū Isrā'īl"). While most Muslim exegetes regard the Yahūd and their relig-

restriction did not apply to them: "Say [O Muḥammad]: I find not in that which is revealed unto me aught forbidden to an eater to eat thereof, except it be carrion, or *blood poured forth*, or swine ..." Remarks 'Ikrima: "Were it not for this verse, the Muslims would have observed concerning the veins in meat what the Jews observe."[20] "What the Jews observe" in this connection is also associated by Muslim tradition with the *halakhic* kashering process of salting and soaking meat in order to extract the blood. The Mālikī Ibn Khuwayzmindād (or Ibn Khuwayzī Mandād) declared: "Blood is forbidden as long as [the avoidance or removal of it] does not entail pervasive inconvenience (*mā lam ta'umm bihi al-balwā*), such as in the case of blood on one's person or garment [which must be removed before prayer]; but blood is permitted whenever [the avoidance or removal of it] *does* entail pervasive inconvenience, such as in the case of blood in meat and its arteries."[21] 'Ā'isha narrated:

> We would cook [meat in] pots (*kunnā naṭbakhu al-burma*) during the lifetime of the Messenger of God, and the pots would become suffused with blackness from the blood (? *ta'lūhā al-ṣufra min al-dam*).[22] We would dine on this fare without reservation, because taking care [to eliminate the blood from the meat] is an encumbrance and involves much difficulty, and [our] religion has been divested of encumbrances and difficulties (*li-anna al-taḥaffuẓ min hādha iṣrun wa-fīhi mashaqqa, wa'l-iṣr wa'l-mashaqqa fī al-dīni mawḍū'*).[23]

Al-Qurṭubī comments on this *ḥadīth* as follows: "This is a basic principle of Islamic law: whenever the community of believers finds the execution of a commandment (or: the performance of a ritual – *adā'*

---

ious system as a (according to some, evolutionary) continuation of the Banū Isrā'īl and their religious system, there is a small dissenting minority, which includes the eleventh century jurist of the Ẓāhirī *madhhab*, Abū Muḥammad 'Alī b. Aḥmad b. Ḥazm, that denies this continuum (see Adang, *Muslim Writers*, 94–109).

20 Ṭabarī, 8:94 (no. 10959): "*law lā hādhihi al-āya la-tatabba'u al-Muslimūn [min?] 'urūq al-laḥm mā tatabba'hā al-Yahūd.*"

21 Qurṭubī, 2:197.

22 The color indicated by the root *ṣ.f.r.* in its various forms is not always easy to establish. In different contexts it might denote black, yellow, orange (saffron) or even – considering that the *baqaratun ṣafrā'un* of Q. 2:69 almost definitely refers to the Pentateuch's red heifer – light or bright red (and thus we could perhaps read here that "the pots were suffused with the *redness* of the blood").

23 Qurṭubī, 2:197.

'ibāda) oppressive, they are made exempt from that commandment (*saqaṭat al-'ibāda 'anhā*)."[24]
In order to flesh out the full significance of the dietary provision regarding the sciatic vein for the general effort to paint the Israelites as antonymous to Islamic *rukhṣa,* we need to consider the triad of verses from Sūrat Āl 'Imrān reputedly connected to it (we have already quoted part of the first verse):

> All food was lawful to the Children of Israel, save that which Israel forbade himself before the Torah was revealed (*min qabli an tunazzala al-Tawrātu*). Say [O Muḥammad, to the Jews]: Produce the Torah and read it to us if you are truthful! Whosoever forges a falsehood concerning God (*man iftarā 'alā Allāhi*) after this, such are the wrong-doers. Say: Believe God, and follow the religion of Abraham, the upright – he was not of the idolators (Q. 3: 93–5).

What was this polemic about? Al-Ṭabarī and al-Qurṭubī survey the range of interpretations, which are separated by subtle but significant nuances. The material is extensive and confusing (perhaps even to the compilers themselves, as we shall see), and we shall do our best to summarize and simplify it.

All exegetes and traditionists agree that before the theophany at Sinai every kind of animal was *ḥalāl* (permitted) for the Israelites (as it had been for mankind in general since Noah),[25] and that the bone of contention in these verses concerned the questions whether, when, why and by whom particular foodstuffs were eventually forbidden to them. There is also a general consensus among the commentators that the

---

24 Ibid. This is a basic principle of Jewish law as well. Note that al-Qurṭubī's statement is not couched in a way that necessarily limits its application to the Prophet's time. Even if *rukhṣa per se* is confined to the period of revelation and is a prerogative of the Deity – and this is far from clear (see above, chap. 2, n. 40) – the concessionary spirit that characterized it continued to inform the unfolding of *fiqh* and the creation of *sharī'a,* and a method often difficult to distinguish from *rukhṣa* was regularly employed by jurists over the centuries when faced with problematic situations.

25 Recall the first of al-Qurṭubī's examples of abrogation in the Biblical tradition (in the context of his refutation of Jewish arguments against *naskh*): "God the Exalted declared to Noah upon his exit from the ark, 'Behold, I have made all beasts food for you and for your descendents, and I have given you free rein [to consume] these just as [you have heretofore eaten] herbage – with the exception of blood, which you shall not eat.' Then, subsequently, God forbad Moses and the Children of Israel a great many animals."

Jews are portrayed in this passage as guilty of lying (specifically, to Muḥammad). What did they lie about?

According to one group of opinions, the Jews averred that they were expressly commanded by God in the Torah to refrain from eating the meat surrounding the sciatic tendon.[26] Such a claim, testifies al-Ṭabarī, is a calumny against God:

> This was in no way forbidden to them by God in the Torah. Rather, they forbade it to themselves in conformity with [the practice of] their father [Jacob-Israel] and then afterwards ascribed its prohibition to God (*ḥarramūhu ʿalā anfusihum ittibāʿan li-abīhim thumma aḍāfū taḥrīmahu ilā Allāh*). God, the Mighty and Majestic, therefore gave them the lie, instructing His Prophet thus: "Say to them, O Muḥammad: 'If you [Jews] are truthful, then bring forth the Torah and read it (*atū bi'l-Tawrāt fa-utlūhā*): we will then see whether that [prohibition] is found in it or not!'" [This was done in order] that their deceit might be shown clearly to anyone ignorant of their affair (*li-yatabayyana kidhbuhum li-man yajhalu amrahum*).[27]

A second batch of interpretations accuses the Jews of what is essentially the same dissimulation, but in connection with a different victual:

> ... from Ibn Jurayj, from ʿAbd Allāh b. Kathīr, who said: We heard that [Jacob] suffered from an illness, and they say that it was sciatica. He said: Lord, my favorite foods are camel meat and camel milk (*luḥūm al-ibil wa-albānahā*). If you make me well, I will prohibit these to myself! Ibn Jurayj said: ʿAṭā' b. Abī Rabāḥ said: Israel (i.e., Jacob) forbade the meat and milk of camels.[28]

---

26 Many Jews avoid sirloin to this day, since such meat borders on the *gid ha-nasheh* (see Mishna Ḥullin, 7:2 and 5; Genesis Rabbah, 78:6).

27 Ṭabarī, 4:4.

28 Ibid., 4:7. A similar explanation is attributed to the Prophet himself, who is approached by a group of Jews (*ʿaṣāba min al-Yahūd*) who challenge him to "tell us about the food our father Israel had prohibited to himself prior to the revelation of the Torah" (*yā Abā Qāsim, akhbirnā ayy al-ṭaʿām ḥarrama Isrā'īl ʿalā nafsihi min qabli an tunazzala al-Tawrāt*). Muḥammad replied, "I adjure you by the One who revealed the Torah to Moses! Are you aware that Israel-Jacob (*Isrā'īl Yaʿqūb*) became deathly ill, and that his illness continued for a long time (*ṭāla saqamuhu*), and that he vowed a vow to God that if He would cure him of his illness he would abjure his most beloved food and drink, and that his favorite food was camel flesh, and his favorite drink camel milk?" They answered, "By God, that's right!" Ṭabarī, 4:9. In other versions, this question is part of a larger quiz, which Muḥammad passes easily – see Ibn Isḥāq—Guillaume, 255, and Wheeler, *Prophets,* 115–6. This is one of the ubiquitous "*miḥan al-Yahūd,*" see Wheeler, "Israel and the Torah," 71 and n. 22. See also

Some reports describe how Jacob's sciatica was aggravated by the ingestion of camel flesh,[29] others how the "physicians" prescribed avoidance of camel flesh to combat his sciatica,[30] still others how eating the part of the camel containing the sciatic tendon had made him ill in the first place,[31] and a lone opinion that the only food that relieved his sciatica was camel flesh.[32] As a consequence of at least one of these situations – conclude these interpretations – Jacob solemnly swore off camel meat (and milk) forever, his descendents following suit. This is what actually transpired, but the Jews claimed otherwise. They maintained that none other than God Himself had forbade them these camel products through the medium of official Torah revelations. "If so," Muḥammad is instructed by Allāh to demand of them, "then produce the Torah and read it to us!" (Q. 3: 93). For – so we are assured by the commentators – "they lied: it is not in the Torah."[33] "Such was never prohibited in the Torah."[34]

---

ibid., p. 72, where a report of al-Tirmidhī is cited to the effect that "Israel was a nomad, and his sciatic sinew became afflicted, and he found nothing that would ease his pain except camel meat and milk, so this he prohibited." It may be fruitful to analyze such statements in light of the negatively valenced Israelite sedentarization process – adumbrated in the agricultural fare they demand to be fed – depicted in Q. 2: 61. The prohibition of camel meat and milk referred to in these many passages may also reflect the Jewish prohibition on the consumption of any meat and dairy products together, a rule the Biblical derivation of which is also problematic.

29 Ṭabarī, 4: 8.

30 Qurṭubī, 4: 119: "*lammā aṣāb Ya'qūba 'irqu al-nasā waṣafa al-aṭṭibā' lahu an yajtanib luḥūm al-ibil.*"

31 Ṭabarī, 4: 9.

32 Qurṭubī, 4: 118: "*kāna yaskunu al-badw fa-ishtakā 'irq al-nasā fa-lam yajid shay'an yulā'imuhu illā luḥūm al-ibil wa-albānahā, fa-li-dhālika ḥarramahā.*" The idea seems to be that he would symbolize his gratitude for the cure by abstaining from the food that helped cure him, or, perhaps, that – having been the only food that agreed with him during his illness – camel milk and meat reminded him of being sick, and so he avoided it from then on.

33 Ṭabarī, 4: 5: "*wa-kadhabū: laysa fī'l-Tawrāt.*"

34 Qurṭubī, 4: 120. See, however, Leviticus, 11: 1–4 (where there is no connection to Jacob): "And the Lord spoke to Moses and Aaron, saying to them: Speak to the Children of Israel thus: These are the creatures that you may eat from among all the land animals: any animal that has true hoofs, with clefts through the hoofs, and that chews the cud – such you may eat. The following, however, from among those that either chew the cud or have true hoofs, you shall not eat: the camel – although it chews the cud, it has no true hoofs: it is unclean for you ..." The claim of late *taḥrīf* – i.e. that the Jews have altered their scriptures

"God did not forbid Israel or his offspring sciatic tendons or camel flesh and milk," elaborates al-Ṭabarī, addressing himself to the Jews on God's behalf. "Rather, this was something that Israel forbade to himself and to his descendents[35] without God ever having forbidden it in the Torah ... And you, O community of Jews (*yā ma'shar al-Yahūd*), you prevaricate in assigning such a scriptural prohibition to Him, and you slander God and assert regarding Him that which is untrue."[36]

> Say, O Muḥammad, to the Jews who allege that God prohibited tendons, camel meat and camel milk in the Torah: "Bring the Torah and read it!" So that their endemic mendaciousness and the falsehoods they spread concerning God will be disclosed to anyone unaware of their true nature ... Allāh informed His Apostle of the Jews' libelous claims about Himself in this matter so that Muḥammad's knowledge of the subject would serve as an argument against them (*ḥujja lahu 'alayhim*). For inasmuch as many of their own people were ignorant of this issue, and since Muḥammad was illiterate and not even a member of their folk, one would certainly have expected him *not* to know [the truth about these foods and their prohibition] (i.e. that God had nothing to do with the matter). And this was one of the most powerful proofs to them that he was the Prophet of God (*wa-kāna dhālika lahu min a'ẓam al-ḥujja 'alayhim bi-annahu nabī Allāh*).[37]

So far we have surveyed two different interpretations of Q.3:93–5, both of which divest God of responsibility for dietary restrictions that Islamic tradition saw as one more example of the *athqāl* and *aghlāl* (burdens and chains) that characterize Judaism. In both cases – that of

---

since the coming of the Qur'ān – might possibly be made in this case, but I have not encountered it. We shall see momentarily that many *muḥaddithūn* take the opposite stance – that the prohibition on camel flesh *is* in the Torah though the Jews tried to hide it – and in the context of his commentary on Q.6:145 al-Ṭabarī adduces the opinions of several *ṣaḥāba* and *tābi'ūn* to the effect that Allāh prohibited the camel (*al-ba'īr, al-ibil*) to the Jews in the Torah (see below).

35 This is, in a sense, another variant: instead of the Children of Israel abstaining from such foodstuffs in order to perpetuate their venerable ancestor's custom, the initiative is taken away from them and given to Jacob. He enjoins his children and the future generations to observe this precept (see Ṭabarī, 4:4: "*fa-inna dhālika ḥarāmun 'alā wuldihi bi-taḥrīm Isrā'īl iyyāha 'alā wuldihi*"; Qurṭubī, 4:119: "*inna Isrā'īl qāla ḥīna aṣābahu 'irq al-nasā: wa'llāhi la-in 'āfānī Allāhu minhu lā ya'kuluhu lī walad*").

36 Ṭabarī, 4:10.

37 Ṭabarī, 4:9. These lines appear in the exegesis of the final verse of our triad: "Say: Believe God, and follow the religion of Abraham, the upright; he was not of the idolators."

the ban on sciatic tendons and that of the proscription of camel products – the purported Jewish claim that God Himself had enacted those laws and inscribed them in the Torah is declared spurious. A third and final analysis of the significance of this Qur'ānic passage takes what appears, at least at the outset, to be the opposite tack. According to this approach, the Jews insisted that God and the Torah were specifically *not* involved in their decision to abstain from the sciatic tendon and/or camel products, that they had established this practice solely in order to imitate their father Jacob's behavior (*wulduhu ḥarramūhu istinānan bi-abīhim*),[38] and that they continued to maintain it to this day entirely of their own accord. "God did not prohibit anything to us," they would say. "Rather, *we* prohibited to ourselves that which Israel prohibited to himself."[39] The challenge from the Muslim side in *this* case to "produce the Torah and read it" is issued for a purpose diametrically antithetical to that envisioned by the earlier analyses. Here the objective is to confirm that the sacred document does indeed contain the prohibitions in question. To elucidate this position, Q. 3: 94 is paraphrased by al-Ṭabarī:

> And bring, O Jews – if you deny [that Allāh forbad these foodstuffs] – bring the Torah and read it, if you are telling the truth when you say that God did not forbid these things to you in the Torah, and that you yourselves prohibited them solely in conformity with Israel's denial of them to himself.[40]

The facts were otherwise: "*God* forbad them those very things that Israel had denied to himself ... and that they had subsequently forbidden to themselves in honor of Jacob's self-denial."[41] "God prohibited [the sciatic tendon and/or camel products] to the Jews in the Torah ... and then said [in refutation of their claims to legislative independence]: 'No one has forbidden this but Me! (*mā ḥarrama hādhā ghayrī*).'[42]

To sum up this third and final understanding of the polemic reflected in Q. 3: 93–5: the Jews allege that (a) Jacob forbade himself the sciatic tendon and/or camel products; (b) Jacob's offspring turned their father's personal vow into a family – and eventually a tribal and national – tradition; and (c) God had nothing to say on this subject at

38 Ṭabarī, 4: 3.

39 Qurṭubī, 7: 102: "*Inna Allāha lam yuḥarrim 'alaynā shay'an, wa-innamā naḥnu ḥarramnā 'alā anfusinā mā ḥarrama Isrā'īl 'alā nafsihi.*"

40 Ṭabarī, 4: 4.

41 Ibid., 4: 3.

42 Ibid.

Sinai, and the Jews have continued observing this precept (or these precepts) on their own authority to this day. The Muslims accept (a) and (b), but reject (c). According to their version of Biblical historiography, God confirmed and reinforced the heretofore tradition-based Jewish self-prohibitions of tendons and camels through the medium of canonization. He enshrined these statutes in the Torah.[43]

If the reader is dizzy, so was al-Ṭabarī. Attempting to make some sense out of this jumble of mutually exclusive theories – and trying especially to reconcile the claim advanced by certain Muslim *mufassirūn* that the dietary restrictions in question are *not* found in the Torah with the claim of other commentators that they most definitely are – he took the road of compromise: "The position closest to the truth (*awlā al-aqwāl fī dhālika*) is that ... [the given foodstuff] was prohibited to the Children of Israel prior to the Torah on account of their father Jacob having forbidden it to them, whereas God had yet to intervene through revelation of any kind (*[lā] fī tanzīl wa-lā bi-waḥy*). [Thus matters remained] until the Torah was revealed, at which time God forbade them in it what He wished and permitted them in it what He wished (*ḥarrama Allāhu 'alayhim fīhā mā shā'a wa-aḥalla lahum fīhā mā shā'a*)."[44] This is a decision not to decide.[45]

---

43 In this sense, too, Jewish experience as portrayed here is the photographic negative of Muslim experience: whereas in Islam religion gets easier over time (as we saw in chap. 2), in Judaism religion gets harder over time (for which tendency see below, the conclusion of chap. 7, especially p. 142–3).

44 Ṭabarī, 4: 5.

45 All of this confusion did not arise out of the blue. The Biblical passage itself leaves room for ambiguity, indeed, for the specific type of ambiguity that informs the intra-Islamic debate we have been outlining. The Hebrew original of the first clause of Genesis, 32: 33 is open to two possible renderings (especially when isolated from the remainder of the verse, a common phenomenon in Midrashic methodology): *'al ken lo yokhlu Benei Yisra'el et gid ha-nasheh* could mean either (1) "Therefore the Children of Israel *do* not eat the sciatic sinew [which is upon the hollow of the thigh, because (the 'man') had touched the hollow of Jacob's thigh at the place of the sciatic sinew"]..." or (2) "Therefore the Children of Israel *must* not eat the sciatic sinew ..." (see, for instance, Exodus, 12: 43, where *kol ben nekhar* lo yokhal *bo* means not "no stranger *will* eat of it" but "no stranger *may* eat of it"). The first reading would be consistent with the first Islamic exegetical claim we have been discussing – that the avoidance of the sciatic tendon is a tribal tradition of the Children of Israel that was never enjoined upon them by God – because it relates an anecdote rather than issuing a command ("... the Children of Israel *do* not ... because the man had touched ..."). The second reading is consistent with the second Islamic asser-

In the end, however, al-Ṭabarī's diplomatic approach is justified, because a minute's probing reveals that the various attitudes surveyed

---

tion we have delineated – that God strengthened an already extant Israelite custom by transforming it into an official Biblical precept – because "the Children of Israel *must* not," comprises an unmistakable command (the "narrator" in the Pentateuch is its divine Author, and no one else is quoted in this verse). The anonymous but much respected work *Sefer HaḤinukh*, which enumerates and elucidates the 613 Biblical precepts (and which was probably composed in Barcelona not long after the time of al-Qurṭubī), addresses this very question in its entry on the *mitzvah* of avoiding the sciatic tendon in terms strikingly similar to the internal Islamic deliberations we have surveyed: "The words *lo yokhlu* [in Genesis, 32:33] are not intended as narrative (*lo ne'emar derekh sipur*), as if to say, 'because this event happened to the father the children refrain from eating the tendon' (*mipnei she-era' davar ze ba-av nimna'im ha-banim mi-le'ekhol gid*). Rather, it is a warning from God that they *must* not eat it" (H. D. Chavel, ed., *Sefer HaḤinukh* [Jerusalem: Mosad HaRav Cook, 5716], 57). More than this: while delving into the intricate details involved in observing the law of *gid ha-nasheh*, the Talmud plays host to the following debate. "Rabbi Judah said: 'Was not the sciatic tendon forbidden at the time of the sons of Jacob?' [The other rabbis] said to him: 'Does [the verse] say, "Therefore the Children of *Jacob* do not eat ..."? No. It says, "Therefore the Children of *Israel* do not eat ..." – and they were not called "the Children of Israel" until Sinai. Thus [we must disagree with you, Rabbi Judah, and affirm that] the prohibition [against eating the sciatic tendon] was issued at Sinai [and was not observed by Jacob's immediate descendents], but was inserted into its present position [in the story of Jacob wrestling with the angel] in order to inform us of the original reason for its prohibition.' Rava raised an objection [to the claim that they were not called "Children of Israel" until Sinai]: 'Is it not written, "And the *Children of Israel* carried Jacob their father [down to Egypt]..."? [Genesis, 46:5 – thus they were styled "Children of Israel" long before the Theophany].' [The rabbis answered:] 'That was immediately after the event [of Jacob's renaming, and therefore the new name was specially emphasized (??)].' Rabbi Aḥa the son of Rava [came to the aid of his father and] said to Rabbi Ashi: 'In that case, the prohibition should have been instituted from that moment [when they were first referred to as "Children of Israel,"] onward [instead of being instituted at Sinai]!' Rabbi Ashi replied: 'Was the Torah revealed piecemeal?! (*ve-khi Torah p'amim p'amim nitna?* – [this is not the twenty-odd years of intermittent, circumstance-tied, often abrogating and abrogated messages sent down discontinuously by Allāh to Muḥammad in the Islamic revelatory *process*! – ZM]).'" And so the Talmudic debate continues ... (Ḥullin, 101b).

The present writer has argued elsewhere against the claims of Geiger, Muir, Goldziher, Wensinck, Schacht, Rosenthal, Wansbrough, Crone and others that many specific Islamic ritual regulations, and even the legal debates and methodologies surrounding them in the *fiqh* literature, were influenced by – when they were not virtual carbon copies of – Jewish *halakha* ("Dead Tradition: Joseph Schacht and the Origins of Popular Practice," *Islamic Law and So-*

thus far are not as disparate as they seem. Ultimately, they amount to the same fundamental statement: restrictions are bad things. This is easily seen when we ask why – according to the third and final approach detailed above – God saw fit to give His stamp of approval to the austere and unpleasant practice of sciatic tendon removal and/or eschewal of gourmet dromedary products?[46] Is He not, after all, the unsurpassed advocate of ease and inveterate enemy of hardship? The answer to this question is unanimous among those who support this third thesis: far from an *endorsement* of such burdensome observances, Allāh's imposition of the same upon the Banū Isrā'īl shows that He views severity in religion as a curse – a curse eminently suited for smiting Israelites. God's ratification through revelation of the hardships that the Jews had placed upon themselves was His way of punishing

---

ciety 10: 3 [September 2003]; "First Blood: Purity, Edibility and the Independence of Islamic Jurisprudence," *Der Islam* 81: 1 [April 2004]). When – as in the cases examined in those essays – the energies of Muslim jurists were directed entirely toward the *internal* elaboration of their *own* system of law, with no reference whatsoever to Jewish norms; and when, on top of this, few if any parallels can be found in the *halakha* to the deliberations and conclusions of the *fuqahā'*; in such situations one is certainly not justified in asserting Jewish influence. In the present instance, however, in which the efforts of Muslim exegetes are consciously and avowedly focused on the elucidation not of Muslim but specifically of *Jewish* law and tradition (Qur'ānic exegesis having functioned as a segue into this endeavor); and in which the parallels in Jewish *midrash halakha* are extremely clear and strong; in such a situation one is no less unjustified in *not* asserting (primarily unidirectional Jewish → Muslim) influence. The internal Islamic debate on the subject of *'irq al-nasā* outlined in the works of al-Ṭabarī, al-Qurṭubī and elsewhere is unquestionably a high-fidelity echo of the internal Jewish (Talmudic and post-Talmudic) debate on the subject of *gid ha-nasheh* (and this says much about the profound extent of intellectual exchange between Muslims and Jews in both *maghrib* and *mashriq*). The main difference lies in the use to which this issue was put by Muslim traditionists and commentators: unlike the Jewish case, here the question is valenced, as we have seen, and is made into an important milestone in the historic saga of macrocosmic *rukhṣa-naskh*. We shall encounter an even more powerful example of this phenomenon below, in the final chapter.

46 We saw that camel products were considered a delicacy by Jacob, a portrayal which obviously bears witness to the tastes of the authors of these anecdotes more than it does to those of their protagonist. As for the rigors involved in removing the sciatic tendon, the Mishna determines that "butchers are not deemed trustworthy in the matter [of removing the sciatic tendon]" because it is extremely difficult to extract properly (Mishna Ḥullin, 7: 1). One receives forty stripes for eating the sciatic tendon deliberately (Ibid., 7: 3).

them for their crimes (*innamā ḥarramnā dhālika 'alayhim 'uqūbatan bi-baghyihim*).[47]

What crimes? Well, for one, the crime of placing hardships upon themselves. There is a persistent undercurrent in the Islamic sources on this subject of "You asked for it, you got it." "God forbade the Jews in the Torah that which Israel had forbade himself," explains al-Ṭabarī, "as a penalty for the injustices they had perpetrated against themselves and for their oppression of their own souls (*bi-baghyhim 'alā anfusihum wa-ẓulmihim lahā*)."[48] Admittedly, the Islamic term *ẓulm al-nafs* has a semantic latitude that encompasses transitive as well as reflexive intent, and sometimes it combines the two (witness Moses' lament/reproof: "O my people! You have wronged yourselves [*ẓalamtum anfusakum*] by choosing the calf. So turn in penance to your Creator ..." Q. 2:54).[49] Nevertheless, it is unquestionably significant that the literal meaning of the expression concerns harm done to oneself (al-Qurṭubī, commenting on the phrase *ẓulm al-nafs*, explains that "we say of anyone who does something that redounds to his detriment: 'you have aggrieved your own soul'").[50] Thus, for instance, when the Qur'ān speaks of the Israelites' reticence to partake of the smorgasbord furnished by their Lord in the wilderness – and accuses them, in consequence, of bringing their troubles down upon their own heads – it employs similar terminology:

> And we caused the white clouds to give you shade, and sent down upon you the manna and quails, saying: Eat of the good things wherewith We have provided you – We wronged them not, but they were wont to wrong themselves (*wa-mā ẓalamūnā wa-lākin kānū anfusahum yaẓlimūn* – Q. 2:57).[51]

---

47 Ṭabarī, 8:102.

48 Ṭabarī, 4:4.

49 There is in this both the sense of sinning against oneself and the sense of sinning against heaven. Similarly, when Mā'iz b. Mālik of the Aslam tribe came to the Prophet to confess having committed adultery, he fell to his knees and cried: "O Messenger of God! I have darkened my soul through fornication!" (*qad ẓalamtu nafsī wa-zanaytu* – Muslim, *Kitāb al-Ḥudūd*, 29:1692). He has sinned against God, his wife and himself all at once. See also the similar usage attributed to the Queen of Sheba, Q. 27:44 (Lassner, *Queen of Sheba*, 66).

50 Qurṭubī, 1:385: "*yuqālu li-kulli man fa'ala fi'lan ya'ūdu 'alayhi ḍararuhu: innamā asa'ta ilā nafsika.*"

51 Or: "They wronged *Us* not, but they were wont ..." It is interesting that the Biblical story here alluded to contains a piquant example of such "watch what you ask for" theology: "Say [O Moses] to the people: 'Be ready for tomorrow,

Our claim, then, that at least one of the Deity's motivations for entering Jacob's special diet onto the divine law books was to penalize his descendents "for the injustices they had perpetrated against themselves and their oppression of their own souls" through the adoption of difficult practices, is not entirely without foundation. In Q. 16: 118, indeed, the two notions of self-oppression and divine prohibition are combined and causally related: "And unto those who are Jews, We have forbidden that which We have already related to you (i.e. certain tasty foods); We wronged them not, but they wronged themselves."[52] The Banū Isrā'īl, by augmenting their religion with all sorts of superfluous and unreasonable constraints, had fashioned and foreshadowed their own punishment, which the Lord then took up and meted out to them measure for measure. This divine policy is well encapsulated in the Prophet's warning: "Do not take upon yourselves excessive hardships, lest God inflict hardship upon you" (*lā tushaddidū 'alā anfusikum fa-yushaddida Allāhu 'alaykum*).[53] Because they had adopted unnecessary stringencies not enjoined upon them by Allāh – in this case, with regard

---

and you shall eat meat, for you have kept whining before the Lord and saying, "If only we had meat to eat! Indeed, we were better off in Egypt!" Very well: the Lord will give you meat, and you shall eat. You shall eat not one day, not two, not even five days, or ten, or twenty, but a whole month – until it comes out of your noses! (*'ad asher yetze me-apkhem* – Numbers, 11: 18–20).'" Following a similar principle, because Pharaoh had hardened his heart, the Lord hardened Pharaoh's heart even more (Exodus, chapters 8 and 9). This is also a familiar Qur'ānic motif/rhythm: "When [the hypocrites] fall in with those who believe, they say: 'We believe!'; but when they go apart to their own devils they declare: 'Lo! We are with you; we were only mocking.' Allāh will mock *them*, and leave them to wander blindly on in their contumacy" (Q. 2: 14–15). "Whosoever is in error, let God increase him in error!" (Q. 19: 76). Many punishments in the Islamic version of hell involve the sinner being forced to commit a transgression that s/he had committed in life, but this time *ad nauseum* and *ad infinitum.*

52 "*ḥarramnā mā qaṣaṣnā 'alayka*" presumably refers to Q. 6: 147, which we shall examine presently. The verses leading up to this one further clarify its import in this connection: "So eat of the lawful and good food which Allāh has provided for you, and thank the bounty of your Lord if it is Him you serve. He has forbidden to you only carrion and blood and swine-flesh and that which has been sacrificed to other than Allāh ... And utter not, concerning that which your own tongues qualify (as legally edible or inedible), the falsehood: 'This is lawful and this is unlawful' (*hādhā ḥalālun wa-hādhā ḥarāmun*), forging thereby a fabrication concerning Allāh. Lo! Those who invent a lie about Allāh will not succeed" (Q. 16: 114–16).

53 Baghawī, 4: 137; Kister, "Concessions," 91.

to *'irq al-nasā* and *luḥūm al-ibil* – Allāh therefore "went them one better" and etched those same stringencies into scriptural stone, rendering prohibitions that had been merely optional up to that point strictly mandatory from then on. God hurts those who hurt themselves.[54]

In this connection, we should make our way back momentarily to the microcosmic plane of intra-Islamic *rukhṣa-naskh*, and recall the manner in which *tahajjud* became temporarily obligatory for the community of believers. According to al-Ṭabarī, at first the Prophet alone had been commanded to "rise at night" and engage in supererogatory supplications. However, word soon got out about Muḥammad's extraordinary practice and the Muslims assembled in front of his house/mosque in the moonlight, seeking to imitate their Excellent Exemplar. He went out to them affecting a stern mien and demanded that they disperse, "fearing lest nocturnal devotions be prescribed for them also." "Take upon yourselves only those acts of which you are capable!" he had cautioned them. But it was too late. Allāh had marked the gathering and descried the eagerness, and He forthwith imposed the obligation to "rise at night" upon the entire *umma*. The results, as we saw, were disastrous, and *naskh* had eventually to be deployed to relieve the exhausted Muslim community.

This process parallels, in telescoped fashion, what we have just witnessed in the historical macrocosm (or the Jewish microcosm). The Muslims sought to follow Muḥammad's *sunna* and add an extra set of devotions to their litany; the Jews sought to follow Jacob's *sunna*[55] and augment the category of unkosher foods. As a consequence, God *obligated* the Muslims in that which they had *volunteered* to do, just as he had obligated the Jews in that which *they* had volunteered to do.[56] In

54 This notion is further confirmed and elaborated below, especially in chapter 7.

55 This is al-Ṭabarī's usage, as we saw: "*wulduhu ḥarramūhu* istinānan *bi-abīhim.*" The Talmud explains Isaiah's statement, "The Lord sent a word unto Jacob, and it hath lighted upon Israel" (*davar shalakh be-Ya'kov ve-nafal be-Yisra'el* – Isaiah, 9:7) thus: "The Lord sent a word [*davar* can also mean a thing, or even damage (like *dever, hadbara*)] unto Jacob ..." – this is [the injury to his] sciatic tendon; "... and it hath lighted upon Israel" – for the prohibition thereof has spread throughout Israel (Ḥullin, 91a). Note, in this connection, that Heb. *mila* similarly means both "word" and "cutting" (and thus also circumcision – see above, note 18).

56 *Minhag Yisra'el din hu*, goes the famous Talmudic phrase: "The custom of Israel eventually becomes its law."

neither case was this maneuver successful in the long term: the Muslims soon found themselves hanging by ropes, the Jews shackled by chains. Finally, *rukhṣa* through *naskh* brought deliverance to the fatigued Muslims in the microcosm when the *farīḍa* of *qiyām al-layl* was abolished in favor of a less grueling provision. The Jews in the macrocosm were also offered a means of escape from their incomparably difficult lifestyle: through the abrogation of Judaism by Islam.[57]

57 "God, praise Him, forbade [the Jews] all these things in the Torah in punishment for their lying... then God abrogated all of that in favor of the law of Muḥammad (*thumma nasakha Allāhu dhālika kullahu bi-sharīʿati Muḥammadin*) permitting them that which had been forbidden to them and removing the straitness (*ḥaraj*) through Muḥammad, and He obligated all people in the religion of Islam, in that which it permits and that which it forbids, in that which it commands and that which it proscribes" (Qurṭubī, 7: 103).

7. Ask Not

The Banū Isrā'īl Heap Hardship upon Themselves

The "you asked for it, you got it" motif is nowhere better illustrated than in the traditional commentary surrounding the "flagship verses" of Sūrat al-Baqara:

> When Moses said to his people: "God commands you to sacrifice a cow," they replied: "Are you making game of us?" "God forbid that I should be so foolish!" he rejoined. "Call on your Lord," they said, "to make known to us what kind of cow she shall be." Moses replied: "Your Lord says, 'Let her be neither an old cow nor a young heifer, but in between' – do, therefore, as you are bidden." "Call on your Lord," they said, "to make known to us what her color shall be." Moses replied: "Your Lord says: 'Let the cow be yellow (alternately: orange, red, or even black – *ṣafrā'*)[1], a rich hue pleasing to the beholder.'" "Call on your Lord," they said, "to make known to us the exact type of cow she shall be; for to us all cows look alike. If God wills we shall be rightly guided." Moses replied: "Your Lord says: 'Let her be a cow not subjected by ploughing the soil or watering the tilth,[2]

---

1 For speculation by an unidentified exegete that *ṣafrā'un* here means black, see Ṭabarī, 1:490 (al-Ṭabarī himself confutes this notion). The heifer in the Jewish case is definitely red (*t'mimah be-admumiyut* – RaSHI to Numbers, 19:2) and may not have even two black hairs (ibid.). The Talmud goes so far as to warn that in case the creature refuses to come along and one wants to encourage it by bringing out a fellow cow, the latter must not be black (Yoma 2a). See above, chap. 6, n. 22. Genesis Rabbah to Numbers 19:2 plays on the formulation: "Instruct the Children of Israel to bring *unto you* a red cow …" and reads into these words a divine promise to Moses: "This cow will forever bear your name, and will be known as 'the cow that Moses offered in the desert.'" Bona fide crimson cows being an extreme rarity in all periods (the Talmud claims there were ten throughout history), modern Hebrew has bestowed this honor on the ladybug instead, naming it *parat Moshe Rabbenu*, "Our Master Moses' Cow."

2 According to a minority opinion among the commentators, *innahā baqaratun lā dhalūlun* tuthīr al-arḍa *wa-lā tasqī al-hartha* means rather "a cow not subjected which, *though she plough the soil*, does not water the tilth" (see Qurṭubī 1:428). The presence of the "not watering the tilth" clause, absent from the list

> a cow whole and without blemish." "Now you have come with the truth," they answered, and they sacrificed it, though they had nearly failed to do so. And when you slew a man and fell out with one another concerning him, God made known what you concealed. We (Allāh) said: "Strike him with part of it!" Thus does God restore the dead to life and show you His signs that you may grow in understanding (Q. 2: 67–73).

To make sense of this typically cryptic passage, and of its elucidation and elaboration in the *tafsīr*,[3] we need to recollect at least two Biblical prescriptions and adduce a minimum of two Rabbinic anecdotes. The first Biblical prescription is taken from Numbers 19:

> The Lord spoke to Moses and Aaron, saying: This is the law of the Torah that the Lord has commanded: Instruct the Children of Israel to bring unto you a red cow without blemish, in which there is no defect and *upon which no yoke has been laid*... And whoever comes into contact *in the open field with one who has been slain by the sword* or who died naturally, or with a human bone or with a grave, shall be unclean seven days. And they shall take for the unclean person from the ashes of the burnt purification (i.e. the immolated cow, seasoned while burning with cedar wood, hyssop and scarlet stuff) and fresh water shall be added to them in a vessel. And a clean person shall take hyssop, dip it in [the resultant solution], and sprinkle it on ... him who touched bones or a corpse ...

The second Biblical prescription is found in Deuteronomy 21:

> If, in the land that the Lord your God is giving you to possess, *someone slain is found lying in the open field*, the identity of the slayer not being known, then your elders and magistrates shall go out and measure the distance from the corpse to the nearby towns. The elders of the town found to be nearest the corpse shall then take a calf *which has never been worked, which has never pulled in a yoke*, and bring it down to a rugged wadi which is *neither tilled nor sown*. There, in the wadi, they shall break the calf's neck (or: decapitate it) ... Then all the elders of the town nearest to the corpse shall wash their hands over the calf whose neck was broken ... and they shall declare: "Our hands did not shed this blood ..."

---

of Biblical criteria for a qualified red heifer and irrelevant in most of Arabia, might possibly supply ammunition to those who claim that the Qur'ān is a product of riparian Iraq.

3 Its elucidation and elaboration in the *fiqh* is focused on the institution of *qasāma* – a collective oath of innocence taken by residents of a locality in which (or closest to which) a murdered corpse has been found – and has been covered comprehensively by Patricia Crone, "Jāhilī and Jewish Law." See also Ruud Peters, "Murder in Khaybar: Some Thoughts on the Origins of the Qasāma Procedure in Islamic Law," *Islamic Law and Society* 9 (2002).

From the Babylonian Talmud (Kiddushin 31a) we have this quaint anecdote:

> Rav 'Ula was asked to what lengths one should go in honoring father and mother. He answered: Come and see what a certain heathen from Ashqelon by the name of Dama b. Netina did. Once the sages sought to purchase from him precious stones for the priestly ephod, and were willing to pay 600,000 pieces – Rabbi Kahana taught: 800,000 pieces – but the key [to the storehouse where the gems were kept] was under his father's pillow, and he refused to wake his father [and lost the sale] (*ve-haya hamafte'akh munaḥ taḥat me-ra'ashotav shel aviv ve-lo-tzi'aro*). The following year God rewarded him [for honoring his father to such a degree] and a red heifer was born in his herd. The sages of Israel came to his house [seeking to buy the heifer]. He said to them: "I know that were I to ask for it I could obtain any price from you, but I ask nothing of you except the money I lost [last year] by honoring my father."

Finally, the midrash (Pesikta Rabbati 14) delivers the following story:

> It once happened that Israel was in need of a red heifer but could not find one. Finally they found what they were looking for in the possession of a heathen. They said to him, "Sell us your cow." He replied, "I will part from it for three (alternately: four) gold pieces." The Israelites answered: "We will pay what you ask." [Since they had accepted so readily without even bargaining] the heathen divined, while they had gone off to fetch the sum, how greatly they were in need of his cow, and [upon their return] he said to them, "I will not sell it to you." The Israelites persisted: "Perhaps you are seeking a higher price? ..." – and [they negotiated with him] until they agreed to pay him one thousand gold pieces. What did that wicked man do? He summoned a friend of his, also a gentile, and said to him: "Watch now how I put one over on the Jews! (*bo ur'e hay'akh ani mesaḥeq ba-yehudim*). I will take the yoke and secretly place it on my cow (thus rendering the creature invalid for use in the all-essential purification ceremony), and I will take their money [and give them a worthless beast in exchange]." He took his yoke and placed it on the cow all night long. On the morrow, when he brought the cow out [to the Israelite representatives], they began to examine it and noticed that two hairs which had been standing on end the previous day were now flattened, and that the cow had become cross-eyed [from looking at the yoke]. They said to [the owner of the cow]: "Keep your cow, and save such games for your mother!" (*ṭol paratkha sḥok be-imkha*). [Amazed at their discovery of his ruse, the cow owner] began to intone, "Blessed be He who chose this nation!" Then he hung himself.[4]

4 See also Yerushalmi Pe'ah, 1:1, in connection with this and the previously adduced gemara.

From these Judeo-classical ingredients – modified to suit Islamic theology, conflated and concatenated to resolve a specific exegetical difficulty, and supplemented by the creative imagination of the *quṣṣāṣ* (storytellers) – Muslim tradition produced the following widely circulated narrative (we translate here at some length from one of the many versions recorded by al-Ṭabarī):

> We were told by Mūsā, who said: 'Amrū related to me that Asbāṭ[5] related to him that he had it from al-Suddī [that the circumstances surrounding the revelation of Q. 2:67–73 were as follows]: There was a man of the Children of Israel who was very wealthy,[6] and he had a lone daughter and a nephew of meager means. The nephew asked his uncle for his daughter's hand in marriage, but the uncle refused. Enraged, the young man declared: "I will kill my uncle, inherit his property, marry his daughter, and benefit from his blood money!" (*la-aqtulanna 'ammī wa-la-akhudhanna mālahu wa-la-ankaḥanna ibnatahu wa-la-akulanna diyatahu*).[7] In the meantime merchants had arrived from abroad to trade with one of the Israelite tribes, and the young man approached his uncle and said: "O Uncle! Set out with me [to the territory of that tribe] and help me do business with these men, perchance I shall make a profit. For when they see you with me, they are sure to grant me [their business]."
>
> So the uncle set out with his nephew at night, and when they arrived at [the territory of] that tribe, the young man killed his uncle, [left his body lying there] and returned home to his people. On the morrow he came [to his uncle's house] pretending to seek his uncle, as if he didn't know where he was and couldn't find him. Setting out in search of him, he found [his corpse] surrounded by a large crowd of people. "You have killed my uncle!" he cried. "Now pay me his blood money!" (*qataltum 'ammī fa-*

5 Asbāṭ is a proper name but also the plural of *sabaṭ* (Heb. *shevet*) meaning either "grandchild" or "Israelite tribe." It is perhaps noteworthy that the *matn* following this *isnād* consists of a story involving the territorial constellation of Israelite tribes (*asbāṭ*) in the Holy Land, together with a judgement by Moses, another name gracing the transmission chain. Mūsā ← 'Amrū ← Asbāṭ ← al-Suddī is, however, a very common *isnād* preceding anecdotes that may be characterized as belonging to the genre of *Isrā'īliyyāt*.

6 Some versions give him the name 'Āmīl.

7 Presumably the nephew was the heir since the uncle had no male offspring. According to other recensions of this *ḥadīth* the wealthy man "had no children, and he had a relative who was his heir" (*la yakun lahu walad wa-kāna lahu qarīb wa-kāna wārithuhu*). There is no spurned marriage proposal in those versions, and the only motive for murder is money (that may also be the only *true* motive, of course, in the recension we are currently examining).

addū ilayya diyatahu).[8] And he began weeping and strewing dust on his head and calling out, "Oh, Uncle!"

The nephew hauled [the representatives of that tribe] before Moses, and Moses decreed that they must pay him the blood money.[9] They, however, beseeched him: "O Messenger of God! Postpone the implementation of your decree[10] until such time as we discover the actual perpetrator. For by God, even though the sum is paltry [when divided among us], we do not want the shame of this blot upon our name." It was in allusion to this series of events that God, may He be praised and extolled, revealed: "And when you slew a man and fell out with one another concerning him, God made known what you concealed" (Q. 2: 72. The remainder of our anecdote relates, in somewhat roundabout fashion, *how* God made known what had been concealed). Moses responded to them: "[Very well, in that case,] God commands you to sacrifice a cow!" (Q. 2: 67). The tribal representatives were perplexed: "We ask you about a murdered man and about the identity of his murderer, and you tell us to sacrifice a cow? Are you mocking us?! (*nas'aluka 'an al-qatīl wa-'amman qatalahu wa-taqūlu tadhbaḥū baqaratan – a-tahza'a binā?*). Moses responded: "God forbid that I should be so foolish!"

Ibn 'Abbās said: "Had the Children of Israel then simply gone out and taken the first cow available and slaughtered it, this would have sufficed for them (because in the revelation so far, God had merely commanded them to "sacrifice a cow" – any cow). Instead, they insisted on making the matter more difficult and pestering Moses [with additional questions geared to further focusing the commandment, and in retaliation for this] God did indeed make the matter more difficult for them (*wa-lākinuhum shaddadū wa-ta'annatū Mūsā fa-shaddada Allāhu 'alayhim*).[11]

8 The whole first section of this tale has no rabbinic parallel, so far as I can tell, although it certainly reads like a common ancient literary topos. This part of the story leads up to a *demand for the wergild* on the part of the scheming nephew. Given the trans-linguistic wordplay often characterizing Qur'ān-Tawrāt commentary (see above, chap. 5, notes 2 and 28; below in the present chapter, n. 37; and chap. 8, n. 21), could there possibly be any significance to the fact that the hero of the previously cited anecdote in Talmud Qiddushin is cryptically named Dama b. Netina – literally: "Blood/Money [*dam/damim*], son of Give"? Could this in any way have contributed to the nephew's demand, especially as formulated in alternate versions of our *ḥadīth*: "Give me the blood"?

9 *'Iṣma* or no, here is an erring prophet (of course, some Muslim theories of prophetic infallibility allow for errors of this type).

10 This *ud' lanā* (from the root *d.'.*), especially considering its placement in the story, may well be influenced by the repeated *ud'u lanā* (from the root *d.'.w*) of Q. 67–71.

11 For this particular sort of measure-for-measure rhythm, see above, chap. 6, n. 51.

(After asking their series of questions – recorded in Q.2:68–71 – which led to the progressive circumscription of the precept, the Children of Israel were finally satisfied and declared to Moses: "Now you have come with the truth!" [Q.2:71]). They then set out in search of [a cow that fulfilled all the recently revealed divine requirements] but could not find one. Now, there was a man of the Children of Israel who was among the most reverential of people toward his father (*min abarr al-nās bi-abihi*). A man once came to see him bearing an exquisite pearl. "Will you buy this pearl from me for 70,000?" he asked.[12] But the [first man's] father was sleeping at the time, and the key [to the vault where the money was kept] was under his head (*fa-kāna abūhu nā'iman taḥta ra'sihi al-miftāḥ*), so the young man (*al-fatā*) replied: "As you are! If you will but be patient until my father wakes up, I will buy that pearl from you for 80,000!" The owner of the pearl shot back: "Wake your father now, and I will give it to you for 60,000!" And the bargaining in this vein continued until the pearl owner offered to sell his merchandise on the spot for 30,000 and the young man offered to buy it when his father woke up for no less than 100,000. When the visitor persisted, the young man finally exploded: "No, by God! I will never buy this pearl from you for any price!" And he refused to wake his father.

And God compensated the young man for the loss of that pearl by granting him that cow [that the Children of Israel had so far failed to find] (*fa-'awwaḍahu Allāhu min dhālika al-lu'lu' an ja'ala lahu tilka al-baqara*). The Children of Israel then passed by, and they espied the very cow they were seeking at his house. They offered to trade him [the price of?] a cow for his cow, but he refused. Then they doubled their offer, but he still refused, and they kept adding to the sum until it reached [the worth of?] ten cows, but he was adamant in his refusal. They said: "By God! We will not leave you alone until we take this cow off your hands!" and they brought him before Moses. "O Prophet of God!" they addressed him. "We finally found the cow in this fellow's possession, but he refuses to sell it to us – and we gave him a good price!" (*wa-qad a'ṭaynāhu thamanan*). Moses said to the man: "Sell them your cow!" The man replied: "O Messenger of God – I've a greater right to my property [than they do]!" (*anā aḥaqqu bi-mālī*). Moses said: "You are right."[13] He turned to his people: "Satisfy your comrade!" So they offered him the weight of the cow in gold, but he refused; and they multiplied their offer as before, until they reached the sum of ten times the weight of the cow in gold. To this the young man agreed, and he sold them his cow and took its price.

Moses then commanded [the elders of the tribe accused of responsibility for the murder of the uncle]: "Sacrifice it!" And they did so. Then he said: "Strike him with part of it!" (Q.2:73). And they struck [the uncle's corpse]

12 Here the hero is buyer; in the Rabbinic version, seller.

13 *Ṣadaqta.* Again, a prophet stands corrected.

> with a hunk of flesh from between the cow's shoulder blades, and he revived. They asked him: "Who killed you?" He answered: "My nephew – for he schemed: 'I'll kill him, take his money and marry his daughter!'" Then the uncle dropped dead again.[14] And they took the lad (i.e. the nephew – *al-ghulām*) and killed him.[15]

As usual, there is more going on in this lengthy passage in terms of sources, influences and references than we can possibly tackle here. The major points, however, may be touched upon. First, and most conspicuous, is the highly imaginative amalgamation of two Biblical precepts that are, in their Judaic context, entirely unrelated: *para aduma* (the red heifer) and *'egla 'arufa* (the decapitated calf).[16] A number of suggestive similarities between the two institutions no doubt facilitated this merger (although these similar features do not seem to have impressed the rabbis, as there is no more connection between the two ordinances in the Talmud or midrash than in the Torah). As we saw above in the Pentateuchal excerpts, in both cases the animal in question must never have pulled the plough.[17] Both passages refer to an encounter with someone slain lying in the field. Both bovines are slaughtered as part of a ceremony designed to lift the stain of death impurity: the cow literally (its ashes combined with immersion water cleanse "the father of fathers of all ritual pollution" – *avi avot ha-ṭum'a* – incurred through contact with the dead) and the calf metaphorically (murder is the ultimate moral impurity). Neither animal is killed in the framework

---

14 Crone – who only alludes to this story, and who makes the strange claim that "Sūra 2:63 ff is a paraphrase of Deuteronomy 21:1–9" (Crone, "Jāhilī and Jewish law," 176) – notes interestingly in another connection that in pseudo-Jonathan the "decapitated calf" ceremony has become a magical method for identifying the killer: after the calf is slaughtered, worms will emerge from its excreta and crawl over the guilty party (ibid, 167).

15 Ṭabarī, 1:481–2 (no. 980). Though it is ubiquitous in medieval *tafsīr*, many latter day Muslim commentaries on the Qur'ān either ignore or deny the legitimacy of this story, as part of their campaign against the *Isrā'īliyyāt* (see above, chap. 4, end of n. 8). These modern exegetes generally propose that the referent object of "when you killed a man ..." (Q. 2:72) is Jesus.

16 This was already recognized by Hirschfeld (Hartwig Hirschfeld, *New Researches into the Composition and Exegesis of the Qoran* [London: Royal Asiatic Society, 1902], 108).

17 A stipulation (repeated, as we saw, in Q. 2:71) that also reminds us of the Qur'ānic/Bedouin anti-agrarian motif, especially when we note that the wadi where the calf's neck is to be broken must similarly be "neither tilled nor sown" (*asher lo ye'abed ve-lo yizare'a* [Deut. 21:4] – a veritable "*wādin ghayr dhī zar'in*" [Q. 14:37]). See above, chap. 6, n. 28.

of the sacrificial system of the Tabernacle/Temple cult. Their age requirement is close (*'egla bat shnatah u-fara bat shnatayim*),[18] and both must be virgins.[19] All of these comparable characteristics and associations probably *paved the way* for the fusion of the two institutions in Islamic tradition. But the immediate impetus for such conflation was more likely a two-pronged exegetical problem.

First, what is the connection between the divine-human dialogue regarding the heifer (Q. 2:67–71) and the pair of verses immediately following it (Q. 2:72–3: "And when you slew a man and fell out with one another concerning him ... We said: 'Strike him with part of it!'...")? On the face of it, the juxtaposition of these passages is meaningless. Yet Q. 2:72–3 makes no sense in isolation either. Second, when Moses brought the Israelites news of God's injunction: "Allāh commands you to sacrifice a cow!", what made them respond: "Are you making fun of us?!" Given the prevalance of sacrificial rites in so many societies and religions throughout the ancient world, on top of the well-known centrality of the same to the Israelite Temple cult, the Jews' rejoinder to

---

18 Mishna Para, 1:1; Tractate Rosh HaShana 22a; Numbers Rabbah, 19:1: "A one year old calf and a two year old cow." This is the sole Rabbinic statement I have found that contains references to both institutions, and even here there is no real connection being made between them: we have to do rather with a convenient mnemonic or legal aphorism (the Bible's crimson cow is compared to, and seen as atonement for, another calf – the Golden Calf [Numbers Rabbah, 19:4] – and so is the Qur'ān's bright yellow (= golden?) cow [see Qurṭubī, 1:422]). The red heifer can nevertheless be older than two years according to other sources, whereas the calf cannot (see Para, 1:1–2; Gittin 60a; according to Para 1:1, however, the majority of sages claim that even the calf can be slightly older: "A two year old calf and a three year old cow"). Even though the *halakha* does not permit Jews to "take a [red] calf and let it grow into a [red] cow" (Yalquṭ Ḥuqat 8), the "cow-as mature-calf" idea may have influenced the Islamic story that we shall cite presently of a boy who grows up to be a man and goes to look for his childhood calf that has grown up to be a red cow, and then sells it to the Israelites who use it to for *'egla 'arufa/qaṣāma* purposes.

19 At least no one must have seen them mounted. "Let *that which has born no fruit*" says the Talmud regarding the *'egla 'arufa* (Soṭa 46a), "be killed in a place that bears no fruit, in order to atone for [the murdered man] who will bear no more fruit." In Mishna Para 2:1 we read that "Rabbi Eliezer says, If the red heifer for the sin offering were with young, it is valid; but the sages declare it invalid." A strikingly similar debate in the *tafsīr* (see, e.g., Qurṭubī, 1:425 and 428) regarding whether "the cow" needs to be a virgin follows the rabbis in connecting the scriptural "subjection to a yoke" (Qur'ānic *dhalūl*) either with being mounted by the male or with the hard work involved in carrying the pregnancy to term.

Moses seems strange – another *non sequitur.* True, we could perhaps argue that the general decline of sacrifice as a religious device by the advent of Islam (and Islam's own restriction of rampant *jāhilī* sacrifice to a handful of occasions, especially *'īd al-aḍḥā/qurbān* and *yawm al-aḍḥā*), rendered the practice somewhat strange in the eyes of those responsible for the content of the Qur'ān, and that they projected their feelings onto their protagonists. But this is an argument of which pious Muslim commentators could not avail themselves.

We might also propose that those who brought the Qur'ān into being were at least dimly aware of the ubiquitous portrayal of the red heifer in Jewish sources as an exasperatingly unfathomable precept:

> A heathen queried Rabbi Yoḥanan ben Zakkai: "These rites which you perform look like mumbo-jumbo to me (*ilin milei de-aton 'avdin nir'in keman kshafim*). You bring close and burn a heifer, mash it, take its ashes, and if one amongst you is polluted through contact with a [human] corpse, you sprinkle him [with a solution of those ashes and flowing water] on the third and seventh day of his impurity and declare: Lo, thou art clean!" (*taharta*). (The rabbi provided a bogus answer that satisfied his challenger, who thereupon departed, at which point) his students said to Rabbi Yoḥanan: "Master, you have fobbed this fellow off with a twig – but what will you say to us?" The rabbi answered: "By your lives! Neither does the corpse pollute, nor does the water [mixed with the heifer's ashes] purify. Rather, the Holy One, blessed be He, stated: 'I have enacted a law and ordained an ordinance (*ḥuqa ḥaqqaqti gzeira gazarti*) and you may not transgress my commandment,' [as it is written regarding the red heifer]: "This is the *law* of the Torah ..." [*zot* ḥuqat *ha-torah*].' "[20]

> The apparel of those occupied in the preparation of the heifer, from the beginning until the end of the process, is contaminated, whereas the [ash-water mixture derived from] the heifer itself purifies apparel! [What sense does that make?]. The Holy One, blessed be He, said [in response]: 'I have enacted a law and ordained an ordinance, and you are not authorized to transgress my ordinance!' (*ḥoq ḥaqqaqti gzeira gazarti i ata rashai la'avor 'al gzeirati*).[21]

---

20 Tanḥuma Ḥuqat 8; Psikta de-Rav Kahana (Dov Ber Mandelbaum [ed.], New York: Jewish Publication Society, 1986), 1: 74. See also RaSHI to Numbers, 19: 2: " 'This is the *law* of the Torah ...' – [This emphasis is] on account of the fact that Satan and the nations of the world disparage Israel, saying: 'What kind of commandment is this, and what possible meaning can it have?!' (*mah ha-mitzvah ha-zot u-mah ṭa'am yesh bah*); therefore the Lord designated it a *ḥoq*, by which term He intended to convey that 'This is My decree, and you have no right to reflect upon it!' "

21 Numbers Rabbah, 19: 1; Ḥullin 29b; see also Qohelet Rabbah, 5: 5.

Ḥoq/ḥuqa/ḥuqim is the Rabbinic label for divine statutes which are incomprehensible to human reason.[22] The ritual of the red heifer is considered by the Talmud and midrashim to be the preeminent example of this type of commandment, inscrutable even to the most sagacious of scholars. History's wisest man, King Solomon, is made to admit as much in a Rabbinic paraphrase of Ecclesiastes 7:23: "All these things I mastered, *but the issue of the red heifer – I researched and inquired and investigated it*; I thought I could fathom it, but it eludes me."[23] It is possible, then, that a vague (or not so vague) Muslim awareness of this pervasive Judaic perception of *para aduma* as the epitome of incomprehensibility is what lurks behind the reaction of the Banū Isrā'īl in Q. 2:68: "Are you making game of us?" – that is, "What kind of crazy commandment is this?!" Since the Qur'ān is almost invariably formulated as a terse summary or shorthand reminder of phenomena it assumes are known in greater detail to most of its readers/hearers, it would not be out of character for the text to expect us to fold into Moses' original communication – "God commands you to sacrifice a cow" – the entire panoply of obscure rituals and internal contradictions notoriously associated by Jewish and perhaps pan-Semitic tradition with the red heifer. In such a case it would not be surprising for the Qur'ān's Israelites to have reacted to what sounded to them like a great deal of tangled rigamarole by asking Moses if he was pulling their leg.[24]

22 It has been argued that the traditional Judaic division of the Pentateuchal code into rational and non-rational commandments was influenced by Mu'tazilism (see above, chap. 1, n. 5), but whether this claim is founded or not, the Talmudic/Midrashic passage just cited shows that the notion of an inscrutable divine injunction was alive and well known long before the arrival of Islam.

23 Numbers Rabbah, 19:3. Moses was nevertheless said to have been initiated into its secret logic, ibid. 19:4.

24 As Rabbi Yoḥanan's students had, in a sense, reacted to his initial exposition in the above excerpt. It should not be argued against this attempt to discover the original intent of the Qur'ān here that the verses following "Are you making game of us?" show the Jews *themselves* complicating matters and helping to construct an incorrigible institution, and that the Qur'ān would not present the Jews as cultivating complication immediately after displaying surprise at it. This would be to accept the traditional exegetical take on Q. 2:68–71 according to which the trio of questions posed by the Jews led to the difficult nature of the heifer precept. But Rabbinic sources do not see the multiplicity of the creature's specifications as the problematic or curious aspect of this commandment, but rather the underlying irrationality of the procedure itself, and this may be the outlook actually reflected in the Qur'ān. Of course, it is entirely possible that the Qur'ān has indeed merged the precepts of *para aduma* and *'egla 'arufa*

But the *mufassirūn* do not opt for this explanation either, for theirs is a diametrically antithetical agenda, as we shall soon see.

The solution provided by Muslim tradition to this textual problem takes yet another leaf from the book of Rabbinic methodology: the widely applied principle of scriptural exegesis known as *'ayn muqdam u-me'uḥar ba-Torah* – "there is [not necessarily] a proper chronological progression in [every narrative of] the Torah."[25] Al-Qurṭubī lists a series of his predecessors' suggestions regarding the proper way to understand Q. 2: 67–73, all of which come down to this: either (1) "His words: 'When you slew a man and fell out with one another concerning him ...' (Q. 2: 72) were revealed *before* His command to sacrifice the cow" (Q. 2: 67) (*wa-yajūzu an yakūna qawluhu "wa-idh qataltum nafsan" fī nuzūl muqaddaman wa'l-amr bi'l-dhabḥ mu'akhkharan*); or (2) the verses were indeed revealed in the order in which they are currently found in the Qur'ānic codex, but they should be *understood* as if Q. 2: 72 preceded Q. 2: 67.[26] This suggested reordering underlies – or, perhaps more plausibly, is a product of – the lengthy *ḥadīth*-story at the center of this discussion. That account, it will be recalled, began with a murder and an argument about it (purportedly alluded to in Q. 2: 72: "When you slew a man and fell out with one another concerning him ..."), followed by an appeal to Moses to allow the allegedly offending tribe time to investigate and home in on the actual killer. God/ Moses decide to save the tribe the trouble: if they sacrifice a cow, the Prophet intimates, the murder mystery will unravel (the first half of Q. 2: 67). This statement makes little sense to the tribal leaders – "What does a cow have to do with a murdered man?" (*mā al-baqara wa'l-qatīl?*)[27] – and so they protest: "Are you making game of us?" (the second half of Q. 2: 67). Moses assures his people that he is deadly serious, and they then begin to delve into the particular features of the sacrificial victim (Q. 2: 68 through the first half of Q. 2: 71). When they finally feel that they have grasped the matter, they go off in search of just

and that the *ḥadīth* in the *tafsīr* is a product of – and not the motivation for construing – this scriptural conception.

25 See, e.g., Pesakhim 6b; Brakhot 7b. This principle is, I think, even more suited to the Qur'ān – a book in which chronological narrative is a rarity and in the redaction of which under the *khulafā al-rāshidīn* chronology played no known role – than to the Bible, a book which contains a more-or-less orderly exposition of purported historical events.

26 Qurṭubī, 1: 422.

27 Ṭabarī, 1: 483.

the right animal. They find it with a certain fellow, and now we are in Talmudic territory (about which more in a moment). After much haggling they purchase the rare specimen for an exhorbitant price and slaughter it (*fa-dhabaḥūhā*... – the second half of Q. 2: 71). Following Moses' instructions, they then strike the corpse with a chunk of the cow's tissue, and the dead man comes to life temporarily in order to finger his despatcher (here we skip over Q. 2: 72 ["When you slew a man..."] – which, as we saw, has been lifted out of its place by the exegetes and parachuted down at the beginning of the pericope – and conclude with Q. 2: 73: "We said: 'Strike him with part of it!' Thus does God restore the dead to life and show you His signs that you may grow in understanding").[28] Thus, by (1) combining the Pentateuchal precepts of *para aduma* and *'egla 'arufa,* (2) slightly rearranging the Qur'ānic text, and (3) filling in the blanks with either Rabbinic or homegrown anecdotes, the *tafsīr* has smoothed over the rough spots disturbing Sūrat al-Baqara's banner passage.

Before we take up the most important aspect, for our purposes, of this exegetical enterprise, it remains to point out several interesting discrepancies between al-Ṭabarī's *ḥadīth* and its probable Jewish progenitors. One immediately apparent anomaly is the involvement of Moses, whose presence in this tale is indicative of the overall haziness – or else

28 It is noteworthy that the *uḍribūhu* of Q. 2: 73 could easily connote the "dashing" of polluted persons with red heifer ash-water: *mei nida lo* zoraq *'alav ṭame yihye* (Numbers, 19: 13). If we add to this the Biblical usage "and they shall take for the unclean person *some of* the ashes from the fire of the cleansing (*ve-lakḥu la-ṭame* me-*'afar srefat ha-ḥaṭat*) to which fresh water shall be added in a vessel, and a clean person shall... sprinkle it... on him who touched the bones..." (ibid., 19: 17–18), we begin to understand the probable reason why Q. 2: 73 is formulated: *qulnā: uḍribūhu* bi-ba'ḍihā – that is, "and We [God] said: dash him [*scil.,* the contaminated man] with some of it [*scil.,* the ash-water]." If this is the true intent of Q. 2: 73 – and I lean toward thinking it is – then we can almost do away with the bold re-ordering and conflation of the exegetes and argue that Q. 2: 67–73 reflects only the *para aduma* and not the *'egla 'arufa* (I say "almost" because we still haven't made sense of Q. 2: 72: "And when you killed a man and argued about it...". This requires further study). It should also be pointed out that our *ḥadīth*'s manner of fusing these two precepts entails the notion that Israel was willing (albeit reluctantly, as a result of Moses' urging) to pay out extravagant sums – what sometimes sounds like a large portion of the national revenue – for the expiation of a single murder. This perhaps smacks more of the norms characterizing classical Arabian than classical Israelite society, in which latter no outlay was too great to acquire the *para aduma* (not the *'egla 'arufa*) because "it is the purification of all Israel."

the radical midrashic and trans-chronistic quality – of the Islamic perception of Jewish sacred history. The story clearly takes place in the Holy Land: the nephew leaves his uncle's body in what can only be the *territory* (Heb. *naḥala*), and therefore the jurisdiction, of another tribe. In one version we read that "his heir killed him, then carried his body and dumped it in a tribe not his own" (*iḥtamalahu wa-alqāhu fī sabaṭ ghayr sabaṭihi*)[29] – clearly indicating a district rather than a nomadic band – and in another the uncle's murderers are even said to have sought damages from "the people of that city" (*ahl al-madīna*).[30] Moreover, the Biblical institution of *'egla 'arufa* (the calf whose neck is broken in collective expiation for an unsolved murder), which, as we saw, most probably impacted on our Islamic anecdote, only obtains in the Land of Israel ("If, *in the land that the Lord your God is giving to you to possess*, someone slain is found lying in the open field ..."[Deut. 21: 1]). Since other early Muslim sources seem to be aware that Moses died without crossing the Jordan,[31] his appearance here is curious.

A few other minor metamorphoses that occurred during the transfer of these *topoi* from Judaic to Islamic tradition should be noted. The Talmud's righteous gentile, Dama b. Netina – who refused to wake his father even for the sake of a large profit and who was rewarded for such fealty through the birth in his herd of a red heifer – has become an Israelite in our *ḥadīth*. The heathen of the midrashic variant – who, grasping the importance of his cow to the Jews, jacked up the price to 1000 gold pieces and then tried to bamboozle his buyers by clandestinely placing a yoke on the creature – has also undergone an interesting transformation, and shows up variously disguised in anecdotes recorded by al-Ṭabarī and al-Qurṭubī. In the first of these we read that

> [the Children of Israel] could not find a cow that answered to the description they had been given (by God – *allatī nu'itat lahum*) save only in the possession of an old lady who had orphans in her care (*'inda 'ajūz 'indahā yatāmā wa-hiya al-qayyima 'alayhim*). When she realized that [the Israelites] could not purify themselves without her cow, she doubled the price (*lamma 'alimat annahum lā yazkū lahum ghayrahā aḍ'afat 'alayhim al-thaman*). They went to Moses and told him that they could not find a cow with the required characteristics except in the possession of so-and-so, and that she had demanded double the price. Moses said to them: "God tried to

29 Ṭabarī, 1:479 (no. 978).

30 Ṭabarī, 1:507 (no. 1075).

31 E. g., Newby, *Last Prophet*, 143.

> make it easier for you, but you made it harder on yourselves!" (*inna Allāha qad kāna khaffafa 'alaykum fa-shaddadtum 'alā anfusikum*). "Now go," continued Moses, "and pay her her due!"[32]

Al-Qurṭubī brings us what he sees as "the long and short" of the many similar anecdotes told in connection with "that cow":

> A son was born to a man of the Children of Israel, and this man also had a calf. He sent the calf off into the woods, and said: "O God! I commend this calf to Your care on behalf of this boy" (*innī astawdi'uka hādhihi'l-'ijla li-hādhā'l-ṣabī*).[33] Years went by and the man died, and when the son grew up his mother, to whom he was extremely dutiful, said to him: "When you were a child, your father commended a calf to the care of God on your behalf. No, go and fetch it." The young man went out searching, and when [what had meanwhile grown into] the cow saw him she walked right up to him – even though she had been reared in the wild (*wa-kānat mustawḥisha*) – and he took hold of her horns. He began to lead her back to his mother, and on the way he met the Children of Israel (*sic.*).[34] They saw that his cow possessed all of the characteristics regarding which they had been commanded, so they bargained with him and he demanded an exhorbitant price (*fa-sāmūhu fa-ishtaṭṭa 'alayhim*). Now, the actual worth of the cow – according to what has been narrated by 'Ikrima – was three dinars. The Children of Israel went to Moses and complained: "This fellow has raised the price through the roof!" Moses replied: "Satisfy his demand." And they bought it from him for its weight [in gold].[35]

Two main differences between these Islamicized versions and the Rabbinic original are important. First, as in the case of Dama b. Netina, here too the protagonist's identity has been changed. In the midrashic tale he is a greedy and malicious idol-worshipper; in the *tafsīr* he becomes either an elderly female guardian of orphans (of uncertain religio-national affiliation),[36] or, alternately, a wholesome young Israelite

32 Ṭabarī, 1:480 (no. 979).

33 It is perhaps worth mentioning in this connection that the scapegoat is, at least in the Bible (Levit., 16:10), also sent out into the wilderness (as an atonement for all Israel), and is occasionally linked by Rabbinic literature (e.g., Tanḥuma Ḥuqat, 7) with the red heifer as another salient instance of a *ḥoq* (see above, p. 125–6).

34 Here, as in many other instances in Islamo-classical literature (some of which we have cited above), the "Banū Isrā'īl" are conceived almost as a *Gestalt*, perhaps parallel to the use of "Knesset Yisrael" in Rabbinic literature. The "Children of Israel" can come over to your house, sit in your living room and haggle with you (see above, p. 121).

35 Qurṭubī, 1:430.

36 The statement that "when she realized that [the Israelites] could not purify

who cares for his mother (which latter might herself be called, after the death of her husband, an elderly female guardian of orphans).[37] This shift facilitated a negative portrayal of the Banū Isrā'īl, who did not scruple to take the milk out of the mouths of babes but were too miserly to offer the providers of those indigent children generous compensation until Moses compelled them to do so ("Pay her her due!"). Based on the second anecdote cited above, Muḥammad b. Ka'b al-Quraẓī – a descendent of Jews (who may therefore be presumed to be familiar with their character and whose testimony against his own ancestors carries more weight than would that of a pure-bred Arab) – accuses the Children of Israel of being too cheap to procure the animal necessary to carry out God's command.[38]

---

themselves without her cow, she doubled the price" sounds like she is being envisioned as a gentile.

37 And thus these two *aḥādīth* probably represent the same story told from different points of view, a common phenomenon in *ḥadīth/sīra/tafsīr* (recall that in the first version we cited from al-Ṭabarī there was also a girl orphaned as a result of the death of her father). How did the heathen of the midrash become the old lady (*'ajūz*) of the *ḥadīth*? The basic whisper-down-the-lane effect no doubt played a role in such transformations as did various processes of creative adjustment, not to mention the possibility of the existence of a plethora of versions in the source tradition (i.e. there may have been a Jewish variant that has not come down to us in which the hero was in fact an elderly woman). That having been said, I should like to offer an alternative speculation in a philological-phonetic vein. Pesikta Rabbati's – and the most common Rabbinic – term for heathen is *'akūm*, an acronym for *'oved kokhavim u-mazalot* (a worshipper of stars and constellations). The earliests (Cairo genizah) manuscripts/fragments of the Talmud and other Rabbinic literature show that though rarer than today, such acronyms were in fact already in use long before sixteenth century Christian censorship increased their frequency (by forcing publishers to replace designations like *nokhri* and *goy* with *'akūm*). Since we know that a Hebrew word like *'akūz* (buttocks) corresponds to the Arabic word *'ajuz* (buttocks), the *k* becoming a *j* (see below, chap. 9, n. 79); and since at least some early Muslim exponents seem to have been impressed by, and also to have played with, the orthography and phonetics of Hebrew texts (see above, chap. 5, notes 2 and 28, and below, chap. 8, n. 21); and finally, since the Rabbinic acronym in question appears in many editions and manuscripts with a *zayin* – the second letter of *mazalot* – added after, or even replacing, the *mem* at the end; given all this, it is at least possible that a Muslim scholar perusing the Hebrew text of this Midrash (which I am increasingly convinced that at least some of them did) was inspired (for reasons we shall mention forthwith) to transform *'akūm/'akūmaz/'akūz* into *'ajūz* (an old lady).

38 Qurṭubī, 1:431: "*wa-hādhā ikhbār 'an tathbīṭihim fī dhabḥihā wa-qillat mu-*

In the end, however, the Jews do pay, and pay dearly, a denouement which points up the second important difference between the Judaic and Islamic versions of our anecdote: whereas in the midrash the idol-worshipper's plot backfires in his face and the Jews emerge with their finances intact, in both of the *tafsīr* stories the owner of the cow – whether Israelite or gentile – gets the better end of the bargain and the Jews are forced to empty their coffers. This element, in turn, brings us to the real central thrust of the hermeneutical activity surrounding Q. 2:67–73, a thrust that comes to the fore most clearly in the numerous amplifications and elaborations of the previously cited statement of Ibn 'Abbās: "The Children of Israel insisted on making the matter more difficult and pestering Moses, and God [in retribution] did indeed make the matter more difficult for them."[39] Of the plethora of (relatively similar) expositions devoted to this subject in the exegetical literature, we will confine ourselves to a brief examination of two. We begin with one of al-Ṭabarī's recapitulations:

> (Q. 2:67–71 comprises) a report from Allāh regarding the three acts of foolishness (*jahla*) committed by this nation.[40] For if, when Moses first conveyed to them God's commandment to sacrifice a cow (in Q. 2:67), they had sacrificed whatever animal was easiest to procure that answered to the description "cow" (*ayyatahā tayassarat mimmā yaqa'u 'alayhi ism baqara*), this would have fulfilled their obligation, since at that point they had not been charged with making use of a cow that possessed any specific characteristics [Q. 2:67: "God commands you to sacrifice *a cow*"]. But when they insisted on asking for clarification regarding [the cow's] particular traits, God announced to them that she must be of a certain age as opposed to any other age, i.e., that she must be half-way between an old cow and a young heifer (Q. 2:68).
>
> Now if, after the issue of [the cow's] age had been settled, they had been satisfied with that and had simply slaughtered the nearest cow that met those age requirements (*adnā baqara bi'l-sann allatī buyyinat lahum*), this would have fulfilled their obligation, since at that point, while they had been charged with making use of a cow of a certain age, they had not been

bādaratihim ilā 'amr Allāhi li-qhalā thamanihi. We shall hear more from Ibn Ka'b, and talk more about his lineage, in chapter 9.

39 These words were inserted, the reader will recall, in the tale told above by al-Ṭabarī (p. 120–21).

40 Al-Ṭabarī's choice of the term *jahla* is almost certainly a literary allusion to Moses' angry response to his people: "God forbid that I should be among the foolish!" (*a'ūḏu bi'llahi an akūna min al-jāhilīn* – Q. 2:67). In other words, it was not he but *they* who were the fools, as we shall see presently.

restricted to making use of a cow of a certain *color.* But when they insisted on asking for clarification regarding the cow's color, God announced to them that she must be of a rich yellow color that pleases the eye (Q. 2: 69).

Now if, after the issue of [the cow's] color had been settled, they had been satisfied with that and had simply gone out and found the nearest cow that met those age and color requirements, this would have sufficed for them, since at that point, though they had been charged with making use of a cow of a certain age and a certain color, nothing had been said to restrict them to a cow that had not been used for particular types of work or that was unblemished in body or hair. But when they refused to be satisfied with anything other than a detailed description of the cow's characteristics which would set her off clearly from all other cattle on earth, and thereby sought to make their lives difficult (*fa-lammā abū illā an takūna mu'arrafa lahum bi-nu'ūtihā [wa-? al-?] mubīna bi-ḥudūdihā allatī tufarriqu baynahā wa-bayna sā'ir bahā'im al-arḍ fa-shaddadū 'alā anfusihim*) – then God [gave them what they wanted and indeed] made their lives difficult, in [retaliation for] their constant questioning of, and disputing with, their Prophet (*bi-kathrat sū'ālihim nabiyyahum wa-ikhtilāfihim 'alayhi*).[41] Therefore did our Prophet [Muḥammad] say to his community: "Leave me be regarding that which I have abandoned for your sake (*dharūnī mā taraktukum*),[42] for those that came before you were destroyed because they asked too many questions and disputed with their prophets. If I command you to do something, do it; if I forbid you to do something, don't do it."[43]

---

41 See Q. 2: 107: "Or do you wish to put questions to your Messenger, as Moses was questioned aforetime ...?" The Israelites of the Qur'ān regularly pepper Moses (and Muḥammad) with annoying, nitpicky questions, just as the Pharisees of the New Testament regularly peppered Jesus with annoying, nitpicky questions. The Hebrew Bible itself sometimes shows them in a similar light, and is probably the ultimate source of the other two cultures' portrayals. Wherever one looks, then, the Jews seem to justify their Islamic cognomen: *aṣḥāb al-mas'ala* – the people who incessantly ask questions, and cannot leave well enough alone!

42 Other versions (see Muslim, *Kitāb al-Faḍā'il, Bāb Wujūb Tark Sū'ālihi bi-Kathra,* 37: 131) have "*mā turiktum.*" The import of this statement seems to be: "Do not look a gift horse in the mouth!" or "Let well enough alone when you see that I have refrained from imposing upon you a given difficult obligation."

43 Ṭabarī, 1: 492. See general statements condemning the asking of too many questions in Bukhārī, 24: 555, Muwaṭṭa, 56: 8 (20) and elsewhere. The choice of the red-heifer issue as the locus for a diatribe against question-asking has a Rabbinic basis as well. As we saw above in Talmud and Midrash, the inquiries of various parties concerning the underlying rationale of the *para aduma* ritual are all shown to be futile, the common answer they receive – that in this case God's orders must be followed blindly – clearly implying that there was no point in

You asked for it, you got it: the Banū Isrā'īl could not resist probing further into the divine injunction vouchsafed unto them, and such relentless needling resulted in the addition of yet another impossible precept to their already arduous religion. This time, as our previously cited variants (al-Ṭabarī's tale of the old woman and al-Qurṭubī's story of the matured youth) make sure to emphasize, the Jews' stubborn inability to leave well enough alone caused them to be hit where it hurts most: in their pockets. Having goaded God by their incessant questioning into narrowing the pool of qualified cows to such a point that the required animal became an extreme rarity, they were forced to expend unheard of sums to obtain it. From one angle, this increasing specification of criteria and the resultant inconvenience was seen as "a punishment from God for their vexing interrogation of their prophet" (*'uqūbatan min Allāhi lahum 'alā mas'alatihim allatī sa'alūhā nabiyahum ta'annutan minhum lahu*).[44] But there is another mechanism at work here.

The tradition with which al-Ṭabarī concludes his above summary may be found, *inter alia,* in *Ṣaḥīḥ Muslim* under the heading: "Chapter on Venerating [One's Prophet] and Not Asking Him Too Many Questions." There Muslim's *shāriḥ* (commentator), the famed thirteenth-century Shāfi'ī jurist Abū Zakariyyā' Yaḥyā Muḥyī l-Dīn al-Nawawī, delivers himself of the following exposition:

> The intent of the *aḥādīth* in this section is that the Prophet Muḥammad, may God's peace and blessings be upon him, forbad his followers to ask too many questions [concerning God's commandments] – or to ask *any* questions concerning practices which they were *not* commanded.[45] He warned against such behavior in order to save [his flock] from its potential consequences, for [excessive questioning] can sometimes lead to the pro-

asking the question in the first place (this is also reminiscent of the Lord's rejoinder to Moses who – seeing in a vision the future dismemberment of Rabbi 'Aqiva by the Romans for teaching the Law – is beside himself: "This is the Torah, and this its reward?" "Be silent!" God tells him. "For thus have I decreed" [Menaḥot, 29b]). In Jewish tradition, then, it is the *meaning* of the red heifer ritual that it is useless, even counterproductive, to probe; the *manner* of its execution, on the other hand, is a legitimate and even essential subject of discussion. According to Islamic tradition, specifically the latter is what the Jews should have avoided. Still, the connection is quite palpable.

44 Ṭabarī, 1:489.

45 ? *Wa'l-ibtidā'bi'l-sū'āl 'ammā lā yaqa'u.* There are many instances in the *ḥadīth* in which overly zealous Companions approach the Prophet with suggestions for new pious precepts and practices (often purportedly learned from the Jews). They are almost invariably rebuffed.

hibition of a thing to the Muslims as a result of which they will suffer hardship (*annahu rubbamā kāna sababan li-taḥrīm shay'in 'alā al-Muslimīn fa-yalḥaquhum bihi al-mashaqqa*). This much was made clear in [the Prophet's] words, may God's peace and blessings be upon him, in the first report [recorded in this chapter]: "The Muslim who commits the *greatest crime* is he who inquires about a thing that was not prohibited to the people, after which it became prohibited as a result of his inquiry" (*a'ẓam al-Muslimīna jurman man sa'ala 'an shay'in lam yuḥarram 'alā al-nāsi fa-ḥurrima min ajli mas'alatihi*).[46] One of the lessons of [both of these *ḥadīths*] is that oftentimes the questioner will not like the answer he receives, and his life will be made worse by it. Therefore did God the Exalted reveal in this connection His lofty words: "O you who believe! Do not ask about things which, if made known to you, would give you trouble; and if you ask about them while the Qur'ān is being revealed, they will indeed be made known to you ..." (*lā tas'alū 'an ashyā' in tubda lakum tasu'kum, wa-in tas'alū 'anhā ḥīna tunazzalu al-Qur'ānu tubda lakum* – Q. 5: 101).[47]

---

46 Emphasis added. See a slightly different version of this statement in Baghawī, 1: 89: "The Muslim who commits the greatest crime *against his fellow Muslims* is he who inquires about a thing that was not prohibited to the people, after which it became prohibited as a result of his inquiry."

47 Muslim, *Kitāb al-Faḍā'il,* 37: 132 [2358]). Commenting on the verse with which al-Nawawī concludes (Q. 5: 101), al-Ṭabarī initially entertains the notion that (at least the first clause) refers to the insulting and irritating interrogations Muḥammad was often subjected to by unbelievers, such as "[If you are a Prophet], then what is my father's name?" or "My she-camel is lost: tell me where it is!" (just as Saul asked the Prophet Samuel about the location of his straying she-asses – Samuel 1, chapter 9. Note also that a group of Jews is depicted in a report of al-Bukhārī's as hesitating to ask the Apostle a theological question for fear that "he might give them a reply which would displease them" [*Kitāb al-'Ilm,* 3: 127]). Ultimately, however, al-Ṭabarī favors the claim that Q. 5: 101 was revealed in reference to Muslims who would over-analyze the precepts revealed by Allāh to His Apostle, or, even more significantly, who would ask questions that would (must we add "as it were"?) *prompt the revelation from On High* of more, and more difficult, prescriptions – Ṭabarī, 7: 107 ff. Al-Nawawī would appear to be drawing the intriguing implication from the middle part of the verse ("and if you ask about them while the Qur'ān is being revealed, they [i.e. the answers in the form of difficult precepts] will be made known to you") that the twenty-three years of Muḥammad's prophethood was a "dangerous," because fluid, time: as we saw above in chapter 1, both Jews and Companions can be "instigators of revelation" during this dynamic period, an idea that flies in the face of al-Qurṭubī's – and what occasionally even looks like al-Ṭabarī's – predestinarian conception of *naskh* (see above, chap. 1, notes 8, 25, 27; chap. 3, n. 8; and below, n. 51). Ibn Isḥāq's claim that it was preeminently *Jewish* questions that led to most of the revelations that

As al-Qurṭubī explains it, this latter verse was sent down as a result of an incident that occurred in connection with an immediately preceding revelation, the well known directive obligating Muslims in the *ḥajj*: "It is a duty to God imposed upon humankind to perform the pilgrimage to the holy House..." (Q. 3: 96). Upon hearing this, one of the believers piped up and queried: "O Messenger of God – every year?" Muḥammad was silent. The inquisitive fellow persisted: "Must we perform the pilgrimage *every year?*" Again the Apostle said nothing. Then, after an interval, he declared: "No! And had I answered in the affirmative, you would indeed have been obligated [in an annual *ḥajj*]" (*law qultu na'am, la-wajabta*).[48] At that moment Allāh revealed: "O you who believe! Do not ask about things which if made known to you would give you trouble..."[49]

It is al-Qurṭubī, as well, who offers up the most intriguing characterization yet for our purposes of the dialogue conducted between the Jews and God concerning the cow. "From this passage," he writes, "we derive proof that an injunction may be abrogated even before it is carried out" (*fī hādhā dalīl 'alā jawāz al-naskh qabla waqt al-fi'l*)."[50] In other words, each divine response to each Israelite inquiry recorded in Q. 2: 67–71 constituted nothing less than a repeal of a previously enacted statute (even if that statute was perceived as having remained in force for no longer than a few moments: this is speed *naskh*). When Allāh instructed the Jews to sacrifice a cow – any cow – this revelation immediately established a bona fide religious precept and created what was designed to be a permanent cultic institution.[51] When, in response

eventually became the Qur'ān – see above, p. 16 – undermines this conception even further. The Qur'ān's self-referential description (in Q. 5: 101) of scriptural revelation as a volatile, participatory process is fascinating.

48 Instead – because the Prophet refrained from responding – Muslims are required to perform the pilgrimage only once in a lifetime, if they are able.

49 Qurṭubī, 6: 289.

50 Qurṭubī, 1: 425. We have already met this theoretical sub-species of *naskh*, see above, chapter 2, n. 23.

51 Thus argues al-Qurṭubī, contradicting his own predestinarian schema of *naskh*. He, too, after all – like the earlier *mufassirūn* – accuses the Jews of being a pain in the side of their Prophet (*hādhā ta'nīt minhum*) and expressly states that "had they simply obeyed [God's original] command and sacrificed any cow they found, this would have achieved the intended result" (*law imtathalū al-amr wa-dhabaḥū ayya baqara kānat la-ḥaṣala al-maqṣūd*). It was, then, Jewish incorrigibility that brought about these divine legislative reforms; had the Jews acted properly, the outcome would have been otherwise (see above, n. 47). The

to Israelite cross-examination, God provided further specifications regarding the cow's age, this new communication cancelled out the previous dispensation and introduced a whole new law – and so on. Once again, Judaism and Jewish legal history function as the mirror image of Islam and Muslim legal history: whereas *naskh* in the Islamic microcosm, as we have argued above (in chap. 2), was almost always an instrument of *rukhṣa,* designed to make life easier for the Muslims, *naskh* in the Judaic microcosm is shown here (and elsewhere) as an instrument of *tashdīd,* designed to make life harder for the Jews.

There is no doubt that we have reflected in all this a perception of the evolution of Jewish religion that draws upon genuine historical elements. The Israelite interrogation of Allāh in Q. 2: 68–71 may be said to epitomize and synopsize the way in which the Oral Law (the Talmud) acted on the Written Law (the Torah). "Thou shalt not boil a kid in its mother's milk," the Pentateuch famously enjoins on three separate occasions (Exodus, 23: 19 and 34: 26; Deut. 14: 21). These words could certainly have been read as a straightforward ban on what was considered a callous and heart-hardening practice (the commentator Ibn Ezra even asserts that it was an ancient Ishmaelite practice): cooking a baby goat in the very maternal fluid that was intended to sustain it. This commandment could then have been classified with other purportedly humane (and essentially "rational") prescriptions – such as shewing away the mother bird before taking her eggs (Deut., 22: 6) or not slaughtering animals on the same day with their young (Levit., 22: 28)[52] – and that would have been the end of the matter. Instead, centuries of dissection and deliberation gradually erected a vast, ramified and infinitely complex sub-section of the dietary code concerned with avoiding the consumption of dairy and meat products together – all on the foundation of this lone simple rule.[53]

---

only way out of this contradiction is to posit that all instances of Israelite refractoriness were also built into Allāh's primeval plan for the unfolding of history, a notion that al-Qurṭubī himself never entertains and that would take us down the road toward some of the sillier extremes of predestinarian apologetics.

52 It is in fact thus classified by certain commentators. Others, however, do not even see this last ordinance as connected to humaneness.

53 The dietary code is another example, according to most, of a *ḥoq,* a rationally inexplicable commandment. It is interesting that while Muslim tradition exhibits a profound interest in Jewish dietary law (see below, chapter 8), the separation of – and three-to-six hour waiting period between ingesting – meat and

Much the same may be said for the institution of the Sabbath: "The seventh day is a day of rest unto the Lord your God," declares Exodus, 20:10, "you shall do no work." The rabbis, however, did not leave it at that: exactly which kinds of activity were permitted and which forbidden on the seventh day? they wondered. Soon 39 "archetypes of work" had grown up around this single Biblical precept, followed by hundreds and eventually thousands of derivative categories that together form the sprawling and immeasurably intricate system of Jewish Sabbath law. If at the very outset "resting on the Sabbath" may well have been a flexible, general notion that – with certain important exceptions – could have meant almost anything an individual Israelite wanted it to mean (just as at the outset the Qur'ānic cow to be sacrificed could have been any cow an Israelite happened upon), centuries of Rabbinic discussion and analysis led to an enormously detailed array of specific acts to be avoided or performed, which together can sometimes make the Sabbath anything but restful![54] This process was repeated to a greater or lesser extent in the case of almost every divine injunction issued to the Israelites, and that is basically how *halakha* came into being.[55] Thus did the Jews – in the eyes of those many early

milk required by that law is nowhere alluded to in the literature I have consulted.

54 The present author, an observant Jew who struggles daily to adhere to these numerous "thou shalts" and "thou shalt nots," should not be suspected of rendering here a negative value judgement of halakhic proliferation. The opposite is the case (see my "Three Shāfi'īs in Search of Water," *Der Islam* 82 [2005]). The real irony is that Islamic tradition is itself a strong proponent of such proliferation, and may in fact be dubbed Judaism's premier partner in this regard. See next note.

55 It is also, of course, how *sharī'a* came into being: a *faqīh* like al-Nawawī spends no less than *one hundred and twenty five pages* of his celebrated *Majmū'* elaborating the jurisprudence and positive law that sprung from the single small seed of a sub-section of Q. 5:6 – "If you find not water, go to clean high ground and daub some of it on your faces and hands." Even though Q. 2:177 avers that "It is not righteousness that you turn your faces towards the East or the West...", the *fuqahā* spend a great deal of time and effort elucidating issues of correct *qibla* orientation. The same could be said for literally thousands of other Qur'ānic- and *ḥadīth*ic- (and *ra'y*-) based precepts, from prayer to inheritance to commerce to menstruation to pilgrimage to testimony to divorce: the vast sections of the Muslim law code that concern all of these topics evolved through a process of juristic inquiry and deliberation not at all dissimilar to that employed by the rabbis. (Note Muḥammad's famous statement that "[t]he scholars (*ulamā'*) of my community are the prophets of the

Muslims who were aware to one degree or another of such developments – make their religion unbearable.[56]

---

people of Israel" [Ignaz Goldziher, *Introduction to Islamic Theology and Law,* trans. Andras and Ruth Hamori (Princeton: Princeton University Press, 1981), 66], and see also above, chap. 1, n. 11, where 'Umar b. al-Khaṭṭāb interrogates the Deity regarding the prohibition on wine in a manner all but identical to that of the Israelites in the present chapter, and with strikingly similar results. He, too, asks a series of unsolicited questions – or, more accurately, makes *exactly three requests for further clarification of a divine commandment* – as a result of which a particularly difficult precept is defined and established. Could the Islamic prohibition on intoxicating beverages have been avoided had 'Umar only kept silent?). Scholars like al-Ṭabarī, al-Qurṭubī and their informants were an integral part of this branching process of legally-oriented scriptural exegesis (what the Jews call *midrash halakha*). More than this: as we saw (above, p. 14), at least in the eyes of Ibn Isḥāq, none other than *Jewish questions* were primarily responsible for the content of Muslim scripture. In a sense, then, the Qur'ān would not even exist but for Israelite *ikthār al-su'āl.* Despite all this, the Banū Isrā'īl and Yahūd are consistently excoriated in Islamo-classical literature for this indomitable penchant of theirs.

56 The Qur'ān's rendering of the *baqara* incident represents, more than anything else, its condemnation of such unnecessary metastasis. No phenomenon better illustrates the lengths to which the Jews went in elaborating the precept of the red heifer than the existence of *masekhet para* – the Talmudic "Tractate of the Cow." Bearing in mind that *Sūrat al-Baqara* is almost entirely concerned with Jews/Israelites; and that the central and most problematic character trait of the Jews, in the view of Islamic tradition, is their indefatigable drive to complicate matters and make religion burdensome; and that, indeed, this trait was seen as so significant that its encapsulation in Q. 2: 67–71 caused this latter to become the eponymous passage of the entire chapter; and that so much of the exegetical material surrounding this passage is informed by an atmosphere of derision and mockery; and finally that, as we have seen and shall see in greater depth below, many Muslim scholars were familiar in varying degrees even with the *halakhic* sections of the Talmud; given all of this, are we not justified in suggesting that the title "The Chapter of the Cow" may be nothing less than a parody on "The Tractate of the Cow"?

8. Homely was Their Food

Jewish Dietary Law as Divine Retribution

An over-inquisitive spirit and excessive severity in religious law were not the sole sins in recompense for which the Israelites were saddled with numerous prohibitions. They gave God many other reasons to make their lives miserable. In this connection, al-Qurṭubī adduces an interesting opinion to the effect that:

> God did not prohibit [the sciatic tendon] to the Jews in the Torah, but rather He prohibited it *after* the Torah, in retaliation for their injustices and unbelief. Every time the Children of Israel would commit a heinous offense, God would forbid them a delicious food.[1]

This conception is most fully elaborated in the commentaries elucidating the next set of verses we shall examine, a set culled from two different Qur'ānic chapters (Sūrat al-Nisā' and Sūrat al-An'ām). These separate passages are regularly linked to each other by the exegetes, and both are tied back, together and separately, to the passage from Sūrat Āl 'Imrān (regarding the food which Israel forbade himself – Q. 3: 93–5) that we analyzed above in chapter 6. They read as follows:

> Because of the wrongdoing of the Jews; and because of their hindering of many from Allāh's way; and because of their taking of usury (though they were forbidden it); and because of their devouring people's property falsely – because of all this, We forbade them the good things which had previously been lawful for them (Q. 4: 160–1).
>
> Unto those who are Jews We forbade every animal with claws; and of oxen and sheep We forbade them the fat thereof, save for that fat which is on the back or the entrails, or that which is mixed with the bone. Thus did We reward them for their rebellion. Lo! We are surely truthful (Q. 6: 147).

Especially with regard to the latter excerpt, the commentaries list a variety of opinions concerning the specific gastronomic prohibitions im-

1 Qurṭubī, 4: 119: "*lam yuḥarrimhu Allāhu fī'l-Tawrāt 'alayhim wa-lākin ḥarramahu ba'd al-Tawrāt bi-ẓulmihim wa-kufrihim, wa-kānat Banū Isrā'īl idhā aṣābū dhanban 'aẓīman ḥarrama Allāhu ta'ālā 'alayhim ṭa'āman ṭayyiban.*"

posed by God upon the Jews, and we shall survey these speculations first. Following the exegetes we divide our discussion into two categories: (1) the species of animals that constitute forbidden food, and (2) the types of fat that may and may not be consumed.

Basing themselves on the clause "every animal with claws (*kulla dhī ẓufurin*)," al-Ṭabarī and al-Qurṭubī – as well as the *ḥadīth* transmitters they cite (especially Mujāhid, Qatāda and Sa'īd b. Jubayr) – lay down what they believe to be the fundamental Biblical criterion for distinguishing between legally edible and legally inedible creatures: "Forbidden to the Jews were those beasts and birds that do not have separated toes (*al-bahā'im wa'l-ṭayr mā lam yakun mashqūq al-aṣābi'*)."[2] Chewing the cud – a *sine qua non* of *kashrut* according to Leviticus, 11:3 – is not mentioned,[3] but this in itself does not lead to any discrepancies with the *halakha* (at least not in terms of the sample species adduced in these and other Qur'ānic commentaries), probably because the only animal prohibited in the Pentateuch for dereliction of cud-chewing is the swine, and the Jewish policy on pigs was well-known. Differences arise due to another factor.

Arabic *ẓufur* can mean a human nail, an animal claw or a bird's talon.[4] Most translations of the Qur'ān render it by "claws" (the remainder offer "undivided hoof," probably under the influence of Bible reading).[5] But *ẓufur* is etymologically related to – or, at the very least,

2 Ṭabarī, 8:96. Echoes al-Qurṭubī: "'*dhī ẓufur – mā laysa bi-munfarij al-aṣābi' min al-bahā'im wa'l-ṭayr.*" In ruminants this is what the Bible calls cloven hoofs. The reader might want to quickly peruse – and keep handy – the eleventh chapter of Leviticus (and see the parallel list in Deut., 14:3–19).

3 It is mentoned elsewhere in *fiqh*, in the context of purity law, where matter regurgitated by ruminants is considered by most authorities to be an *'ayn al-najāsa* (see, e.g., Muḥammad b. al-Ḥasan al-Shaybānī, *Kitāb al-Asl* [Cairo: Mujtama' Majlis Dā'irat al-Ma'ārif, 1966], 1:72; Saḥnūn b. Sā'īd al-Tanūkhī, *al-Mudawwana al-Kubrā* [Beirut: Dār al-Kutub al-'Ilmiya], 1:125–6).

4 The root *ẓ-f-r* appears in only one other place in the Qur'ān: "It is He who has restrained their hands from you and your hands from them in the midst of Mecca, after giving you victory over them (*ba'd an aẓfarakum 'alayhim* – Q. 48:24). The meaning "to be triumphant" or "successful" for the verb *ẓafira* is probably a back formation from the noun, as it is with nails/claws/talons that one *seizes* victory.

5 Pickthall, Arberry, Maulana Muhammad Ali and Zohur al-Hoque have "claws"; Abdullah Yusuf Ali, Sale and Dawood have "undivided hoofs." In both cases, the singular is correctly taken to indicate the plural. The English word "hoof" is from the Old Norse "hofr" and thus probably connected to Arabic *ḥafara* (to dig – as well as to Arabic *khuff*, shoe, foot) and Hebrew

phonetically evocative of – the Hebrew word for bird: *tzipor* (as well as the Arabic word for sparrow, *'uṣfur*), itself either the source or derivative of *tziporen,* "nail."[6] It may well be for this reason that the Muslim traditionists and commentators add a dimension to the Jewish dietary restrictions not found in the Biblical (or Talmudic) version: the application of the litmus-test of "separated toes" to birds:[7]

> Al-Qāsim – Ḥusayn – Ḥajjāj – Ibn Jurayj – Mujāhid, who said regarding [the Qur'ānic phrase] *kulla dhī ẓufurin*: "The ostrich and the camel, fissures, fissures" (*al-na'āma wa'l-ba'īr shaqqan shaqqan*). I (Ibn Jurayj? Al-Ṭabarī?) asked al-Qāsim b. Abī Bazza, who had reported this to me: "What did [Mujāhid] mean by 'fissures, fissures'?" He answered: "This means every animal the feet of which are not genuinely cloven" (*kullu shay'in lam yafrij min qawā'im al-bahā'im*). He went on to explain: "[Any species the feet of which] are genuinely cloven, the Jews eat. The feet of chickens (*al-dajāj*) and of sparrows (*al-'aṣāfīr*) are genuinely cloven, and the Jews eat them. The hooves of camels and of ostriches are not genuinely cloven, and neither are the feet of geese (*al-wazzīn*) or of ducks (*al-baṭṭ*), and consequently the Jews do not eat camels (*al-ibil*) or ostriches or geese or ducks, or anything else that lacks truly cloven feet, and for the same reason they do not eat the wild ass (*ḥimār waḥshī*).[8]

This *ḥadīth* is difficult, but we can attempt to reconstruct its context. Mujāhid, it seems, was holding forth one day on the implications of Q. 6: 147, according to which God forbade the Children of Israel any creature with claws. "Carnivores, in other words, are off limits to Jews," he explained. "What *can* Jews eat?" a member of his audience

---

ḥafar, which also means to dig. A hoof is thus the particular hallmark of land animals, who "dig up" the earth by walking on it.

6 The etymological dictionaries neither confirm nor deny either of these connections. They do, however, derive *tzipor* from *tzafar,* "to chirp, whistle," and this last (though they neglect to mention this as well) is intimately related to *shofar,* a horn (which is why in modern Hebrew to honk one's horn is "*litzfor*"). A horn is the same sort of modified epidermic protuberance as a finger-nail/toenail or talon (*tziporen*). Thus, whether *tziporen* contributed to *tzipor,* or, alternately, was formed by it, either way they are closely connected, and thus the relationship of *ẓufur* to birds. Heb. *ṭofer* (claw) also enters into this mix.

7 The Bible utilizes the criterion of "split hooves" to divide kosher from non-kosher *quadrupeds*, not fowl. A list of permitted and forbidden birds is given in Leviticus, 11: 13–19, based on no known principle (though there has been speculation). Since not all species delineated by the Biblical text can be properly identified, the *halakhic* classification of birds for dietary purposes has always been tricky.

8 Ṭabarī, 8:97.

wondered in response. "Why, ruminants, of course," came the answer, "the overwhelming majority of which have cloven feet. Thus Allāh permitted the Jews to eat only animals possessing cloven feet." "But wait a minute," persisted the listener, "ostriches and camels have cloven feet, and Jews can't eat *them*!" Mujāhid parried this riposte: "Ostriches and camels? Fissures, my dear boy – fissures!" That is: what seem to you to be bona fide divisions in the feet of these two creatures are in truth mere cracks, and that is why these animals are forbidden as food to Jews.

The hoof of a camel appears to be split from the top, but underneath it looks more like one solid pad. Ostrich feet have a large main toe and a much smaller side toe, but they only walk on the former, which may therefore be considered their actual (undivided) foot.[9] As for the remainder of the creatures adduced in the latter part of this *ḥadīth*, (which emanates from a period several generations after Mujāhid): the feet of ducks and geese are webbed, and the onager has a hoof like a horse. Thus, taking all this information together, we can conclude that the (somewhat hazy) general rule of "lack of true clovenness" has been brought to bear by these *muḥaddithūn* in order to identify non-kosher animals whether they walk or fly. This method led to some interesting results.

The Torah as we know it specifically prohibits camels, faulting their feet.[10] Donkeys – though not mentioned in the text – were declared off limits by the *halakha* for the same reason. Ostriches (*bat ha-ya'ana*) are also banned by name in the Bible,[11] together with nineteen other birds,

9 So claim the zoologists. My own personal observations of the ostriches in the children's zoo in the park in front of my house do not confirm this. The idea may alternatively be that the two "prongs" that make up the ostrich's foot do not function independently of one another and/or are not genuinely divided, and thus form a single surface in a manner that is at least analogous to the camel's under-pad. Qatāda does indeed aver that "*ẓafara yad al-ba'īr wa-rijlihi wa'l-na'ām ayḍan kadhālika*," which I take to mean that the feet of camels and of ostriches are similar in that they are both a single, indivisible whole. Alternately, Qatāda could be referring to the fact that they both have nails. *W'Allāhu a'lam.* One factor calling into question our interpretation of Mujāhid's maxim: *al-na'āma wa'l-ba'īr shaqqan shaqqan* as referring to legally insignificant fissures in the feet of the ostrich and camel is the already cited determination that Jews are forbidden to eat *al-bahā'im wa'l-ṭayr mā lam yakun* mashqūq al-aṣābi', in which the root *sh.q.q.* refers specifically to *full-fledged divisions* in feet that *are* legally significant. The contrast may, however, merely reflect inconsistancy of usage. *W'Allāhu a'lam.*

10 Leviticus, 11:4.

11 Leviticus, 11:16.

but with no reference to their manner of locomotion. As for ducks and geese, however: Jews have always eaten these (geese were even a staple dish on Solomon's daily menu).[12] It may be significant, therefore, that while most of the authorities cited by al-Ṭabarī and al-Qurṭubī consider all of the above animals to be unkosher according to Jewish law, Ibn 'Abbās – "the rabbi of this community"[13] – harbors what appears to be a dissenting opinion. He asserts that Jews are not permitted to consume "camels, ostriches and other *land animals* of a similar sort" (*wa-naḥwa dhālika min al-dawābb* – Ibn 'Abbās evidently saw the ostrich as a land animal, not a bird, due to its cursorial capabilities and/or because it is grounded). He says nothing of geese or ducks.[14] Al-

12 See I Kings, 5:3. Sa'īd b. Jabīr, perhaps carried away by the overall category of fowl, even adds the cock (*al-dīk*) to the list of foods forbidden to Jews (Ṭabarī, 8:96). This bird does not even have webbed feet, and indeed, Sa'īd claims that every animal whose toes *are* separated (*kullu shay'in mutafarriq al-aṣābi'*) was prohibited to the Jews. Al-Ṭabarī's modern editor suggests that the text here is corrupt, but that may be because he hasn't read Mishna Ḥulin 3:6, where the Rabbis declare unclean (i.e. inedible) "any bird that parts its toes [in pairs when set upon a cord – *kol 'of ha-ḥoleq et raglav* – because this means it is a predator]." Sa'īd read this Mishna wrong – perhaps because he was not privy to the Gemera's gloss on it – but it is certainly noteworthy that he read it at all. Al-Ṭabarī's informants display a similarly impressive familiarity with other non-Pentateuchal bird-related provisions based on rabbinical decree (*mitzvot de-rabbanan*) when they note that Jews were forbidden to eat birds that are not endowed with "spurs" (*alladhī lā ṣīṣīya lahu* – Ṭabarī, 3:384. This is the *etzba' yetera* of the same Mishna [Ḥulin, 3:6]).

13 *Ḥabr hādhihi'l-umma* – Muḥammad b. Ismā'īl al-San'ānī, *Subul al-Salām: Sharḥ Bulūgh al-Marām* [Cairo: Al-Maktaba al-Tijāriya al-Kubrā, n.d.], 1:65; 'Abd al-Razzāq, 1:102 (505); and throughout the literature; see also Newby, *Last Prophet*, 124. Some have rendered *ḥabr* differently (see Adang, *Muslim Writers*, 13, n. 85) and he may have received the title in view of his exceptional status as – in Arthur Jeffery's phrase – "Übermensch des Tafsīr" (Jeffery, *Materials for the History of the Text of the Qur'ān* [Leiden: E. J. Brill, 1937], 15); but see al-Ṭabarī's definition of the term (Ṭabarī, 6:339) which is unequivocal. Ibn 'Abbās seems, in general, to know more about Judaism than most of his contemporaries, and was an "avid collector and transmitter of biblical legends" (Adang, *Muslim Writers*, 8). On his knowledge of the Torah – and that of other famous Companions such as Abū Hurayra, 'Alī, Zayd b. Thābit and Salmān al-Fārisī, see Nabia Abbott, *Studies in Arabic Literary Papyri* (Chicago: University of Chicago Press, 1967), vol. 2, p. 9 ff. Ibn 'Abbās, however, surpasses them all by far.

14 Ṭabarī, 8:96. See Qurṭubī, 7:102, where Ibn 'Abbās explains that he has lumped camels and ostriches together because "ostriches have hooves like camels" (*li'anna al-na'āma dhāt ḥufr ka'l-ibil*). Another minority opinion hearkens back to the Jacob thesis: Ibn Zayd avers that what was forbidden to the Jews ac-

Qurṭubī evinces no preference in this matter, but al-Ṭabarī comes down strongly in favor of the majority outlook – the one that includes the prohibition on geese and ducks – affirming that "God forbade the Jews *kulla dhī ẓufur* (that is, every species of animal the feet of which are not truly cloven), and it is not permissible to exclude any creature from the general rubric contained in this text save those which the scholarly consensus has seen fit to exclude" (*fa-ghayr jā'iz ikhrāj shay'in min 'umūm hādhā al-khabar illā mā ajma'a ahl al-'ilm annahu khārij minhu*).[15] The Muslim version of this area of Jewish *kashrut* is thus more restrictive than the Jewish version, and both are by far more demanding than Islamic dietary law, which is summarized in the verse preceding the one we have been parsing: "Say: I find not in that which is revealed unto me aught forbidden to an eater to eat thereof, except it be carrion, or blood poured forth, or swine – for that is surely unclean – or any abomination which was sacrificed to other than Allāh" (Q. 6: 146).[16]

The middle section of Q. 6: 147 concerns fat: "... and of oxen and sheep We forbade them the fat thereof (*ḥarramnā 'alayhim shuḥūmahumā*), *save for that fat which is on the back or the entrails*, or that which is mixed with the bone." A comparison of this verse with Pentateuchal parallels yields confusing results. Leviticus, 7:22–3 reads: "And the Lord spoke to Moses, saying: Speak to the Children of Israel, saying: You shall eat no fat (*ḥelev* – hard, coarse fat; suet) of ox or sheep or goat." So far we have a match. In the Biblical version, however, the

---

cording to Q. 6: 146 was "*al-ibil fa-qaṭ*" (Ṭabarī, 8: 97, Qurṭubī, 7: 102). Still another speculation – somewhat closer to the Biblical mark – is that Allāh forbade the Israelites "every bird with talons and every land animal with hooves" (*kull dhī mikhlab min al-ṭayr wa-kull dhī ḥāfir min al-dawābb* – Qurṭubī, 7: 102). This would leave out geese and ducks, and although – again – no common criterion is mentioned for "unclean" birds in the Pentateuch, still, most of them are in fact birds of prey.

15 Ṭabarī, 8: 97.

16 This list is given four times in the Qur'ān (Q. 2: 173; 5: 3; 6: 145; 16: 115). Islamic dietary law is not, however, as simple as it seems in Muslim scripture: see Michael Cook, "Early Islamic Dietary Law," in *Jerusalem Studies in Arabic and Islam*, 7 (1986); and Ersilia Francesca, *Introduzione alle Regole Alimentari Islamiche* (Rome: Istituto per l'Oriente C. A. Nallino, 1995). Qur'ān commentators, especially of the Shī'ite persuasion, have often pointed out, and made rather feeble attempts to resolve, the apparent contradiction between the traditional Islamic notion that Jewish dietary law is far more demanding than its Muslim counterpart and the statement in Q. 5: 5 that "... the food of those who have been given the book is lawful for you *and your food is lawful for them* ..." (see, e.g., Majlisī, 77: 42–3).

breakdown of fat into kosher and non-kosher types is tied to the procedures of the sacrificial cult, and specifically to the regulations governing burnt offerings: "If anyone eats the fat of animals from which offerings by fire may be made to the Lord, he shall be cut off from his people" (Leviticus, 7: 24). Those portions of an animal's fat that would be destined for immolation on the altar, were the animal to be designated a sacrificial victim, may not be eaten by Israelites anywhere.[17] What portions were these? Leviticus, 7: 3–5 itemizes them:

> All [the animal's] fat shall be offered: the whole broad tail (Leviticus 3: 9 adds: ... which shall be removed close to the backbone); the fat that covers the entrails (3: 9 adds: ... and all the fat that is about the entrails); the two kidneys and the fat which is upon them at the loins; and the fatty protuberance on the liver, which shall be removed with the kidneys. The priest shall turn all these into smoke on the altar as an offering by fire to the Lord; it is a guilt offering. All males of the priestly line shall eat thereof.

Thus, the types of fat prohibited to Jews as food are: the fat on the entrails (*ha-ḥelev ha-mekhase et ha-qerev*), the fat on the kidneys (*ha-ḥelev ʿal ha-kelayot*) and the fatty "protuberance" on the liver (*ha-yoteret ʿal ha-kaved*). (Tail/backbone fat [*alya*], although indeed offered up on the altar, is nevertheless excluded from the category of prohibited-because-sacrificed fats due to complex anatomical reasons).

Now, we have seen the Qur'ānic qualification: "[We forbade them the fat of oxen and sheep] save for that fat which is on the back *or on the entrails* (*illā mā ḥamalat ẓuhūruhumā aw al-ḥawāyā*)." Regarding the first point – the fat on the back – the Qur'ān is in agreement with Jewish law, as we saw immediately above.[18] The purported exception of entrails, however, presents a problem. Al-Ṭabarī devotes several pages to this subject,[19] citing authorities who go into detail regarding internal organs the fat of which was supposedly exempt from the Biblical dietary prohibition against *ḥelev/shaḥm*. These privileged viscera comprise: the fat on the innards (*shaḥm* [or: *tharb*] *al-ḥawāyā*), the fat on the kidneys (*shaḥm al-kilyatayn*), the fat on the liver (*shaḥm al-kabd*),

17 The Mishna (Yoma 6: 7) calls these portions *aymurim*.

18 Al-Shāfiʿī is said by al-Qurṭubī to have employed the linguistic-anatomical distinctions arising out of Q. 6: 147 to rule that if a Muslim man swore a pious oath not to eat fat, he could still eat the fat of the back, relying on God's exclusion of that fat from the general category of fat (in the law of the Torah! – Qurṭubī, 7: 103).

19 Ṭabarī, 8: 98–103.

the fat on the intestines (*shaḥm al-ma'bar*), and more. All of these, say the Muslim exegetes, may be eaten by Jews. In other words, the Qur'ānic verse and its accompanying commentaries present a position that is more-or-less the mirror image of that set out in the Pentateuch.[20] The Biblical text establishes the rule that entrail fat may *not* be consumed, but that all other fat *may* be consumed; the Qur'ān claims that the Biblical text establishes the rule that entrail fat *may* be consumed, but that all other fat may *not* be consumed.

We can venture an educated guess about what led to this strange contrariety. As we saw, right after detailing the fats of the various internal organs that are to be broiled on the altar as part of the guilt offering (*asham*), the previously adduced Levitical passage concludes with the words: *kol zakhar ba-kohanim yokhlenu,* which literally translates: "all males of the priestly line shall eat thereof" (Leviticus, 7:6). Given this statement's placement immediately following the list of fats, one's first impression upon reading it is that the priests are being instructed to eat those various portions of entrail-lard directly after the oblation is offered (the more so as *yokhlenu* can modify a plural as easily as a singular object), as if the altar were a stove and the sacrificial ceremony a sacerdotal barbecue. What this verse really means, in extended context, is: "*only* the males of the priestly line *may* eat of it" – as opposed to the remainder of the Israelites, who may not do so – and the "it" in question refers to the guilt offering itself, and specifically to the parts of it that were *not* immolated, not to the entrail fats, which had been burnt to a crisp on the altar. In isolation, however, this concluding statement could conceivably have been understood as enjoining upon the priests the ingestion of the fats enumerated in the verses prior to it, and – since in this particular spot in the text there is nothing to indicate otherwise – an extrapolation could plausibly have been made from the priests to the rest of the Israelites. Here, perhaps, is the root of what became the Qur'ānic and *ḥadīthic* notion that Jews *could* eat the fat of animal innards, the sole instance so far in which *halakha* is made to look less restrictive, not more restrictive, than it actually is.[21]

20 Modern Qur'ān commentators – from George Sale in the early 18th century to Zohurul Hoque at the outset of the 21st – persist in sending readers to Leviticus 7:3 as a reinforcement for Q. 6:147 without qualification of any kind.

21 It should be remembered, however, that since the Qur'ān also *added* a prohibition to the Jewish rule-book against ingesting all other fat – a prohibition which is not found in Torah or Talmud – then in terms of the overall issue of fat consumption, Islam still makes Judaism out to be more restrictive than it ac-

Let us quickly remark upon a few more fat-related points connected to historical *rukhṣa-naskh*. First, it should be noted that the issue of Jacob's *sunna* versus Allāh's *farḍ* as the source of Jewish dietary restrictions crops up here, too. Commenting on the last part of

---

tually is. If this matter was indeed misconstrued in the way we have hypothesized, then – combined with apparent Qur'ānic plays on Pentateuchal phrases like "*samiʿnā wa-ʿaṣaynā*" (see above, chap. 5, notes 2 and 28, chap. 6, n. 37) – it militates for the notion that at least some members of even the earliest generations of Muslims were exposed to, and could comprehend, the actual text of the Hebrew Bible (converts would not have misunderstood this passage). Perhaps, then, Stillman's pronouncement that "needless to say, [medieval Arab-Muslim thinkers] did not know Hebrew" is somewhat overgeneralized (Norman Stillman, "The Judeo-Islamic Historical Encounter: Visions and Revisions" in Tudor Parfitt [ed.], *Israel and Ishmael: Studies in Muslim-Jewish Relations* [Richmond: Curzon Press, 2000], 6. Tradition credits Zayd b. Thābit with learning Hebrew in two weeks [e.g. Abū Dāwūd, *Kitāb al-ʿIlm,* 25: 3638]). Note also, for instance, the assumption that the burning bush was specifically off to Moses' left (e.g., Qurṭubī, 11: 145–6: "*... idh baṣara bi-nār min baʿīd ʿalā yasār al-ṭarīq*"). I am unaware of any midrash that makes such a claim, and, if anything, the Lord's Presence should have been to the right (as the Qur'ān itself seems to indicate: "And when [Moses] came to it, he was called from the right side of the valley in the blessed spot of the bush ..." [Q. 28: 30]). The Biblical text, however, quotes Moses as saying to himself: asura *na ve-er'e et ha-mar'e ha-gadol ha-ze, maduʿa lo yivʿar ha-sne* ("I shall *turn aside* to see this marvelous sight – why is the bush not consumed?" Exodus, 3:3). Given the cross-lingual word-play we have already encountered, it seems at least possible that in the mind of a creative and free-associating Arab-Muslim reader/translator, Hebrew *asura* evoked Arabic *yasār* (or even, perhaps, Arabic "*suriya,*" a designation of ancient vintage for a "land on the left" [*bilād al-shām(āl)* as opposed to *al-yaman*]). For the issue of when and where Muslim scholars had access to which Arabic translations of the Bible, see Lazarus-Yafeh, *Intertwined Worlds,* chapter 5, and Adang, *Muslim Writers,* chapters 1 and 4 (in both works the earlier literature on the subject is cited). Al-Qurṭubī, for one, appears to have been privy to at least certain portions of the Biblical text in one form or another, and Ibn Isḥāq's *Kitāb al-Mubtada'* (as reconstructed by Newby) is full of lengthy quotes from the Pentateuch, Prophets and Writings. In an oral culture where memorization was the premier mode of retention, it is quite possible that when, in the earliest period of Islam, the Jews would "read the Torah in Hebrew and translate it for the people of Islam into Arabic" (according to a widely circulated *ḥadīth*), the Muslims present would absorb much Biblical material verbatim. The question of the possible routes along which information about Judaism and Jewish law was transmitted into Muslim milieus is, however, beyond the scope of the present study. Facile assumptions should not be made (see my "Dead Tradition," 294–5). Libson's *Jewish and Islamic Law* offers some new and intriguing suggestions on this score, especially in chapter 5, and Lassner's discussion of the issues involved (*Queen of Sheba,* chapter 6) is highly enlightening.

Q. 6:147 – "... thus did We reward them for their rebellion. Lo! We are surely truthful" – al-Ṭabarī writes (in first person, speaking for God):

> We are surely truthful regarding the information just provided [in the first two-thirds of the verse] about those Jews, that We forbade them the fat, and prohibited to them the meat of all livestock and fowl that We have mentioned prohibiting to them (i.e. *kulla dhī ẓufurin*), and We are truthful regarding all else that We relate. And [the Jews] are the liars, claiming as they do that all of this was forbidden by Israel to himself, and that they subsequently prohibited it to themselves as a result of his self-prohibition.[22]

Indeed, in this context we have what may be yet another indication of the superiority of Ibn 'Abbās's knowledge of matters Judaic over that of his Muslim contemporaries and successors. Ibn Isḥāq reports that "someone above suspicion told me from 'Ikrima from Ibn 'Abbās that he used to say: 'What Israel forbade to himself was the two lobes of the liver, the kidneys and the fat (except what was upon the back), for that used to be offered in sacrifice and the fire consumed it.'"[23] Though it involves a bit of telescoping or prolepsis (Jacob didn't offer formal sacrifices in the Temple), Ibn 'Abbās's statement is essentially on the mark both in terms of the items forbidden and the reason for their prohibition.

The second point to be made concerns the legal question whether fat – despite the prohibition on its consumption – may legitimately be used in other ways. Here we have an instance of what might, at first glance, be construed as anti-*rukhṣa* on the macrocosmic plane. In Leviticus, 7:24, we read: "Fat from animals that died a natural death or were torn by beasts (in a word: carrion) *may be put to any use* – but you must not eat of it (*ḥelev nevela ve-ḥelev ṭerefa ye'ase le-khol melakha ve-akhol lo tokhluhu*)." Amplifying this statement, in Tractate Pesakhim of the Talmud Rabbi Huna sets up the general principle:

> Every place [in the Torah] where it is written, "He shall not eat," "You shall not eat" or "they shall not eat," both a prohibition on eating and a prohibition on deriving benefit are intended (*eḥad isur akhila ve-eḥad isur hana'a*), unless scripture explicitly makes an exception to this rule, as it does in the case of carrion, for it is written: "You shall not eat anything that

22 Ṭabarī, 8: 102. Similarly, al-Suddī maintains: "*'shuḥūmahā': al-tharb wa-shaḥm al-kilyatayn, wa-kānat al-Yahūd taqūl: innamā ḥarramahu Isrā'īl fa-naḥnu nuḥarrimuhu*" (Ṭabarī, 8: 98).

23 Ibn Isḥāq — Guillaume, 255–6.

has died a natural death; give it to the stranger among you to eat, or you may sell it to a foreigner" (Deut., 14:21).[24]

In *Ṣaḥīḥ* Muslim and elsewhere we encounter the following *ḥadīth*:

> ... from 'Aṭā' b. Abī Rabāḥ, from Jābir b. 'Abd Allāh, that he had heard the Messenger of God proclaim – in the year of the Conquest (630 CE) when he was in Mecca – "Verily, God and His Messenger prohibit the sale of wine, swine, idols and carrion." It was then said to him, "O Messenger of God! What of the *fat* of carrion, with which the hulls of ships are coated, hides are greased and light is given to the people [through candles]? (*a-ra'ayta shuḥūm al-mayta fa-innahu yuṭlā bihā al-sufun wa-yudhanu bihā al-julūd wa-yastaṣbiḥu bihā al-nās?*). The Prophet replied, "No – this is forbidden." Then he said: "May God fight the Jews! For when God, the Mighty and Majestic, forbade them the fat of [carrion], they would melt it down, sell it, and enjoy the proceeds" (*qātala Allāhu al-Yahūd! Inna Allāha 'azza wa-jalla lammā ḥarrama 'alayhim shuḥūmahā, ajmalūhu thumma bā'ūhu fa-akalū thamanahu*).[25]

The Pentateuch, as we just saw, did indeed make a specific point of forbidding the consumption of carrion fat,[26] but in the same breath per-

24 Pesakhim 21b. On the following page, none other than the sciatic tendon is brought in evidence against Rabbi Huna's ruling, for we are commanded not to eat it – and no explicit permission to put it to other use is forthcoming from the Pentateuch – yet the Mishna (ḥullin, 7:2) affirms that "one may send to a gentile [presumably, for a price] a thigh wherein is still the sciatic tendon." This riposte is parried, *inter alia,* with the help of sacrificial blood, regarding which the Bible also instructs "You must not eat of it" (Deut., 12:16 and *passim*) – and regarding which there is similarly no statement of exception – but which, after flowing from the Temple altar into the brook of Kidron, was nevertheless collected and sold to gardeners as fertilizer (Yoma 5:6).

25 Muslim, *Kitāb al-Musāqa wa'l-Muzāra'a, Bāb Taḥrīm Bī' al-Khamr...*, 22:13 (1581). This is a widely syndicated report transmitted through a variety of *asānīd* (see the editor's note on the bottom of Ṭabarī, 8:99 for the many references). Al-Ṭabarī cites its final sentence in two separate reports – solely for the purpose of proving that fat was prohibited to the Children of Israel – even though he joined the Shāfi'iyya as part of the juristic minority that permitted the use (though not the sale) of fat (see al-Nawawī's commentary to this *ḥadīth*). "May God fight against the Jews!" is an allusion to Q. 9:30. See also 'Imād al-Dīn Ismā'īl b. 'Umar b. Kathīr, *Tafsīr Ibn Kathīr* (Cairo: Maktabat Awlād al-Shaykh li'l-Turāth, 2000), 2:185, who echoes R. Huna almost verbatim: "*inna Allāha lam yuḥarrim 'alā qawm akl shay'in illā ḥarrama 'alayhim thamanahu.*"

26 Of course, *no* part of an animal that died naturally could be eaten, but since Leviticus 7:25 warned that "if anyone eats the fat of *animals from which burnt offerings may be made* to the Lord, he shall be cut off from his people," one might perhaps have concluded that the fat of carrion, which was *not* eligible to

mitted any other use of this product. The Talmud, as we also observed, reinforced this right. Muḥammad, according to the above tradition, found (what certainly sounds like) this same "loophole" deceitful and distasteful, and attributed it – not to God, as the Bible does – but to the Jews themselves, who managed to wriggle out of the divine prohibition and turn a profit. It is important to note that even in this sole instance of what may appear to be a reversal of the *rukhṣa* trend (Jews permitted themselves to use carrion fat to grease their hides and make their candles whereas Muslims could not do so) things are not as they seem at first glance. God did not here send down a new revelation in the context of Islam to replace an old revelation vouchsafed unto the Jews (as was the case with menstruation, booty, urine, *lex talionis,* inedible animals, etc.). Rather, Muslim tradition asserts that Muḥammad simply corrected an age-old abuse of the Jews in connection with the commercial exploitation of fat, making sure it did not insinuate itself into Islam.

Finally, we must bear in mind that all of these complex rules, regulations, distinctions and classifications regarding fat *consumption* were abrogated with the coming of the Qur'ān.[27] "The correct opinion," states al-Qurṭubī, "is that God the Mighty and Majestic removed this prohibition through Islam (*rafa'a dhālika al-taḥrīm bi'l-Islām*)." Al-Qurṭubī supports this assertion, *inter alia,* with the help of the following *ḥadīth* (recorded – as he points out – in the *ṣaḥīḥān* of al-Bukhārī and Muslim):

> ... from 'Abd Allāh b. al-Mughaffal, who said: We were laying siege to the [Jewish] fortress of Khaybar (in 628 CE), and somebody threw a sack of fat [over the wall – evidently a Jew who had stored it up intending to sell it]. I leapt upon it and said: By God, I won't give anyone even a bit of it [but will eat it all myself]! Then I turned around, and there was the Messenger of God, smiling (*fa-iltafattu fa-idhā rasūl Allāh mubtasiman*).[28]

The Prophet's smile said it all: Muslims, unlike Jews, were permitted to feast on fat.[29] Another link in the heavy chain of *ḥaraj* had been broken.

---

be sacrificed on the altar, could in fact be consumed. Verse 7:24 – "carrion may be put to any use, but you must not eat it" – may be seen as preempting this possibility with a special reminder.

27 There is a minority opinion, attributed to Mālik and Ibn al-Qāsim, that the consumption of fat is frowned upon (*makrūh*) in certain circumstances.

28 Qurṭubī, 7:103–4. See the parallel version in *Mughnī,* 1:82. The permission to eat things previously forbidden is additionally alluded to in Q. 5:5: al-yawm *uḥilla lakum al-ṭayyibātu* ...

29 A responsum recorded by the 15th century CE *faqīh* Aḥmad al-Wansharīsī

Of the two passages excerpted at the outset of this section – Q. 4: 160–1 and Q. 6: 147 – we have so far focused primarily on the latter, where an important aspect of the "what" of Jewish religious rigor is spelled out (the dietary restrictions). For more information about the "why" of such divinely imposed hardships, we must turn our attention to the former passage, which we reprint here:

> Because of the wrongdoing of the Jews; and because of their hindering of many from Allāh's way; and because of their taking of usury (though they were forbidden it); and because of their devouring people's property falsely – because of all this, We forbade them the good things which had previously been lawful for them (Q. 4: 160–1).

We have already seen that one of the premier malfeasances of the Banū Isrā'īl in punishment for which they were burdened with difficult ritual and social observances was their own predilection for arduous practices. (Another crime of which they are accused in this connection – and which we also noted briefly above – is that of trying to whitewash the embarrassing fact that large portions of their religious system are the result of divine wrath. Note the vicious cycle). The commentary on Q. 4: 160–1 offers additional examples of the Jewish misdeeds that provoked God to visit them with *dīn al-'usr.*[30] Al-Ṭabarī enumerates some of these, employing Qur'ānic phraseology:

---

deals with the question: "May the Jews sell meat they reject as *terefah* to the Muslims? And are the Muslims allowed to eat it?" Answer: "Yes to both questions. The fact that the Jews may not eat these parts does not mean the Muslims cannot." Camilla Adang, "Fatwās as a Source for the Study of Relations between Muslims and non-Muslims in the Islamic West," in Nili Cohen and Andreas Heldrich (eds.), *The Three Religions* (Munich: Herbert Utz Verlag, 2002), 176.

30 "*Ḥarramnāhu 'alayhim 'uqūbatan minnā lahum wa-thawāban 'alā a'mālihim al-say'a wa-baghyīhim 'alā Rabbihim*" (Ṭabarī, 8: 101). See also Wheeler, "Israel and the Torah," 83–4. Wheeler writes: "Because of their disobedience, the Israelites forfeit the promise made to Abraham and receive stricter laws reminding them of their transgression." See Ezekiel 20: 25: "I (God) gave them (Israel) laws that were not good and rules by which they could not live." While it is doubtful, given the context, that this refers to the regulations of the Pentateuch (the commentators offer a variety of explanations), still, it may have often been read that way, especially by Christians, and could have thus filtered into Muslim tradition. In general, the tenor and even terminology of Allāh's excoriation of Israel in Qur'ān and *ḥadīth* is particularly reminiscent of parts of Ezekiel. The Qur'ānic cooptation (in Q. 2: 63) of the Jewish legend according to which "God held [Mount Sinai] above their heads like a ceiling and said: "If you accept my Torah well and good; if not, there shall be your grave! (i.e. I will,

> By this verse Allāh the Exalted intends to say: "We have prohibited to the Jews – who broke the covenant they had made with their Lord,[31] and disbelieved the signs/messages of God (*kafarū bi-ayāt Allāh*),[32] and killed their prophets,[33] and slandered Mary,[34] and perpetrated [other crimes] recorded in God's book – tasty foods and other things which were once permitted to them, in order to chastise them for their wickedness."
>
> And by "their hindering of many from Allāh's way" He means their subversion of many people, and their leading of God's servants mightily astray from His religion and from the right road that He has prescribed for them (*ṣaddihim ʿibād Allāhi ʿan dīnihi wa-subulihi allatī sharaʿahā li-ʿibādihi ṣaddan kathīran*). Their subversion of believers from the path of God consists of their false statements concerning God, and their false claims regarding what they have received from God, and their corruption of the text of scripture and distortion of its straightforward meaning (*tabdīluhum kitāb Allāh wa-taḥrīf maʿānīhi ʿan wujūhihi*). And the greatest of these subversions was their repudiation of the apostleship of our Prophet Muḥammad, and their unwillingness to reveal to those ignorant of the matter what they know [from their scriptures] of his affair.[35]

An interesting association is made in connection with another transgression for which the Jews are taken to task in this verse: "... and because of their devouring people's property falsely."[36] "This means," explains al-Ṭabarī, "that they would take bribes in [exchange for a favorable] judgment (*kānū ya'khudhūna min al-rishā ʿalā'l-ḥukm*),[37] as God

---

drop the mountain – Shabbat 88a)," may also connect up to the Muslim idea that God *imposed* the Torah upon the Israelites as a punishment.

31 For Israelite violation of the covenant see Q. 5: 13, 2: 83–5 and *passim.*

32 This may refer either to the miracles performed for the Israelites in Egypt and the wilderness, which impressed them but little (see Q. 2: 49–75) or to the revelations vouchsafed unto Muḥammad (see Q. 2: 41). The Jews disdained both. Some of the formulations in this and the ensuing passages we will adduce owe a debt, of course, to the New Testament, as well as – ultimately – to the Biblical prophets themselves.

33 Q. 2: 61, 2: 91, 3: 112, and elsewhere. See below, Conclusion, n. 10.

34 Q. 4: 153.

35 Ṭabarī, 6: 32. Many Muslim sources claim that Muḥammad's advent was predicted in the Bible (see Lazarus-Yafeh, *Intertwined Worlds,* 75–111; McAuliffe, "Prediction" and, e.g., Q. 6: 20. See also above, chap. 5, n. 15, as well as the commentaries to Q. 2: 89).

36 See also Q. 5: 62.

37 Cf. "You shall not subvert the needy in their disputes. Keep far from a false charge; do not bring death on the innocent and righteous, for I will not acquit the wrongdoer. Do not take bribes, for bribes blind the clear-sighted and upset the pleas of the just" (Exodus, 23: 6. See also Deut., 10: 17 and 17: 19).

says about them in His Book: 'You see many of them vying with one another in sin and transgression and the devouring of illicit gain' (Q. 5: 62). And another way they would devour the peoples' property was by taking sums for writing books that they claimed had come from God,[38] and taking interest even though this was forbidden to them. And God punished them for devouring all of these vile victuals (*al-ma'ākil al-khasīsa*) by prohibiting to them the consumption of many delicious foods which were previously permitted to them."[39] Measure for measure.

38 Q. 2: 79: "Therefore woe unto those who write the scripture with their own hands and then say, "This is from Allāh," that they might purchase a small gain therewith. Woe unto them for that which their hands have written, and woe unto them for what they earn thereby." See also the commentaries to Q. 5: 63 – "Why do not the rabbis and doctors of the law (*al-rabbāniyūn wa'l-aḥbār*) prohibit them from uttering sinful words and eating things forbidden (*wa-aklihim al-suḥt*)?" – according to which the "forbidden food" in question is ill-gotten gain of a similar type.

39 Ṭabarī, 6: 33. Qurṭubī speaks of the Jews' "seizing of the peoples' money unlawfully and on false pretenses" (*istiḥlāluhum amwāl al-nās bi'l-bāṭil* – Qurṭubī, 7: 104).

9. Turning the Tables

The Muslim-Jewish Polemic over Sexual Positions

Although the myriad ties that bind Jewish and Islamic tradition have attracted the attention of scholars for almost two centuries, much of this profoundly significant sub-discipline remains unexplored. One avenue of inquiry often indicated but seldom pursued involves the exploitation of Jewish legal sources for purposes of illuminating aspects of Islamic jurisprudence. Rarer still, if extant at all, are attempts to clarify difficult issues in *Jewish* law with the help of Muslim juristic or exegetical material. In this section, we will endeavor to apply both of these methods to a specific problem bearing on *rukhṣa-naskh*. Along the way, we shall encounter evidence of an astonishing degree of interaction and/or overlap between the learned classes of early Islam and those of Rabbinic Judaism.

Sins of the Fathers: The Jewish Stance

We begin with a *ḥadīth*:

> ʿAbd Allāh b. ʿAlī reported that a group of the Prophet's Companions were sitting around one day, and a Jew was nearby (*wa-rajul min al-Yahūd qarībun minhum*), and one of the Companions said to the others: "I have sex with my wife lying down." Another said: "I have sex with her standing." A third said: "As for me, I take my wife while she's on her side[1] or on all fours" (*ʿalā janbihā wa-bārikatan*). The Jew came over and exclaimed: "You people are no better than animals! (*mā antum illā amthāl al-bahāʾim*). We Jews have intercourse in only one position" (*innamā naʾtīhā ʿalā hayʾatin wāḥidatin*). [In response to this,] Allāh revealed: "Your wives are a tilth for you; come to your tilth in any manner you

1 Or: on her back – see below, note 29.

please ..." (*nisā'ukum ḥarthun lakum fa'tū ḥarthakum annā shi'tum* – Q. 2:223).[2]

What is the actual Talmudic position on sexual positions? The answer is somewhat complicated. Seeking to address one of the classical conundrums of theodicy – the phenomenon of congenital defects – Tractate Nedarim of the Babylonian Talmud offers the following:

> Rabbi Yoḥanan b. Dahabai said: The ministering angels revealed four things to me: (1) Why are cripples born? Because [their parents] "overturn their table" (*ḥigrin mipnei ma havin? Mipnei she-hofkhim et shulḥanam*). (2) Why are mutes born? Because [their fathers] kiss [their mothers] on "that place" (*viz.* the genitalia). (3) Why are children born deaf? Because [their parents] talk during intercourse (*mipnei she-mesaprim bi-sh'at tashmish*). (4) Why are children born blind? Because [their fathers] look at "that place."[3]

Having registered Rabbi Yoḥanan's purportedly heaven-sent schema of sexual crimes and their pre-natal punishments, the Gemara proceeds to raise several objections to it. The first of these focuses on a single clause: the notion that talking during intercourse is a sin, the wages of which are – measure for measure – hearing-impaired offspring. An anecdote is adduced in which Ima Shalom, the wife of the famous first century Tanna Rabbi Eliezer b. Horkinus (Hyrcanus), is asked why her children are so beautiful (*yefefin be-yoter*). She responds:

> [My husband] does not have relations with me[4] at the beginning of the night, or at the end of the night, but only in the middle of the night. And

2 Ṭabarī, 2:534. The commentators suggest a variety of alternate circumstances for the revelation of this verse, as we shall see.

3 Nedarim, 20a. Earlier on the same page we read that "he who looks at the heel of a woman [a euphemism, we are soon told, for the 'filthy place' (*bayt ha-ṭinofet*)] will have degenerate children" (*banim she-aynam mehuganim*).

4 The Hebrew has *ayno mesaper 'imi*, "does not converse with me" (RaSHI glosses: *ayno meshamesh*, "does not have intercourse"), an interesting choice of euphemism given the context. Cp. the *double entendre* "intercourse" itself, and cf. RaSHI to Berakhot 3a, according to whom "*isha mesaperet 'im ba'ala*" – one of the signs of the third watch of the night – apparently refers to conversation and nothing more. Given Ima Shalom's association of this metonymic metaphor with the phases of the night, and also the fact that the RaSHI of Tractate Nedarim is not really RaSHI but rather a posthumous recapitulation of the "spirit" of his commentary, one is tempted to speculate that the great commentator himself did not have our passage from Nedarim squarely in mind when he glossed the clause "*isha mesaperet 'im ba'ala*" in Berakhot, and that that clause should perhaps be rendered differently (*scil.*, "women having relations with their husbands"). However, it is somewhat hard to credit the idea that marital

> when he has relations (*ukhshehu mesaper*) he uncovers a handbreadth and covers a handbreadth, and he is as one driven by a demon.[5] I asked him: Why do you act thus? He answered: So that my mind will not wander to another woman, and our offspring be illegitimate.[6]

Even the proper translation of this conjugal exchange, let alone its correct interpretation, is far from clear, but the Talmud is primarily interested in the fact that it took place at all: here is the greatest rabbinic luminary of his generation in full palaver with his wife at the height of passion, and what's more, his children turn out perfect. This parry is quickly riposted – the angel who spoke to R. Yoḥanan was referring to *general speech* as being harmful to progeny, whereas Ima Shalom and her husband were discussing pertinent matters of the bed (*mili de-tashmish*) – but a new refutation is offered in its place, this time addressing the entirety of R. Yoḥanan's sexually restrictive "revelation" and invalidating its underlying premise:

> R. Yoḥanan [b. Zakkai] said: These are the words of R. Yoḥanan b. Dahabai, but the sages said: "The law is not according to R. Yoḥanan b. Dahabai, but rather, whatever a man wishes to do with his wife, he may do (*kol ma she adam rotze la'asot be-ishto 'ose*). It is like the case of meat that comes

---

love-making was a sufficiently common feature during the hours of approximately three to five o'clock in the morning that it could function as an effective sign of the third "watch" of the night. The conversation between a waking couple, on the other hand (people rose much earlier than today), might be overheard in a densely crowded or acoustically conducive neighborhood. Thus, RaSHI's interpretation in Berakhot does indeed make more sense in the end.

5 "Uncovering a handbreadth and covering a handbreadth" may mean that he was extraordinarily modest and exposed no more of his wife's skin than necessary (the RoSH agrees, and even ventures that this approach is reminiscent of the notorious "intercourse through a sheet" [*she-lo yehene be-kiruv basar dugmat derekh sadin*]). Similarly, the description of the husband as one who appeared "driven by a demon" may be meant to imply that he had intercourse in a reluctant, forced manner, and not out of love or lust. More likely, however, especially given R. Eliezer's explanation of his actions to his wife ("so that my mind will not wander to another woman"), these depictions indicate the diametric opposite: that Ima Shalom's husband undressed his wife in a tantalizing fashion, bit by bit, in order to heighten the excitement and keep his thoughts focused strictly upon her, and that he had intercourse with her with great passion and vehemence, as one possessed by a demon (this notion is supported by one of the two interpretations suggested by RaSHI: *she-ba eleha be-koakh ve-dome ke-mi she-shed kof'o*).

6 Nedarim, 20b. Fantasizing about another woman while having relations with one's wife is seen as quasi-adultery, and the offspring concieved by such an encounter therefore acquires the (legally irrelevant) status of a quasi-bastard.

> from the butcher's stall: if he desires, he can eat it salted; if he desires, roasted; if he desires, cooked; or if he desires, boiled (*mashal le-basar ha-ba mi-bayt ha-ṭabaḥ: ratza le-okhlo be-melakh, okhlo; tzali, okhlo; mevushal, okhlo; shaluq, okhlo*). (Another simile suggested for the same purpose is that of) a fish bought from the fisherman (which one can prepare in any number of ways)..."
>
> A woman came to Rabbi [Yehuda HaNasi] and said, "Rabbi, I set him (*viz.* my husband) a table, and he overturned it!" (*'arakhti lo shulḥan ve-hofkho*). Rabbi[7] responded, "My daughter, the Torah has permitted you [to your husband]; what can I do for you? Another woman came to Rav with the same complaint, and he replied, "How is this [situation] different from [that of] a fish?" (*mai shna min binita?*) [in the second simile, above].[8]

The upshot of this discussion is, then, that all sexual positions are permissable according to Jewish law, as the Tosafot commentary to the above passage emphasizes: "It is written: 'When a man takes a wife [and cohabits with her ...' – Deut., 22: 13]. She is thus 'taken' by him, in order to do with her as he wishes" (*hi lekukha lo la'asot bah kol ḥeftzo*).[9]

But a question remains: is anything else covered by the all-encompassing *carte blanche*, "whatever a man wishes to do with his wife, he may do"? Is anal intercourse also included under this rubric? The answer to this question depends on how we understand the pivotal expression, "overturning the table" (*hafikhat ha-shulḥan*). R. Yoḥanan b. Dahabai had claimed that the sin of fathers (or parents) who "overturn their table" is visited upon their children, who are born lame. RaSHI explains: "'Overturn their table' means [his] face to [her] back (*panim ke-neged 'oref*), for [this refers to those who] have 'abnormal intercourse' with their wives" (*she-ba'im al-neshotayhen she-lo ke-darkah.*

7 Rabbi Yehuda HaNasi – patriarch of Judea, descendent of David, redactor of the Mishna (d. early third century CE) – is often referred to simply as "Rabbi."

8 Nedarim 20b. RaSHI comments on *binita*: "a fish, that he may eat any way he wants." Tosafot: "A fish, that he may fry or boil as he pleases." The comparison of the female sexual partner to various victuals is common, of course, in both ancient and recent times. Angolan tribesmen explained their promiscuity/polygyny to the anthropologist studying them by saying that they were "not able always to eat of the same dish" (Will Durant, *The Story of Civilization* [New York: Simon and Schuster, 1935], vol. 1, p. 40). Early twentieth century American slang called an attractive woman a "dish" as well.

9 The Tosafot is a running commentary to the Talmud composed between the eleventh and thirteenth centuries CE by a number of contributors who saw themselves as direct and indirect disciples of the most famous commentator, RaSHI (R. Shlomo ben Yitzḥaq, d. 1105 CE).

"*Bi'a she-lo ke-darkah*" is Talmudic code for anal penetration). The thirteenth century commentator R. Asher b. Yeḥiel (RoSH) seconds this interpretation, and adds a sort of karmic justification: "'Overturn their table' refers to buggery (*leshamesh she-lo ke-darkah*), and this is measure for measure: since he causes her pain in her knees, [his] offspring will be crippled in the legs" (*she-maṭriaḥ otah 'al arkuvoteha le-fikhakh ha-banim nekhe [sic] raglayim*).[10] Tosafot and Rabbenu Nissim – the two remaining commentaries printed on the Talmudic page – agree that the referent is anal intercourse. Since, as we saw, the Gemara goes on to decree unequivocably in favor of the right to engage in "table inversion" and against the notion that such activity harbours any

10 Aside from the obvious question why the infant must suffer for his father's (or parents') wrongdoing, one does want to inquire of the RoSH how it is that Providence's solicitousness for the woman's welfare stops short of concerning Itself with the life-long anguish she will experience as a result of raising a crippled child. If the focus of R. Yoḥanan b. Dahabai's statement is solely on the retribution meted out to the *man* for his actions (such that "*hofkhim et shulḥanam*" refers to the father's act alone), which it may well be (and which, according to the RoSH's point of view, it *must* be, for he paints the wife as victim, not perpetrator); and if we understand R. Yoḥanan to be saying that the physically challenged child is not necessarily the product of the specific deviant instance of cohabitation under scrutiny (and thus, of course, we are forced to understand him from the RoSH's point of view, for the RoSH sees "table inversion" as referring to anal sex. This reading is also supported by the remainder of R. Yoḥanan's equations, which involve actions – kissing, conversing, looking – which do not engender offspring); if all this be true, then one slim possibility suggests itself: that the RoSH is envisioning a polygamous situation, in which the *man's* offspring – by any woman, not necessarily the one with whom he engages in problematic love-making – will be afflicted for his crime. This is farfetched, however, and still leaves many ethical questions unanswered (among them: why should *any* wife be made to pay for her husband's perversions with another spouse?). It is more probable that the RoSH is merely elucidating the internal logic of a position that he knows will ultimately be defeated, and/or that he sees the whole passage as more hortatory and homiletical than reflective of any rigid reality. Tosafot proffers a similar explanation to that of the RoSH, but with a significant twist: "Because *they* alter their sexual practice in connection with the thighs, *their* children are damaged in the thighs." Here, the measure for measure idea is maintained, but blame is cast on both partners: because they regularly engage in anal intercourse (*meshamshim miṭatam she-lo ke-darkam*), when they do eventually conceive through *vaginal* intercourse, the fetus may be defective (I say "may be" because R. Yoḥanan's schema, even if meant to be taken literally, does not necessarily involve a set of one-to-one correspondences: handicapped people happen, in retrospect, as a result of their parents' prurience; but such sexually immoral behavior does not automatically lead to a physically challenged child).

negative consequences for future offspring, the conclusion is that the *halakha* permits heterosexual sodomy.

Confirmation of this conclusion may be had from a different quarter. The Mishna in Tractate Yevamot entertains the (largely hypothetical) scenario of two men who had betrothed a wife each, and, having decided to celebrate their weddings in tandem, inadvertantly switched brides on the eve of the nuptials and consummated the marriage with the wrong women.[11] The procedure in such a case involves, *inter alia,* the return of the wives to their proper husbands, but only after a celibate interval of three months. This interregnum (similar to the *'idda* period in Islamic law) is designed to ensure that no child was conceived on that midsummer night of unintended wife-swapping.[12] To this requirement, however, the Gemara raises an objection: "But surely no woman is impregnated by her first sexual encounter!" (*ve-ha ayn isha mit'aberet be-bi'a rishona* – such, evidently, was the belief at the time, at least in certain circles: conception could not occur during the same sexual act in which the hymen was perforated). A rejoinder to this protest is brought in Rava's name: "But wasn't Tamar impregnated by her first sexual encounter?!"

Tamar was the daughter-in-law of Judah, the fourth son of Jacob. She had been married to Judah's firstborn, Er, but "Er was evil in the sight of the Lord, and the Lord took his life." Er having died childless, the obligation of Levirite marriage fell upon Onan, his younger brother, and Judah instructed him: "Go in unto your [deceased] brother's wife and do your duty by her as a brother-in-law, and provide offspring in your brother's name." But Onan was loathe to bring children into the world who would not be recognized as his own, and so he performed coitus interruptus and "spilled [the seed] on the ground" (onanism). This act was similarly displeasing to the Lord, and Onan shared his elder brother's fate. As the years went by subsequent to these events, Tamar saw that Judah was in no hurry to dispatch his third and last son, Shelah, on the mission that had – so it no doubt appeared – led to the demise of his other two. In desperation, she dis-

11 Half of this scenario, of course, took place in the story of Jacob, who mistook Leah for Rachel on his wedding night and "came in unto her" (Genesis, 29: 18–26), so it may not have been perceived as entirely theoretical.

12 Such a child would be considered illicit – a *momzer* – and illicit individuals are subject to certain unique restrictions in Jewish law. Were the brides returned immediately to their lawful husbands and permitted to them sexually, the status of any issue would be unknown.

guised herself as a harlot and stood by a fork in the road until her father-in-law passed by on the way up to shear his sheep. She caught his eye, he went in unto her, and nine months later she was delivered of twins.[13]

Thus – returning to the Talmudic deliberation – Rava could adduce the example of Tamar as a woman who conceived on the first try, and thereby support the original ruling of the Mishna (regarding the marital mix-up) requiring a three-month waiting period after the initial instance of erroneous intercourse before the brides may be returned to their rightful spouses. The reader is no doubt ready with the same rejoinder to Rava immediately offered by the Talmudic text: "But what of Tamar's previous husbands, Er and Onan?" The first of these presumably, and the second definitely, slept with her, and thus her virginity was a thing of the distant past by the time she cohabited with Judah. The Gemara answers this challenge on Rava's behalf: "[Er and Onan] engaged [solely] in anal intercourse [with Tamar]" (*shimshu she-lo ke-darkan*).[14]

One's initial impression upon exposure to this Talmudic "analysis" of the Biblical narrative is that the deadly sin of Er and Onan was sodomy (an act in which the seed also goes to waste), and that sodomizing the female is therefore prohibited. The Tosafot commentary indeed posits this interpretation, only to rebut it with the help of the discussion in Tractate Nedarim that we already examined above:

> It sounds from this as if anal intercourse is forbidden (*mashma' de-asur leshamesh she-lo ke-darkah*). And yet we read in the second chapter of Nedarim: "A woman came to Rabbi [Yehuda HaNasi] and said, 'Rabbi, I set [my husband] a table, and he overturned it!' (*'arakhti lo shulḥan vehofkho*). Rabbi responded, 'My daughter, the Torah has permitted you [to your husband] – what can I do for you?'" From that exchange we establish the legal conclusion (that anal intercourse is permissable). We know that "he overturned the table" refers to anal intercourse (*ve-hofkho hayynu she-lo ke-darkah*), because [this method of coition] causes the woman pain [which is why she came complaining to Rabbi], as it is written: "[And Dina, the daughter whom Leah had borne to Jacob, went out to visit the daughters of the land.] And Shekhem the son of Ḥamor the Ḥivite, the prince of

---

13 Genesis, chapter 38.

14 And thus her virginity remained intact until her father-in-law had vaginal intercourse with her. Yevamot, 34–a. Onan is thus perceived as having "spilled the seed" not so much through coitus interruptus as by having intercourse in an orifice unhelpful for reproduction.

the land, saw her; and he took her, and lay with her, and *ill-treated* her" (*va-yiqakh otah va-yishkav otah va-*ye'aneha, Genesis, 34: 2) – he "ill-treated" her by having unnatural intercourse with her.[15] Similarly, [we can demonstrate the association of anal intercourse with physical discomfort (or emotional anguish) from Laban's adjuration of his son-in-law Jacob (Genesis, 31: 49–50): "May the Lord keep watch between you and me, when we are out of sight of each other:] if you *ill-treat* my daughters (*im* t'ane *et benotai*)..."[16] Nor can "overturning the table" signify a situation in which the woman is on top and the man is underneath (as the first of two opinions attributed to RaSHI in Nedarim had proposed),[17] for then she would have had no reason to [come to Rabbi and] complain (since she experiences no physical or emotional distress in such a situation).[18]

Having established that "table inversion" is a metaphor for heterosexual sodomy (for this was the only act which could have impelled the anonymous woman in Nedarim to bring a grievance before Rabbi) and therefore that such sodomy is legitimate (because Rabbi made clear to the woman that her husband had every right to "overturn her table"), Tosafot now takes up an additional argument for the licitness of anal intercourse:

Moreover, we read in the chapter on The Four Methods of Judicial Execution in Tractate Sanhedrin that R. Eliezer said in the name of R. Ḥanina: "A pagan (*oved kokhavim*) who has anal intercourse with his wife has committed a capital offense."[19] [The Gemara there] immediately raises the fol-

15 See Genesis Rabbah, 80: 5: "'And he lay with her' – this is natural (i.e. vaginal) intercourse; 'and he ill-treated her' – this is unnatural (i.e. anal) intercourse." Shekhem raped Dina in both these manners.

16 For a lone speculation – among many others to the contrary – that the "ill-treatment" referred to in this imprecation is anal intercourse, see the various commentaries to Yoma, 77b.

17 This was the position demanded by the demonic Lilith, Adam's wife before Eve in Jewish legend (Lassner, *Queen of Sheba,* 21). The second opinion ascribed to RaSHI in the same place (Nedarim 20a) is that the referent is anal intercourse. Since the RaSHI commentary to Tractate Nedarim is considered somewhat unreliable – a sort of pseudo-RaSHI, probably penned by students or persons even further removed from the great commentator – Tosafot may well be implying that the first of these two contradictory opinions related in RaSHI's name (that "table turning" means the wife on top) is an erroneous attribution.

18 Or, as Tosafot puts it while commenting on Tractate Sanhedrin, 58b, "['Table inversion'] does not refer to [a situation in which] she is on top and he is underneath, for what does she lose by this?" (*de-ma mafsedet be-khakh?*).

19 The actual formulation, found in Sanhedrin, 58b, is: "A Noaḥide who has anal intercourse with his wife is liable" (*ben Noaḥ she-ba 'al ishto she-lo ke-darkah*

lowing objection: "Is it possible that a pagan should be liable to the death penalty for this when a Jew who commits the identical transgression is *not* liable [to the same, or any, punishment for it]?" (Now this rhetorical question only makes sense if by stating that a Jew is) "not liable" [to punishment if he engages in anal intercourse the Gemara actually] intends to say [that a Jew is] "not prohibited" [from engaging in anal intercourse].[20] For were anal intercourse in fact forbidden to a Jew, then it would indeed be logical to assume that a pagan could be executed for the same deed, since [the legal principle regarding pagans is that] "their admonition is their death," as in the case of robbery and the rest [of the Noaḥide laws. In such a case the Gemara's question – "Is it possible that a pagan should be liable to the death penalty for sodomy when a Jew who commits the identical transgression is *not* liable?" – would be meaningless] (*de-i ika isur be-Yisrael*

ḥayav). A Noaḥide is a pre- or non-Israelite descendent of Noah – father of all humankind after the flood – and is bound, according to Jewish law, by some seven general minimum standards of behavior (*sheva' mitzvot b'nei Noaḥ*), including prohibitions against murder, theft, idolatry and forbidden sexual relations (*gilui 'arayot*). Tosafot's usage "*oved kokhavim*" literally means a star-worshipper. Other versions of, or references to, this statement in rabbinic literature substitute the term "a Cuthean," another cognomen for non-Jews. "Liable" is shorthand here for "liable to the death penalty."

20 This is somewhat difficult, and I will attempt to explain it here and again in the text. Some acts in Jewish law are not punishable after the fact, but are nevertheless forbidden before the fact (*paṭur aval asur*). Tosafot is saying that the only situation which would appear illogical enough to induce the rabbis of Gemara Sanhedrin to wonder aloud about the condemnation of the pagan to death for anal intercourse, is a situation in which Jews were perfectly free to engage in that same act. Such a discrepancy would certainly strike the rabbis as strange. Were Jews merely *not liable to punishment* for anal coition *a posteriori*, but nevertheless *forbidden* to do it *a priori*, there would be no reason to marvel about the *execution* of gentiles for the same crime: this level of discrimination between Jew and non-Jew was considered par for the course (i.e. there are numerous legal scenarios in which if a Jew and a non-Jew both commit the same transgression, the non-Jew will be more severely punished). But if Jews are not only *not liable to punishment* for sodomy, but are in fact *fully allowed* to perform this act in the first place, *then* the claim that gentiles should perish for the same sexual deviation certainly piques one's curiosity: for *that* level of discrimination between Jews and non-Jews is not plausible according to the principles of *halakha*. All of this being assumed, then, let us now admit the fact that the rabbis' curiosity was in fact piqued: a question (the very question we are currently scrutinizing) was indeed provoked in their minds by R. Ḥanina's opening proposal that pagans who have anal sex must die. That question, we recapitulate, would only have arisen if the law were perceived to provide that Jews are *entirely permitted* to practice anal intercourse. Since the question did arise, Tosafot concludes that they are in fact so permitted. Q. E. D.

niḥa de-meḥayev be-oved kokhavim mita de-azharatan zo hi' mitatan kemo be-gezel ve-sha'r devarim).

In the rough and rudimentary legal system (known as "the Noahide Laws") dreamt up by Judaism for the remainder of mankind as the minimum criterion of civilization, punishments were not graduated to fit crimes. All perpetrations of these fundamental felonies – murder, blasphemy, theft, incest, ripping a limb off of a live animal, neglecting to set up law courts, and more – equally carried death in their train.[21] Thus it is entirely plausible that a transgression for which a Jew would only be flogged (or even just scolded) would theoretically warrant stoning if committed by a pagan. But if so (Tosafot is asking), then how understand the Gemara's objection in Sanhedrin: "Is it conceivable that a pagan should be liable to the death penalty for [anal intercourse] when a Jew who commits the same transgression is *not* liable [to punishment for it]?" After all, as we have just seen, such a breakdown is eminently conceivable! Thus, the Gemara's perturbation only makes sense if we assume a certain looseness of usage and in place of "a Jew is not *liable*" (i.e. after the fact) for engaging in sodomy we substitute "a Jew is not *prohibited*" (i.e. in the first place) from engaging in sodomy. A situation in which gentiles are executed for an act altogether *permitted* to Jews certainly should raise a rabbinic eyebrow and provoke further deliberation. In other words, the necessary assumption behind the Gemara's objection is that anal intercourse is an entirely licit act for Jews according to the *halakha*.[22] Tosafot concludes its discussion of this topic with a statement of Rabbenu Yitzḥaq:

> [Anal intercourse] is not considered the [evil] act of Er and Onan unless one engages in it on a regular and constant basis and specifically for the purpose of "spoiling the seed" [in order to avoid impregnation] (*ela ke-she mitkaven lehashḥit zera' ve-ragil la'asot ken tamid*). But if every so often

21 See Sanhedrin, 57a.

22 See also Tosafot to Sanhedrin 58b (opening words: *Mi ika midi*...), where the conclusion is similarly formulated: "[Anal intercourse] is not forbidden [to a Jew] unless he engages in it consistently in order that his wife should not become pregnant and lose her beauty (*ela 'ose kakh tadir she-lo tit'aber ve-yakḥish yofyah*). But if most of his relations with his wife are 'natural' (i.e. vaginal) but occasionally he is driven by his passion to desire her in the 'unnatural' (i.e. anal) manner, this is permissable." Tosafot does not follow up on the conundrum it itself identified, *scil.*, how a fully permitted act for a Jew could be a capital offense for a gentile (the Gemara in Sanhedrin ultimately challenges the notion that non-Jews are to be executed for anal intercourse).

> one is driven by one's passion to have anal intercourse with one's wife, this is permissable (*aval be-aqra'i be-'alma u-mit'ave lavo 'al ishto she-lo ke-darkah shari*), as we read in Tractate Nedarim: "Whatever a man wants to do with his wife, he may do ..."[23]

Tosafot in all the above-cited passages is only interested in establishing this one legal fact, and therefore does not enter into the question whence the notion is derived in the first place that gentiles are prohibited from engaging in anal intercourse. Bereishit Rabba (18:5) fills in the gap, tracing this interdiction to – or at least finding support for it in – Genesis, 2:24: "Therefore shall a man leave his father and mother and cling unto his wife, and they shall be as one flesh." Only that type of "clinging," extrapolates the midrash, which leads to the fusion of a married couple into "one flesh" (i.e. their offspring) is acceptable. Or, as the Jerusalem Talmud formulates the same point, "only that locus through which the two of them generate 'one flesh'" is permitted (*mi-makom she-shenayhem 'osim basar eḥad*).[24] Anal intercourse not leading to reproduction, it is beyond the pale. This goes for all sons of Adam with the exception of that small group for whom a novel set of norms was inaugurated at Sinai.

Finally, Rabbinic Judaism makes its position clear in the matter of heterosexual sodomy with the help of a comparison to homosexual sodomy. Leviticus, 18:22 warns: "Do not lie with a male as one lies with a female" (*ve-et zakhar lo tishkav mishkevei isha*). The Gemara plays upon the plural-sounding form of the word *mishkevei* and renders this verse slightly otherwise for exegetical purposes: "Do not lie with a man in *the ways* that one lies with a female." "Scripture," continues the Gemara, "is here affirming that are *two ways* to lie with a female" (*shnei mishkavot ba-isha*). RaSHI explains that the Talmud's intent is that for an assortment of legal purposes, anal intercourse is considered equivalent to vaginal intercourse (such that, for instance, if a married women is consensually sodomized by a man other than her husband, these two paramours are guilty of adultery). Now, the verse stipulates that a man must refrain from doing with men what he normally does with women. From this we can deduce the inverse correlate: that a man is *permitted*

---

23 Rabbenu Yitzḥaq was one of the preeminent Ba'alei HaTosafot (contributors to the commentary currently under examination) and – like many of his fellow contributors – a grandson of RaSHI.

24 Yerushalmi Qiddushin, 1:1.

to do with women that which he is *forbidden* to do with men. And what is that? Anal intercourse.[25]

Sodomy and Calumny: The Intra-Islamic Polemic

We have so far surveyed the classical Judaic attitude to variations on the theme of vaginal sex in the missionary position. The recurrent motto epitomizing this attitude is: "Whatever a man desires to do with his wife, he may do." Almost without exception, as we have seen, the medieval commentators on the Talmud include under this catch-all rubric the act of anal intercourse. What is the Islamic outlook on diverse sexual positions and deviant modes of coition? The launch-point for any discussion of this subject is the opening line of the 223rd verse of the

25 This is an application of the pervasive Talmudic principle, "by inference from a negative precept a positive precept may be extracted" (*mi-klal lav ata shome'a hen*). The famous MaHaRSHA (Morenu HaRav Shemu'el Adels, d. 1631 CE) employed a similar method to justify Rabbi Yehuda HaNasi's response in Nedarim to the woman who came complaining of "table inversion." Rabbi said to her (it will be recalled), "My daughter, The Torah has permitted you to your husband – what can I do for you?" Upon what did Rabbi base this statement? After all, no Biblical verse says as much. The MaHaRSHA explains: "Once the Torah forbade both 'natural' and 'unnatural' intercourse with an illicit woman [a conclusion reached by combining the many Biblical pronouncements against adultery and incest with the information gleaned from Levit. 18:22 that there are two official ways to sleep with a woman], we can conclude that with a licit woman (i.e. one's lawfully wedded wife) both of these acts are permissable (for related approaches to, and uses of, Genesis 18:22 – including speculation as to the two "ways" a man might sleep with another *man* – see Yevamot, 83b and Gittin, 85a). Note, in this connection, the tail end of a famous *ḥadīth*, in which a close relative of such logic is evident: "... [The Prophet informed a group of his Companions:] Sexual intercourse is a virtuous act (*wa-fī buḍ'i aḥadikum ṣadaqa*). They said: O Messenger of God! Shall one of us satisfy his passion (*shahwatahu*) and receive a reward for this? He answered: "What do you think: were he to do so in forbidden circumstances, would this not obligate him in punishment? In the same fashion, if he does so in permitted circumstances, should this not bring in its train a reward?" (*a-ra'aytum law waḍa'hā fī ḥarāmin a-kāna 'alayhi wizrun? Fa-ka-dhālika idhā waḍa'hā fī'l-ḥalāli a-lā kāna lahu ajrun?* – Abū Zakariyā' Yaḥyā Muhyī al-Dīn al-Nawawī, *Matnu'l-Arba'īn al-Nawawiya fī'l-Aḥādīth al-Ṣaḥīḥa al-Nabawiya* [Cairo: Muṣṭafā al-Bābī al-Ḥalabī wa-Awlāduhu, n.d.], 29, no. 25. A similar version may be found in the same scholar's *Riyāḍ al-Ṣāliḥīn* [Beirut: Dār al-Kutub al-'Ilmiya, 1999], 52 [13:120]).

second chapter of the Qur'ān: "Your wives are a tilth for you; come to your tilth as you please ..." (*nisā'ukum ḥarthun lakum fa'tū ḥarthakum annā shi'tum*). The occasion for the revelation of these words is variously identified by the exegetical literature (the uncharacteristically large number of alternate scenarios proposed as the *sabab al-nuzūl* for Q. 2:223 testifies to the considerable importance of, and interest in, this issue in early Islam). The conflicting opinions regarding the referent of this clause and the particular acts it prescribes and proscribes are organized by the *tafsīr* into what is essentially a debate over the legality of anal intercourse. By closely examining this debate we shall not only map out an additional route of macrocosmic *rukhṣa-naskh* and witness a truly remarkable degree of intertexture between Judaic and Islamic tradition, but we may even gain new insight into the meaning and significance of the Talmudic discussion just outlined.

First, let us look at some of the more common suggestions regarding the circumstances under which Q. 2:223 descended into the world. We have already cited (at the outset of this chapter) the *ḥadīth* depicting Companions of the Prophet engaged in "locker room talk" about their favorite sexual positions. They are upbraided by a Jew, only to be subsequently supported in their uninhibited latitudinarianism by God Himself. In fact, almost all the *aḥādīth* surrounding the revelation of "Your wives are a tilth for you ..." ascribe the debut of this license to make love multifariously either directly or indirectly to Jewish provocation. The most oft-repeated of such sketches involves an instance of what might be called "*hijra* culture shock":

> Ibn 'Abbās said ... What happened was that the community of *anṣār* had been idolators (*ahl wathan*) living side-by-side with the community of Jews.[26] These last being a People of the Book, [the Yathriban polytheists]

26 Espying seven strangers at Mīna during the pilgrimage of 620–1 CE, Muḥammad approached them and inquired as to their tribal affiliation. Upon receiving the reply, "Banū Khazraj," the Prophet enthused: "Ah! Then you are confederates of the Jews?" "We are," responded his interlocutors, thereby furnishing their questioner with a segue into the subject of monotheism (see Muir, *Life of Mohammad,* 114). The Aws were allied with the Banū Qurayẓa and Banū al-Nadhīr, the Khazraj with the Banū Qaynuqā', but the people of Yathrib used to be addressed collectively as al-Khazraj, and that is probably what is intended in the above anecdote. "God had prepared the way for Islam," writes Ibn Isḥāq, "in that [the Khazraj whom Muḥammad met at al-'Aqaba] lived side-by-side with the Jews who were people of the scriptures and knowledge, while they themselves were polytheists and idolators ..." (Ibn Isḥāq—Guillaume, 197). Ibn 'Abbās reported: "If the child of a woman became sick [in pre-Islamic

saw them as superior to themselves in knowledge and would imitate many of their ways (*yarūna lahum faḍlun ʿalayhim fīʾl-ʿilm fa-kānū yaqtadūna bi-kathīr min fiʿlihim*). A norm of the People of the Book was that they would only have intercourse with their wives with the latter lying on their backs (i.e. in the missionary position – *ʿalā ḥarf*),[27] this being the [method of intercourse in which] the woman is least exposed (*wa-dhālika astar mā takūnu al-marʾa*).[28] The community of *anṣār* (proleptically speaking) adopted this norm of theirs. The Qurashites, on the other hand, used to cohabit with their wives in a manner unknown to/deplorable in the eyes of

---

Yathrib] she would vow that if the child survived she would convert it to Judaism, such that when the Banū al-Naḍīr were expelled there were some children of the Ansār among them..." (Abū Daʾūd, *Kitāb al-Jihād*, 14: 2676). It may be the great extent to which these Arabs were under the influence of their Jewish neighbours that led Sale to describe the proselytes gained by Muḥammad in or around the year 620CE as "six of the inhabitants of Yathrib of the Jewish tribe of Khazraj" (Sale, "Preliminary Discourse," 36).

27 Alternately, "on one side" or "in one manner" (see Lane, *s. v.* "*ḥarf*," 550, col. 2). Although "*ʿalā ḥarf*" might also mean "on the side"; and although what may be a synonym for this, "*ʿalā junūbihinna*," appears in an alternate recension of this report; and finally, although we might be able to cajole both these phrases into directly connoting the missionary position by imagining a man and woman "side-by-side" (i.e. facing each other with the man on top); still, keeping in mind the aforementioned statement of the Jew to the conversing Companions ("We Jews have intercourse in *only one position*" [*innamā naʾtīhā ʿalā hayʾatin wāḥidatin*]), we might also translate "in one manner," or, perhaps, "on one side," i.e. with the women lying on their backs (so the meaning is essentially the same). See Ṭabarī, 2: 533, where "*munḥarifatan*" is offset against "*muḍtajiʿatan*," which latter often indicates recumbency *on one's side*, and the *ḥadīth* with which we began this chapter, where "*muḍtajiʿatan*" seems to harbor a meaning distinct from "*ʿalā janbihā*." On the other hand, see Ṭabarī, 2: 535, where "*ʿalā janb*" is listed as an alternative to "*qāʾiman aw qāʿidan*," and Q. 3: 190, which promises triumph to "those who remember Allāh standing, sitting and [lying] on their sides [*qiyāman wa-quʿūdan wa-ʿalā junūbihim*": in both cases, roots which we are used to associate with "the side" seem to signify lying down. The upshot seems to be, at any rate, that under Jewish influence the Yathriban Arabs went over to having sex solely in the missionary position.

28 The missionary position is "the method of intercourse in which the woman is least exposed/most covered up" either because her genitalia are less visible to her partner, or because if he lies flat upon her he looks at her face and does not see her body, whereas when cohabiting "from behind" both the orifice and much of the body are in plain ("*ẓāhir*" = *ẓahr*, the back) view, especially if the man's torso is vertical and the woman's horizontal. The Jewish manner of intercourse is thus the most modest of all (and recall, in connection with "*astar*," Ima Shalom's husband, R. Eliezer b. Horkinus, who would "uncover a handbreadth and cover a handbreadth").

[the inhabitants of Madīna], enjoying them from the front *and* from behind, as well as thrown down on the ground [or: prostrate] (*kānū yashraḥūna al-nisā' sharḥan munkaran*[29] *wa-yataladhdhadhūna minhunna muqbilātin wa-mudbirātin wa-mustalqiyātin*). When the Emigrants came to Madīna, one of their men married a woman of the Helpers, and made to do the same with her (*viz.* to take her in a manner other than the mission-

29 The explanation offered by al-Qurṭubī's modern editor for "*kānū yashraḥūna al-nisā' sharḥan*" is "*sharaḥa al-rajul jariyatahu idhā waṭa'ahā nā'imatan 'alā qafāhā,*" i.e. that it describes a man having intercourse with his female partner while she lies on her back (al-Ṭabarī's editor confirms: "*sharaḥa al-rajul imra'tahu idhā salaqahā* [= throws her down on her back] *fa-waṭa'hā nā'imatan 'alā qafāhā*" – Ṭabarī, 2: 537, n. 2. Lane defines *sh.r.ḥ.* in this context as "he threw, or laid, upon her back, and then compressed, his female slave or a young woman" and *Lisān al-'Arab* agrees: "*wa-sharaḥa jāriyatahu idhā salaqahā 'alā qafāhā thumma ghashiyahā*"). But if that is the meaning, then what is the word "*munkaran*" doing here (in al-Qurṭubī's recension)? If "*sharḥan*" signifies the missionary position – the specific posture considered legitimate by all parties concerned (including the Jews and soon-to-be *anṣār*) – then what reason could there be to declare it "reprehensible" (let alone "unknown," the other possible translation of *munkaran*)? Even if we translate "*kānū yashraḥūna al-nisā' sharḥan*" as "they used to strip their wives totally naked" and assume that this approach was seen as antithetical to the modesty characterizing the Jewish/Yathriban way (which, as we saw, was considered "*astar mā takūnu al-mar'a*"), there is still no place for censure since Allāh is clearly understood to have approved *all* sexual positions and practices – with the possible exception of heterosexual sodomy – at the end of the *ḥadīth* (by the revelation of Q. 2: 223). And it would certainly be hard to describe the practice of coition in the nude as "strange" or "unknown" to anyone.

"*Munkaran,*" the problematic term, appears in at least three different editions of al-Qurṭubī's commentary, so it is probably not a misprint (although the parallel story in al-Ṭabarī's *Jāmi'* reads "*kānū yashraḥūna al-nisā'* bi-Mekka, *wa-yataladhdhadhūna*...," so a scribal error committed during the period between these two *mufassirūn* is a possibility). One solution that comes to mind is that we should render "*yashraḥūna al-nisā' sharḥan*" as simply "cohabit with their wives" (i.e. in a generic sense, unconnected to any particular posture) and retranslate the entire sentence thus: "The Qurashites used to cohabit with their wives in a reprehensible manner, enjoying them both *vaginally and anally* [as opposed to 'from the front and from behind']." The reprehensible element of this in al-Qurṭubī's eyes would then be anal intercourse, an act of which he is a vehement opponent, as we shall see. This runs into another problem, however: the end of the *ḥadīth* explicitly restricts the permission forthcoming from Allāh to the performance of *vaginal* intercourse from a variety of angles, and does so using the same phraseology we are attempting to parse: "*muqbilātin wa-mudbirātin wa-mustalqiyātin, ya'nī bi-dhālika mawḍi' al-walad.*" If we extrapolate from the end of the *ḥadīth* back to the middle, which seems logical here, then the sentence we are striving to decipher cannot refer to anal sex.

ary, probably from behind). She rebuked him for this (*ankarathu 'alayhi*), and insisted: "We have intercourse only on one side/in one manner. So either do it that way or leave me alone!" The matter became serious between them [or: word of their affair spread][30] and eventually reached the ears of Muḥammad, upon which Allāh revealed: "Your wives are a tilth for you; come to your tilth however you please." That is to say, from the front, from behind, as well as prostrate – in each case the intent being via the [orifice] whence the child emerges (*ya'nī bi-dhālika mawḍi' al-walad*).[31]

The *anṣār* were thus momentarily torn between two opposing influences in the matter of conjugal relations: the restrictive and puritanical convention of the Madīnan Jews versus the "anything goes" approach of the Meccan Emigrants. God stepped in and settled the affair, apparently in favor of the Qurashites. But confusion remained regarding the particulars of each party's position: what *exactly* was advocated by the *Yahūd*, what by the *muhājirūn*, and most importantly, what was decreed by Allāh Himself? What specific sexual positions had originally stood in the dock awaiting judgement, and what, in precise and detailed terms, was the verdict?

As exemplified by the ultimate clause in the passage cited above, the prevailing opinion amongst Companions and commentators held that the latitude granted by "come to your tilth as you please" was limited to any position in *vaginal* intercourse (*ya'nī bi-dhālika mawḍi' al-*

Despairing, I called Etan Kohlberg. His tentative suggestion seems to me to be correct: even if the adjective *munkaran* was added to the text by al-Qurṭubī (which it may well have been, for the term does not appear in any of the versions of this *ḥadīth* found in the cannonical collections), it nevertheless probably refers to a practice strange and/or reprehensible not in the eyes of al-Qurṭubī or the report's narrator (Ibn 'Abbās), but *in the eyes of the Yathribans.* (The interpolation of "*munkaran*" may also have been influenced by the *mufassir*'s knowledge that the *anṣārī* woman will ultimately reprove her *muhājir* husband further down in the passage ["ankarathu *'alayhi*"] for importing the Meccan manner of intercourse to Madīna). If this is the significance of *munkaran* here, then we should indeed understand "*yashraḥūna al-nisā' sharḥan*" as connoting intercourse in general, and should then translate the passage as we have done: "The Qurashites used to cohabit with their wives in a manner unknown to/deplorable in the eyes of [the inhabitants of Madīna], enjoying them [vaginally] from the front *and* from behind..."

30 Al-Qurṭubī's text reads: "*sharā amruhumā,*" but the same report in the commentary of Ibn Kathīr has "*sarā amruhumā,*" which seems to fit better.

31 Qurṭubī, 3: 81–2. See also Muslim, *Kitāb al-Nikāḥ, Bāb Jawāz Jimā'at Imra'tahu fī Qublihā min Quddāmihā wa-min Warā'ihā,* 39:2592; and Baghawī, 27:83).

walad). A strong minority, however, stubbornly maintained that Q. 2:223 constituted permission to engage in anal intercourse as well:

> ʿAṭā b. Yasār related: A man had anal intercourse with his wife during the lifetime of the Messenger of God (*aṣāba rajūl imraʾtahu fī dubrihā ʿalā ahdi rasūl Allāh*), and the people condemned him for this and said, "Plug up her anus!" (*athfirhā*). But Allāh revealed: "Your wives are a tilth for you; come to your tilth as you please."[32]

That the legal status of anal sex was an extremely unstable and "loaded" issue may be gauged both by the vehemence of the exchanges recorded and by the fact that almost every authority quoted in favor of the position condoning that act is also shown either personally disavowing this attribution or being exonerated of it by others. Thus we read, for instance, that:

> ... Ibn ʿAwn reported from Nāfiʿ (the Persian *mawlā* of ʿAbd Allāh b. ʿUmar and an almost peerlessly reliable traditionist), who said: It was Ibn ʿUmar's practice to remain silent whenever the Qurʾān was being recited (*kāna Ibn ʿUmar idhā quriʾa al-Qurʾān lam yatakallim*). One day I recited [in his presence]: "Your wives are a tilth for you; come to your tilth as you please," and he piped up and asked: "Do you know in what context this verse was revealed?" I replied, "No." He said, "It was revealed in reference to having intercourse with women in their anuses" (*nazalat fī ityān al-nisāʾ fī adbārihinna*).[33]

On the other hand, however:

> Abū al-Naḍr said to Nāfiʿ, the *mawlā* of Ibn ʿUmar: "You talk too much! (*qad akthara ʿalayka al-qawl*). For you say about Ibn ʿUmar that he issued a judgment allowing anal intercourse with women" (*aftā bi-an yuʾtā al-*

---

32 Ṭabarī, 2:537 (3471). Since the only vocalization provided by my edition of *Jāmiʿ al-Bayān* is a hamza over the alif, it is difficult to know whether we should read *athfirhā* in command form, as we have done, or, alternately, *athfarahā*: "he has plugged up her anus!" It might also be translated: "tie an *izār* (a waist-wrapper) between her legs."

33 Ṭabarī, 2:535 (3464), where another version shows Nāfiʿ "holding the Qurʾānic codex for Ibn ʿUmar, when the latter reached the verse, 'Your wives are a tilth ...,' and said: "[This constitutes permission] to have anal intercourse with her" (*an yaʾtīhā fī dubrihā*). Similarly, Zayd b. Aslam reported that Ibn ʿUmar said: "A man had anal intercourse with his wife, after which his conscience bothered him (*atā imraʾtahu fī dubrihā fa-wajada fī nafsihi*), so Allāh revealed: 'Your wives are a tilth ...'" (Ṭabarī, 2:536–7 [3470]). On the historicity of Nāfiʿ, and the claim – especially interesting for our purposes, as will become clear below – that he was invented by Mālik b. Anas, see G. H. A. Juynboll, "Nāfiʿ, the *Mawlā* of Ibn ʿUmar," *Der Islam* 70 (1993). Harald Motzki has argued against his thesis in "*Quo vadis, ḥadīt*-Forschung?" *Der Islam* 73 (1996).

nisā' fī adbārihinna). Nāfi' replied: "[Those who ascribe such a statement to me] slander me! I'll tell you how the matter was: Ibn 'Umar was once reviewing the Qur'ān in my presence (*'araḍa 'alayy*[34] *al-muṣḥaf yawman wa-anā 'indahu*). When he reached "Your wives are a tilth ...", he said: O Nāfi'! Do you know what this verse refers to? We Qurashites used to bend our women prostrate and take them [vaginally] from behind (*innā kunnā ma'shar Quraysh nujabbī al-nisā'*).[35] When we arrived at Madīna and married *anṣārī* women, we wanted to do with them what we had done with our other (i.e. Meccan) wives. But [the Madīnan women] were loathe to do that and it grieved them, for they were used to being taken on their sides/in the missionary position (*fa-idhā hunna qad karihna dhālika wa-a'ẓamnahu wa-kāna nisā' al-anṣār innamā yu'tīna 'alā junūbihinna*). And God sent down, "Your wives are a tilth ..."[36]

Here Nāfi' protests (perhaps under pressure) that he has been misquoted: he had related a piece of normatively significant scriptural exegesis in the name of his master, and certain disreputable elements had twisted it to serve their own perverted ends.[37] Other sources saddle the *mawlā* himself with the responsibility for this distortion: Mūsā b. Ayyūb al-Ghāfiqī told Abū Mājid al-Ziyādī that Nāfi' had related regarding Ibn 'Umar that he relied on Q. 2: 223 to sanction heterosexual sodomy. Abū Mājid replied: "Nāfi' lied! I myself regularly associated

34 Thus has al-Qurṭubī's modern editor vocalized this word, although it might be better to read it *'alā*.

35 This second form of the root *j-b-y* is commonly employed to describe the *sujūd* or prostrate position of the *rak'a*. Thus al-Qurṭubī's editor defines this term: "*nujabbī al-nisā' – ay na'tīhinna mankibīn 'alā wujūhihinna.*" The association between the nomenclature of sexual positions and prayer positions may perhaps be echoed in the *ḥadīth* with which we opened this chapter – where Companions speak of having intercourse with their wives "lying down, standing, on her knees (*bārikatan*) and on her side/back (*'alā janbihā*) – if we compare it roughly to the positions of the *rak'a*, or to verses like Q. 3: 190, which speaks of "those who remember Allāh standing, sitting and [lying] on their sides (*qiyāman wa-qu'ūdan wa-'alā junūbihim*)." The "*rak'a* position" is a sexual term well known in the *adab*.

36 Qurṭubī, 3: 82. For the possible renderings of "*'alā junūbihinna*" see above, note 27. Abū al-Naḍr's opening accusation that Nāfi' "talks too much" may perhaps be understood in the sense of "you have a big mouth!" In other words, *we* know that Ibn 'Umar sanctioned the sodomizing of women, but there is no reason to go sharing this information with the entire town!

37 The ambiguousness of the concluding phrase of the first report, "*fī adbārihinna*" – which can signify either "in their anuses" or "from the rear [but in the vagina]" – probably also played a role in this dispute, as we shall see it do more than once below.

with Ibn 'Umar, and I once heard him say: 'I haven't looked at my wife's vagina for quite some time!'" (*mā naẓartu ilā farj imra'tī mundhu kadhā wa-kadhā*).[38]

---

38 Ṭabarī, 2:536 (3467). The import of Ibn 'Umar's reputed statement in this context is difficult to establish. It could mean that he hasn't seen his wife's genitals for a long while because he only performs intercourse with her in the missionary position. One problem with this option is that it would exclude dorsal *vaginal* intercourse, as well, during which the vulva is presumably even more visible than in the course of anal sex; another problem with this proposed solution is the inconsistency: the phrase "for quite some time" indicates that Ibn 'Umar did not *always* refrain; a third problem is that abstaining from an act does not necessarily entail forbidding it. The second possibility – that Ibn 'Umar's statement signifies that he had a predilection toward celibacy, or at least an aversion to perversions like gazing at the pudendum, and thus was not the type of man to support a lascivious indulgence like anal intercourse – is even less plausible, as Ibn 'Umar is portrayed all over the *ḥadīth* and *fiqh* literature as a veritable Cassanova, who was wont to entertain multiple concubines in the space of a few hours and whose preferred method of breaking the Ramaḍān fast was intercourse (*kāna yafṭūru bi'l-jimā'* – sometimes, due to his extreme impatience and powerful sex drive, even before sundown). A third alternative – that Ibn 'Umar hadn't viewed his wife's reproductive organ for some time because he preferred to sodomize her and therefore focused on her *anal* orifice – would obviously defeat the purpose of the report.

This sends us back to the first option: that Ibn 'Umar only cohabited with his wife face-to-face and thus was never visually exposed to her private parts. This may garner further support from the association of "table inversion" with the other undesirable act of "looking at that place" (and "kissing that place") in R. Yoḥanan b. Dahabai's statement cited at the outset of this section. Indeed, Abū Mājid's quotation of Ibn 'Umar encourages us to view the association of these two clauses in that same Talmudic passage as less random than the modern reader – infused with notions of sexual egalitarianism and conjuring up images of cunnilingus – might have assumed. R. Yoḥanan juxtaposes these dirty deeds because from his perspective (and from that of his contemporaries) the rear entry coital position is the most common instance in which a man might be inclined to observe, or even osculate, his wife's genitalia. Visual and oral contact with the female pudenda are lumped together with posterior vaginal intercourse in the Talmud because there is at least a probable causal connection between these acts. Thus – returning to the *ḥadīth* – by affirming that he "had not seen his wife's genitals for quite some time" Ibn 'Umar was intimating that, despite his fierce libido, he has limited himself to the missionary position for a good while now. Furthermore, one could argue that such an interpretation is helped rather than hindered by the inconsistency reflected in the temporal delimitation: the fact that Ibn 'Umar had in the past been used to engage in anal intercourse but had then ceased doing so indicates that the famed Companion had reached the conscious conclusion that there was something wrong with this act. (Alternately, Abū Mājid's attribution of this statement to Ibn 'Umar may represent an attempt to explain away the fiercely contradictory reports re-

Ibn 'Abbās, for his part, admitted that Ibn 'Umar had ruled in favor of buggery, but attempted to excuse him: "By God, Ibn 'Umar may be forgiven for his delusion (*inna Ibn 'Umar w'Allāhi yughfaru lahu wahmuhu*)," because it is easy to confuse the terminology for rear entry vaginal intercourse ("*mudbirātin*") with that for anal intercourse ("*fī adbārihinna*") in the previously cited "*hijra* culture shock" narrative – and that was evidently how Ibn 'Umar had erred.[39] Mālik b. Anas, making no such apologies, upheld the veracity of Nāfi''s alleged assertion regarding his master's position in the face of virulent opposition. When he was told that the people were narrating from Sālim b. 'Abd Allāh (Ibn 'Umar's son) the claim that "that slave (or that lout) lied about my father!" (*kadhaba al-'abd aw al-'ilj 'alā abī*), Mālik responded: "I testify that Yazīd b. Rūmān related to me from [none other than] Sālim b. 'Abd Allāh [himself], who said that he heard from the mouth of [his father] Abd 'Allāh b. 'Umar [the very ruling] which Nāfi' transmits from him." Another challenge was mounted against Mālik in this connection:

> al-Hārith b. Ya'qūb narrated from Abū'l-Ḥabbāb Sa'īd b. Yasār that he once asked Ibn 'Umar what he thought about the fact that Sa'īd and his comrades would purchase slave-girls *wa-nuḥammiḍu lahunna.* "What is *tamḥīḍ?*" asked Ibn 'Umar (employing the *maṣdar* of the verb Sa'īd had just used). "The buttocks" (*al-dubr*), his interlocutor clarified.[40] Ibn 'Umar exclaimed: "Uf uf! Does a believer do such things?!"

This report portrays the scion of the second caliph as disgusted by the thought of sodomy, and thus undermines the view that he ruled it permissible. But Mālik was not found wanting in this case either. He swore that Rabī'a had informed him that the self-same Sa'īd b. Yasār had related from Ibn 'Umar exactly what Nāfi' had related from him (i.e. that he had sanctioned anal intercourse).[41]

garding the latter's position. Abū Mājid would thus be implying that Ibn 'Umar harboured – in the general manner of al-Shāfi'ī after him – both a *qadīm* [earlier] and *jadīd* [later] opinion on the subject of anal intercourse).

39 Qurṭubī, 3:81.

40 *Ḥamaḍa*, like Hebrew *ḥamatz*, means to go sour. Embarrassed, Lane does not translate the second form of this verb, defining it instead in Arabic: "*atā al-mar'a fī dubrihā,*" and speculating that this slang connotation is connected to the root's base meaning: "as though he shifted from the better of the two places (i.e. orifices) to the worse thereof, by reason of preposterous desire," just as wine sours and becomes vinegar, a poorer version of itself.

41 Ṭabarī, 2:536. For another, nearly identical, version of Ibn 'Umar's censure of

The high level of instability surrounding this issue is perhaps best encapsulated by al-Qurṭubī's citation of a statement by Ayyūb, who heard Nāfiʿ quoting Ibn ʿUmar, who supposedly explained Q. 2:223 as follows: "'Come to your tilth as you please': this means have intercourse with her in ..." (*qāla: ya'tīhā fī*). Al-Qurṭubī hurriedly (and unconvincingly) appends al-Ḥumaydī's completion of Ibn ʿUmar's statement: "that is, [in] the vagina" (*yaʿnī al-farj*), but the unresolved controversy is clearly reflected in this dangling sentence.[42] The considerable acrimony generated by this controversy – instances of which we have already observed – is well captured by the following dialogue:

> Rūḥ b. al-Qāsim reported: I was present when Abū Mulayka was asked about [anal intercourse], and I heard him say: "I wanted to perform it with one of my concubines yesterday, and I experienced difficulty, so I facilitated it with some oil or grease" (*qad aradtuhu min jāriya lī al-bāriḥa fa-iʿtāṣa ʿalayya fa-istaʿintu bi-duhn aw bi-shaḥm*). I turned to him and exclaimed: "God be Praised! I heard Qatāda report that Abū Dardā' said: 'Does anyone but an infidel do such a thing?!'" Abū Mulayka replied: "God curse you, and Qatāda, too!" I said: "I will never again relate anything from you!" But I later repented of this.[43]

Aside from Ibn ʿUmar, many other Companions, Successors and third and fourth generation luminaries were simultaneously pressed into the service of both sides of this polemic. This widespread "fickleness" manifests itself not just in conflicting reports, but even in emendations of the texts of those reports. Al-Ṭabarī adduces a narration of Ibn Jurayj, who transmitted the decree of Mujāhid: "Have intercourse with women in their behinds in whatever fashion" (*a'tū al-nisā' fī adbārihinna ʿalā kulli naḥwin*). The modern editor of *Jāmiʿ al-Bayān* steps forward at this point, inserting the word *ghayr* into square brackets between *fī* and *adbārihinna* and asking us to read: "Have intercourse with women *anywhere but* in their behinds in whatever fashion." The editor justifies this interpellation by claiming: "It is well known that Mujāhid does not hold such an opinion," an assertion he supports by sending us

---

Saʿīd b. Yasār, see Qurṭubī, 3:84. Mālik himself often transmitted directly from Nāfiʿ.

42 The same abrupt conclusion to this *ḥadīth* is found in Bukhārī, *Kitāb al-Tafsīr*, 6:60 (50). Since almost no one anywhere in the corpus of *ḥadīth* or *fiqh* feels the need to euphemize descriptions of vaginal intercourse, the chances are that al-Ḥumaydī is being disingenuous and that the intended continuation (or implication) here was: "in her anus."

43 Ṭabarī, 2:536.

to the fourteenth-century Qur'ān commentary of 'Imād al-Dīn Ismā'īl b. 'Umar b. Kathīr, where Mujāhid – Ibn 'Abbās's prize pupil – is shown relating two interpretations of his master antagonistic to anal sex.[44] Now, it is true that al-Ṭabarī does not classify the report of Ibn Jurayj together with those adduced specifically to legitimate anal intercourse; and it is also true that Mujāhid's statement as recorded in that report probably makes more sense as modified by the editor (its import would then be: "have intercourse with women any way you like, as long as you avoid the anus," a formulation quite familiar to anyone who has perused this literature and an example of which is attributed by al-Ṭabarī elsewhere to Mujāhid himelf: "*ya'tīhā kayfa shā'a wa-attiq al-dubr wa'l-ḥayḍ*").[45] Despite these compelling points, however, one still has to wonder about that missing *ghayr.*[46]

Another symptom of the inconstancy characterizing this topic is the "spin" often applied by later discussants to the relevant statements of earlier figures. 'Aṭā' b. Abī Rabāḥ reminisced that he and some others had once entertained the question of posterior penetration at the house of Ibn 'Abbās, and that the latter had come out and settled the debate by pronouncing: "Have intercourse with them whencesoever you wish, from the front and from behind" (*a'tūhunna min ḥaythu shi'tum, muqbilatan wa-mudbiratan*). A man who overheard this anecdote of 'Aṭā''s approached him and enthused: "In other words, sodomy is permitted!" 'Aṭā' vigorously rejected this interpretation, insisting that "[Ibn 'Abbās] meant the vagina – from the front and from behind *in the vagina!*" (*innamā yurīdu al-farj: muqbilatan wa-mudbiratan* fī'l-farj).[47] One factor militating *against* 'Aṭā's explication of his master's statement, and *for* the hopeful inference of his interlocutor, is an invalidation of anal sex imputed elsewhere to Ibn 'Abbās, in which he derives the divine interdiction of this act from the verse preceding Q. 2:223. There God instructs His flock of believers that after women have ceased menstruating and ritually cleansed themselves, their menfolk should "go in unto them *in the place that Allāh has commanded you*" (*fa'tūhunna* min ḥaythu amarakum Allāh). Thus, argues Ibn 'Abbās, there is a specific orifice set aside for intercourse by heavenly fiat, and therefore "one must not abandon the vagina in favor of an-

44 See Ṭafsīr Ibn Kathīr to Q. 2:223.
45 Ṭabarī, 2:533 (3451).
46 Ṭabarī, 2:534–5 (3461).
47 Ṭabarī, 2:535 (3461). We shall hear more on the subject from Ibn 'Abbās below.

other venue" (*lā yujāwiz al-farj ilā ghayrihā*).[48] The nature of Ibn 'Abbās's manipulation of the phrase *min ḥaythu* here allows us to offset this report against the report 'Aṭā attempted to rationalize above, where the same diction is employed: "*a'tūhunna* min ḥaythu *shi'tum, muqbilatan wa-mudbiratan.*" These two traditions should accordingly be seen as contradictory accounts of the opinion of Ibn 'Abbās: if he is portrayed in the second *ḥadīth* as understanding the scriptural formulation *a'tūhunna* min ḥaythu *amarakum Allāh* to mean "have intercourse with them *in the orifice* that God has commanded you," then his encouragement in the first *ḥadīth* to *a'tūhunna* min ḥaythu *shi'tum* should logically signify "have intercourse with them *in whatever orifice* you wish."[49]

Some of those who came out against anal intercourse were accused of not practicing what they preached. Zayd b. Aslam was told that Muḥammad b. Munkadir prohibited sodomy. In response, Zayd testified that that same Muḥammad had confided in him that he himself would regularly engage in it (*ashhadu 'alā Muḥammadin la-akhbaranī annahu yaf'aluhu*).[50] When Qatāda heard that 'Amrū b. Shu'ayb had berated a bedouin for buggering his wife, he could not believe it: "Him?! [He] who excels all others at 'the insertion of that which is inserted into either of the orifices'?!" (*fuḍḍila 'alā'l-nāsi bi-īlāj al-wālij fī al-sabīlayn?* [this is an unmistakable and quite humorous play on the primary category of pollutive "event" in the Muslim purity code: *khurūj al-khārij min al-sabīlayn,* "the emergence of that which emerges from either of the orifices" – *viz.*, the substances secreted by vagina/penis and anus (or ureter)]).[51]

The Prophet Muḥammad himself was, of course, no exception to such contradictory reporting: in this area, as nearly everywhere, he plays both thesis and antithesis. On the one hand, we possess *ḥadīths* like the following, recorded by al-Ṭabarī:

---

48 Ibid., 2:533 (3449).

49 The employment of the expression *min ḥaythu* to mean "via the orifice that..." in *aḥādīth* attributed to Ibn 'Abbās is also on display in his proverbial recapitulation of this whole subject: "Guide your 'producer' to the place of 'production'" (*asiq nabātaka min ḥaythu nabātahu*), see below.

50 Ṭabarī, 2:535–6 (3465). This is either an accusation of hypocrisy against Muḥammad b. Munkadir, or evidence that he could not have made the statement against anal intercourse that certain parties ascribe to him. The echoes of the Islamic Creed in the diction of Zayd's statement seem like deliberate irony.

51 Qurṭubī, 3:86.

> People from Ḥimyar came to Allāh's Apostle asking about various things. One of them said: "O Messenger of God! I am a man who loves women (*innī rajul uḥibbu al-nisā'*) – what do you say about that?" God, may His name be Exalted, revealed the answers to most of [the Ḥimyarites'] questions in the Chapter of the Cow, and concerning what the man had asked He revealed: "Your wives are a tilth for you; come to your tilth as you please" (Q. 2:223). The Messenger of God [then explained the meaning of this revelation to the man,] saying: "Come to her from the front or from behind – so long as it is through the genitals" (*a'tihā muqbilatan wa-mudbiratan idhā kāna dhālika fī'l-farj*).[52]

This "man who loved women" may strike a piquant pose, but his self-description makes little sense in context. He can, I suppose, be forced to fit his surroundings if we understand his statement as a euphemism employed out of politeness to the Prophet, who nevertheless immediately divined its more particular significance – that the man was fond of a plethora of sexual positions – and answered him (with God's help) appropriately. It is more likely, however, that we have to do with a simple scribal error, or, alternatively, with a deliberate bowdlerization, in either case facilitated by orthographical resemblance. The earliest recension of this report most probably did not read "I am a man who *loves* women" (*uḥibbu al-nisā'*), but "I am a man who *bends women prostrate and copulates with them from behind*" (*ujabbī al-nisā'*). The continuation of the question – "What do you say about that?" – as well as the Deity's and His Oracle's subsequent answers, both make more sense that way. Support for this speculation may also be had from the commentary of Ibn Kathīr, where the identical tradition is adduced but with a single difference: a dot appears under what was the letter *ḥā'* in al-Ṭabarī's version, so that it now reads "*innī rajul* ajubbu *al-nisā'*."[53] Since the closest the root *j.b.b.* comes to anything remotely sexual is its occasional use in the second form to designate date-palm fecundation, this does not seem right either. But it is, as it were, a *step* in the right direction: back to the original *ujabbī* (from the root *j.b.y.*). This latter is, at any rate, the usage on display in yet another narration concerning Q. 2:223, which, like the previous one (however it is read), shows the Prophet opposing anal intercourse:

52 Ṭabarī, 2:540 (3478).

53 See Ibn Kathīr's commentary to Q. 2:223, some twelve lines from the beginning.

> From Umm Salama, the wife of the Prophet, who reported: A man married a woman and wanted *an yujabbīhā* (= to have intercourse with her from behind while her head and body were lowered and her buttocks raised).[54] The woman refused, saying: "Not until I ask the Messenger of God!" Umm Salama said: So she came and told me about it. I informed the Messenger of God, who said: "Summon her!" When she arrived the Messenger of God recited to her "Your wives are a tilth for you ..." (and then went on to epitomize and qualify): "One orifice only, one orifice only" (*ṣimāman wāḥidan, ṣimāman wāḥidan*).[55]

So far, then, Muḥammad has been portrayed as a determined foe of rectal copulation. But another *ḥadīth* quotes the same Prophet's spouse to the opposite effect:

> From 'Abd al-Raḥmān b. Sābiṭ, who said: I said to Ḥafṣa [daughter of 'Abd al-Raḥmān b. Abī Bakr][56]: "I wish to ask you something, but I am embarrassed to do so." Ḥafṣa responded: "Ask, my dear son, about whatever is on your mind!" He continued: "Well, I wish to ask you about cohabiting with women in their anuses" (*urīdu an as'alaka 'an ghishyān al-nisā' fī adbārihinna*). She replied: Umm Salama related to me: "I asked the Messenger of God about that, and he recited: "Your wives are a tilth for you; come to your tilth any way you please."[57]

An additional narration, already cited above, buttresses the claim that the Apostle approved of anal intercourse:

> 'Aṭā b. Yasār related: A man had anal intercourse with his wife during the lifetime of the Messenger of God (*aṣāba rajūl imra'tahu fī dubrihā 'alā ahdi rasūl Allāh*), and the people condemned him for this and said, "Plug up her anus!" (*athfirhā*). But Allāh revealed: "Your wives are a tilth for you; come to your tilth as you please."[58]

---

54 See above, note 35.

55 Ṭabarī, 2:538–9 (3476). See the recension of al-Zuhrī: *in shā'a mujabbiyatan wa-in sha'a ghayr mujabbiyatan, ghayr anna dhālika fī ṣimām wāḥid* (sometimes written: *simām wāḥid,* with a *sīn,* the idea – "plugging up" – being the same. Qurṭubī, 3:81).

56 There may be some confusion here, since the phraseology used by 'Abd al-Raḥmān b. Sābiṭ here to introduce his question is found verbatim in many other places as a similar preamble to a question put to Ḥafṣa, the Prophet's wife. This is immaterial for us at the moment, however.

57 Ṭabarī, 2:535 (3468).

58 See also above, n. 33: "A man had anal intercourse with his wife, after which his conscience bothered him (*atā imra'tahu fī dubrihā fa-wajada fī nafsihi*), so Allāh revealed: 'Your wives are a tilth...'"

Having adduced two anti-sodomy and two pro-sodomy Prophetic traditions, we now – as in the cases of Ibn 'Abbās and Ibn 'Umar above – come to a report the vague and vacillating nature of which seems deliberately designed to mesh these conflicting conceptions into a single narrative, or at least to telescope the process whereby (what may have been) the originally pro-anal position of the Prophet was subsequently "spun" in order to extract from it an anti-anal position:

> From Khuzayma b. Thābit, that a man asked the Prophet, may God's peace and blessings be upon him, regarding intercourse with women in their anuses, or about the cohabitation of a man with his wife in her anus (*'an ityān al-nisā' fī adbārihinna aw ityān al-rajul imra'tahu fī dubrihā*). The Prophet responded: "Both are permissible" (*ayyu ḥalāl*). But when the man turned to go, [the Prophet] called him back, or he commanded someone else to call him back, and [Muḥammad] said [to the man]: "Now, what did I intend? Did I say, 'both *holes* [are permissible]' or 'both *openings* [are permissible]' or 'both *receptacles* [are permissible]'? (*kayfa? Qultu fī ayyu al-khurbatayn aw fī ayyu al-kharzatayn aw fī ayyu al-khuṣfatayn?*). [No. I said only: '*both* are permissible,' by which I meant that both *angles of approach* – not both *orifices* – are acceptable]. So from behind her in her genitals, yes; but from behind her in her behind, no.[59]

Yet another "personality split" of the sort we have been analyzing involves Mālik b. Anas. We have seen him above repeatedly championing the cause of Nāfi', who was adamant that his mentor Abd Allāh b. 'Umar considered anal intercourse licit. Moreover, Mālik himself is said to have ruled in favor of this position – *scil.* that "coition in the buttocks is allowed" (*al-waṭ' fī'l-dubr mubāḥ*) – in a work he reputedly wrote known as "the secret book" (*fī kitāb lahu yusammā kitāb al-sirr*).[60] Yet

59 Shāfi'ī, *Umm*, 5: 186. This *ḥadīth* is doubly difficult, because our first impression is that Muḥammad's referent in replying that "both are permissible" is the two scenarios described by the questioner. But these two scenarios are really two ways to describe the same phenomenon, so that doesn't make sense. Furthermore, I am not positively certain that the Prophet's "clarification" to the man should be punctuated with a question mark. Either way, however, the final import of the report is the same.

60 Qurṭubī, 3: 83. Or: "the book of secrets." Unless this is a calumnious invention, which certainly seems possible (Mālik had many detractors), it sounds like a private manual for circulation among Mālik's inner circle, the members of which – being more knowledgable, and less conservative and excitable, than the general populace – could be exposed to the genuine, unpolished principles and provisions of the law. This is reminiscent of Averroes "Double Truth" – one for the masses, the other for the intellectual elite – with the significant difference that "the secret book" probably contained what Mālik saw as the *most* "ortho-

we also read that when Ibn Wahb and ʿAlī b. Ziyād informed Mālik that people in Egypt were representing him as having declared the sodomizing of women permissible, he exploded:

> They tell lies about me, they tell lies about me, they tell lies about me! Are you not Arabs? (*a-lastum qawman ʿaraban?*). Does not God the Exalted say: "Your wives are a *tilth* for you"? Well, is the "tilth" located anywhere but in the birthplace?! (*hal yakūnu al-ḥarth illā fī mawḍiʿ al-manbit?!*).[61]

So far, then, nothing certain can be said about the subject of anal intercourse in early Islamic legal thought except that it divided scholars and aggravated tempers.

Reaping what you sow: Judaism and Islam meet in the middle[62]

Mālik's defense of his own decency with which we closed the previous section wielded the argument that scripture's employment of an agricultural metaphor in Q. 2: 223 is not fortuitous. Women, in their capacity as participants in coition, are compared to an arable tract of land which, when sown, brings forth crops. The purported implication is that one may copulate with a female partner only through that orifice which, when inseminated, will generate offspring. Parallels to such hermeneutical reasoning are recorded in the name of several authorities. Al-Ṭabarī opens his commentary to Q. 2: 223 with the explanation that "God means by this, may His name be exalted, that your wives are cultivable fields for [the production of] your children (*nisāʾukum muzdaraʿ awlādikum*); for we know that *ḥarth* denotes *muzdaraʿ*."[63] Al-Qur-

---

dox" position. Al-Qurṭubī himself counters that "Mālik was too noble to keep a 'secret book.'"

61 Qurṭubī, 3: 84.

62 Goitein alone has noted the interaction between the Judaic and Islamic traditions in the matter of sexual positions. He devotes little more than a paragraph to it ("Ha-dat ha-zoʿefet," 7), in which he correctly alludes to Islam's portrayal of Judaism as more restrictive than it actually was in this area, but he is too short on space (and too genteel) to say much else.

63 Ṭabarī, 2: 532. Al-Suddī seconds: "As for the 'tilth,' that is the field that one ploughs" (ibid.). Arabic *ḥ.r.th.* is Hebrew *ḥ.r.sh.* As a verb they both mean to plough, and both can harbour a sexual connotation, or at least a connection to women. Samson said to the Philistines, referring to their collusion with his

ṭubī, displaying his fierce antipathy toward the anal act, advances a similar argument, crowning it with a poetic stanza:

> These traditions establish the permissibility of all [sexual] positions and postures, so long as coitus takes place in the location of the "tilth" (*hādhihi'l-aḥādīth naṣṣun fī ibāḥat al-ḥāl wa'l-hay'āt kullahā idhā kāna al-waṭ' fī mawḍi' al-ḥarth*). In other words, [have intercourse] in whatever way you like: from behind (*min khalfin*), from the front (*min quddāmin*), on her/your/both of your knees (*bārikatan*), thrown down (*mustalqiyatan*) and recumbent (*muḍṭaji'atan*). But as for cohabitation elsewhere than in the customary venue of cohabitation (*al-ityān fī ghayr al-ma'tī*), this has never been permitted, and it is not permitted [now] (*mā kāna mubāḥan wa-lā yubāḥ*).
>
> The Qur'ānic usage "tilth" proves that intercourse other than in the proper locus of intercourse is forbidden. For "tilth" is a simile indicating that [women] are "farmlands for [the cultivation of] progeny" (*muzdara' al-dhurriyya*).[64] Scripture's choice of this term is designed to restrict the license [to engage in various types of love-making] to coition via the female reproductive organ, as it is that [organ] which constitutes the fertile field [for the procreation of] future generations, and the male seminal drop is comparable to the seed (*wa'l-nuṭfa ka'l-badhr*). Thus did Tha'lab sing: "Wombs are plantations ploughed by us mates/Ours is to sow while God germinates" (*innamā al-arḥām araḍūn lanā muḥtarithāt/fa-'alaynā al-zar' fīhā wa-'alā Allāh al-nibāt*).[65]

Ibn 'Abbās also reputedly applied this literary analysis. According to one report he prohibited coition through the anus, insisting that "the 'tilth' is via the vagina, whence will emerge the progeny" (*innamā al-ḥarth min al-qubul alladhī yakūnu minhu al-nasl*).[66] Elsewhere we read that when a man pressed him to sanction sodomy based on the scriptural warrant to "Come to your tilth as you please," Ibn 'Abbās admonished him: "Watch out! Is there a 'tilth' in the anus?" (ī *wayḥak! wa-fī'l-dubr min ḥarth?*).[67] His aphoristic motto, with which he summed up his position on this subject, was: "Guide your 'producer' to the place of 'production'" (*asiq nabātaka min ḥaythu nabātahu*).[68]

---

wife: "Had you not ploughed with my heifer, you would not have guessed my riddle!" (Judges, 14:18).

64 The word *dhurriya* itself, of course, comes from an agriculturally connected root, *dh.r.r.*, meaning to strew or scatter (seed).

65 Qurṭubī, 3:82.

66 Ṭabarī, 2:534 (3457).

67 Ibid., 2:535.

68 Ibid., 2:534. Or: "Guide your 'producer' to the place whence *it itself* was pro-

Even before Ibn 'Abbās, the Prophet himself, in one of the dozen or so anti-anal traditions tied to his name, reportedly authorized intercourse "in whatever position you prefer, so long as it is *in the birthplace*" (*fī mawḍi' al-walad*).[69]

At this point, the reader is asked to recall the midrash's justification for the primeval, universal proscription of anal sex (to which the Jews were eventually made the sole exception). Rabbi Ḥanīna was cited in Bereishit Rabba as having deduced this pristine ban from Genesis, 2:24: "Therefore shall a man leave his father and mother and cling unto his wife, and they shall become one flesh." Only that type of "clinging," the rabbi inferred, which leads to the fusion of a man and woman into "one flesh" (i.e. their offspring) is acceptable. The Jerusalem Talmud, as we also saw, seconds this notion: "Only that locus through which the two of them generate 'one flesh'" is permitted (*mi-maqom she-shnay-hem 'osim basar eḥad*).[70] Intercourse must be had, in short, in the orifice designed to initiate gestation when fertilized. Anal penetration does not fit the bill.

The similarity in content and method is striking. Both traditions – Judaic and Islamic – home in on a scriptural passage connected to copulation, and literalize its central metaphor (*ḥarth*, *basar eḥad*).[71] Both

---

duced." Ibn 'Abbās additionally argued that were anal intercourse permitted, the institution of abstinence during menses would be upended, because "if this entrance is blocked, you can just come in through the other entrance!" (*idhā ishtaghala min hāhunā ji'ta min hāhunā* – ibid., 2:535). The association with menstruation is made by others, as well – such as Qatāda, who enjoined his fellow Muslims to "enter through the passage whence the menstrual blood exits" (ibid., 2:533) – and derives, in part, from the juxtaposition between the Qur'ān's most important reference to the feminine flow (Q. 2:222) and the verse we are currently scrutinizing.

69 Qurṭubī, 3:82.

70 Yerushalmi Qiddushin, 1:1.

71 A plain reading of Genesis, 2:24 could easily lead to the conclusion that "they shall become as one flesh" refers to the extreme closeness ideally created between a couple after years of marriage (the Talmud reiterates in a variety of contexts that "his wife is like his own body" [*ishto ke-gufo*]. The famous R. Aryeh Levin once explained to a physician that "My wife's foot is hurting us"). Still, RaSHI's gloss – that "one flesh" refers to their child in common – is not far removed from that plain meaning, and may well be an integral part of it. "Tilth" in the context of Q. 2:223, although a clear reference to the male perspective of women as objects of the sex act, seems to require some exegetical initiative before it can be construed as a direct reference to the reproductive power of the female genitalia. In this case, too, however, the interpretation of

sets of exegetes then enlist that literalized metaphor to represent female fertility, and, by extension (or reduction), the female genitalia. Both go on to exploit that representation in order to establish, or at least reinforce, the prohibition on anal sex. And both instances constitute the sole attempts in their respective religious literatures to anchor this prohibition in Sacred Writ. Indeed, so analogous are the procedures performed by Talmud and *tafsīr* in this connection that the latter gives the impression of being a full-fledged transposition of the former: the same melody played in another key, or a different instrument.

This impression is strengthened when we discover that the identical phenomenon takes place, and even more clearly, on the other side of the debate. As we saw, the Gemara only once sought to ground the legality (for Jews) of heterosexual sodomy in the Torah, and it did so by comparing and contrasting this act to homosexual sodomy. Leviticus, 18:22 admonishes: "Do not lie with a male as one lies with a female." Since the verse stipulates that a man must *refrain* from doing with a man what he normally – and, by inescapable inference, licitly – does with a woman, we can deduce from it the inverse correlate: that a man is *permitted* to do with women what he is *forbidden* to do with men. And what is that? Anal intercourse.

The lone attempt by a Muslim sage to derive the right to engage in rectal penetration from the Qur'ān proceeds as follows:

> It is narrated in the name of Muḥammad b. Ka'b al-Quraẓī, that he saw no problem with [anal intercourse] (*kāna lā yarā bi-dhālika ba'san*), and would interpret in support of this (*wa-yata'awwalu fīhi*) the words of God, the Mighty and Majestic: "Do you come to the males among the creatures and leave the wives that God has created for you?" (Q.26:165–6). Said Ibn Ka'b: "The meaning [of this verse] is, 'You incline to intercourse with males and forsake the same with your wives' (*tatrukūna mithl dhālika min azwājikum*). Now were the equivalent [of homosexual coition] when practiced with females *not* permitted, then [the scriptural analogy] would be invalid (*wa-law lam yubaḥ mithl dhālika min al-azwāj la-mā ṣaḥḥa dhālika*). Nor can the legitimacy of [intercourse through] the *other* orifice (i.e. the vagina) be considered analogous [to the homosexual act], but rather the significance of the verse can only be: "[Your sin is that] you do this (i.e. sodomize men) while abandoning its licit counterpart (i.e. so-

---

the *mufassirūn* certainly does not stray too far from the straightforward significance of the text, and may conceivably be essential to it, or at least indivisible from it.

domizing women)" (*taf'alūna dhālika wa-tatrakūna mithlhu min al-mubāḥ*).[72]

This time the correspondence between the two exegetical procedures is unmistakable, and quite fascinating. Rabbinic tradition chose the premier anti-homoerotic passage in the Torah and – taking advantage of the fact that it sets up heterosexual cohabitation as the licit mirror image of the iniquitous homosexual act – reversed the verse's polarity, expanded on the physical mechanics involved, applied the principle that "by inference from a negative precept a positive precept may be extracted," and duly reached the conclusion that anal intercourse with women is authorized by God. Point by point, the Islamic interpretation cited above conducts the self-same operation using the premier anti-homoerotic passage in the Qur'ān.[73]

---

72 Qurṭubī, 3:83.

73 It is interesting in this connection that Ibn 'Abbās is cited as authorizing his fellow believers to "*ya'tīhā kayfa sha'a mā lam ya'mal 'amal qawm Lūṭ*" (Ṭabarī, 2:533 [3450]). Similarly, the Prophet is made to decry anal sex as "*al-lūṭiya al-ṣughrā*" (Qurṭubī, 3:85. Ṭāwus avers that homosexual sodomy evolved from heterosexual sodomy: "*kāna bad' qawm Lūṭ ityān al-nisā' fī adbārihinna*" – ibid.). Although Wansbrough rarely adduces, and on no occasion delves into, particular examples in order to support his broad claim that Jewish hermeneutical techniques were adopted and adapted by Islam in "a fairly uncomplicated process of direct appropriation" (Wansbrough, *Qur'ānic Studies*, xi) – or his even more sweeping proclamation that "certainly the exegetical techniques employed in Rabbinic Judaism and Sunnī Islam were identical" (*Sectarian Milieu*, 110) – it must be admitted that the instance we are currently examining represents at least one link in the chain supporting his statement. Others have expressed similar (and similarly unsupported) opinions about the relationship of the two legal and exegetical systems, from Goldziher and Margoliouth to Cook and Crone. Judith Romney Wegner has made some compelling (together with some less than compelling) arguments regarding the connection between the methodologies of *halakha* and *sharī'a* in her erudite "Islamic and Talmudic Jurisprudence: The Four Roots of Islamic Law and their Talmudic Counterparts" in Ian Edge (ed.), *Islamic Law and Legal Theory* (Aldershot: Dartmouth, 1996). I find her – and Wansbrough's – comparison between *ijmā'* and *hakol* particularly unconvincing. See also R. Brunschvig, "Herméneutique Normative dans le Judaïsme et dans l'Islam," *Atti della Academia Nazionale dei Lincei* 372 (1976); G. R. Hawting, "An Ascetic Vow and an Unseemly Oath? *Īlā* and *ẓihār* in Muslim Law," *BSOAS* 57 (1994) and idem., "The Role of the Qur'ān and *ḥadīth* in the Legal Controversy about the Rights of a Divorced Woman during her 'Waiting Period' (*'idda*)," *BSOAS* 52 (1989). The case to which this note is appended, together with many other examples of clear-cut cooptation by Islamic sources of Jewish legal discussions and conclusions, represents a challenge to Calder's claim that pursuing the ultimate

Moreover, the man made responsible for this fancy bit of hermeneutical footwork on the Muslim side is Muḥammad b. Ka'b b. Sulaym al-Quraẓī (d. ca. 738 CE). As his *nisba* indicates, this *muḥaddith* and scriptural exegete was descended from the ill-fated Jewish tribe of Banū Qurayẓa, whose men were all executed and women and children sold into slavery after the Battle of the Trench (627 CE). His father, Ka'b, was a boy at the time of his tribe's debacle, and some years after being indentured he converted to Islam. Ka'b must have shared the record of his experiences with his son Muḥammad, for the latter is the authority relied upon by the historian al-Wāqidī for the most detailed and lengthy of his accounts of the Banū Qurayẓa affair.[74] But his tribe's tale of woe was apparently not all that Ka'b passed down to his son: he seems also to have herited to him Talmudic methods of scriptural exegesis that he himself had imbibed as a youth. These methods came in handy later on at least one occasion: when Ibn Ka'b sought Qur'ānic sanction for anal intercourse.

Indeed, it is clear that in this case Ibn Ka'b (or pseudo-Ibn Ka'b) must have absorbed – whether from his father or from some other Jewish source – more than just methodology. His detailed replication of the

(alien) provenance of particular norms or principles of Islamic law is a futile exercise (Norman Calder, *Studies in Early Muslim Jurisprudence* [Oxford: Clarendon Press, 1993], chapter eight). The semantic and etymological correspondence between "Mishna" and "Sunna," already noticed by Sale ("Preliminary Discourse," 120), is clearly not fortuitous (see above, chap. 6, n. 45), although Crone once again goes too far in claiming that "[t]he order of the subjects in the Mishna and the Muslim lawbooks is related" (Patricia Crone, *Roman, Provincial and Islamic law* [Cambridge: Cambridge University Press, 1987], 20).

74 Abū 'Umar Muḥammad b. 'Umar al-Wāqidī, *Kitāb al-Maghāzī* (ed. Marsden Jones. London: Oxford University Press, 1966), 2:455–59. In his own *Kitāb al-Maghāzī* (not extant but drawn upon by others) Abū Ma'shar Najīḥ b. 'Abd al-Raḥmān al-Sindī made liberal use of Ibn Ka'b's narratives. It may be of relevance to our discussion that one of his other main authorities is none other than Nāfi', the pivotal figure in the defense of "*dubr.*" Muḥammad b. Ka'b was a prominent second generation traditionist, an important source of *Isrā'īliyyāt* and one of the teachers of Muḥammad b. Isḥāq (see Newby, *Last Prophet*, 5, 76, 77, 84, 130, 131 and 132), which latter was himself criticized for using Jewish converts as sources for his *Sīra* (ibid., 6). It is interesting that while Ka'b al-Aḥbār, the most famous Jewish convert-informant, maintained that *Isaac* was the son sacrificed by Abraham, Muḥammad b. Ka'b, already two generations into Islam, insisted that it was Ismā'īl (ibid., 76–7). Also, his account of the number and order of the plagues in Egypt does not tally with the Biblical version (ibid., 130).

rabbinic argument for the legality of anal sex, and his agile superimposition of the same onto the terms and texts of the Islamic canon, constitutes indisputable evidence that he (or his later Muslim "pseudopigrapher") had delved deeply at some point into the specific Talmudic *sugya* (discussion) surrounding this subject. And since it seems highly doubtful that, of all topics, the legal status of anal intercourse was the sole *halakhic* or hermeneutical issue into the complexities of which his father (or other teachers) chose to initiate him, we are well within our rights to suggest that Muḥammad b. Ka'b – though a pious, educated, second-generation Muslim – was no less a Torah scholar than a Qur'ān scholar.[75]

Were anyone still inclined to call these concurrences coincidental – or to perceive in them mere distant echoes of indirect cross-cultural influence – what follows should serve to disabuse them of that notion. We can, indeed, open this phase of our investigation not only with an irrefutable example of the "transference" of a normative issue from the Judaic to the Islamic tradition, but with an uncharacteristically emphatic Muslim acknowledgement of that transference. R. Yoḥanan b. Dahabai, it will be recalled, had claimed that the ministering angels had revealed to him that cripples are born "because [their parents] 'overturn their table.'" Al-Ṭabarī records the testimony of Muḥammad b. Munkadir (whom we previously met as one of the many authorities whose posi-

75 Ibn Ka'b is not exempt from (what may have been) the campaign to acquit important figures of the advocacy of anal intercourse. Al-Ṭabarī cites a report according to which Ibn Ka'b asserted that the intent of Q. 2: 223 is "*a'tihā muḍtaji'atan wa-qā'imatan wa-munḥarifatan wa-muqbilatan wa-mudbiratan – kayfa shi'ta* idhā kāna fī qubulihā" (Ṭabarī, 2: 533), and he is credited, as well, with transmitting the aforementioned motto of Ibn 'Abbās: "Guide your 'producer' to the place of 'production.'" By suggesting that Ibn Ka'b was a Torah scholar, we obviously intend a far more profound level of knowledge than that adumbrated by *ḥadīth*ic statements to the effect that, e.g., "the first Muslims read not only the Qur'ān, but the Torah" (Newby, *History*, 76) – unless we want to posit that most of the first Muslims were Jews. In other words Ibn Ka'b was, more accurately, a *Talmud* scholar (had space permitted, we could have shown him above, in chapter 7, delving into the minutest particulars of the red/yellow heifer rite, as well). Ka'b al-Aḥbār is often shown in the *ḥadīth* interpreting excerpts from the Torah for various Companions, and he – or the historical elements he represents – may sometimes have done so in great depth. Even in the pre-Islamic period we read about "a woman of the Kath'am tribe named Fāṭima bint Murr, who was the prettiest of all women, in the full bloom of her youth, the most pious and *well read in the scriptures*" (Ibn Sa'd, *Ṭabaqāt*, 104).

tion on anal intercourse was the subject of disagreement), who heard Jābir b. 'Abd Allāh relate the following:

> The Jews used to say: If a man has relations with his wife in her genitals from behind, his offspring will be deformed (*idhā jāma'a al-rajul ahlahu fī farjihā min warā'ihā kāna waladuhu aḥwal*). In response to this Allāh, may His name be exalted, revealed: "Your wives are a tilth for you; come to your tilth any way you please."[76]

A nearly identical version of this *ḥadīth*, also related by al-Ṭabarī in the name of Jābir through Muḥammad al-Munkadir, recounts that

> the Jews asserted that if a man has intercourse with his wife in her vagina from the rear, and they conceive a child together, that child will be deformed" (*idhā atā al-rajul imra'tahu fī qublihā min dubrihā wa-kāna baynahumā walad kāna aḥwal*). So God, the Mighty and Majestic, sent down: "Your wives are a tilth ..."[77]

Al-Ṭabarī himself sums up his lengthy commentary on the relevant section of Q. 2:223 with the conclusive declaration: "This verse descended as a response to what the Jews used to tell the Muslims, *viz.* that if a man has intercourse with his wife from the rear in her vagina the child will emerge deformed."[78]

Several points must be made regarding these highly significant snippets. First, we have here what is a great rarity in the legal – as opposed to the legendary – realm: an acknowledged locus of intersection between the two religious traditions. Even if these reports represent a back-projection of conversations that took place at a later time, in Iraq or elsewhere, if we combine them with the relatively clear calques we have witnessed so far we may take it as confirmed that members of the Muslim community deliberated with members (or at least ex-members)

---

76 Ṭabarī, 2:538 (3475). "*Aḥwal*" literally means "crooked, twisted, contorted" (and therefore also connotes cunning); the meaning "squinty-eyed" appears to be a later derivation of this.

77 Ibid. See also Qurṭubī, 3:81. This report is found in five out of the six cannonical collections of *ḥadīth*, in the "marriage" (*nikāḥ*) and "Qur'ānic Commentary" (*tafsīr*) sections (see editor's note number 2 on Ṭabarī, 2:538 for exact references). One of the interesting differences between these two *aḥādīth* is the claim of the first that *his* offspring will be deformed, as opposed to the claim of the second that *their* offspring will be deformed. This may parallel the two different interpretations (with their different implications) of the RoSH and Tosafot regarding *hafikhat ha-shulḥan* discussed above in note 10.

78 Ṭabarī, 2:542: "*hādhihi'l-āya nazalat fī-mā kānat al-Yahūd yaqūluhu li'l-Muslimīn idhā atā al-rajūl al-mar'a min dubrihā fī qublihā jā'a al-walad aḥwal.*"

of the Jewish community about the types of sexual positions that were acceptable in the eyes of God. The element of interaction and even direct dialogue is strongly present in these traditions:

> Murra al-Hamadānī reported that he had been told by Ḥuṣayn, that a Jewish man met a Muslim man and asked him: "Do any of you have intercourse with your wives while on your knees [or: while they are on all fours]?" (*a-ya'tī aḥadukum ahlahu bārikan?*). The Muslim answered, "Yes." He then informed the Messenger of God about this [exchange], and the verse "Your women are a tilth..." was revealed.[79]

We have already met the priggish Jew who interrupted and censured the uninhibited *ṣaḥāba* as they freely expatiated on their favorite sexual positions, and there is also this:

> Rabī'a explicated the expression *anā shi'tum* [of Q. 2:223], asserting that it means: "Via whatever conduit you want" (*min ayna shi'ta*). It was told to us – and only God knows the truth – that the Jews said: "The Arabs come at their wives [vaginally] by way of their buttocks, and this practice leads to the birth of deformed children" (*inna al-'arab ya'tūna al-nisā' min qibali a'jāzihinna, fa-idhā fa'alū dhālika jā'a al-walad aḥwal*). God gave the lie to this idle talk of theirs (*fa-akdhaba Allāhu uḥdūthatuhum*), saying: "Your wives are a tilth for you; come to your tilth however you please."[80]

---

79 Ṭabarī, 2:533 (3453).

80 Ṭabarī, 2:534 (3460). *A'jāz* is the plural of *'ajūz* (= rump, buttocks), related to Hebrew *'akuz* which has the same meaning. There is a slim possibility that the expression "*min qibali a'jāzihinna*" in this *ḥadīth* means not "by way of the buttocks" (i.e. vaginal intercourse from behind) but "in the buttocks," in which case we would annex it to the minority opinion we are about to take up. In what is, albeit, an unrelated anecdote, Jews – or at least ideal Jews – are portrayed as wary of even *looking* at a woman's hindparts. Glossing Q. 28:25 – "And one of [Jethro's daughters] came [to Moses], walking bashfully..." – al-Qurṭubī first quotes 'Amrū b. Maymūn who reassures us that "[Ṣafūryā b. Shu'ayb = Tzippora daughter of Jethro, soon to be wife of Moses] was not a brazen woman, of the type that goes out and comes in" (*lam takun salfa'an min al-nisā' kharrāja wallāja*), and then explains, citing Ibn 'Abbās, that "When [Tzippora] came bearing her father's message [urging Moses to dine with them], Moses followed her back to her home. And between the place where Moses was (i.e. the well whence he had watered the daughters' flocks) and her father's house was a distance of 12, 000 cubits, and while they were walking the wind blew and pressed Tzippora's dress up against her body such that the contours of her derrière became visible (*fa-habbat rīḥ fa-ḍammat qamīṣahā fa-waṣafat 'ajīzatahā*). This distressed Moses, and he said to her: 'Walk behind me, please, and guide me with your voice... for I am an Hebrew man, and I do not look at the buttocks of women" (*innī rajūl 'ubrānī lā anẓuru fī adbār al-nisā'* – Qurṭubī, 13:217). On Moses at Midian see Wheeler, *Moses*, chapter two.

In contrast to the six or seven examples enumerated so far, the following *ḥadīth* paints a slightly different picture of the Jewish critique, by tweaking only one component of the by now familiar claim:

> From Zayd b. Aslam, who reported that the Jews used to say: If a man has relations with his wife in her anus, his offspring will be born deformed (*idhā jāma'a al-rajul ahlahu fī dubrihā kāna waladuhu aḥwal*). In response to this Allāh, may His name be exalted, revealed: "Your wives are a tilth for you; come to your tilth as you please."[81]

This last report brings us to our second observation regarding the phenomenon of cultural convergence that we have so far been examining. In the previous versions adduced, the Jews are portrayed as objecting to rear-entry *vaginal* intercourse, and asserting that such an act leads to the birth of blemished children. As al-Ṭabarī reaffirms: "This verse [i.e., Q.2:223] was revealed in condemnation of a group among the Jews that condemned intercourse with women in their vaginas from behind" (*nazala fī istinkār qawm min al-Yahūd istankarū ityān al-nisā' fī aqbālihinna min qibali adbārihinna*).[82] The narration in the final block quote above, however, depicts the Jews as taking exception to *anal* – not inverted vaginal – sex.

In other words, the Islamic exegetical literature is internally conflicted over this issue, and therefore pursues its habitual dialectic. What, the *mufassirūn* wondered, was the exact Jewish point to which Q.2:223 formed the counterpoint; and what, concomittantly, was the specific intent of that counterpoint? Was Jewish opposition to *anal* intercourse subsequently quashed by divine sanction of the same? Or was it Jewish circumscription of proper coital posture to the missionary position that was overthrown, by celestial authorization to perform *vaginal* intercourse "from any angle you like" (*kayfa shi'tum; min ayya wajh shi'tum; ibāḥat al-ḥāl wa'l-hay'āt kullahā idhā kāna al-waṭ' fī mawḍi' al-ḥarth*)? Far from being a theoretical exercise, this exegetical polemic and its ultimate outcome harboured important practical-legal ramifications for the intimate lives of hundreds of millions of Muslims for centuries to come. In the end, the preponderance of commentators (and jurists) followed (or fabricated) the preponderance of *ḥadīth* reports in opting for the latter understanding of the Jewish claim: that it stigmatized extra-missionary *vaginal* copulation. God accordingly had

81 Ṭabarī, 2:536 (3469). The idea is obviously that offspring conceived vaginally on *another occasion* will be born deformed.

82 Ṭabarī, 2:537.

revealed Q. 2:223 in order to give Muslims free reign regarding various postures in *vaginal* intercourse (*ya'tīhā kayfa sha'a mā lam ya'mal 'amal qawm Lūṭ*).[83] On this view – which ultimately prevailed in *sharīʿa* no less than in *tafsīr* – the subject of anal sex had never even been broached by the Jews. Since the Jews are not shown condemning it, Allāh's retort to them cannot be construed as approving it, and anal intercourse remains prohibited in Islamic law to this day.

The Talmudic parallel to the *tafsīr*'s debate in this case pitted the "epiphany" of R. Yoḥanan b. Dahabai against the corrective administered by the majority of sages. R. Yoḥanan's vision had vilified "table-turning" and made it the cause of birth defects; the remainder of the rabbis had overruled him, offering the husband full fiat to sleep with his wife "in any manner he wishes." Here, too, however, further clarification is necessary. What purportedly sinful act, decorously disguised by the metaphor "table turning," was afterwards authorized by the sages (and, in the end, by Jewish law as well)? As we saw, the overwhelming majority of Talmudic commentators take "table inversion" (*hafikhat ha-shulḥan*) to signify anal intercourse, and view the invalidation of R. Yoḥanan's karmic schema by his colleagues as positive permission to engage in that act.[84] Anal intercourse is therefore, at least in principle, permitted by the *halakha* down to the present day.

But our balance is off. Where is the *opposing* Jewish interpretation of the Talmudic term "table-turning" that would correspond to the *first* (and finally victorious) of the two Muslim renderings of the Jewish position, *viz.*, that it denounces not anal, but rear-entry *vaginal* intercourse? Even without this counterweight in place, the parallels so far surveyed are more than sufficient to establish the extremely close relationship between the two sets of discussions and narratives. To complete our picture, however, and demonstrate the thoroughgoing congruency of the Muslim and Jewish treatments of this topic, we require that missing piece of the puzzle. As it happens, we have it.

At the end of the fourth order of the Mishna (Nezikin), a minor tractate known as Kallah is appended in most printed editions of the Babylonian Talmud. Tractate Kallah (not to be confused with its far

83 The formulation in parentheses is attributed to Ibn 'Abbās, Ṭabarī, 2: 533 (3450).

84 A lone opinion attributed to RaSHI – one of two positions ascribed to him – holds, as we saw, that "table inversion" refers to the woman being on top. The other position given in his name is that it connotes sodomy.

younger and far longer sibling, Kallah Rabbati) is made up, for the most part, of extremely early Tannaitic material, and large portions of it appear to have been composed by a student of R. Eliezer b. Horkinus ("the Great"), who died sometime around the beginning of the second century CE (and who, as we saw above, was said by the Talmud to engage in passionate – as well as garrulous – sexual relations with his wife, Ima Shalom).[85] The material collected in Tractate Kallah may well have been extant, then, at least in some form, long before the redaction of the Mishna itself, let alone the Gemara.

Now, as we know, the relevant clause in the seraphic teaching vouchsafed unto R. Yoḥanan b. Dahabai as recorded in Gemara Nedarim reads:

> ... Why are cripples born? Because [their parents] "invert their table" (*ḥigrin mipnei ma havin? Mipnei she-hofkhīm et shulḥanam*).

In Tractate Kallah, however – almost certainly the source of Nedarim's citation – what is likely to be the original version of R. Yoḥanan's statement includes an additional phrase not found in the later recension:

> R. Yoḥanan said ... Why are cripples born? Because [their parents] "invert their table," *engaging in the act of animals* (*ḥigrin mipnei ma havin? Mipnei she-hofkhim et shulḥanam ve-'osim ke-ma'ase behemot*).[86]

What it means to engage in the "act of animals" (*ma'ase behemot*) is obvious: rear-entry vaginal intercourse.[87] The beast has not been born that performs anal sex, and we therefore now know how the earliest layer of rabbinic literature defines "table-turning": coition in the vagina from

---

85 See above, p. 156–7. On the dating of Tractate Kallah, see Michael Higger's critical edition of the same, *Massekhtot kallah, ve-hen massekhet kallah ve-massekhet kallah rabbati* (New York: Debe Rabanan, 1936), introduction, pp. 12–15.

86 Kallah, 1:8. The word "*ve*" ("and") conjoining "*hofkhim et shulḥanam*" with "*'osim ke-ma'ase behemot*" indicates the elucidation – not the augmentation – of the former by the latter: "engaging in the act of beasts" is an elaboration of "table inversion," not an additional transgression.

87 The nomenclature has not changed: today's crude colloquialism for this sexual position is "doggy style" (the rabbis, however, preferred "animal style," *inter alia* because they were convinced that dogs have intercourse "back to back" as a special punishment for violating Noah's rule of abstinence while on the ark (see Sanhedrin, 108b and Genesis Rabbah, 20:3. Dogs do in fact sometimes get stuck that way after intercourse, which may be what the rabbis were referring to. Other Jewish sources claim that it was mice that violated the prohibition on maritime relations).

behind, what the Muslim sources call *fī qublihā min dubrihā, fī farjihā min warā'ihā, ẓahruhā li-baṭnihā ghayr mu'ājazatan*, etc.[88] Here, then, is the missing piece of our puzzle: a dissenting Jewish interpretation of "table-turning" to match the majority (but not unanimous) Muslim understanding of the same idea. And now is the time to summon back our opening anecdote about the *ṣaḥāba* and the Jew for its third and final appearance:

> 'Abd Allāh b. 'Alī reported that a group of the Prophet's Companions were sitting around one day, and a Jew was nearby, and one of the Companions said to the others: "I have sex with my wife lying down." Another said: "I have sex with her standing." A third said: "As for me, I take my wife while she's on her side or on all fours" (*'alā janbihā wa-bārikatan*). The Jew came over and exclaimed: "You people are no better than animals! (*mā antum illā amthāl* al-bahā'im). We Jews have intercourse in only one position." [In response to this,] Allāh revealed: "Your wives are a tilth for you; come to your tilth any way you please."

Note the point at which the Jew could take it no more: *bārikatan* – rear-entry vaginal intercourse; and the derogatory comparison he chose: *bahā'im* (= *behemot*) – those who have sex like animals. Here (and, in fact, throughout this chapter) Islamic tradition has stepped in to strengthen our claim – opposed by the entire tradition of Jewish Talmudic learning and commentary down to the present day – that the "table-turning" or *hafikhat ha-shulḥan* of Tractate Nedarim connotes not sodomy but *ma'ase behemot* (*bārikatan*), that is, vaginal coition from behind.

It is interesting to note in this connection that the explanations employed by the Talmudic commentators to bolster their assertion that "table-turning" refers to anal intercourse can often just as easily be made to fit the alternate theory: that this phrase refers to rear-entry *vaginal* intercourse. It will be remembered, for instance, that the RoSH tacks on a "measure-for-measure" justification to the notion that "table inversion" produces lame children: "Since he causes her pain in her knees, his offspring will be crippled in the legs." Vaginal sex from behind, of course, "causes her pain in the knees" no less than sodomy. Or in the case of RaSHI's interpretation, to wit: "'Overturn their table' means [his] face to [her] back (*panim ke-neged 'oref*), for this refers to

88 The first two formulations have already been cited; the last belongs to 'Ikrima, Ṭabarī, 2:534 (3458).

those who have abnormal (= anal) intercourse with their wives." Here again, "his face to her back" describes rear-entry genital no less than rectal penetration, and a midrash that employs the same terminology makes this plain: "All creatures have intercourse face to back (*panim ke-neged 'oref*) ... except for three that copulate face to face, because the Divine Presence communicated with them: human beings, snakes and fish."[89] In this midrash *panim ke-neged 'oref* refers specifically to *genital* coition from behind – we are talking, after all, about animals again – and thus at least the first part of RaSHI's statement could support our alternative (vaginal) interpretation of Nedarim's statement.

Nothing more is needed than what has been adduced thus far, I think, to prove our point regarding the twinning – or, rather, the cloning – which took place between the Judaic and Islamic discussions of this topic. But there *is* more. It will be remembered that as an illustration of the rabbinic rejection of R. Yoḥanan's four-part equation, the Talmud adduced the example of a woman who approached R. Yehuda HaNasi and complained: "Rabbi! I set my husband a table, and he overturned it!" Rabbi responded: "My daughter, the Torah has permitted you to him, so what can I do for you?" Now we turn to a *ḥadīth* of Sa'īd b. Jubayr:

> Ibn 'Abbās reported: Once 'Umar came to the Prophet and cried, "O Messenger of God! I am undone!" (*halaktu*). Muḥammad replied: "And what is it that has 'undone' you?" 'Umar said: "This night I have overturned my saddle!" (*ḥawwaltu raḥlī al-layla*). [Muḥammad] said nothing in response, and God sent down: "Your wives are a tilth for you; come to your tilth as you please."[90]

Tables or saddles, it makes little difference: 'Umar sits in for the woman, Allāh and His Apostle for the rabbi. The connection is clearer

---

89 Genesis Rabbah, 20:3. A snake – *the* snake – was spoken to after the incident of the forbidden fruit, and God ordered the whale to spit out Jonah.

90 Ṭabarī, 2: 540; Qurṭubī, 3: 82. "*Ḥawwaltu raḥlī*" could also conceivably be translated "I have *switched* my saddle," but given the context "overturned" fits better. At any rate the intent is the same. Note 'Umar in his traditional role – in which he is joined (indeed, surpassed) only by the Jews – of what we have styled an "instigator of revelation" (see above, chap. 1, n. 11 and especially chap. 2, n. 33). Here the comparable role played by 'Umar and the Banū Isrā'īl/Yahūd is made abundantly clear. And note that once again 'Umar manages to elicit a divine declaration bestowing sexual freedoms – a subject in which both he and his son were highly interested – on the entire *umma* (as was the case with cohabitation after a nap during Ramaḍān, see above, pp. 39–40).

still when we compare 'Umar's diction – *ḥawwaltu raḥlī.* – with that of the Muslim traditions quoting the Jews to the effect that copulation from behind produces deformed children. The word we translated in those traditions as "deformed" is *aḥwal,* literally: twisted, crooked. This makes the association of 'Umar's statement with Jewish *halakha* and *haggada* (law and lore) more than manifest, and we can combine the two *ḥadīth*ic statements to yield the following equation: *idhā* ḥawwala *al-rajulu raḥlahu kāna waladuhu* aḥwal – if a man *twists around* his "saddle," his child will be born *twisted.*[91]

But can this same combination find confirmation on the Jewish side? Is there a parallel in the Talmud to this karmic play on words? Neither the phraseology in Gemara Nedarim nor that in Tractate Kallah help us at first glance, for the Hebrew verb employed in each of these sources for "overturning" the table is *hofkhim* while the description of the infant's defect is *khiger* (lame), these roots being unrelated. Rather, for gratification on this score we must turn to the later and larger twin of Tractate Kallah, Kallah Rabbati. There (in chapter 1, section 23) we find the following:

> He who has intercourse in a seated position will be seized with *dayriya*; if he allows her to be on top of him, this is the way of brazenness (*derekh 'azut*), and he will be seized with *diliriya*;[92] if they cohabited while both faced the same direction (*shimshu shenayhem ke-eḥad*)[93] this is the **crooked** way (*harei ze derekh* ***'ikesh***) ... and therefore the child will come out **crooked** (*u-mitokh kakh ha-velad yetze* ***'ikesh***).[94]

91 The fact that *raḥlahu,* his saddle, rhymes with *ahlahu,* his wife, may have played some small role in this, too. It is interesting to note the freedom with which medieval Jewish authors, for their part, when borrowing Muslim literary material, would replace Arabic-Islamic proper names with those of well-known Hebrew-Jewish figures ('Ā'isha became the prophetess Deborah, 'Umar Rabbi 'Aqiva, Abū Ḥanīfa and al-Shāfi'ī Ravina and Rav Ashi, etc. – see Hava Lazarus-Yafeh, "Judaism and Islam," in *Some Religious Aspects,* 82–3).

92 These are two illnesses which I am currently unable to identify.

93 I take this to connote rear entry vaginal intercourse, in which both parties face the same direction (as opposed to the missionary position, in which they face opposite directions. There may be other ways to understand, or even translate, "*shimshu shenayhem ke-eḥad*").

94 Though Kallah Rabbati is probably a late, even post-Islamic compilation, it certainly contains much older material. This passage should additionally be compared, of course, to the *ḥadīth* we have repeatedly adduced about the Companions and the Jew: he rebukes them for indulging in more-or-less the same sexual postures.

Here, as in the case of *ḥawwaltu – aḥwal*, we have a direct semantic-grammatical relationship between the problematic act and the eventual fate of the offspring, heightening the sense of "as you sow, so shall you reap." In fact, we might easily have detected this "measure for measure" notion at work – at least semantically, if not etymologically – in the previously cited Kallah and Nedarim versions, as well: a *khiger* was often, before leg-braces and surgery, an individual forced to walk on all fours – like an animal. Because the parents had *had sex* the way animals do (with the mother, moreover, on her hands and knees, on all fours), the child will be made to *walk* the way animals do. Or, looked at another way, because the parents had *inverted* the proper order of things, their progeny will also be *inverted*.

The original impetus to sketch out this alternative understanding of the Talmudic discussion of sexual positions came from the author's incidental exposure to the *tafsīr* material on the same subject. This material had clearly (and, to a certain extent, avowedly) grown out of the corresponding rabbinic discussions, but it had nevertheless maintained a decidedly different emphasis – and attributed to the Jews *themselves* a decidedly different emphasis – than that unanimously held by the medieval Talmudic commentators. The overwhelming majority of traditions collected in the Muslim exegetical literature upheld the idea that Judaism did not even support variations in *vaginal* intercourse, let alone permit anal intercourse. The Jewish interpreters of the Talmud (and the Jewish *halakhic* authorities in their wake), on the other hand, believed that Rabbinic Judaism not only legitimated all variations in vaginal intercourse, but that it sanctioned anal sex, as well. The truth, as we have suggested, may well be somewhere in between these two poles: the Talmud definitely prefers the sages' outlook ("whatever a man wants to do with his wife he may do") to that of R. Yoḥanan (who stigmatized "table turning"), but since their respective positions – as we have been arguing – in all likelihood concerned not anal but rear entry vaginal intercourse, this preference is not tantamount to the acceptance of sodomy, and is, in fact, irrelevant to it.

The more important point, however, is that we were stimulated to call into question the traditional Jewish reading of a set of Talmudic passages (passages with significant implications for *halakha*) by examining material in the Muslim *tafsīr* that essentially duplicated those passages in every way except one. Upon further inquiry, it became apparent that not only could the rabbinic deliberations in question *suffer* the interpretation indirectly put upon them by the Muslim exegetes, but in fact they made more sense that way than they did when read through the glasses of the medieval Jewish commentators. It was almost as if in this particular instance the Islamic sources were doing exactly what they have always claimed to be doing: preserving an earlier and more correct understanding of the Jewish religion than the Jews themselves had done.[95] At any rate, all of the above represents a till-now non-existent enterprise – the study of Talmud with the help of *ḥadīth* – which is (I hope I have shown) more than worthy of being brought into existence.[96] That the corollary is also true – that the present author's grasp of the often difficult *ḥadīth* and *tafsīr* material reviewed above (indeed, throughout this work) was greatly facilitated by his familiarity with the corresponding Talmudic discussions – goes without saying. Our stubborn segregation from one another harms even our self-understanding.

---

95 I say "almost as if" for good reason: the age-old Islamic assertion that Islam not only retains, but in a sense even constitutes, those elements of Judaism which God had originally prescribed in the uncorrupted Torah, does not jibe with the current discovery. In the present case the "original" outlook attributed to Jews by the *tafsīr* is itself a position that Islamic doctrine believes must be superseded. Still, though the opinion *directly* attributed to the Jews is seen that way, the opposing, *Islamic* outlook – which also has its roots in rabbinic material and is represented by the *tafsīr*'s connecting of 'Umar's saddle reversal specifically with rear entry *vaginal* intercourse – may indeed be an echo of an original, and since lost, rabbinic conception. The controversial theories of Rabbi Abraham son of Maimonides included the claim that Islam "preserved many elements of the practices and teachings of the ancient Jewish sages" which were abandoned by the rabbis once such practices had spread among heretical Christian sects (Lazarus-Yafeh, "Judaism and Islam," 89. R. Abraham, however, mostly had Sufism in mind).

96 Such a project may be viewed as an extended application of Lazarus-Yafeh's statement that the relationship between Judaism and Islam resembles "a palimpsest, layer upon layer, tradition upon tradition, intertwined to the extent that one cannot really grasp one without the other, certainly not the later without the earlier, *but often also not the earlier without considering the shapes it took later*" (cited in John Reeves, "Some Explorations of the Intertwining of Bible and Qur'ān" in Reeves, *Bible and Qur'ān,* 43. The emphasis is his). A number of scholars have begun re-examining Biblical texts with the help of Qur'ān, *ḥadīth* and *tafsīr* (see ibid., as well as the literature listed there on p. 44, n. 4; also Brian Hauglid, "On the Early Life of Abraham" in ibid., 87: "[N]on-biblical tradition such as we find in Islam may retain certain biblical elements Jews or early Christians did not choose to emphasize." See, as well, Andrew Rippin, "Interpreting the Bible through the Qur'ān" in G. R. Hawting and Abdul-Kader A. Shareef [eds.], *Approaches to the Qur'ān* [New York: Routledge, 1993]). We have attempted in this chapter to apply a similar methodology to rabbinic literature.

Review

Let us, in closing, recapitulate in summary form the parallel developments we have traced in this chapter, following the order of the narrative components as they appear in the Talmudic text:

(1) *Talmud*: R. Yoḥanan b. Dahabai claims that the angels assert that a man's offspring will be crippled if he and his wife "overturn their table."

Tafsīr: Jābir b. ʿAbd Allāh claims that the Jews assert that a man's offspring will be deformed if he has relations with his wife from behind.

(2) *Talmud*: The rabbis reject this purportedly angelic equation, ruling instead that: "Whatever a man wishes to do with his wife, he may do."

Tafsīr: Allāh rejects this purportedly Jewish equation, ruling instead that: "Your wives are a tilth for you; come to your tilth as you please."

(3) *Talmud*: The rabbis elucidate their own statement, explaining that "It is like meat: if he desires, he can eat it salted; if he desires, roasted; if he desires, cooked; or if he desires, boiled."

Tafsīr: Muḥammad elucidates God's statement, explaining that "If you desire, you may cohabit with her from the front; if you desire, from behind; if you desire, recumbent; or if you desire, on all fours" (*in shi'ta fa-muqbilatan wa-in shi'ta fa-mudbiratan wa-in shi'ta fa-muḍtaji'tan wa-in shi'ta bārikatan*).

(4) *Talmud*: The illustrative anecdote is told of a woman who came before Rabbi Yehuda HaNasi and complained, "I set my husband a table, and he overturned it!" Rabbi, however, sanctions the husband's deed. Another woman approaches Rav with the same complaint, and he, too, authorizes the act, again employing the food analogy ("How is this situation different from that of a fish [which one may cook however one wishes]?").

Tafsīr: The illustrative anecdote is told of ʿUmar b. al-Khaṭṭāb, who came before the Prophet and complained, "I am undone! This night I have overturned my saddle!" Allāh, however, sanctions his (husbandly) deed. Another man approaches Muḥammad with the same issue: "I am a man who bends women prostrate and copulates with them from behind – what do you say about that?" God and his Prophet give the nod to this man, too, again employing the analogy of the "tilth."

(5) *Talmud*: The Talmudic commentators wrestle with the question what is meant by the "table inversion" that the woman had complained to Rabbi about (and that R. Yoḥanan b. Dahabai had spoken of as causing birth defects) but which Rabbi and Rav had nevertheless sanctioned. The overwhelming majority is of the opinion that the referent is anal intercourse, which is thus permitted to Jews but still forbidden to gentiles. This latter point is supported by Bereishit Rabba and the Jerusalem Talmud, which draft Genesis, 2:24 to the cause: "Therefore shall a man leave his father and mother and cleave unto his wife, and they shall become one flesh." Only that type of "cleaving" in that specific orifice which leads to the creation of "one flesh" (the child) is acceptable.

Tafsīr: The exegetes and traditionists wrestle with the question what is meant by the "saddle inversion" that 'Umar had complained about (and that the Jews had spoken of as causing birth defects) but which Allāh and Muḥammad had nevertheless sanctioned. The overwhelming majority is of the opinion that the referent is rear entry vaginal intercourse, and they thus forbid the believers to practice anal intercourse (after all, they are gentiles!). They support this prohibition by drafting Q. 2:223 to the cause: "Your wives are a tilth for you..." Like a field that, when seeded, yields crops, only that orifice which produces offspring when inseminated can be a legitimate sexual target.

(6) *Talmud*: A single citation in a minor tractate supports our contention that the "table inversion" authorized in Tractate Nedarim refers not to anal but to rear-entry vaginal intercourse. From this perspective, a different basis for the legitimacy of heterosexual sodomy is required, and it is found in Leviticus, 18:22, which admonishes: "Do not lie with a male as one lies with a female." Since the verse commands men to *desist* from doing with men what they normally – and, by ineluctable implication, lawfully – do with women, we can deduce the inverse correlate: that men are *allowed* to do with women what they are *barred* from doing with men: *viz.*, engage in anal intercourse.

Tafsīr: A minority of *mufassirūn* and *muḥaddithūn* (or is it a silenced majority?) holds that the sexual *carte blanche* granted by God to Muslims in Q. 2:223 includes the right to engage in anal intercourse. At least one member of this camp, however – perhaps as a nod to the argument that the "tilth" represents the reproductive organ – sought an alternate scriptural foundation for the right to engage in rectal penetration, and found it in Q. 26: 165–6: "Do you come to the males among the creatures and leave the wives God has created for you?" Remarks the commentator in question (Muḥammad b. Ka'b): "The significance of this verse can only be: "[Your sin is that] you do this (i.e. sodomize men) while abandoning its licit counterpart (i.e. sodomizing women)" – in other words, feel free to perform with women what you must refrain from performing with men, i.e. anal intercourse.

It should be clear by now that we have to do here not with two similar stories, or with two stories one of which has been influenced in varying places and in varying degrees by the other. Rather, they are the same story, from beginning to end: one version in Hebrew, the other in Arabic. The term consistently employed by *ḥadīth* and *tafsīr* for the sexual act (of any kind) is *ityān*, "coming to" a woman. This is almost assuredly a direct translation of the Talmudic term no less ubiquitously deployed for the same purpose: *bi'a*, "coming to" a woman. There are a great many examples of such corresponding usage, but perhaps no philological parallel in the literature on this topic is so intriguingly eerie than that connected to the consultation which took place in the Talmudic narrative *between* stages 1 and 2 above. There, it will be recalled, the Gemara relates that "someone asked" a question of Ima Shalom, the wife of R. Eliezer b. Horkinus, regarding proper behavior during marital relations. Across the length and breadth of *ḥadīth* and *tafsīr* a plethora of the Prophet's wives – from Ā'isha to Ḥafṣa to Maymūna to Umm Ḥabība to Zaynab and beyond – are regularly showered with questions regarding the Apostle's (and therefore the proper) behavior in diverse circumstances. When it comes to a topic like ours (i.e. coital postures), which is subsumed under the overall category of sexual norms – a category concerning which Muḥammad's wives are considered the peerless experts and are ever and anon consulted – we should certainly expect to find the Prophet's spouses well and widely represented. However, throughout the lengthy treatments of al-Ṭabarī, al-Qurṭubī and others regarding Q. 2: 223, amongst all of the authorities cited and anecdotes adduced, only one wife of the Prophet ever puts in an appearance, and she does so for the sole sake of fielding questions (in her case, too, asked by an anonymous interrogator) about correct and incorrect conduct during sexual intercourse. Her name is Umm Salama – Ima Shalom.[97]

---

97 See above, pp. 180–1. In Muslim tradition Umm Salamah – whose given name was Hind – was taken to wife by the Prophet after her husband, Abū Salamah,

The significance of all of this for macrocosmic *rukhṣa-naskh* should not be lost on anyone. Indeed, it might be said that Jews and Muslims basically agree in assessing the relationship between their respective communities' attitudes toward sex. "Ten measures of fornication came down to the world," states the Talmud (Qiddushin 49b), "and nine of them were taken by Arabia" (and remember Rabīʿa's claim that "the Jews said: 'The Arabs come at their wives by way of their buttocks ...'").[98] We heard the *ḥadīth*, for its part, quote a Hebrew who proudly protests that "We Jews have intercourse in only one position!" and adduce many similar demonstrations of Jewish sexual reserve. The Jews saw the Arabs as lechers; the Arabs saw the Jews as prudes.[99]

What is ironic about this is that from almost all the evidence we have examined thus far in this chapter, the opposite appears to be the case, at least in the legal sphere. From the point of view of the medieval Talmud commentators, and therefore that of Jewish law as well, the rabbis had already established the right of Jews to perform anal intercourse long before the advent of Islam. The Islamic consensus regarding heterosexual sodomy, on the other hand, has been sketched out above and is well reflected in the following statement recorded by al-Baghawī: "God will turn His face from him that goes in unto another man, or into a woman via her rear" (*rajul... atā imra'a fī duburihā*).[100] It is true that we may hypothesize, as we have done, that the Talmudic

was martyred at Uḥud. "Abū Salamah" is also the way Muslim legend renders the name of King David's rebellious son, Avshalom (Absalom).

98 Above, p. 191. It is worth investigating whether the use of the term "Arab" instead of Muslim in many of these *ḥadīth*ic citations of Jewish statements is indicative of their authenticity and relative antiquity.

99 Cf., however, the statements regarding the "inordinate passion" of the Jews which led them to sanction marriage to half-sisters (above, p. 58) and their reprehensible practice of public nude bathing (above, p. 72). Note also, for instance, that many Biblical-Talmudic tales – especially those concerning figures considered prophets by Islamic tradition – were censured by Muslim exegetes as overly risqué. The Jews as purveyors of sexual vice, license and libertinism forms a common motif in modern Muslim fundamentalist literature, a phenomenon no doubt originally influenced not so much by Islam's classical sources as by elements of Christian anti-Semitism, as well as by Palestinian Arab exposure to some of the radical experimental communities of early Zionism which were characterized – especially when compared with their conservative Muslim neighbors – by considerable immodesty and promiscuity. See also, in this connection, n. 15 of the Conclusion.

100 Baghawī, 25:112; see also Abū Da'ūd, *Kitāb al-Nikāh*, 11:2157. Both pronunciations, *dubr* and *dubur*, are found in vocalized texts (and in the dictionaries).

commentators got it wrong, and that the rabbis of Nedarim, Yevamot and elsewhere intended to sanction not anal but rear-entry *genital* sex. But even so, this would not account for the portrayal of the Jews as more sexually straitlaced than the Muslims.[101] For as we have seen, there is no argument over the fact that the Talmud *did* permit any and all positions and postures in *vaginal* intercourse.[102]

So what factor does explain the depiction of Jews by Islamic classical literature as conservative and repressed in matters libidinous? The answer is not far to seek, for we have encountered this phenomenon – or something quite similar to it – on many an occasion during our investigation thus far. In order for the macrocosmic *rukhṣa-naskh* pro-

101 It is also true that in the context of another area of sex-related law, we read about a man who approached Muḥammad and said: "O Messenger of God! I have a concubine, and I do not wish to get her with child, but I do want what every man wants (*urīdu mā yurīdu al-rijāl* – i.e. to reach orgasm. Alternately: "I intend what every man intends"), so I practice withdrawal (*aʿzil ʿanhā* – and ejaculate outside her). But the Jews say that the act of withdrawal is "the minor infanticide" (*al-mawʾūda al-ṣughrā*). "The Jews lie," responded the Prophet – and he sanctioned the practice. (Abū Dāʾūd, *Kitāb al-Nikāḥ,* 1:501). Besides containing another intriguing instance of "transposition" – the Jews are shown describing the crime of onanism in terms of a purported pre-Islamic Arabian institution uprooted by the Qurʾān – this report, like those we have been examining, also raises the question of Islamic exaggeration of Judaic restrictiveness. The referent here is almost certainly the Talmudic notion (connected to the situation of Tamar which we scrutinized above, p. 161) that coitus interruptus – "threshing inside but winnowing outside" (*dash mi-bifnim ve-zoreh mi-bakhutz*) – is unacceptable. In truth, however, far from declaring it a form of proto-murder, we saw Rabbenu Yitzḥaq rule there that unless pursued as a deliberate and persistent policy (as was the case, admittedly, with the man who queried Muḥammad at the beginning of this note), "spilling the seed" in the context of, e.g., anal intercourse, was perfectly alright. Moreover, the Muslim outlook on this practice may not be as lenient as the above quoted *ḥadīth* would have it, for we also read that "some of the Companions asked the Prophet about *ʿazl,* and he said: 'that is the hidden infanticide'" (*dhālika al-waʾd al-khafiy* – Muslim, *Nikāḥ,* 24:141 [1442]; cp. Wāqidī, 1:413). On *ʿazl* and birth control in general, see Basim Musallam, *Sex and Society in Islam* (Cambridge: Cambridge University Press, 1983); and earlier, G. H. A. Juynboll, "The ḥadīth in the Discussion of Birth Control," reprinted in Juynboll, *Studies,* 1:374–9, as well as Graf's article cited there. Also Goitein, "Ha-dat ha-zoʿefet," 7–8.

102 We cannot, however, rule out the possibility that Muslims came into contact with particularly puritanical Jewish circles who did decry sexual positions other than the missionary, an attitude reflected not just in the statement of R. Yoḥanan b. Dahabai, but in the passage in Kallah Rabbati cited above, pp. 198–9.

cess to work, and in order for it to serve the ends of Muslim teleology or "master narrative,"[103] Judaism has to be more demanding and restrictive than Islam. Historical alleviation-via-abrogation is conceived by Islamic doctrine as a one-way street, beginning with the conclusion of the Torah and ending with the conclusion of the Qur'ān. In our current case, the traditions making up the *tafsīr* perform an interesting feat of acrobatics to maintain this linear procession: they make the internally *rejected* opinion of R. Yoḥanan b. Dahabai into the official Jewish position, while presenting (a co-opted version of) the Talmudic sages' alleviative response – which *did* in fact become the official Jewish position – as the official *Islamic* position, revealed by God through His Prophet *in opposition* to the Jews. In other words: what might be called *microcosmic rukhṣa-naskh within* the Jewish milieu (the rabbis' "relaxation" of R. Yoḥanan's frigidity) has been metamorphosed into another instance of *macrocosmic rukhṣa-naskh* characterizing the grander scale of human history (Islam's relaxation of Judaic frigidity). Thus, even if the final conclusion of all of the legal deliberations we have followed above is that the *halakha* is in fact *more* sexually permissive than the *sharīʿa,* in Islamic literature that conclusion has been reversed: the Jews are shown to be the more puritanical of the two communities, and the revelations sent down to Muḥammad to have mitigated that puritanism for Islam.

The Muslims have turned the tables on us.

103 Donner, *Narratives,* 129.

Conclusion

One of the many important tensions that arise out of the material examined in this study is that between the Banū Isrā'īl as past paradigm and the Yahūd as present reality. Although the two terms are often used interchangeably – and although there is almost always a clear sense in Islamic classical texts of the unbroken continuity between the Israelites of yore and the Jews of recent times (whenever those times might be) – nevertheless, there are a number of levels on which this distinction has significance.[1] One of these concerns the nature of social intercourse and cultural-intellectual exchange between Jewish and Muslim circles in the early centuries of Islamic history, and the effect of such contacts on the extent of correspondence between the Muslim conception of Judaism and the Jewish conception of Judaism.

More than once in the course of this study the reader, confronted with instances of intra-Islamic dispute over what Jews claimed or Judaism prescribed, may have found him or herself wondering: why not just ask a Jew? Wouldn't this have settled the argument once and for all? And wouldn't this have avoided a great many misconceptions? The answer is that they did consult Jews. The sources analyzed in this essay – containing as they do on many occasions surprisingly accurate allusions to midrashic lore, unmistakable rehearsals of Talmudic *sugyot* (cases, discussions), intimate acquaintance with rabbinic hermeneutical methods and extensive familiarity with intricate *halakhic* minutiae – leave no room for doubt that al-Ṭabarī, al-Qurṭubī and/or many of the previous authorities they cite maintained direct contact with relatively learned Jewish circles (or at least with converts emanating therefrom) in Iraq, Syria, Egypt, al-Andalus and elsewhere.[2] If so, however, then

1 A notable difference that we shall *not* pursue here between the two terms is that whereas on a small few occasions the Banū Isrā'īl are depicted in a positive light (see below, n. 7), the Yahūd, as far as I can tell, never are.

2 One might add to this list of locations Arabia in the time of Muḥammad and the Rāshidūn Caliphs, bearing in mind, however, the longstanding questions regarding the historicity of the Jewish (and even the initial Muslim) presence there. The Biblical knowledge displayed by certain *muḥaddithūn* and *mufassirūn* (and, indeed, by the Qur'ān itself) is also impressive, and often includes al-

what accounts for the persistence of these same luminaries in asserting, for example, that Jews pluck each other's eyes out, or don't eat duck, or excise urine-splattered flesh, or forego booty in war, or harbour Victorian attitudes to sexuality (or, on the other hand, bathe collectively and shamelessly in the nude), or that the Torah/*halakha* does not prohibit the consumption of camel meat or kidney fat but does forbid the use of sand as a substitute for water, or that Jews cannot pray individually outside of the synagogue or that they are (or were) required to slaughter a yellow heifer if they find an unidentified corpse in the field? Surely it was a simple enough matter to question members of the local Jewish community or even just observe their behavior in order to discover what provisions they did and did not follow.[3]

---

most word-for-word translations of Pentateuchal passages. On the question which Muslim scholars had, or did not have, an Arabic translation of the Hebrew Bible in front of them, see Lazarus-Yafeh, *Intertwined Worlds,* chapter 5.

3 As Goitein puts it, comparing such Muslim misconceptions to the fantastic ideas found in Greek and Roman literature regarding the Jews: "Every one of those authors could have informed himself about the true nature of this nation had he troubled himself to walk only a few blocks from his house! Instead these [Greek and Roman] masters, who presumed to represent themselves as the pinnacle of human civilization, were content to copy and transmit from generation to generation over the course of centuries inane and stupid legends, without making the slightest attempt to examine themselves or search out the truth" (Goitein, "Ha-dat ha-zo'efet," 151. Goitein distinguishes between a "prescientific" period of Muslim writing on Judaism, on the one hand, and the more accurate descriptions rendered in later times by the likes of al-Mas'ūdī and al-Bīrūnī [whose expositions have been well covered by Adang; and see also in this connection Franz Rosenthal, "The Influence of the Biblical Tradition on Muslim Historiography" in Bernard Lewis and P. M. Holt, *Historians of the Middle East* (Oxford: Oxford University Press, 1962), p. 42–3]).
This simple method of investigation – talking to genuine Jews – might have been helpful in honing Muslim knowledge concerning Jewish *lore* no less than Jewish law. Al-Qurṭubī (2:37), for instance, relates on the authority of al-Suddī that "When the Messenger of God mentioned Solomon among 'those who were sent to mankind' (*al-mursalīn*), the Jewish rabbis said: 'Behold, he claims that the son of David was a prophet! By God, he [Solomon] was nothing but a sorcerer'" (*sāḥir* – see also Ṭabarī, 1: 623 ff; Ibn Isḥāq—Guillaume, 255. The insults borne by previous Prophets often functioning as a model for what Muḥammad had to endure, it is noteworthy that Allāh's Apostle was also called a *sāḥir* by his detractors, and this is one of the "standard scriptural epithets employed to denigrate a prophet" [Wansbrough, *Sectarian Milieu,* 5 and 15]; see, for instance, Q. 27: 14). While it is true that Solomon is not considered a prophet by Jewish tradition – and while he was certainly given wizardly capabilities in the Midrash (he even had a magic ring) – al-Suddī's description is at

One reason that this method was not generally employed – or, at least, did not serve to eliminate the outstanding contradictions between

most a caricature of any possible rabbinic response. A discussion with Jews could easily have rectified this misconception regarding their attitude to Solomon (on Solomon in Qur'ān and certain *tafāsīr* with Jewish parallels, see Geiger, 83; Newby, *Last Prophet,* 161–71; Tottoli, *Biblical Prophets,* 35–8 and the literature cited there in n. 50; A. H. Johns, "Solomon and the Horses: The Theology and Exegesis of a Koranic Story," *Mélanges de l'Institut Dominicaine des Études Orientales du Caire* 23 [1997]; and especially Lassner, *Queen of Sheba, passim.* Some Muslim traditions envision a succession of demon kings, all of them named Solomon, ruling the world before the creation of Adam – see Sale, "Preliminary Discourse," 57).

A more blatant example of such fabrications is found in Fakhr al-Dīn al-Rāzī's commentary on Q. 18:60 ff: "As for the son of Manasseh, it is said that prophethood came to him before it came to Moses son of 'Amram. The people of the Torah allege that he is the one who was searching to be taught this knowledge (*viz.*, the 'right guidance' vouchsafed unto 'one of God's servants,' Q. 18:65–6), and that Khiḍr [= the said servant] is the one who scuttled the ship, killed the boy, and fixed the wall, Moses b. Manasseh being with him. *This is the opinion of most of the Jews*" (translated in Wheeler, *Prophets,* 226. Emphasis added). While Elijah, who is loosely associated with Khiḍr, is often compared to Moses (son of 'Amram, however, not Manasseh – see, e.g., Exodus Rabbah, 44:1 and Matthew, 17:4), this is a far cry from al-Rāzī's claim. The latter has no basis, so far as I know, in Jewish (or Christian) sources, which are not aware of a Moses son of Manasseh. Unless one wants to posit a conspiracy among his Jewish or ex-Jewish informants to dupe al-Rāzī, this appears to be another case of Islamic fantasy about what Jews believe – a fantasy which could have been quickly exposed through a few conversations with Jews (interestingly, a similar claim regarding the identity of Khiḍr's companion is attributed to Nawf al-Bikālī by al-Bukhārī [5:279 (4725)], and is refuted, not surprisingly, by Ibn 'Abbās). In Hebrew "Menasheh" is only a weak letter "nun" away from "Moshe," and that letter is suggestively written in superscript in Judges 18:30. See Newby's excellent discussion of the possible provenance of this unknown figure in *Last Prophet,* 112–16.

A more well-known illustration of such misconceptions or inventions involves Muḥammad's reported adoption of the Jewish Fast of Atonement (*'āshūrā'*, from Heb. *'asor,* the tenth [day of the first month – Levit. 23:27]). "When Muḥammad asked the Jews what was the origin of the Fast, they said that it was in memory of the delivery of Moses out of the hands of Pharaoh and the destruction of the tyrant in the Red Sea. '*We* have a greater right to Moses than they,' responded the Prophet; so he fasted like the Jews, and commanded his people to fast also" (Ṭabarī, *Annales,* 1:1281). This inaccurate notion regarding the provenance and significance of Yom Kippur could also have been corrected through consultation with Jewish neighbors, just as such exposure might have disabused Muslims of the notion that "the Jews call their Messiah, the son of David, by the name al-Dajjāl" (Geiger, 24; also Sale, "Preliminary Discourse," 62–3); that Leah was sister of Tzippora and daughter of Jethro (Qurṭubī,

the Islamic and Jewish perceptions of Torah law – is connected to *taḥrīf*, the accusation that the Jews/Israelites/Ezra/Priests had corrupted their scriptures, and the related claim that they had added precepts to their religious code that God had never intended. As a result of this outlook, no information Jews gave Muslims in the ninth through twelfth centuries CE (or today, for that matter) could have any real bearing on the truth of God's original revelations to their ancestors over two millennia earlier. But there is another factor in play here.

The Banū Isrā'īl in Islamic tradition are less a historical entity than a moral paradigm. With a number of significant exceptions, their function in Qur'ān, *ḥadīth*, *tafsīr* and elsewhere is to serve as the emblem of all that Muslims should not be.[4] They are also, for related reasons, a re-

---

13:217; but see the compelling argument in this connection of Wheeler, *Moses*, chapter two) and that her first born's name was "Rubil" (Newby, *Last Prophet*, 80 and *passim*); that the Second Temple was destroyed by Antiochus (Ṭabarsī to Q. 17:4–8 [8:516]); that King David had a hundred wives (e.g. Nasafī to Q. 33:38); and that "Wahb b. Munabbih said, on the authority of some of the scholars of the Children of Israel, that the *Shechina* was the head of a dead cat. When it cried out in the ark with the cry of a cat, they were sure of victory, and triumph would come to them" (Newby, *Last Prophet*, 151; this is reminiscent of Apion's accusation that the Jews of antiquity worshipped an ass's head in the Holy of Holies) – all of this, in addition to a host of chronological mix-ups regarding Biblical and post-Biblical history found in the Qur'ān and *tafsīr*, might have been corrected by a minor amount of investigation (I say chronological "mix-ups" in deliberate disregard of the increasingly dominant trend in post-modernist academia, which requires scholars to refrain from assuming the historical precedence of Biblical or Talmudic to Qur'ānic rendering of similar narratives, and to substitute for previously accepted notions of "borrowing" a set of often incoherent and sometimes sycophantic disquisitions on "intertextuality" designed to avoid "privileging" either tradition [this is yet another incarnation of what Andrew Rippin once called the "irenic approach" to Islamic studies]). The Qur'ānic claim that "The Jews say, 'Ezra is the son of God…'" (Q. 9:30 – see Lazarus-Yafeh, *Intertwined Worlds*, chapter 3; Ibn-Isḥāq-Guillaume, 269; Bukhārī, *Kitāb al-Tafsīr*, 6:60 [105]; Ibn Isḥāq-Guillaume, 163; Newby, *History*, 112–16, 190–2) is a still more blatant example of such distortion. The fact that this last assertion is often mitigated, qualified or even wholly abandoned in the *tafsīr* would seem to indicate that at least in particularly egregious cases, Muslim luminaries paid heed to the correctives provided them by Jews or Jewish texts (al-Qurṭubī even quotes the opinion that all Jews who ever made such a claim regarding Ezra are extinct [*lam yabqa Yahūdī yaqūluhā bal inqaraḍū* – Qurṭubī, 8:100]).

4 Near the end of his section on Last Rites in the *Umm*, al-Shāfiʿī furnishes a prime example of *naskh* in the context of *sunna*. He stipulates that "one is not to rise at the passing of a bier, as the rising for such has been abrogated," and butresses this ruling with a pair of prophetic exempla that describe how Allāh's

pository of miscellaneous guilt – "Were it not for the Children of Israel, meat would not spoil" (*law lā Banū Isrā'īla lam yakhnaz al-laḥm*)[5] –

Apostle "used to stand in honor of funeral processions, but later on he sat" or "stood and enjoined standing, then sat and enjoined sitting" (*Umm,* 1:318). Al-Shāfi'ī indicates neither the reason for the original practice nor the occasion for the change of heart, but two cannonical traditions may illuminate the relevant circumstances. The first is from Jābir b. 'Abd Allāh, who reported: "A funeral cortege passed by and the Messenger of God stood up for it. We stood with him, but we protested, 'O Messenger of God, she (the deceased) is a Jewess!' He replied: 'Death is a terrible thing; so if you see a funeral cortege, stand up'" (*inna al-mawta faza'un fa-idhā ra'aytum al-janāza fa-qūmū* – Bukhārī, *Kitāb al-Janā'iz, Bāb Man Qāma li-Janāzat Yahūdī,* 23:198 [no. 1229]). The second *ḥadīth* is narrated by 'Ibāda b. al-Ṣāmit, who recounts that when the Prophet would follow a burial procession, he would remain standing until the body was interred. On one such occasion a rabbi approached him and said, "Why, we do likewise, O Muḥammad!" Upon hearing this the Messenger of God took his seat, exclaiming: "Oppose them!" (*fa-jalasa rasūl Allāh wa-qāla khālifūhum* – Tirmidhī, *Kitāb al-Janā'iz, Mā Jā'a fī'l-Julūs qabla an Tūḍi'a,* no. 941). Christopher Melchert adduces a *ḥadīth* in which the Prophet passed by a Companion leaning back on his left hand and asked, "Will you sit as do those who have incurred God's wrath?" (a clear reference to the Jews, see Q. 1:7. Melchert, "Etiquette," 39, n. 60; see also 'Abd al-Ra'ūf al-Munāwī, *Fayḍ al-Qadīr: Sharḥ al-Jāmi' al-Ṣaghīr* [Cairo: Muṣṭafā Muḥammad, 1938], 3:543). The reference, I would imagine, is to the Passover Seder, where Jews famously recline (hasiva) on their left side (Tractate Pesakhim, 108a: "Leaning backwards is not considered 'reclining,' *nor is leaning on the right side*, lest food enter the trachea instead of the gullet ..."). A selection of similar *mukhālafa* traditions is provided by Kister, "Do not Assimilate." 'Umar continued this tradition, commanding: "Do not imitate the Jews!" (Ignaz Goldziher, "Kämpfe um die Stellung des ḥadīṯ im Islam," *ZDMG* 71 [1907], p. 865), and "Do not compose a Mishna (*mithnāt*) like the Mishna of the Jews!" (Ibn Sa'd, 5:140; see Goldziher, *Muslim Studies,* 2:194). He also thrashed a Muslim for copying out the book of Daniel, shouting with each lash the verse: "We have revealed unto you an *Arabic* Qur'ān!" (Q. 7:42. Patricia Crone, *Slaves on Horses: The Evolution of the Islamic Polity* [Cambridge: Cambridge University Press, 1980], 18. 'Umar is, however, shown on other occasions displaying a keen interest in adopting particular Jewish customs and Torah precepts – see, e.g., Ibn Ḥanbal, 3:387). To confuse matters further, it should be added that the *mufassirūn* occasionally seem to be working with the assumption that the Banū Isrā'īl adhered to the *same* legal principles that post-Muḥammadan Muslims do. See, for instance, Qurṭubī, 15:144, where David's judgment between the "two adversaries" who scaled the wall of his palace and surprised him in his *miḥrāb* (Q. 38:21–4) is adduced in support of one *faqīh*'s opinion that litigation may be conducted in a mosque (cf., however, ibid., 15: 140, where Ibn al-'Arabī, discussing the number of David's wives, clearly distinguishes between "*shar'uhum*" and "*shar'unā*"). This question requires further study.

5 Baghawī, 1:49; Bukhārī, *Kitāb al-Anbiyā',* 55:547. Actually, this particular bit

and an emblematic locus of national suffering: "Plague is a calamity sent to the Children of Israel (*al-ṭāʿūn rijz aw ʿaḏāb ursila ʿalā Banī Isrāʾīl*), so if you hear that it has broken out in a land, do not go there, and if it breaks out in a land where you are, do not depart thence."[6] The Jews had become "an astonishment, a proverb and by-word" (as predicted in Deuteronomy, 28:37), the older brother gone bad whose mistakes were to be learned from and avoided.[7] Just as the doings and say-

---

of guilt may not be so miscellaneous. Although the *ḥadīth* does not allude to it, the sixteenth chapter of Exodus tells the story of the manna in the wilderness and quotes Moses there as instructing the Israelites to "let no one leave any of [the manna] over until morning. But they paid no attention to Moses; some of them left of it until morning, and it became infested with maggots and stank. And Moses was angry with them" (Exodus, 16:19–20). The manna was bread, not meat, but (a) the Midrash claims that it could taste like anything the eater wanted it to, and (b) the word for bread in Hebrew (*leḥem*) is the word for meat in Arabic (*laḥm*). Here, then, may be the basis for the accusation.

6 Muslim, *Kitāb al-Salām, Bāb al-Ṭāʿūn wa'l-Ṭiyara…*, 2218–9. The notion that "plague is a calamity sent to the Children of Israel" is rather irrelevant to the common sense advice and practical instructions regarding quarantine that are the central purpose of this *ḥadīth*, and the "so" therefore appears out of place. But since Muslims do a great many things *with reference to* what the Israelites did, the latter are included here as the archetypal precursor of a plague-smitten people, even though their presence does not seem to fulfill any exemplary or antonymous function. This is pure habit.

7 Thus, in order to warn Muslims against the dangers of sexual temptation, the Prophet Muḥammad is quoted as exhorting: "Fear the world and fear women, for the first trial of the Israelites was by women." (*ittaqū al-dunyā wa'ittaqū al-nisāʾ fa-inna awwala fitnati Banī Isrāʾīl kānat fī'l-nisāʾ* – Baghawī, 2:43). Perhaps this refers to Numbers, 25:1–9, wherein we read that "while Israel was staying at Shittim, the people profaned themselves by whoring after the Midianite women, who invited them to sacrifice to their god…" The Hebrew ringleaders of this movement were publicly impaled at the Lord's command and 24,000 people perished in a subsequent plague. This was certainly a "trial." (The odious manner of worshipping the Midianite Deity Baʿal Peor – prostration with rump facing the idol followed by defecation, according to the Talmud [Sanhedrin 66a] – was related by Maimonides to the Islamic *rakʿa*, though he stressed that the Muslims were unaware of the derivation!). To Muḥammad is also attributed a strong aversion to hairpieces, which he explained, *inter alia*, by the claim that "the Children of Israel were destroyed by the wigs their women wore" (this, too, however, may well reflect an actual encounter with Jews, though more likely in Iraq than in Arabia).

On rare occasions Israelites (usually individuals as opposed to the nation as a whole) may be employed to present a positive example (see, for instance, Q. 3: 113–4. I cannot agree with Hirschberg, Goitein and others who imply that the *Banū Isrāʾīl* – as opposed to the *Yahūd* – are for the most part depicted as righteous or pious in Muslim literature. This is far from being the case). So, for in-

ings of the Excellent Exemplar were proliferated exponentially to function as positive models, so the deeds of the Nefarious Exemplar were

stance, "one of the Israelite prostitutes" (*baghiyy min baghāya Banī Isrā'īl*) who espied a dog circling a well and panting in thirst, took off her boot and, tying it to her veil, lowered it into the well and drew water for the dog (*naza'at khuffahā fa-awthaqathu bi-khimārihā fa-naza'at lahu min al-mā'*). Her sins were forgiven, for "in [charity towards] every creature that has a humid liver there is a reward" (*fī kulli dhāt kabdin raṭbatin ajrun* – Nawawī, *Riyāḍ al-Ṣāliḥīn,* 13: 126; Baghawī, 3: 143). This is, however, a bit of a back-handed compliment given the lady's profession, and it is not insignificant that the following *ḥadīth* in this last source has the Prophet describe how an Israelite woman is being tortured in hell for starving her cat (it was also "a prostitute of the Children of Israel" – the Salomé-like daughter of King Rawād [= Herod] named Baghiyy [= prostitute] – who, according to Ibn Isḥāq, was responsible for the beheading of John the Baptist [Newby, *Last Prophet,* 202]). Despite this link to prostitution, however, the Banū Isrā'īl are elsewhere credited with taking even greater measures to preserve communal morality than the Muslims: "'Ā'isha said: If the Prophet had seen what women have wrought, he would have prevented them from praying in the mosque as the women of the Children of Israel were prevented" (Abū Dā'ūd, 1: 569). More recently, Chief Justice al-'Ashmawī of Egypt credited Israelite tradition with the introduction of *ḥijāb,* quoting Genesis, 24: 64: "Raising her eyes, Rebecca saw Isaac. She alighted from the camel and said to the servant, 'Who is that man walking in the field toward us?' The servant replied, 'That is my master.' So she took her veil and covered herself ..." (Muḥammad Sa'īd al-'Ashmawī, *ḥaqīqat al-ḥijāb wa-ḥujiyyat al-ḥadīth* [Cairo: Maktabat al-Kulliyāt al-Azhariyya, 1995], 60). If the veil *was* a Jewish invention, the virtue that this covering was designed to protect did not remain intact for long: in order to explain why, of all the Prophets, only Jesus did not marry, pseudo-Nawawī adduces the "immorality of the women of the Children of Israel of his time: he [*viz.,* Jesus] could not find a chaste woman fit to marry, for he was sent during the time of the Children of Israel's decline" (*al-sabab fī 'adam ziwāj 'Īsā, 'alayhi al-salām, fasād nisā' Banī Isrā'īl fī zamanihi, fa-lam yajid fīhinna imra'a ṣāliḥa talīqu bi-'ishratihi, li-annahu bu'itha fī zaman inḥiṭāṭ Banī Isrā'īl* – Nawawī, *Majmū',* 19: 12. This source is "pseudo" because only eight or so authentic volumes of the *Majmū'* have come down to us, the remainder of this gargantuan work being reconstructed or "filled in" by later medieval and even modern scholars). Some Israelites are represented as pious practitioners of religion (*EI²,* *s. v.* "Banū Isrā'īl" [Goitein]). While the *ḥadīth* famously envisions "seventy thousand *Jews* of Isfahan" joining the *dajjāl* (the Muslim anti-Christ, who is said by some to be a Jew himself [Muslim, 41: 6995]) in the End of Days, a different eschatalogical tradition depicts "seventy thousand people from the *Banū Isrā'īl*" charging the walls of Constantinople with the cry *Lā Illāha illā Allāh!* and subsequently battling *against* the *dajjāl* (Muslim, 40: 7034). Moralizing anecdotes involving anonymous Israelite individuals and their escapades – a common sub-genre – generally entail no censure of the Jewish People as a whole (e.g. the tale of the partial judge, Qurṭubī, 15: 152–3).

extended vigorously to provide negative models. In this spirit, Muslim writers vied with one-another in multiplying Israelite crimes: "It is told that the Jews killed all the prophets after Moses."[8] "The Messenger of God said: 'The Children of Israel murdered forty-three prophets in a single morning.'[9] Abū 'Ubayda related from 'Abd Allāh [b. 'Umar?]: 'The Children of Israel would kill seventy prophets *every* morning, and then go about their green-grocery.' "[10] In this archetypal capacity of all-

A final point should be briefly made with regard to all of the above (as well as to the hundreds of other Muslim descriptions of Jews and Israelites detailed in this volume). While Islamic tradition generally prefers to consider (and condemn) the *Yahūd* and *Banū Isrā'īl* as a monolithic collective or even as a single corporate organism, yet it should not be forgotten that the Qur'ān itself often takes pains to avoid such crass generalization, regularly accusing (for instance) "a *group among* you [Israelites]" (*farīqan minkum*) – i.e. not all of you – of treason or recalcitrance (or other sins), and not neglecting, after excoriating the Jews for "turning your backs [on God]," to add the qualification: "...except for a few of you" (Q. 2:83). These parenthetical attempts at what might be described (with some irony) as accuracy or fairness warrant further investigation.

8 Qurṭubī, 8:101.

9 Qurṭubī, 4:43–4.

10 Ibid. The Jews as killers of the prophets is, of course, an old and incessant mantra of the New Testament (as well as of the Qur'ān, see verses 2:61, 2:91, 3:21, 3:112, 3:181, 4:155 – compiled by Vernon Robbins and Gordon Newby, "The Relation of the Qur'ān and the Bible" in Reeves, *Bible and Qur'ān,* 33). The Bible knows of only two prophets killed by the Israelites – Zechariah and Uriah – though several others were imprisoned (Muslim tradition has conflated the murder of Zechariah with what some claim was the assassination of John the Baptist's father, Zacharias [see Newby, *Last Prophet,* 202–3]). A minor prophetic figure name Uriahu was also executed by King Jehoiakim (see Jeremiah, 26:20–23). Based on 2 Kings 21:16, however – in which the wicked king Manasseh son of Hezekiah is said to have "filled Jerusalem [with blood] from one end to the other" – Josephus (*Antiquities,* 10:38) claims that "Manasseh killed all the righteous men among the Hebrews, nor did he spare even the Prophets, *everyday putting some to death*" (emphasis added). The Jerusalem Talmud (Sanhedrin, 10:2 [28c]) confines Manasseh's murder spree to Isaiah alone (who was, according to the Aggada, the king's own grandfather). When about to be executed, this prophet uttered the ineffable tetragrammaton and was enveloped by a cedar tree. But Manasseh's men sawed through the tree and killed him (Yevamot 49b). The informants of al-Ṭabarī (15:29ff) and al-Qurṭubī (10:178) know this latter story with minor variations (see also David Sidersky, *Les Origines des Légendes Musulemanes dans le Coran et dans les Vies des Prophètes* [Paris: J. Eisenberg, 1933], 139ff). The number of victims of Dhū Nuwās, the "Jew with two pendulating sidelocks" who persecuted the Christian population of Najrān, was similarly inflated by successive authorities from 20,000 to 21,000 to 70,000 (Qurṭubī, 19:221; cp. the estimates of the number of victims of the plagues Phinehas stopped, Newby, *Last Prophet,* 141).

around bogey-man, the Israelites of Islam need bear no relation to any Jews (or any Israelites) who ever lived. "Allow your beards to grow abundant and long," urged Muḥammad, "clip your mustaches and pluck out (or: dye) your hoary hair – do not resemble the Jews."[11] Abundant and long beards have been, of course, the hallmark of the Jew ever since the time of David's delegation to Ammon, the members of which were humiliated by "clipping off one side of their beards and cutting away half of their garments at the buttocks" (II Samuel, 10:4). This insult led to full-scale regional war, and the "greatly embarrassed" men were ordered by the King to "stay in Jericho until your beards grow back; then you can return" (Ibid., verse 5).[12] Indeed, in the sole

---

To the list of Prophets killed by the Jews according to Islamic tradition should also be added Jesus (although the Qur'ān, perhaps echoing Docetist notions, asserts that they only *thought* they had crucified him, Q. 4: 157), and possibly even the final Apostle of Allāh himself: "Mohammed at first showed great regard to [the Jews], adopting many of their opinions, doctrines and customs; thereby to draw them, if possible, into his interest. But that people, agreeably to their wonted obstinacy, were so far from being his proselytes, that they were some of the bitterest enemies he had, waging continual war with him, so that their reduction cost him infinite trouble and danger, *and at last his life*" (Sale, "Preliminary Discourse," 27, alluding, no doubt, to the poisoned mutton supposedly served Muḥammad by the Jewess Zaynab, whose husband had been slain at Khaybar. Emphasis added).

11 Shāfi'ī, *Umm*, 1:36: "*'a'afū al-liḥya wa-khudhū min al-shawārib wa-ghayyirū al-shayb wa-lā tashabbahū bi'l-Yahūd*." Norman Calder has the following to say about the significance of this tradition (which either he or I have translated incorrectly): "A rare acknowledgement of alien influence is found in a *ḥadīth* cited by Shafi'i, *Umm*, i. 18.5–6. 'The Prophet of God said "Let your beards grow, and your mustaches; and dye your grey hair; do not resemble the Jews."' Here the influence is adversative, and signals once again the difficulties of any claim that parallels indicate influence, for opposites also might indicate influence. That the reference is to the externals of Jewish appearance, and not to the structures of Jewish law, is also significant. (Calder, *Studies*, 217, n. 47). Anyone knowledgeable about the "externals of Jewish appearance" in history will immediately see the problem here. It is, however, just possible that only the last clause – "pluck out/dye your hoary hair" – is being opposed to Jewish practice and it is significant that one report has Anas b. Mālik, the Prophet's personal servant, instructing a young man to shave off his sidelocks, "for this is the fashion of the Jews" (Abū Dāwūd, *Kitāb al-Tarajjul*, 33: 4185).

12 One of the 613 Biblical commandments, recorded in Leviticus 19:27, reads as follows: "You shall not round the corners of your heads, nor mar the corners of your beard" (*lo taqifu p'at roshkhem velo tashḥit et p'at zqanekha*). Based exegetically on this verse is the strict *halakhic* prohibition against cutting or shaving the beard or side-locks, and until the onset of the pervasive use of depilatories and the electric razor (the employment of both of which is forbidden to

mention of facial hair in the Qur'ān, it belongs to an Israelite: "[Aaron] said [to Moses]: O son of my mother, seize me not by my beard ..." (Q. 20: 94).

---

this day by many Jewish legal authorities, despite the lack of blade), one of the most visible marks of the Jew in history has been his long beard. The Talmud calls the beard "the adornment of a man's face" (Baba Metzia, 84a) and disparagingly refers to a male over twenty years of age who doesn't sport one as a eunuch (*hareihu kesaris* – Yevamot 80b). Priests without beards were not privileged to perform the blessing of the people known as *birkat kohanim* or *nesiat kapayim* (Yerushalmi Sukkot 3: 14). Sixteenth century Jewish Kabbalists of Sephardic origin refrained from even *touching* their lengthy beards, lest they thereby cause any hairs to fall out and violate the Biblical commandment (Isaac Luria, *Ba'er Haytev,* 181: 5). The only case in which the *amoraim* of the Talmud permitted even a minor trimming of the beard with forceps was for those who had constant dealings with the Roman authorities (Baba Qama 83a). Israel Abrahams notes that while Jews in Europe were reported occasionally to have clipped their beards with scissors (a practice permitted by certain European *poskim* [the Jewish equivalent of *muftīs*]), "Jews resident in Moslem lands allowed their beards to grow without even trimming them" (Abrahams, *Jewish Life in the Middle Ages,* [New York: Atheneum, 1969], 283 (this probably reflects the influence of the Muslim environment). There is, on the other hand, no technical *halakhic* problem with clipping the mustache (*ha-safa mutar le-galḥo be-ta'ar* – Maimonides, *Yad, Hilkhot 'Avodat Kokhavim,* 12: 8). It is, of course, highly significant that the *ḥadīth* recorded by al-Shāfi'ī (to which this note is appended) appears in Muslim's compendium and other sources with one important difference: "*al-Yahūd*" is replaced by "*al-Majūs*" (the Magians/Zoroastrians). This type of interchangeability is highly common: see, for instance, Ibn-Isḥāq-Guillaume, 270, where an anachronistic, atheistic rebuttal of the *kalām*istic argument from design – "Now, Muḥammad, if God created the world, then who created God?" – is placed in the mouths of Madīna's Jews. In other sources – and even a few paragraphs down in Ibn Isḥāq himself – the culprits are more accurately identified as *mutakallimūn,* with no connection to Judaism. Similar to this is the assertion/admonition that "the Children of Israel perished because they practiced *ra'y* (independent reasoning in jurisprudence)" (*EI*², *s. v.* "Banū Isrā'īl" [Goitein]). The Jews, in other words, are a convenient kerygmatic saddle for sins and heresies, even when such sins and heresies manifestly belong to others.

All this having been said, it should be reiterated that (as we have often seen in this study) many of the early Islamic descriptions of Jewish law and practice are quite accurate (for additional *aḥādīth* that represent Jewish observances more or less correctly, see Kister, "Do not assimilate"). An intriguing conundrum in this regard concerns a statement of al-Zuhrī in which the Prophet is quoted as inquiring, "What do the Jews do with their white hair?" The answer came, "They do not change it[s color] with anything." Muḥammad then enjoined: "So act differently than them (*fa-khālifūhum*), because the most perfect dye with which you can change [the color of] your white hair is *ḥinnā*'" (Juynboll, *Studies,* 4: 69). The Talmud does not ban the dying of hoary locks *per se,* though

One of the results of this paradigmatic conception of the Banū Isrā'īl (and even of the Yahūd) appears to have been a compartmentalization of sorts. The genuine Jews of the here and now (at any given point in history), although unquestionably associated on many levels with the Israelites of Islamic legend, were not necessarily perceived as the purveyors of everything ancient Israel (or ancient Jewry) represented. This meant that, at least at certain times and places, Muslim traditionists, commentators and even jurists may have allowed themselves to engage in anthropological-intellectual adventures involving fraternization with their Jewish counterparts in a relatively positive spirit – almost as if by excoriating the ideal, wrath was diverted from the real.[13]

But this dichotomy also meant that such mettlesome Muslim scholars must have subjected themselves to a "debriefing" upon their return home to mosque or *madrasa*, where a controlled form of cognitive dissonance seems to have assumed command. Whatever knowledge they had obtained from their interfaith encounters regarding the lineaments of Torah law was tested against the asseverations of Muslim scripture and early Islamic tradition concerning the same. Information that passed this test – either by tallying with the statements of Qur'ān and *ḥadīth* or by introducing additional data not addressed by those sources – was incorporated more-or-less accurately into the growing body of knowledge about the Banū Isrā'īl and their laws (and was put

one might infer such a ban from the Rabbinic statement (Shabbat, 94b) that *plucking out* one's white hairs is forbidden on weekdays no less than on the Sabbath (when it violates the rule against "shearing"), because of the Pentateuchal prohibition against imitating the dress or cosmetic procedures of women (*u-modim ḥakhamim le-Rabbi Eliezer be-melakeṭ levanot mitokh sheḥorot she afilu aḥat ḥayav, ve-davar ze af be-ḥol asur mi-shum she-ne'emar: lo yilbash gever simlat isha*). In the *Mishneh Torah*, Maimonides copies out this Talmudic passage more-or-less verbatim, and then adds the following: "Furthermore, [one is also punished by stripes] if he *dyes* his hair black; as soon as he dyes one white hair he is liable" (*ve-khen im tzava' se'aro shaḥor, mi-she-yitzba' se'ar levana aḥat loqe – Yad, 'Avodah Zarah,* 12:10). The *Kesef Mishneh* commentary is perplexed by this Maimonidean addition, and struggles to find a Talmudic basis for it through analogy to the Rabbinic ban on plucking. Does al-Zuhrī's *ḥadīth* buttress the *Kesef Mishneh's* argument for the antiquity of the *halakhic* prohibition on dying white hair? If so, then we have here yet another instance in which the study of Islamic texts can help illuminate the study of Jewish texts.

13 Interestingly, both Muḥammad and Abū Bakr are shown entering "Jewish schools" (*bayt midrās* – Ibn Hishām, 2:144 and 148; Ibn Isḥāq—Guillaume, 260 and 263; Geiger, 9) and arguing with the learned rabbis studying there.

to work explicating Qur'ānic passages concerning Jews). Information that contradicted what Muslim sages already knew from their most sacred texts about the Torah of the Hebrews, was either rejected, ignored or "spun" in such a way as to dovetail with divine revelation and prophetic *sunna.*[14] But while the knowledge obtained in these encounters was often modified, the encounters themselves had a considerable impact on Muslim history and ideology, as we have seen.

All of this is not to say that the widespread preoccupation with the Banū Isrā'īl in the seminal sources of the Islamic religion has been a boon to Muslim—Jewish relations. Little is gained in the context of this essay (indeed, perhaps in any context) by pointing out the obvious fact that the perception of the Children of Israel as the supreme embodiment of evil and excess is not helpful to the promotion of ecumenical harmony. It is sufficient to note what was inspired in the tenth-century Ḥanafite jurist and exegete, Aḥmad b. 'Alī Abū Bakr al-Rāzī al-Jaṣṣāṣ, by this general outlook. Seizing on the recurrent equation epitomized by Qatāda's statement that "[the Jews] were punished for their injustice and rebelliousness by the prohibitions imposed upon them" (*'ūqibū 'alā ẓulmihim wa-baghyihim bi-taḥrīm ashyā' 'alayhim*), al-Jaṣṣāṣ suggests the following lofty application of the principle of *imitatio Dei*: "In this we have proof of the permissibility of intensifying the persecution of [the Jews – *jawāz taghlīẓ al-miḥna 'alayhim*] by making laws prohibiting them many good things as a punishment for their wickedness; for God informs us in this verse (Q. 4:160) that He forbade them many good things as a punishment for their wickedness."[15]

---

14 Sometimes, on the other hand, Qur'ān and *ḥadīth* seem to have been interpreted (and, in the case of *ḥadīth*, also manufactured) so as to accord with what was learned from Jewish sources. The provenance of the "original" impressions – in the Qur'ān itself and the early *ḥadīth* – is sometimes harder to discover, though we have tried our hand in a number of instances above.

15 Jaṣṣāṣ, 2:366. The extensive use to which the classical Islamic conception of the Banū Isrā'īl and Yahūd has been put in the context of the Arab-Israeli/Muslim-Jewish conflict of modern times is well known (see, e.g., Yehoshafat Harkaby, *Arab Attitudes to Israel* [Jerusalem: Israel Universities Press, 1971], which also contains an excellent primary source bibliography, and Bernard Lewis, *Semites and Anti-Semites* [London: George Weidenfeld and Nicolson Ltd., 1986, reprinted with new afterward, 1997], who, however, argues that the Jews in the original narratives were not threatening enough for modern propagandistic purposes, so the classical material had to be embellished. See also Rivka Yadlin, *An Arrogant and Oppressive Spirit: Anti-Zionism as Anti-Judaism in Egypt* [Oxford: Pergam Press, 1989]). Shaykh al-Azhar Ṭanṭawī's

Still, it is important to recognize that the condemnation of the Banū Isrā'īl in connection with the onerousness of their religion is not primarily an indictment of the Banū Isrā'īl: it is primarily an indictment of onerousness in religion. Al-Qurṭubī, after furnishing a long list of Israelite excesses, sums up by saying: "This proves that the wages of sin are prohibitions" (*wa-fī hādhā dalīl 'alā anna al-taḥrīm innamā yakūnu bi-dhanb*).[16] In other words, the purpose of all of the information that he has assembled regarding the burdensome practices of the Children of Israel is to throw into relief the great value of *rukhṣa*, and to discourage Muslims from heading down the road of severity previously traveled by the Jews.[17]

---

post-Six Day War study on the subject (Muḥammad Sayyid Ṭanṭāwī, *Banū Isrā'īl fī'l-Qur'ān wa'l-Sunna* [Cairo: Tawzī' Dār Ḥirā', 1969]) is a particularly elaborate instance. Ṭanṭāwī is interested in portraying the Jews as, *inter alia,* purveyors of loose morals and licentiousness, and this may account for his terse and superficial treatment of the issues we have covered in this study (six pages – out of 476 – which themselves touch only on the barest and most well-known implications of Q. 4: 160 and Q. 6: 147. See also, in this connection, Suha Taji-Farouki, "A Contemporary Construction of the Jews in the Qur'ān" in Nettler and Farouki, *Muslim-Jewish Encounters*). The wide-reaching review of Arab educational text-books conducted by the Jerusalem based "Center for Monitoring the Impact of Peace" – though it must be used with care due to the thinly veiled agenda motivating it – shows clearly that the classical material found in medieval Muslim texts forms the primary ingredient in descriptions of Jews and the Jewish state in today's school curricula in many Muslim lands (see www.edume.org).

16 Qurṭubī, 7: 104.

17 It is the *Drang nach Nachsicht,* the indomitable urge to be lenient woven into Islam's "DNA," that has the best chance of encouraging modern day Muslims to adopt a moderate stance, that is, to consciously choose the more tolerant of the two or more *sharī'a* views usually available to the believer due to the dialectical nature of Islamic jurisprudence. Moreover, in the numerous cases – such as that of the status of religious communities that arose after Islam – where there may be no *makhraj,* no legally legitimate way to avoid the harsher attitude and the persecutory actions it demands, the example of the Prophet's (and God's) finesse and flexibility may nevertheless inspire many in the direction of compromise and moderation (as it already has done, it would seem, on many an occasion in history, such as in the case of the Muslim conquest of India, whose polytheistic inhabitants should have been given the choice of Islam or the sword – at least according to many authorities – but weren't). Allāh and His Apostle regularly "looked the other way" and "turned a blind eye" even in situations where the law was clear, and they are the models of emulation *par excellence.* They were also followed in this, to a large extent, by the early *fuqahā.* Islam is indubitably a religion of rules; but it is also history's unsurpassed advocate of bending the rules.

There is in this an unmistakable message to the Muslim "fundamentalists" of recent times, who would skip over centuries of what they perceive to be shameful *sharīʿa* minimalism and arrive back in the golden age of the *salaf al-ṣāliḥ* (the illustrious early generations) – even, in the dreams of many, before the debut of the *fuqahāʾ* and *madhāhib* themselves. Many of these circles have injected a fierceness and strictness (often coupled with a barbaric cruelty) into Muslim religion that it never knew before. They have done so at least partially as a counteraction to centuries of religious corner-cutting and legal laxity which they see as a deviation from the genuine Islam of the Messenger of God and his Companions.[18] They would do well to take a lesson from the very same passages concerning the Banū Isrāʾīl the sentiments of which they are so fond of exploiting in their endless battle against world Jewry. The preeminent statement conveyed by those passages, especially when combined with the manifold "microcosmic" instances of *rukhṣa* experienced by the first community of Muslims (several of which we surveyed above, in chapter 2), is that true "fundamentalism" – the return to the roots and foundations of the Islamic religion as practiced in the time of the Prophet Muḥammad and his immediate successors – is in fact bound up with nothing so much as a loosening up. Religious corner-cutting and legal laxity were what pristine Islam was all about. Its ways were ways of pleasantness, and all its paths were peace.

18 There are undeniably opposing trends, evident today even within movements generally described as "fundamentalist," in which Islam's leniency and its penchant for "taking the easy way out" serve as a source of pride as well as a tool of *daʿwa*.

Appendix

John Burton on *Naskh*

The immense force exerted by *kalām*-istic theology, though tempered somewhat by Ash'arites and others, has never fully subsided. This rationalist-philosophical outlook, which cannot abide the idea of divine mind-changing (see chap. 1, n. 27), may lie indirectly at the root of an extremely odd feature of John Burton's otherwise erudite and informative study of *naskh* theories (*The Sources of Islamic Law: Islamic Theories of Abrogation*). Unlike the writer of the present volume – who has been occupied solely with the traditional Muslim outlook on these matters – Burton set himself the daunting task of tracing the actual historical development of the methodology of abrogation. Now, we ourselves have spoken above (chap. 1) of the institution of *naskh* (and *jam'*) as deriving, in part, from the Muslim scholarly *perception* of Qur'ānic self-contradiction. We did not venture an opinion as to whether that perception corresponded to reality, that is, whether internal contradiction really does exist in the Qur'ān. Had we done so, however, our position would obviously have been tentative and nuanced (we have to do, after all, with an ancient text that grew up in circumstances largely unknown to us, as well as with the notoriously difficult problem of defining what constitutes "contradiction" in the first place).

Many of the Qur'ānic passages marked by the exegetes as conflicting with one another to this or that degree do indeed appear, to the untrained (but at least objective) eye, to conflict with one another to this or that degree; other purportedly adversarial pairs evince a less blatant contrast. Similarly, a goodly number of the verses harmonized with their supposedly hostile fellows with the tools of *jam'* actually do give the impression of being reconcilable without an excessive amount of effort (that is, the commentators' syntheses seem convincing); whereas in other instances the peace-making between antagonistic passages certainly looks forced. Put briefly: from a detached, critical perspective, it is safe to say that the Qur'ān (like most all voluminous or epic documents that have accumulated over time, religious or otherwise) contains at least a modicum of internal contradiction. However, whereas orthodox Jewish or Christian doctrine – especially after having been merged with Platonic—Aristotelian metaphysics – cannot abide the modern critical conclusion that their sacred writings are punctuated by a variety of co-existing antitheses, orthodox Islamic doctrine – with its early notion of revelation as process and its perception of abrogation as legitimate – is in a position to embrace just such a conclusion regarding its own scripture, and in fact does so.

If I have read him right (and this is admittedly a difficult task given his dense, laconic style and the extreme complexity of the subject matter), Burton's own conception of this issue strangely resembles the combined Judeo-Christian-Hellenic attitude, but with an even more curious twist involving a fundamental self-contradiction that leaves the reader wondering which of Burton's theses is, as it were, *nāsikh* and which *mansūkh*. On the one hand, Burton consistently ascribes the origins of *naskh* to the fact that early Muslim scholars were "scandalized" and "embarrassed" by the idea of contradictory statements in the Qur'ān (pp. 4, 20, 81 and *passim*). On the other, he repeatedly asserts that jurists and exegetes went out deliberately in search of – and forced matters and ignored evidence until they were sure to find – contradiction in as many places in the Qur'ān as possible (pp. 30, 57, 73 and *passim*). This oxymoronic combination is epitomized by the opening sentence of chapter six (entitled: "The Alleged Ḳur'ānic Basis of Naskh"), which follows upon more claims of far-fetched conflict construction by scriptural commentators and *fuqahā'*: "Such alleged conflict between Ḳur'ānic verses as we have just considered must surely have proved a source of considerable embarrassment in the first century to the original heirs of this self-contradicting Islamic heritage" (p. 81). How could, and why would, representatives of the same exegetical and juristic tradition that was "embarrassed" by scriptural self-contradiction put so much effort into "alleging" that same contradiction? Who deliberately discovers, manufactures and multiplies in their Holy Book phenomena of which they are ashamed? (Were one to claim that this was done in order to explain the gradual evolution of a legal position on a particular issue, certainly *jam'* would have been the neater and less "embarrassing" method to apply, and the idea of legislative "evolution" could have been foregone altogether). Surely it makes more sense to posit that when they examined the Qur'ān, Muslim thinkers of all types at least occasionally came across what genuinely appeared to them to be – and what in point of fact actually *are* – bona fide contradictions between different scriptural statements, and that they then struggled to confront the problems such contradictions posed. (They solved these problems, when the expediant employed was the doctrine of *naskh*, in as bold and intellectually honest a fashion as this writer, for one, has encountered in any religious tradition: by averring, at least in the earliest *tafāsīr*, that *God had corrected Himself*).

But Burton, astonishingly, does not seem to believe in the historical reality of intra-Qur'ānic conflict, let alone in the antiquity of the notion of abrogation, and comes across as nothing less than a champion of *jam'*. Beyond what has already been said, he quotes approvingly a modern Muslim opponent of *naskh* who propounds that "when one of [the exegetes of the first century] was faced with a problem in his understanding of certain verses, *imagining that they were in conflict*, he would grasp this principle [*naskh*] to remove his difficulty" (p. 31, emphasis added. See also p. 37, where the institution of abrogation is said to have been "projected back to the earliest generations" [note that, contrary to this assertion, Ibn 'Abbās often wielded *naskh* to handle purported contradictions that al-Ṭabarī, many generations later, preferred to confront with the help of *jam'* – see, e.g., Ṭabarī, 1: 461]). In other words, what the Qur'ān is perfectly willing to admit about itself, as we have seen (*inter alia*, in Q. 2: 106) – *scil.*, that it is a document composed of segments that entered Islamic consciousness at different stages, and that the later, more "mature" material often superseded that which had arrived before it – Burton himself is not willing to concede (this is all the more incomprehensible given that we saw the Qur'ān itself [in Q. 16: 102] defensively justifying such supercessions in the face of outside ridicule. Nor should we forget Q. 3: 6, the similarly self-conscious *mutashābihāt* verse). It will be recalled that Q. 4: 82 urges: "Will they not ponder the Qur'ān? Had it been from other than Allāh, they would have discovered in it much incongruity." Despite this statement, al-Ṭabarī and the vast majority of *mufassirūn* did indeed manage to discover much incongruity in the Qur'ān, for the most part in matters of *ḥalāl* and *ḥarām*, and they often confronted this problem with the help of *naskh*. Burton has also pondered the Qur'ān, but unlike the vast majority of Muslim commentators he, so it would appear, discovers no incongruity there! It is ironic that an early medieval literary genre (classical *tafsīr*) should display such openness to the idea of "process" and to the instability and fluidity of religion in its formative period, while a late twentieth-century century scholar should go beyond even al-Qurṭubī in advocating what sounds very much like *i'jāz al-Qur'ān*.

This impression is actually strengthened after reading Burton's no less difficult but far more rewarding earlier study, *The Collection of the Qur'ān* (1977). Here he argues that what Muslim jurists and exegetes claimed were Qur'ānic variants – whether in the sense of bits of revelation forgotten by certain Companions and preserved by others or in the context of the seven (or fourteen) different "readings" of the scriptural text – have no historical reality, but are essentially back-projections of *fiqh* disputes (or, alternately, devices for rationalizing contradictions between *fiqh*-based provisions – the origin of which Burton, following Schacht, considers to be largely non-Qur'ānic – and Qur'ānic norms, after these last were brought to the fore as the indispensible legal standard by a vociferous minority during Schacht's "secondary stage"). Burton claims that the equally unhistorical method of *naskh* was cooked up retroactively in tandem with the bogus notion of the variant *qirā'āt* in order to pave the way for the proposition that many of the rules advanced by the local *fiqh* schools, but absent from, or even opposed in, the Qur'ān, were in fact previously present in the "Qur'ān source" (the oral reservoir of revelations whence the law was ostensibly derived and of which the *muṣḥaf* – the Qur'ānic codex as we know it – is a sort of distillation). These rules, however (so the "uṣūlīs" claim) were (inadvertantly?) left out of the canon. (Here, as well as in *Sources of Islamic Law* and "The Exegesis of Q. 2: 106" Burton almost invariably employs the same lone example to illustrate his theories: the issue of stoning for adultery. He thus provides the reader no opportunity to test those theories against the "many" rules that Burton would have us believe were fabricated *ex nihilo* – or borrowed wholesale from foreign sources – by the local *fiqh* schools).

Only two of the three types of *naskh* (see chap. 1, n. 3) – *naskh al-tilāwa dūna al-ḥukm* and *naskh al-ḥukm wa'l-tilāwa* – appear relevant to this argument (for they describe the *excision* of textual passages from the canon, while the third type does not), and it often seems that Burton is interested solely in them and does not extend his thesis to "the classical mode of abrogation," i.e., *naskh al-ḥukm dūn al-tilāwa.* (The matter is far from clear, however: contrast the conflicting statements made on pp. 134, 160 [note here the unhelpful qualification "... *especially* by the two theories which posit the absence from the *muṣḥaf* of verses ..."], 164, 235 and *passim*). This limited focus may in fact inform *Sources of Islamic Law* as well: there, too, the issue of whether and to what extent the author includes *naskh al-ḥukm dūna al-tilāwa* in his deliberations and conclusions is fuzzy, but cross-referencing with *Col-*

lection makes one suspect that the third mode of abrogation plays a rather meager role there (the same is true of "The Exegesis of Q. 2: 106," see especially p. 452). If this is the case, then Burton's entire ouevre on the subject of *naskh* harbors little significance for understanding the type of abrogation central both to the thinking of the *fuqahā* and to our present study.

If, however, Burton's theories in *Collection are* meant to apply, even in part, to *naskh al-ḥukm dūna al-tilāwa,* then he rejects the reality of this mode of abrogation as he does the others, and believes that the "uṣūlīs" sought sanction for it in scriptural verses that are actually irrelevant to it (e.g., p. 56; also "The Exegesis of Q. 2: 106," p. 453). Thus, for instance, taking advantage of the semantic ambivalence of the term *āya,* Burton argues that whenever the Qur'ān speaks of "the replacement of one *aya* by another" (e.g., Q. 16: 102) it is referring not to the substitution of one Qur'ānic verse by another, but to "an individual ritual or legal regulation established and hallowed in one religious tradition, the Jewish, and now modified in a later tradition, the Islamic" (p. 237). This suggestion is quite interesting in light of the material assembled in the present volume – following which we might perhaps agree with Burton's interpretation while adding that verses like Q. 2: 106 may well refer to *both* the macrocosmic *and* the microcosmic processes of abrogation simultaneously – but this still does not resolve the difficulties with Burton's own outlook. The maintenance of the fiction regarding *qirā'āt* and *naskh* required, so he says, the concoction of a narrative asserting a *post-Prophetic* collection and redaction of the Qur'ān (because during Muḥammad's lifetime textual variants would not have emerged or would have been quickly quashed). This is a narrative Burton sets out to reject. Hand in hand with his dismissal as fictitious of (a) the thousands of scriptural variants, (b) the redaction of the Qur'ān under 'Uthmān or the *shaykhān,* and (c) *naskh,* comes Burton's punchline at the end of the book: "What we have today in our hands is the muṣḥaf of Muḥammad" (p. 240). That is, while the *Qur'ānic variants* are in truth a back-product of *fiqh* activity, the Qur'ān itself as we currently know it is not: it was extant long before the legal schools came on the scene (in other words, though Burton adopts Schacht's *conclusio e silentio* – that legal traditions not adduced in a juristic dispute did not exist prior to that dispute – with regard to *ḥadīth,* he is not willing to extend it, as his teacher Wansbrough did, to the Qur'ān. See, in this connection, Patricia Crone, "Two Legal Problems Bearing on the Early History of the Qur'an" in *Jerusalem Studies in Arabic and Islam,* 18

[1994], where Crone goes too far, to my mind, in supporting Wansbrough's thesis, stating that "of rules based on the Qur'an from the start we no longer possess a single clear-cut example" [pp. 10–11]). Burton, in a word, believes with Islamic orthodoxy that Qur'ānic content emerged in its entirety while Muḥammad lived (regarding Muḥammad's own historicity he evidently harbors no doubts). He parts with Muslim tradition only in claiming that this soon-to-be scriptural material was also assembled and edited *before* the Prophet's death (see *Collection,* pp. 44, 125, 187, 203 and *passim*). But even if we granted that the Qur'ān was created over a period of less than twenty-three years under the auspices of one talented man, this in no way eliminates the high probability that contradiction crept into that document at various stages, a reality for which the Qur'ān's own embarrassed defensiveness (Q. 16: 102, 5: 101, 3: 6, 87: 7, etc.) is, again, the most unassailable testimony (so are the Jewish assertions – recorded by Muslim authors and confirmed in Geonic and post-Geonic literature – that "parts of [the Qur'ān] contradict other parts" [*yunāqiḍu ba'ḍuhu ba'ḍan*]). In short, whether under Muḥammad or under his successors, a document and a religion forged over time will perforce be accompanied by progress and change, by the phenomenon of later positions opposing and superceding earlier ones, in a word: by *naskh.*

Stranger still (returning to *Sources of Islamic Law*) is the fact that Burton recognizes that "[a]nother consideration in favor of the antiquity of a generalized substitution theory ... is that it must have been prior in Muḥammad's thinking at least, and probably also in that of his contemporaries, to the view they took of the relationship, one to another, of the major religious dispensations originated in the historical prophetic cycle in which Muḥammad claimed to participate" (p. 84). In other words, it makes sense that the Muslim notion of one set of norms replacing another within the *same* religion would arise coterminus with, if not earlier than, the Muslim conception of previous religions replacing each other over time. This sounds right (cf., however, Wansbrough, *Sectarian Milieu*, 41 and 109–19, who envisions the opposite extrapolation: from the phenomenon of successive confessional systems to the institution of internal Islamic *naskh*), and in the same paragraph Burton concludes: "Whether [this early internal substitution theory tied to the concept of a series of abrogating and then abrogated faiths] bore any resemblance to what later came to be known as '*naskh,*' is the most important question of all which our study must confront." Although it is relatively clear that he believes the answer to be negative, in the remaining 230 pages of Burton's book this question is never heard from again. Part of what I have tried to do in the current study is begin grappling with it.

Bibliography

Primary Sources

al-'Ashmawī, Muḥammad Sa'īd, *Ḥaqīqat al-Ḥijāb wa-Ḥujiyyat al-Ḥadīth* (Cairo: Maktabat al-Kulliyāt al-Azhariyya, 1995).

al-'Asqalānī, Aḥmad b. Nūr al-Dīn 'Alī b. Ḥajar, *Fatḥ al-Bārī bi-Sharḥ Saḥīḥ al-Bukhārī* (Beirut: Dār al-Fikr, 1970).

al-'Asqalānī, Aḥmad b. Nūr al-Dīn 'Alī b. Ḥajar, *Al-Iṣāba fī Tamyīz al-Ṣaḥāba* (Cairo: Maṭba'a al-Sa'āda, 1328).

al-'Atā'iqī, Muḥammad, *al-Nāsikh wa'l-Mansūkh* (Cairo: Maktabat Wahba, 2000).

al-'Aynī, Abū Muḥammad Maḥmūd b. Aḥmad, *'Umdat al-Qāri Sharḥ Ṣaḥīḥ al-Bukhārī* (Istanbul: n.p., 1308 AH).

'Aẓīm-Ābādī, Abū al-Ṭayyib Muḥammad Shams al-Ḥaq, *'Awn al-Ma'būd Sharḥ Sunan Abī Dā'ūd* (Beirut: Dār al-Fikr, n.d.).

al-Bājī, Abū'l-Walīd Sulaymān b. Khalaf, *Muntaqa: Sharḥ Muwaṭṭā' al-Imām Mālik* (Cairo: Dar al-Fikr al-'Arabī , 1982).

al-Bayḍāwī, Nāsir al-Dīn Abū Sa'īd 'Abd Allāh b. 'Umar al-Shīrāzī, *Tafsīr al-Bayḍāwī* (Beirut: Dār al-Kutub al-'Ilmiya, 1988).

al-Bayhaqī, Abū Bakr Aḥmad b. al-Ḥusayn b., *Kitāb al-Sunan al-Kubrā* (Beirut: Dār al-Ma'rifa, 1992).

al-Buhūtī, Manṣūr b. Yunus, *Kashshāf al-Qinā' 'an Matn al-Iqnā'* (Riyāḍ: Maktabat al-Naṣr al-Ḥadītha, n.d.).

al-Bukhārī, Muḥammad b. Ismā'īl, *Ṣaḥīḥ al-Bukhārī* (Beirut: Dār al-Fikr, 1991).

al-Dārimī, 'Abd Allāh b. 'Abd al-Raḥmān, *Sunan al-Dārimī* (Cairo: Dār Iḥyā' al-Sunna al-Nabawiya, n.d.).

Dawood, N. J., *The Koran* (London: Penguin Books, sixth edition, 1990).

al-Ghazālī, Abū Ḥāmid Muḥammad b. Muḥammad, *Iḥyā 'Ulūm al-Dīn* (Cairo: Mu'assasa al-Ḥalabī li'l-Nashr wa'l-Tawzī', 1967).

al-Ghazālī, Abū Ḥāmid Muḥammad b. Muḥammad, *Kitāb al-Wajīz fī Fiqh Madhhab al-Imām al-Shāfi'ī* (Beirut: Dār al-Ma'rifa li'l-Ṭibā'a wa'l-Nashr, 1979).

Guillaume, Alfred, *The Life of Muhammad: A Translation of Ibn Isḥaq's "Sirat Rasul Allah"* (Oxford: Oxford University Press, 1955).

al-Ḥalabī, 'Alī b. Burhān al-Dīn, *Insān al-'Uyūn fī Sīrat al-Ma'mūn* (Beirut: Dār Iḥyā' al-Turāb, n.d.).

al-Ḥanbalī, Zayn al-Dīn Abū'l-Faraj b. Rajab, *Fatḥ al-Bārī: Sharḥ Ṣaḥīḥ al-Bukhārī* (Madīna: Maktabat al-Ghurabā' al-Athariyya/Maktabat Taḥqīq Dār al-Ḥaramayn, 1996).

al-Ḥanbalī, 'Abd Allāh Shams al-Dīn, *Ṣafwat al-Rāsikh fī 'Ilm al-Mansukh wa'l-Nāsikh* (Beirut: Dār al-Fikr, n. d.).

al-Ḥāzimī, Abū Bakr Muḥammad b. Mūsā, *Al-I'tibār fī'l-Nāsikh wa'l-Mansūkh min al-Āthār* (n. p., n. d.).

Ibn 'Abd al-Barr, Abū 'Umar Yūsuf, *Al-Tamhīd li-mā fī'l-Muwaṭṭa' min al-Ma'ānī wa'l-Asānīd* (Fez: Tab' Wizārat al-Awqāf, n.d.).

Ibn Abī Shayba al-Kūfī, Abū Bakr 'Abd Allāh b. Muḥammad, *al-Kitāb al-Muṣannaf fī'l-Aḥādīth wa'l-Athār* (Beirut: Dār al-Fikr, 1989).

Ibn (al-)'Arabī, Abū Bakr Muḥammad b. 'Abd Allāh al-Ma'āfirī, *Aḥkām al-Qur'ān* (Cairo: 'Īsā al-Bābī al-Ḥalabī, 1967).

Ibn 'Arabī, Muḥyī al-Dīn, *Radd al-Mutashābih ilā al-Muḥkam min al-Ayat al-Qur'aniya wa'l-Aḥādīth al-Nabawiya* (Cairo: Maktabat 'Ālam al-Fikr, 1988).

Ibn Ḥazm, Abū Muḥammad 'Alī b. Aḥmad, *Al-Muḥallā* (Beirut: Manshūrāt al-Maktab al-Tijārī li'l-Tibā'a wa'l-Nashr wa'l-Tawzī', n.d.).

Ibn Hishām al-Ma'āfirī, Abū Muḥammad 'Abd al-Mālik, *Al-Sīra al-Nabawiyya* (Cairo: Maktabat al-Kulliyāt al-Azhariyya, n.d).

Ibn Isḥāq, Abū Ja'far Muḥammad b. Ya'qūb, *Al-Uṣūl min al-Kāfi*, (Beirut: Dār al-Ta'rīf, 1401).

Ibn Kathīr, 'Imād al-Dīn Ismā'īl b. 'Umar, *Al-Bidāya wa'l-Nihāya* (Beirut: Maktabat al-Ma'ārif, 1966).

Ibn Māja, Muḥammad b. Yazīd al-Qazwīnī, *Sunan* (n.p.: 'Īsā al-Bābī al-Ḥalabī wa-Shurakā'uhu, n.d.).

Ibn Nujaym, Zayn al-'Ābidīn b. Ibrāhīm, *Al-Baḥr al-Rā'iq: Sharḥ Kanz al-Daqā'iq* (Beirut: Dār al-Kutub al-'Ilmiya, n.d.).

Ibn Qudāma al-Maqdisī, Abū Muḥammad 'Abd Allāh b. Aḥmad b. Muḥammad ("Muwaffaq al-Dīn"), *Kitāb al-Mughnī* (Beirut: 'Ālam al-Kutub, n.d.).

Ibn Rushd, Muḥammad, *Bidāyat al-Mujtahid wa-Nihāyat al-Muqtaṣid* (Fez: al-Maṭba' al-Mawlawiya, 1909).

Ibn Sa'd, Muḥammad, *Al-Tabaqāt al-Kubrā* (Leiden: E. J. Brill, 1905–40).

Ibn Shaddād, Bāhā al-Dīn, *Dalā'il al-Aḥkām* (Damascus: Dar Qutayba, 1992).

Ibn Sulaymān, Muqātil, *Kitāb Tafsīr al-Khams Mi'at Āya min al-Qur'ān al-Karīm* (ed. Isaiah Goldfeld. Shfar'am: Al-Mashriq Press, 1980).

Ibn Sulaymān, Muqātil, *Tafsīr* (Cairo: Al-Hay'a al-Miṣriyya al-'Āmma li'l-Kitāb, 1978).

al-Iṣbahānī, Abū Nu'aym Aḥmad b. 'Abd Allah, *Ḥilyat al-Awliyā' wa-Ṭabaqāt al-Aṣfiyā'* (Beirut: Dār al-Kitāb al-'Arabiyya, 1967).

al-Ishbīlī, Aḥmad b. Muḥammad b. Faraḥ al-Lakhmī, *Mukhtaṣar Khilāfiyāt al-Bayhaqī* (Riyāḍ: Maktabat al-Rushd, 1997) al-Jaṣṣāṣ, Abū Bakr Aḥmad b. ʿAlī al-Rāzī, *Aḥkām al-Qurʾān* (Beirut: Dār al-Kutub al-ʿIlmiya, 1994).

al-Majlisī, Muḥammad Bāqir, *Biḥār al-Anwār* (Beirut: Muʾassasat al-Wafāʾ, 1983).

Mālik b. Anas, *al-Muwaṭṭāʾ* (Cairo: Dār Iḥyāʾ al-Kutub al-ʿArabiya, 1918).

Maulana Muḥammad ʿAlī, *The Holy Qurʾān: Arabic Text, English Translation and Commentary* (Lahore: Ahmadiyyah Anjuman Ishaʾat al-Islam, 1998 [First Edition 1917]).

al-Māwardī, Abūʾl-Ḥasan ʿAlī b. Muḥammad b. Ḥabīb, *al-Ḥāwi al-Kabīr* (Beirut: Dār al-Fikr, 1994).

al-Munāwī, ʿAbd al-Raʿūf, *Fayḍ al-Qadīr: Sharḥ al-Jāmiʿ al-Ṣaghīr* (Cairo: Muṣṭafā Muḥammad, 1938).

Muslim b. al-Ḥajjāj, *Saḥīḥ Muslim* (Beirut: Dār al-Maʿrifa, 1994).

al-Nabhānī, Taqī al-Dīn, *Al-Khilāfa* (Aman: Ḥizb al-Taḥrīr, n.d.).

al-Nabhānī, Taqī al-Dīn *al-Shakhsiyya al-Islāmiyya* (Beirut: Dār al-Umma, 1994).

al-Nasāʾī, Aḥmad b. Shuʿayb, *Al-Sunan al-Kubrā* (Bombay: Dār al-Qayyima, 1985).

al-Nawawī, Abū Zakariyāʾ Yaḥyā b. Sharaf Muḥyī al-Dīn, *Kitāb al-Majmūʿ (Sharḥ al-Muhadhdhab)* (Cairo: Al-Azhar, n.d.).

al-Nawawī, Abū Zakariyyāʾ Yaḥyā b. Sharaf Muḥyī al-Dīn, *Rawḍat al-Ṭālibīn* (Beirut: Dār al-Kutub al-ʿIlmiya, 1992).

al-Nawawī, Abū Zakariyāʾ Yaḥyā b. Sharaf Muḥyī al-Dīn, *Sharḥ Saḥīḥ Muslim* (Cairo: Maṭbaʿat al-Ḥalabī, 1349 AH)

al-Nawawī, Abū Zakariyāʾ Yaḥyā b. Sharaf Muhyī al-Dīn, *Matnuʾl-Arbaʿīn al-Nawawiya fīʾl-Aḥādīth al-Ṣaḥīḥa al-Nabawiya* (Cairo: Muṣṭafā al-Bābī al-Ḥalabī wa-Awlāduhu, n.d.).

al-Naysābūrī, Abū Bakr Muḥammad b. Ibrāhīm b. al-Mundhir, *Al-Awsaṭ fīʾl-Sunan waʾl-Ijmāʿwaʾl-Ikhtilāf* (Riyāḍ: Dār al-Ṭayba, 1993).

al-Naysābūrī, Niẓām al-Dīn Ḥasan b. Muḥammad al-Qummī, *Tafsīr Gharāʾib al-Qurʾān* (Beirut: Dār al-Fikr, 1996).

al-Qārī al-Harawī, ʿAlī, *Fatḥ Bāb al-ʿInāya* (Aleppo: Maktab al-Maṭbūʿāt al-Islāmiya, 1968).

al-Qasṭallānī, Abūʾl-ʿAbbās Aḥmad b. Muḥammad, *Irshād al-Sārī fī Sharḥ al-Bukhārī* (Cairo: Dār al-Kutub, 1325 AH).

al-Qurṭubī, Abū ʿAbd Allāh Muḥammad b. Aḥmad b. Abī Bakr al-Anṣārī, *Al-Jāmiʿ li-Aḥkām al-Qurʾān* (Cairo: Al-Maktaba al-Tawfiqiya, n.d.).

al-Qurṭubī, Abū ʿAbd Allāh Muḥammad b. Aḥmad b. Abī Bakr al-Anṣārī, *Jāmiʿ li-Aḥkām al-Fiqhiyya* (Beirut: Dār al-Kutub al-ʿIlmiya, 1994).

al-Sallām, Abū ʿUbayd b. Qāsim, *Kitāb al-Nāsikh waʾl-Mansūkh,* ed. John Burton (Cambridge: The Trustees of the E. J. W. Gibb Memorial Foundation, 1987) al-San'āni, Abd al-Razzāq, *al-Muṣannaf* (Beirut: Dār al-Kutub al-'Ilmiyya, 1972).

al-San'ānī, Muḥammad b. Ismā'īl, *Subul al-Salām: Sharḥ Bulūgh al-Marām* (Cairo: Al-Maktaba al-Tijāriya al-Kubrā, n.d.).

al-Sarakhsī, Shams al-Dīn, *Al-Mabsūṭ* (Beirut: Dār al-Fikr, 1989).

al-Shāfi'ī, Muḥammad b. Idrīs, *Kitāb al-Umm* (Beirut: Dār al-Fikr, n.d).

al-Shāfi'ī, Muḥammad b. Idrīs, *al-Risāla* (Beirut: Dār al-Kutub al-'Ilmiyya, n.d)

al-Shawkānī, Muḥammad b. 'Alī, *Nayl al-Awṭār: Sharḥ Muntaqā al-Akhbār min Aḥādīth Sayyid al-Akhyār* (Cairo: Mujtama' Majlis Dā'irat al-Ma'ārif, 1953).

al-Shaybānī, Muḥammad b. al-Ḥasan, *Kitāb al-Asl* (Cairo: Mujtama' Majlis Dā'irat al-Ma'ārif, 1966).

al-Shaybanī, Muḥammad b. al-Ḥasan, *Kitāb* al-*Ḥujja 'alā ahl al-Madīna* (Beirut: al-Mazru' Bināyat al-Īmān, 1983).

al-Shīrāzī, Abū Isḥāq Ibrāhīm b. 'Alī, *Al-Muhadhdhab fī Fiqh al-Imām al-Shāfi'ī* (Beirut: Dār al-Qalam, 1992).

al-Sijistānī, Abū Dā'ūd Sulaymān b. al-Ash'ath, *Sunan Abū Dā'ūd* [Aleppo: Maṭba'at Muṣṭafā, 1952],

al-Suyūṭī, 'Abū al-Faḍl 'Abd al-Raḥmān b. Abī Bakr Jalāl al-Dīn, *Al-Durr al-Manthūr fī'l-Tafsīr bi'l-Ma'thūr* (Cairo: Dār Iḥyā' al-Kutub al-'Arabiyya, 1314)

al-Ṭabarī, Abū Ja'far Muḥammad b. Jarīr, *Ta'rīkh al-Rusul wa'l-Mulūk* (Ed. M.J. de Goeje *et al*, Leiden: E.J. Brill, 1879–1901).

al-Ṭabarī, Abū Ja'far Muḥammad b. Jarīr, *Jāmi' al-Bayān 'an Ta'wīl Āy al-Qur'ān* (Beirut: Dār al-Fikr, 1988).

al-Taḥāwī, Abū Ja'far Aḥmad b. Muḥammad, *Sharḥ Ma'ānī al-Athār* (Beirut: 'Ālam al-Kutub, 1994).

al-Tamīmī, 'Abd al-'Azīz b. Ibrāhīm, *Kitāb al-Nīl wa-Shifā' al-'Alīl* (Jedda: Maktabat al-Irshād, 1985).

al-Ṭanṭāwī, Muḥammad Sayyid, *Banū Isrā'īl fī'l-Qur'ān wa'l-Sunna* (Cairo: Tawzī' Dār Ḥirā', 1969).

al-Tanūkhī, Sahṇūn b. Sā'īd, *al-Mudawwana al-Kubrā* (Beirut: Dār al-Kutub al-'Ilmiya).

al-Tanūkhī, Abū 'Alī al-Muḥassin b. 'Alī, *Al-Faraj ba'da al-Shidda* (Beirut: Dar Ṣādir, n. d.).

al-Tibrīzī, Walī al-Dīn, *Mishkāt al-Maṣābīḥ* (Lahore, Mālik Sirāj al-Dīn, n.d).

al-Tirmidhī, Abū 'Īsā Muḥammad, *Ṣaḥīḥ al-Tirmidhī* (Cairo: Al-Maṭba'a al-Miṣriya bi'l-Azhar, 1931).

al-Wāqidī, Abū Muḥammad b. 'Umar, *Kitāb al-Maghāzī* (ed. Marsden Jones. London: Oxford University Press, 1966).

Yusuf Ali, Abdullah, *The Holy Qur'an: Text, Translation and Commentary* (Elmhurst: Tashrike Tarsile Qur'an, 2001).

Zayd, Muṣṭafā, *Al-Naskh fī'l-Qur'ān al-Karīm* (Beirut: Dār al-Fikr al-'Arabī, n.d.).

al-Zamakhsharī, Jār Allāh Maḥmūd b. 'Umar, *Al-Kashshāf 'an Ḥaqā'iq Ghawāmiḍ al-Tanzīl* (Cairo: Maṭba'a al-Ḥalabī, 1966).

Secondary Sources

Abbott, Nabia, *Aishah: The Beloved of Mohammad* (Chicago: University of Chicago Press, 1942).

Abbott, Nabia, *Studies in Arabic Literary Papyri* (Chicago: University of Chicago Press, 1967).

Abrahams, Israel, *Jewish Life in the Middle Ages,* (New York: Atheneum, 1969).

Adang, Camilla, "Fatwās as a Source for the Study of Relations between Muslims and non-Muslims in the Islamic West," in Nili Cohen and Andreas Heldrich (eds.), *The Three Religions* (Munich: Herbert Utz Verlag, 2002).

Adang, Camilla, *Muslim Writers on Judaism and the Hebrew Bible* (Leiden: E.J. Brill, 1996).

Ahmad, Barakat, *Muḥammad and the Jews: A Re-examination* (New Delhi: Vikas Publishing House, 1979).

Astren, Fred, "A Tribute to Professor William M. Brinner" in Benjamin Hary *et al* (eds.), *Judaism and Islam: Boundaries, Communication and Interaction* (Leiden: E.J. Brill, 2000).

Astren, Fred, "Depaganizing Death: Aspects of Mourning in Rabbinic Judaism and Early Islam" in Reeves, *Bible and Qur'ān.*

Ayoub, Mahmoud M., "Dhimmah in Quran and Hadith," *ASQ* 5 (1983).

Bashear, Suliman, *Arabs and Others in Early Islam* (Princeton: The Darwin Press, 1997).

Bell, Richard, *The Origin of Islam in its Christian Environment* (London: Frank Cass, 1968).

Ben Shammai, Haggai, "Jew Hatred in the Islamic Tradition and Koranic Exegesis," in Shmuel Almog (ed.), *Anti-Semitism through the Ages* (trans. Nathan Reisner, London: Pergamon, 1988).

Ben-Ze'ev, Yisra'el, *HaYehudim be-'Arav* (Jerusalem: Aḥi'asaf, 1957).

Bosworth, C. E., "The Concept of Dhimma in Early Islam" in Benjamin Braude and Bernard Lewis (eds.), *Christians and Jews in the Ottoman Empire* (London: Holmes and Meier, 1982).

Bouman, Johan, *Der Koran und die Juden: Die Geschichte einer Tragödie* (Darmstadt: Wissenschaftliche Buchgesellschaft, 1990).

Bousquet, G.H. and G.W., "L'influence Juive sur les Origines du Culte Musulman," *Revue Africaine,* 98 (1954).

Bravmann, M. M., *The Spiritual Background of Early Islam* (Leiden: E. J. Brill, 1972).

Brinner, W. M., "Prophets and Prophecy in the Islamic and Jewish Traditions," in Brinner and Ricks, *Studies.*

Brinner, W. M., "The Origin and Use of the Term Isrāʾīliyyāt in Muslim Literature," *Arabica* 46 (1999).

Brinner, William and Ricks, Stephen (eds.), *Studies in Islamic and Judaic Traditions* (Atlanta: Scholar's Press, 1986), and vol. 2 of the same (1989).

Brinner, William, "The Image of the Jew as *Other* in Medieval Arabic Texts" in Ilai Alon *et al* (eds.), *Israel Oriental Studies XIV: Concepts of the Other in Near Eastern Religions.*

Brunschvig, R., "Herméneutique Normative dans le Judaïsme et dans l'Islam," *Atti della Academia Nazionale dei Lincei* 372 (1976).

Bryan, J., "Mohammed's Controversy with Jews and Christians," *Muslim World* 9 (1919).

Burton, John, "The Exegesis of Q. 2: 106 and the Islamic Theories of *Naskh*" *BSOAS* 48/3 (1985).

Burton, John, *The Collection of the Qur'ān* (Cambridge: Cambridge University Press, 1977).

Burton, John, *The Sources of Islamic Law: Islamic Theories of Abrogation* (Edinburgh: Edinburgh University Press, 1990).

Burton, John, "The Collection of the Qur'ān," *Glasgow University Oriental Society* 23 (1969).

Calder, Norman, "*Tafsīr* from Ṭabarī to Ibn Kathīr," in G. R. Hawting and Abdul-Kader A. Shareef (eds.), *Approaches to the Qur'ān* (London: Routledge, 1993).

Calder, Norman, *Studies in Early Muslim Jurisprudence* (Oxford: Clarendon Press, 1993).

Chapira, Bernard, "Légendes bibliques attribuées à Kaʿb al-Ahbar," *Revue des Etudes Juives* 69 (1919).

Cohen, Mark, and Udovitch, Abraham, *Jews among Arabs: Contacts and Boundaries* (Princeton: Darwin Press, 1989).

Cohen, Mark, *Under Crescent and Cross: The Jews in the Middle Ages* (Princeton: Princeton University Press, 1994).

Conrad, Lawrence, "The Dervish's Disciple: On the Personality and Intellectual Milieu of the Young Ignaz Goldziher," *Journal of the Royal Asiatic Society,* 2 (1990).

Conrad, Lawrence, "The Pilgrim from Pest: Goldziher's Study Tour to the Near East (1873–1874)," in Ian Richard Netton (ed.), *Golden Roads: Migration, Pilgrimage and Travel in Mediaeval and Modern Islam* (Richmond, Surrey, 1993).

Cook, Michael, "Early Islamic Dietary Law," *Jerusalem Studies in Arabic and Islam,* 7 (1986).

Courbage, Youssef and Fargues, Philippe, *Christians and Jews under Islam* (London: I. B. Tauris, 1997).

Crone, Patricia and Cook, Michael, *Hagarism: The Making of the Islamic World* (Oxford: Cambridge University Press, 1977).

Crone, Patricia and Hinds, Martin, *God's Caliph: Religious Authority in the First Centuries of Islam* (Cambridge: Cambridge University Press, 1986).

Crone, Patricia, "Jāhilī and Jewish Law: The *Qasāma*," *Jerusalem Studies in Arabic and Islam* 4 (1984).

Crone, Patricia, *Roman, Provincial and Islamic law* (Cambridge: Cambridge University Press, 1987).

Crone, Patricia, *Slaves on Horses: The Evolution of the Islamic Polity* (Cambridge: Cambridge University Press, 1980).

Dickinson, Eerik, *The Development of Early Sunnite* ḥadīth *Criticism: The* Taqdima *of Ibn Abī ḥātim al-Rāzi (240/854–327/938)* (Leiden: E. J. Brill, 2001).

Donner, Fred M., *Narratives of Islamic Origins: The Beginnings of Islamic Historical Writing* (Princeton: The Darwin Press, 1998).

Dozy, R., *De Israëlieten te Mekka: Van Davids tijd tot in de vijfde eeuw onzer tijdrekening* (Haarlem: A. C. Kruseman, 1864).

Durant, Will, *The Story of Civilization* (New York: Simon and Schuster, 1935).

Encyclopedia of Islam, Second Edition (Netherlands: E. J. Brill, 1986–2004).

Faizer, Rizwi S., "Muhammad and the Medinan Jews: A Comparison of the Texts of Ibn Ishaq's *Kitāb Sīrat Rasūl Allāh* with al-Waqidi's *Kitāb al-Maghāzī*," *International Journal of Middle East Studies* 28 (1996).

Fakhry, Majid, *A History of Islamic Philosophy* (New York: Columbia University Press, 1970).

Firestone, Reuven, "The Qur'ān and the Bible: Some Modern Studies of Their Relationship" in John Reeves, *Bible and Qur'ān* (Atlanta: Society of Biblical Literature, 2003).

Firestone, Reuven, *Journeys in Holy Lands: The Evolution of the Abraham-Ishmael Legends in Islamic Exegesis* (Albany: State University of New York Press, 1990).

Fischel, Walter, *Jews in the Economic and Political Life of Medieval Islam* (New York, 1969).

Francesca, Ersilia, *Introduzione alle Regole Alimentari Islamiche* (Rome: Istituto per l'Oriente C. A. Nallino, 1995).

Friedmann, Yohanan, "Classification of Unbelievers in Sunnī Muslim Law and Tradition," *Jerusalem Studies in Arabic and Islam* 22 (1998).

Friedmann, Yohanan, *Tolerance and Coercion in Islam* (Cambridge: Cambridge University Press, 2003).

Fück, Johann, "The Originality of the Arabian Prophet" in Merlin L. Schwartz (ed. and trans.), *Studies on Islam* (Oxford: Oxford University Press, 1981).

Gaudeul, Jean-Marie and Caspar, Robert, "Textes de la Tradition Musulmane concernant le *Taḥrīf* (falsification) des Ecritures," *Islamo-Christiana* 6 (1980).

Geiger, Abraham, *Was hat Mohammed aus dem Judenthume aufgenommen?* (Bonn, 1833), trans. F.M. Young (1896) and currently available – with prolegomenon by Moshe Pearlman – as *Judaism and Islam* (New York: Ktav Publishing House, 1970).

Gilliot, Claude, "Les 'informateurs' Juifs et Chrétiens de Muḥammad," *Jerusalem Studies in Arabic and Islam* 22 (1998).

Ginzberg, Louis, *Legends of the Jews* (Philadelphia: Jewish Publication Society, 1968).

Goitein, S. D, "Who were Muḥammad's Chief Teachers?", *Gotthold E. Weil Jubilee Volume* (Jerusalem, 1952).

Goitein, S. D., "Ha-dat ha-zo'efet: qavim li-dmut ha-yahadut ba-sifrut ha-muslemit ha-qduma" in *Sefer Dinaburg* (Jerusalem: Qiryat Sefer, 1950).

Goitein, S. D., "Isrā'īliyyāt," *Tarbitz,* 6 (1934–5).

Goitein, S. D., "Ha-Banū Isrā'īl ve-Makhloqotehem," *Tarbitz* 3 (1932).

Goitein, S. D., "Muhammed's Inspiration by Judaism" in *Journal of Jewish Studies,* 9 (1958).

Goitein, S. D., *A Mediterranean Society: The Jewish Communities of the Arab World as Portrayed in the Documents of the Cairo Genizah* (Berkeley: University of Califormia Press, 1967).

Goitein, S. D., *Jews and Arabs: Their Contacts through the Ages* (New York: Schocken Books, 1955), esp. Chapter 4.

Goldziher, Ignaz, "Kämpfe um die Stellung des ḥadīṯ im Islam," *ZDMG* 71 (1907).

Goldziher, Ignaz, "Usages Juifs d'apres la Litterature des Musulmans," *Revue des Etudes Juives* 28 (1894).

Goldziher, Ignaz, *Das Buch vom Wesen der Seele* (Berlin, 1907).

Goldziher, Ignaz, *Muslim Studies* (trans. C. R. Barber and S. M. Stern. London: Allen & Unwin, 1971).

Goldziher, Ignaz, *Introduction to Islamic Theology and Law,* trans. Andras and Ruth Hamori (Princeton: Princeton University Press, 1981).

Hakim, Avraham, "Conflicting Images of Lawgivers: *Sunnat 'Umar* and *Sunnat Muḥammad*" in Berg, Herbert (ed.), *Method and Theory in the Study of Islamic Origins* (Leiden: E. J. Brill, 2003).

Hallaq, Wael, *A History of Islamic Legal Theories* (Cambridge: Cambridge University Press, 1997).

Harkaby, Jehosaphat, *Arab Attitudes to Israel* (Jerusalem: Israel Universities Press, 1971).

Hasan, Ahmed, "The Theory of Naskh," *Islamic Studies* 14 (1965).